MESOPOTAMIAN
ARCHÆOLOGY

PLATE I

COLOURED LION AT KHORSABAD

MESOPOTAMIAN ARCHÆOLOGY

AN INTRODUCTION TO THE ARCHÆ-
OLOGY OF BABYLONIA AND ASSYRIA. BY
PERCY S. P. HANDCOCK, M.A. WITH
NUMEROUS ILLUSTRATIONS, ALSO MAPS

LONDON: MACMILLAN AND CO.
LTD., AND PHILIP LEE WARNER,
ST. MARTIN'S STREET. MDCCCCXII

KRAUS REPRINT CO.
New York
1969

DEDICATED TO

A. M. LORD

IN RECOGNITION

OF MANY ACTS OF FRIENDSHIP

PREFACE

IN every department of science the theories of yesterday are perpetually being displaced by the empirical facts of to-day, though the ascertainment of these facts is frequently the indirect outcome of the theories which the facts themselves dissipate. Hence it is that the works of the greatest scholars and experts have no finality, they are but stepping-stones towards the goal of perfect knowledge. Since the publications of Layard, Rawlinson, Botta and Place much new material has been made accessible for the reconstruction of the historic past of the Babylonians and Assyrians, and we are consequently able to fill in many gaps in the picture so admirably, and as far as it went, so faithfully drawn by the pioneers in the field of excavation and research. This work, which owes its origin to a suggestion made by Dr. Wallis Budge, represents an endeavour on the part of the writer to give a brief account of the civilization of ancient Babylonia and Assyria in the light of this new material.

It is hoped that the infinitude of activities and pursuits which go to make up the civilization of any country will justify the writer's treatment of so many subjects in a single volume. It will be observed that space allotted to the consideration of the different arts and crafts varies on the one hand according to the relative importance of the part each played in the life of the people, and on the other hand according to the amount of material available for the study of the particular subject.

No effort has been spared to make the chapters on Architecture, Sculpture and Metallurgy as comprehensive as the limitations of the volume permit, while for

the sake of those who desire to pursue the study of any of
the subjects dealt with in this book, and to work up the
sketch into a picture, a short bibliography is given at
the end.

It has not been thought desirable to amass a vast number of references in the footnotes, and the writer is thereby
debarred from acknowledging his indebtedness to the
works of other writers on all occasions as he would like
to have done.

In addition to the chapters which deal expressly with
the cultural evolution of the dwellers in Mesopotamia,
two chapters are devoted to the consideration of the
Cuneiform writing—its pictorial origin, the history of
its decipherment, and the literature of which it is the
vehicle, while another chapter is occupied with a historical review of the excavations. The short chronological
summary at the end obviously makes not the slightest
pretension to even being a comprehensive summary ; it
merely purports to give the general chronological order
of some of the better known rulers and kings of Babylonia and Assyria to whom allusion is made in this
volume, together with a notice of some of the more significant landmarks in the history of the two countries.

The writer's thanks are due to the Trustees of the
British Museum for permission to photograph some of
the objects in the Babylonian and Assyrian Collections,
and to Dr. Wallis Budge for facilities and encouragement in carrying out the work ; to the University of
Chicago Press for allowing him to reproduce illustrations from the *American Journal of Semitic Languages* and
also diagrams from Harper's Memorial Volumes ; to
M. Ernest Leroux for permitting him to make use of
some of the plates contained in the monumental works
of De Sarzec and Heuzey, and to M. Ch. Eggimann of
the " Libraire Centrale d'art et d'architecture ancienne
maison Morel," for his very kind permission to reproduce two of the plates contained in Dieulafoy, *L'Art*

Antique de la Perse. He is similarly indebted to the Deutsche-Orient Gesellschaft for allowing him to make an autotype copy of one of the plates in Andrae's *Der Anu-Adad Tempel.* He further desires to acknowledge the generosity of Prof. H. V. Hilprecht in allowing him to make use of many of the illustrations contained in his numerous publications, and also of Dr. Fisher for permitting him to reproduce some of the photographs contained in his magnificently illustrated work on the excavations at Nippur. He is very sensible of his indebtedness to these two gentlemen, as also to M. Leroux and the Deutsche-Orient Gesellschaft, for the photographs of excavations in progress are obviously of a unique character and admit of no repetition ; he further desires to express his obligations to Dr. W. Hayes Ward for his most kind permission to copy a number of seal-impressions and other illustrations contained in his recently published work—*Cylinder-Seals of Western Asia.* Lastly, he welcomes the opportunity of acknowledging the kindness of Mr. Mansell for allowing him to publish many photographs of objects in the British Museum and the Louvre contained in his incomparable collection, and for in other ways facilitating the illustration of this volume. Most of the plans and drawings used for this volume are the work of Miss E. K. Reader, who has performed her task with her usual skill.

P. S. P. H.

March, 1912.

ERRATA ET CORRIGENDA

p.   6,   l.   3,   *for* 2500 B.C. *read* 2400 B.C.

p.   6,   l. 18,   *for* 2500 B.C. *read* 2400 B.C.

p. 43,   l.   7   from foot, *read* both French and English explorers

p. 62,   l.   2,   *for* considerable *read* much

p. 89,   l.   5,   *for* ± *read* —

p. 110,   l.   2,   *for* 2500 B.C. *read* 2400 B.C.

p. 125,   l.   7   from foot, *for* or *read* and

p. 130,   l. 23,   *for* 2400 B.C. *read* 2350 B.C.

p. 155,   l. 31,   *for* having *read* have

p. 235,   l.   9   from foot, *for* Sumu-la-ilu *read* Sumu-ilu

p. 247,   l.   1,   *for* 2500 B.C. *read* 2400 B.C.

p. 249,   l. 35,   *after* crudeness *read* these heads

The reference numbers as printed on Plates VII to XI are inaccurate, and should be altered as follows, in agreement with the List of Illustrations and the references in the text :—

	Present number and position		Correct number and position	
ZIGGURAT OF ASHUR-NASIR-PAL . .	VII *Facing* p. 64		VIII *Facing* p. 78	
INSCRIPTIONS ON CLAY . . .	VIII	„ 78	IX	„ 106
RUINED MOUNDS AND COURT OF MEN .	IX	„ 106	X	„ 132
WATER CONDUIT, NIPPUR . . .	X	„ 132	XI	„ 138
EXCAVATIONS IN TEMPLE COURT . .	XI	„ 138	VII	„ 64

CONTENTS

CHAPTER   PAGE

I.   INTRODUCTION—
     (*a*) Land and People   1
     (*b*) Sketch of Babylonian and Assyrian History   28

II.   EXCAVATIONS.   40

III.   DECIPHERMENT OF THE CUNEIFORM INSCRIPTIONS   85

IV.   CUNEIFORM INSCRIPTIONS   95

V.   ARCHITECTURE   119

VI.   SCULPTURE   181

VII.   METALLURGY.   242

VIII.   PAINTING   270

IX.   CYLINDER-SEALS   284

X.   SHELL-ENGRAVING AND IVORY-WORK . .   309

XI.   TERRA-COTTA FIGURES AND RELIEFS . .   317

XII.   STONEWARE AND POTTERY   325

XIII.   DRESS, MILITARY ACCOUTREMENTS, ETC. . .   337

XIV.   LIFE, MANNERS, CUSTOMS, LAW, RELIGION .   364

     SHORT BIBLIOGRAPHY   406

     LIST OF THE MORE IMPORTANT KINGS AND
     RULERS AND A BRIEF CHRONOLOGICAL
     SUMMARY   408

     INDEX   411

ILLUSTRATIONS

PLATE IN COLOURS

PLATE

I. Coloured Lion at Khorsabad . . . *Frontispiece*

PLATES IN HALF-TONE

FACING PAGE

II. Kouyunjik and Nebi Yûnus (two views) . . 42
Nimrûd (Calah) 42
Khorsabad 42

III. Excavations at Nimrûd (Calah) in Ashur-naṣir-
pal's Palace 44

IV. "Fish-God," and Entrance Passage, Kouyunjik 48

V. Doorway at Tellô, erected by Gudea . . 54
South-eastern façade of Ur-Ninâ's building at
Tellô 54

VI. Remains of a Stele in a building under that of
Ur-Ninâ 58
The Well of Eannatum 58

VII. Excavations in the Temple Court, Nippur . 64

VIII. The Ziggurat and Palace of Ashur-naṣir-pal,
Ashur 78

IX. Inscriptions on clay illustrating the sizes and
shapes of the Tablets, etc., used by the Babylonians and Assyrians 106

X. The Ruined Mounds of Nippur . . . 132
Court of the Men from the North-East, Nippur . 132

XI. Water Conduit of Ur-Engur, Nippur . . 138

XII. Portion of the "Vulture Stele" of Eannatum,
Patesi of Lagash 186

XIII. Stele of Victory of Narâm-Sin . . . 192

XIV. Stele engraved with Khammurabi's Code of
Laws 198
The Sun-God Tablet 198

XV. Bas-relief of Ashur-naṣir-pal 202

PLATE		FACING PAGE
XVI.	Bas-reliefs of Ashur-naṣir-pal (four subjects)	204
XVII.	Siege of a City by battering-ram and archers	206
XVIII.	Ashur-bani-pal's Hunting Scenes : Lion and lioness in a garden	218
XIX.	Ashur-bani-pal's Hunting Scenes (two subjects)	218
XX.	Ashur-bani-pal's Hunting Scenes : Hunting wild asses with dogs	220
	Ashur-bani-pal pouring out a libation over dead lions	220
XXI.	Ashur-bani-pal reclining at meat . .	222
	Musicians and Attendants	222
XXII.	Limestone figure of an early Sumerian .	224
	Three archaic stone heads	224
XXIII.	Head and two diorite statues of Gudea ; upper part of female statuette . .	228
XXIV.	Statues of Nebo and Ashur-naṣir-pal ; torso of a woman	230
XXV.	Winged man-headed genii	236
XXVI.	Stone lion of Ashur-naṣir-pal . . .	238
XXVII.	The Kasr lion	240
XXVIII.	Miscellaneous objects of bronze, from Nimrûd	254
XXIX.	Bronze bowl, from Nimrûd . . .	256
XXX.	Decorated arch at Khorsabad . . .	278
XXXI.	Glazed bricks	282
XXXII.	Ivory panels, from Nimrûd . . .	314
XXXIII.	Pottery, from Nimrûd and Nineveh . .	334

ILLUSTRATIONS IN THE TEXT

FIGURE		PAGE
1.	Pictographs	97
2.	Pictographs	99
3.	Late Babylonian " squeeze " of an early inscription	117
4.	Brick-stamp of Narâm-Sin	117
5.	Clay covering of the " Sun-Tablet " . .	117
6.	Restoration of the temple at Nippur . .	137
7.	Restoration of the Anu-Adad temple at Ashur .	144

FIGURE   PAGE

8.   Restoration of Sargon's palace at Khorsabad   . 151
9.   Domed roofs in Assyria   155
10, 11. Terra-cotta drains   159
12. Columnar piers at Tellô   161
13. Large column capital; small column capital   . 165
14. Columns (various)   166
15. Early arch at Nippur   170
16. Early arch at Tellô   170
17. Corbelled arch at Nippur   173
18. Round arch at Babylon   173
19–22. Arched drains at Khorsabad   174
23. Burial-vault at Ashur   176
24. Burial-vault at Ur (Muḳeyyer)   176
24 a. Ziggurat on Assyrian bas-relief   .   .   . 180
24 b. Ziggurat at Khorsabad   180
25. Six early bas-reliefs   182
26. Stele of Ur-Ninâ and mace-head of Mesilim   . 185
27. Two fragments of the "Vulture Stele"; little
        sculptured block (Entemena's reign)   .   . 189
28. Five bas-reliefs, including one of Narâm-Sin   . 194
29. Bas-relief of Sargon, king of Assyria   .   .   . 209
30. Bas-relief of Sennacherib; removal of stone bull . 213
31. Sennacherib at Lachish   215
32. Statue of Esar, king of Adab   223
33. Early stone statue of a woman   224
34. Statue of Manishtusu; seated figure of a woman;
        head of a woman   225
35. Seated figure of Shalmaneser II 231
36. Stone lion-head; figure of a dog; stone figure of
        a human-headed bull inlaid with shell   .   . 234
37. Copper spear-head; hollow copper tube   .   . 243
38. Early copper figures 245
39. Copper figures of Basket-bearers; copper figure
        of Gudea   247
40. Figures and heads of animals in copper and bronze 250
41. Two Assyrian swords; an Assyrian axe   .   . 254
42. Bronze dish   257

FIGURE   PAGE

43, 44.   Bronze gate-bands 259, 260
45.   Silver vase of Entemena   265
46.   Coloured clay relief lion from Babylon   .   . 274
47.   Coloured bull at Babylon; coloured bull at Nimrûd
        (Calah)   275
48.   Three cylinder seals; clay tablet bearing a seal-
        impression   285
49–77.   Impressions from cylinder-seals   .   . 289–307
78–83.   Engravings on shells   310–312
84.   Carved ivory panel from Nimrûd   .   .   . 314
85.   Early terra-cotta figures   318
86.   Terra-cotta figures of later date 320
87.   Terra-cotta figure of a dog   323
88.   Terra-cotta plaque showing dog with attendant   . 323
89.   Stone vase of Narâm-Sin   328
90.   Decorated stone vase of Gudea   328
91.   Three stone vessels, one of which bears an in-
        scription of Sennacherib, and another the name
        of Xerxes; small glass vessel of Sargon   .   . 330
92, 93.   Two early clay pots from Nippur .   .   . 332
94.   Boomerang-shaped weapons   342
95.   Assyrian jewellery.   348
96, 97.   Combs   349
98, 99.   Foot-spearman and Foot-archers of the first
        Assyrian period   350
100–102.   Archers in the reign of Sargon   .   .   . 351
103–105.   Archers in the reign of Sennacherib   .   . 352
106, 107. Assyrian cavalry 354, 355
108.   Assyrian chariotry 356
109.   Assyrian helmets and head-gears   .   .   . 357
110.   Assyrian weapons of offence   358
111.   Battering-rams and shields   360
112.   Naval equipment of the Assyrians   .   .   . 362
113–115.   Babylonian emblems 396, 398

MAPS

(1) Mesopotamia, (2) Babylonia .   .   .   . *Folder at end*

Mesopotamian Archæology

CHAPTER I—INTRODUCTION

(a) LAND AND PEOPLE

THE Mesopotamian civilization shares with the
Egyptian civilization the honour of being one of
the two earliest civilizations in the world, and although
M. J. de Morgan's excavations at Susa the ruined capital
of ancient Elam, have brought to light the elements of
an advanced civilization which perhaps even ante-dates
that of Mesopotamia, it must be remembered that the
Sumerians who, so far as our present knowledge goes,
were the first to introduce the arts of life and all that they
bring with them, into the low-lying valley of the Tigris
and Euphrates, probably themselves emigrated from the
Elamite plateau on the east of the Tigris ; at all events
the Sumerians expressed both "mountain" and "country" by the same writing-sign, the two apparently being synonymous from their point of view ; in support
of this theory of a mountain-home for the Sumerians,
we may perhaps further explain the temple-towers, the
characteristic feature of most of the religious edifices in
Mesopotamia, as a conscious or unconscious imitation in
bricks and mortar of the hills and ridges of their native-
land, due to an innate aversion to the dead-level monotony of the Babylonian plain, while it is also a significant fact that in the earliest period Shamash the Sun-
god is represented with one foot resting on a mountain,

B

or else standing between two mountains. However this may be, the history of the Elamites was intimately wrapped up with that of the dwellers on the other side of the Tigris, from the earliest times down to the sack of Susa by Ashur-bani-pal, king of Assyria, in the seventh century. Both peoples adopted the cuneiform system of writing, so-called owing to the wedge-shaped formation of the characters, the wedges being due to the material used in later times for all writing purposes—the clay of their native soil—: both spoke an agglutinative, as opposed to an inflexional language like our own, and both inherited a similar culture.

A further, and in its way a more convincing argument in support of the mountain-origin theory is afforded by the early art of the Sumerians. On the most primitive seal cylinders[1] we find trees and animals whose home is in the mountains, and which certainly were not native to the low-lying plain of Babylonia. The cypress and the cedar-tree are only found in mountainous districts, but a tree which must be identified with one or the other of them is represented on the early seal cylinders ; it is of course true that ancient Sumerian rulers fetched cedar wood from the mountains for their building operations, and therefore the presence of such a tree on cylinder seals merely argues a certain acquaintance with the tree, but *ceteris paribus* it is more reasonable to suppose that the material earthly objects depicted, were those with which the people were entirely familiar and not those with which they were merely casually acquainted. Again, on the early cylinders the mountain bull, known as the *bison bonasus*, assumes the rôle played in later times by the lowland water-buffalo. This occurs with such persistent regularity that the inference that the home of the Sumerians in those days was in the mountains is almost inevitable. Again, as Ward points out, the composite man-bull Ea-bani, the

---

[1] Cf. Ward, *Seal Cylinders*, p. 24 ff.

companion of Gilgamesh, has always the body of a bison, never that of a buffalo. So too the frequent occurrence of the ibex, the oryx, and the deer with branching horns, all argues in the same direction, for the natural home of all these animals lay in the mountains.

The Mesopotamian valley may, for the immediate purpose of this book, be divided into two halves, a dividing-line being roughly drawn between the two rivers just above Abû Habba (Sippar); the northern half embraces the land occupied by the Assyrians, and the southern half that occupied by the Babylonians. The precise date at which Assyria was colonized by Babylonia is not known, but to the first known native[1] king of Assyria, Irishum, we may assign an approximate date of 2000 B.C. Babylonia proper is an alluvial plain the limits of which on the east and west are the mountains of Persia and the table-land of Arabia respectively. This valley has been gradually formed at the expense of the sea's domain, for in the remote past the Persian Gulf swept over the whole plain at least as far northward as the city of Babylon where sea-shells have been found, and probably a good deal further. It owes its formation to the silt brought down by the two rivers and deposited at the mouth of the Gulf: the amount of land thus yearly reclaimed from the sea in early times is not known, but as Spasinus Chorax the modern Mohammerah, which is now some forty-seven miles inland, was situated on the sea-coast in the time of Alexander, we know that the conquest of the land over the sea has been progressing since his time at the rate of 115 feet yearly.

Thus the physical characteristics of the country in which Babylonian civilization was developed, if it was not actually the place of its origin, form a close parallel to those of Lower Egypt; in Egypt however

---

[1] Cf. Pinches, *Proceedings of the Society of Biblical Archæology*, 1910, p. 42.

such evidence as there is, would indicate the South, or
Upper Egypt as the earliest scene of civilization, the
North being conquered by the Mesniu (Metal-users)
of the South, not only in the battlefield but also in culture and civilization. Both countries have but a small
sea-board where their rivers find an outlet, the Nile into the Mediterranean, and the Tigris and Euphrates
into the Persian Gulf; both countries had emerged
and were yearly emerging out of the sea, for it is certain that at one time the Mediterranean penetrated as
far south as Esneh, while as already mentioned, the
Persian Gulf extended at least as far as Babylon ; we
are accordingly not surprised to find in both the Babylonian and Egyptian cosmologies a tradition which told
of the creation of the world out of a primæval mass
of water, though this idea looms less conspicuously in
the Egyptian than in the Babylonian and Hebrew cosmologies. Both countries also were visited by a yearly
inundation which, while it brought no small amount or
devastation in its train, at the same time deposited the
mud so essential to the enrichment of the soil, the
desolation being checked or at least mitigated in either
country by an elaborate system of irrigation canals, which
same canals were in the summer-time the means of conveying the life-giving water to the dry and thirsty land.
Both Babylonia and Egypt enjoy a warm climate, though
Egypt is much more dry and therefore healthier, and
the corresponding dryness of its soil has preserved the
tangible evidences of its ancient history in a far more
perfect condition than the marsh-country of Lower
Mesopotamia ; and lastly the climate of Egypt is not
subject to the same violent changes of temperature incidental to the seasons in the Valley of the Euphrates.
The evidence of any racial connection between the
earliest known inhabitants of the two countries is very
precarious; as regards their art, their customs and their
language, the Sumerians on the one hand, and the pre-

dynastic and early dynastic Egyptians on the other, show a complete independence of each other; both countries were probably invaded at an early period of their histories by the Semites, who in the case of Mesopotamia completely supplanted their predecessors of different stock, but who were at the same time themselves absorbed by the higher civilization of the Sumerians to which they were the destined heirs, and to the further development of which they themselves were to contribute so largely ; but at what period or periods the Semites swept over Egypt and the north coast of Africa, impressing their indelible and unmistakable stamp upon the foundation-structure of the Egyptian and Libyan languages is not known ; whenever it was, we can safely assume that their advent took place in prehistoric days, for the hieroglyphs and probably also the language of the dynastic Egyptians were the natural development of the language and crude picture-signs of their predecessors, and the theory of a violent break in the continuity of early Egyptian civilization at the commencement of the first dynasty is daily becoming more untenable. We are similarly unable to assign any definite date to the arrival of the Semites in the Mesopotamian Valley, though the Neo-Babylonian King Nabonidus gives us a traditional date for Shar-Gâni-sharri[1] (Sargon) and his son Narâm-Sin, kings of Agade, who, so far as we know, established the first Semitic empire in the country. There were indeed Semitic Kings of Kish before the time of Shar-Gâni-sharri, but the extent of their sway was clearly very limited compared with the far-reaching empire of the rulers of Agade. But there are reasons for doubting the accuracy of the traditional date of 3750 B.C. which Nabonidus assigns to Narâm-Sin, the chief reason being the extraordinary gap in the yieldings of Babylonian excavations between

---

[1] "Sargon" (i.e. Sharru-ukin) was the name given to this ancient king by the later Assyrian scribes.

the time of Shar-Gâni-sharri and Narâm-Sin, and that of
Gudea, the priest-king of Lagash in Southern Babylonia,
who reigned about 2500 B.C.; that is to say, concerning a
period of about 1300 years the excavations have afforded
us practically no information whatever, while both at
the beginning and at the close of that period, we have
abundant evidence of the civilization and history of the
inhabitants of Babylonia; secondly, the style of art characteristic of the time of Gudea and the kings of Ur, as
also the style of writing found in their inscriptions,
presuppose no such long interval between the time of
Sargon and their own day. But there are yet other considerations which are even more potent, and which deserve greater attention than has been up to the present
accorded to them, depending as they do upon the stratification of the ruined mounds themselves. Now it is a
very significant fact that the architectural remains of
Ur-Engur (*circ.* 2500 B.C.) at Nippur, are found immediately above those of Narâm-Sin, for such an arrangement is hardly conceivable if a period of some thirteen
hundred years separated these two rulers. Again, the
excavations carried on by Dr. Banks for the University
of Chicago at Bismâya have been productive of similar
evidence, for immediately below the ruined ziggurat of
Dungi, Ur-Engur's successor on the throne of Ur, large
square bricks of the size and shape characteristic of the
time of Shar-Gâni-sharri were discovered, while among
the bricks a strip of gold inscribed with the name of
Narâm-Sin was also brought to light. The evidence
afforded by the excavations on these two sites would
thus appear to be exceedingly strong against the traditional date recorded by Nabonidus.[1]

It is therefore tempting to reason that that long silent
period, the silence of which cannot be adequately accounted for, had no existence at all, that Nabonidus'
statement is therefore to be discredited, and that Shar-

[1] Cf. however Fisher in *Records of the Past*, Vol. II, part iv, p. 116.

Gâni-sharri and Narâm-Sin probably lived and reigned more than a thousand years later, i.e. about 2650 B.C. On the other hand it is important to remember that the Babylonians were astronomers and mathematicians of no mean order, and that they exercised the greatest possible care in calculating dates, that moreover Nabonidus was a king of Babylonia, and therefore "a priori" likely to be in possession of reliable traditions, if any existed, and further, that he lived 2500 years nearer to the time than we do. The inscription of Nabonidus in question was found in the mound of Sippar near Agade. It says :—
" The foundation corner-stone of the temple E-ulba in
" the town of the eternal fire (Agade) had not been seen
" since the times before Sargon King of Babylonia and his
" son Narâm-Sin. . . . The cylinder of Narâm-Sin, son
" of Sargon, whom for 3200 years, no king among his pre-
" decessors had seen, Shamash the great lord of Sippara
" hath revealed to him." Thus according to Nabonidus, Narâm-Sin lived about 3750 B.C. The archæological evidence is however so strong in this particular case, both negatively in regard to the absence of any tangible evidence of the long interval in question, and positively in regard to the stratification of the mounds containing the relics of these two kings and also in regard to the similarity between the earlier sculptures and inscriptions of Shar-Gâni-sharri and Narâm-Sin and those belonging to the latter half of the third millennium B.C., that we are no longer able to maintain the implicit confidence in the historical accuracy of Nabonidus which early scholars once had.

From the inscriptions of Shar-Gâni-sharri and Na-râm-Sin that have been brought to light, we gather that the authors of these inscriptions were Semites, in other words we learn that the empire of Agade was a Semitic Empire, and since they extended their empire over all Western Asia, the Sumerian power located more in the south must have proportionately dwindled. But their Sumerian predecessors had established their influence and power in Mesopotamia for a long and indefinite time before this date, for Sumerian inscriptions which are almost certainly to be assigned to the pre-Sargonic period give us the names of a large number of early kings and rulers of Babylonia ; their early date is shown by the writing of these inscriptions which bear a more archaic stamp than those of Shar-Gâni-sharri and Narâm-Sin. For just as uninscribed sculptures are relatively dateable by the style of art to which they conform, so that it is possible to provisionally say that this sculpture or cylinder-seal is older than that, because it presents a more archaic and less finished style of art, so is it possible to approximately date un-named and un-dated inscriptions by the style of writing adopted in those inscriptions. We thus have two means at our disposal by which we can assign uninscribed monuments of an early period to their relatively correct places in the evolution of art and culture ; on the one hand the stratum of the ruined mound in which the object in question has been found can often itself be relatively dated by actually inscribed monuments found either in the stratum itself, or in the stratum immediately above or below ; or failing these, by the depth at which the stratum lies below the top of the mound, though this latter alone is a poor criterion owing to the fact that such accumulation will obviously vary in different places. The value of all such evidence however depends on whether or not the strata have been disturbed, as is often unfortunately the case.

The reason why the ruins of Mesopotamian cities have assumed the form of mounds lies in the fact that a conquering chief demolished the clay walls and buildings of his vanquished foe, but instead of clearing the débris away, he built on the top of it ; for his new building operations the new-comer often utilized part of the old material, hence the uncertainty of a date assigned to an object, based on the mere assumption that such object belongs to the stratum in which it has ultimately found itself, without other corroborative evidence. On the other hand we are in these days always able to apply the purely archæological test, which depends upon a close examination of the style of art or the mode of writing.

Some of these pre-Sargonic rulers already alluded to can be arranged in strictly chronological order, i.e. the rulers of the city of Lagash, one of the earliest centres of Sumerian civilization in Babylonia. Lagash lies fifteen hours' journey north of Ur and two hours' east of Warka (the ancient Erech), and it is Lagash which has provided us with more material for our study of early Sumerian life and culture than any other city in the Euphrates valley.

The order of the early pre-Sargonic rulers of Lagash is as follows : Ur-Ninâ, apparently the founder of the dynasty, inasmuch as he bestows no royal title on his father or grandfather, and his successors traced themselves back to him ; Akurgal, Eannatum, Enannatum I, Entemena, Enannatum II, Enetarzi, Enlitarzi, Lugalanda, and Urukagina. But though their chronological order is certain, the length of their reigns is unknown, and their dates can only be approximately ascertained, and even these approximate and relative dates depend entirely on the date of Shar-Gâni-sharri. Assuming the latter's date to have been about 2650 B.C., Ur-Ninâ's date would be roughly about 3000 B.C. Ur-Ninâ the first member of the dynasty has left us a number of his sculptures and stelæ, but there are other nameless works of art discovered either in the neighbourhood or actually in Lagash itself which present a less developed form of art, and where inscriptions are concerned, a more archaic style of writing, while in certain cases the monuments in question were actually discovered in the strata underneath the building of Ur-Ninâ, and with these the history of Mesopotamian art and of the civilization to which it bears such eloquent testimony commences.

RACE

The race to which the Sumerians belonged is not known, but the fact that their language being agglutinative and not inflexional, was therefore neither Aryan nor Semitic, but at least and in this respect akin to the Mongolian languages, of which Turkish, Finnish, Chinese and Japanese are the most illustrious examples to-day, has led certain scholars to seek a connection between some of the Sumerian roots and certain Chinese words, it must however be admitted that this supposed connection is rather hypothetical at present. Further efforts have also been made by Lacouperie and others to establish parallels between Chinese art and culture and those of the Sumerians, but the evidence is not very convincing.

SOIL

As the surface-soil of Babylonia did not originate there, but was brought down by the rivers and deposited by them as their currents lost impetus in approaching the sea, and were thus unable to carry their burden further, it is well to trace this soil to its original source. Both the Euphrates and the Tigris rise in the mountains of Armenia,[1] the geological formation of which is chiefly granite, gneiss and other feldspathic rocks. These rocks were gradually decomposed by the rains, their detritus being hurried rapidly down-stream ; the rivers in the course of their career travel through a variety of geological formations including limestone, sandstone and quartz, all of which contribute something to the silt which is destined to form part of the delta's soil ; the latter being composed mainly of chalk, sand, and clay, is extremely fertile, which won for it a reputation testified to even by the classical writers : thus Herodotus who

[1] Cf. Fisher, *Excavations at Nippur*, p. 1 ; and Prestwich, *Geology* (Map).

flourished in the seventh century B.C. tells us (I, 293) that "of all the countries that we know, there is none which is so fruitful in grain. It makes no pretension indeed, of growing the olive, the vine, or any other trees of the kind ; but in grain it is so fruitful as to yield commonly two hundredfold, and when the production is greatest even three hundredfold. The blade of the wheat-plant and barley is often four fingers in breadth. As for millet and the sesame, I shall not say to what height they grow, though within my own knowledge, for I am not ignorant that what I have already written concerning the fruitfulness of Babylonia, must seem incredible to those who have never visited the country. . . . Palm trees grow in great numbers over the whole of the flat country, mostly of the kind that bears fruit, and this fruit supplies them with bread, wine and honey." However exaggerated this account may be, all ancient writers agree in ascribing to Babylonian soil a fertility and productivity surpassing that of any other country with which they were acquainted.

But the present state of the country is very different from what it was, neglect of cultivation having reduced it once more to a desert waste, or, in the immediate neighbourhood of the rivers, to a pestiferous marsh. The rivers have furthermore varied their courses time and again, though this remark applies more to the sluggish stream of the Euphrates with its low banks, than to the more swiftly flowing Tigris whose current is confined by higher banks, and whose course has consequently undergone less change. At the present time, great efforts are being made to make amends for the neglect to which the once fertile plain of Babylonia has so long been subject, and in the early part of last year (1911) the firm of Sir John Jackson (Limited), contractors and engineers, secured the contract for the building of a great dam at the head of the Hindiyah Canal : this latter is a channel for which the Euphrates has forsaken its own bed, and consequently the Euphrates' bed upon whose banks the city of Babylon lies, is in summer-time perfectly dry, all the water flowing down the Hindiyah Canal except at the time of the inundation. Thus it is that the population have practically ceased to attempt the cultivation of the Euphrates' banks, and have for the most part migrated across country to this canal. The latter however, being quite inadequate for the burden thus thrust upon it by the undivided waters of the Euphrates, has become badly water-logged, and much good land has become swamp. The Turks have been endeavouring for a long time to erect a dam which would drive back part of the water into the bed of the river, and thus at the same time make the regulation of the flow in the canal a possibility, but they have not attained their object. The engineers of Sir William Willcocks were successful in filling up the space between the two arms of the barrage, but the dam was almost immediately breached at another point. When however the scheme now in hand is duly realized, the banks of the Euphrates will once again be dotted with the fertility of bygone days, while the district dependent for its prosperity upon the conditions of the Hindiyah Canal will be similarly improved.

By the side of these rivers flourished the acacia, the pomegranate and the poplar, but the tree which stood the Babylonians in best stead, was the date-palm, from the sap of which they made sugar and also a fermented liquor, while its fibrous barks served for ropes, and its wood, being at the same time light and strong, was extensively used as a building material. So many and so divers were the uses which the date-palm served, that the Babylonians had a popular song[1] in which they celebrated the three hundred and sixty benefits of this invaluable tree. The important part which it played in the life of the early

[1] Cf. *Comptes Rendus, Académie des Inscriptions et Belles Lettres,* 1894, p. 409.

Sumerian population is indicated by the epithet applied
by Entemena to the goddess Ninâ, whom he addresses as
the lady "who makes the dates grow," while various
amphora-shaped vats, and also a kind of oval basin evidently used in the manufacture or preservation of date-
wine were discovered by De Sarzec at Tellô.

The date-tree finds a place on the Assyrian bas-reliefs,
but it must be confessed that the artistic products of the
Babylonians and Assyrians do not afford us so much information as might be expected regarding the flora and
fauna of the country. Vines and palms are of frequent
occurrence on the later bas-reliefs, while oaks and terebinths were also known, for Esarhaddon uses them as
material in his building operations at Babylon, and cedar
trees were regularly procured for the same purpose.

Of the various trees represented on early seals, hardly
any can be identified with any degree of certainty, the
date-palm perhaps being excepted : the reed of the
marshes appears fairly soon, but the fig-tree on the
other hand occurs only in later times, which accords
with Herodotus' intimation that they were not grown
in Mesopotamia in his day ; this notwithstanding, they
must have been known and presumably cultivated
sufficiently early, for amongst the offerings made by
Gudea (2450 B.C.) to the goddess Bau, figs are enumerated, while the olive-tree must also have been known
at an early date, for objects in clay in the form of an
olive belonging to the time of Urukagina are still extant.

The Lotus is sometimes engraved on a seal, always
in the hand of a god, and with other Egyptian elements
it is frequently found on the ivories and bronze dishes
from Nimrûd.

Millet and other cereals have been the subject of
artistic delineation ; flowers of a nondescript character
appear in later times, though the conventional designs

of the rosettes, so familiar in Assyrian art, an example of which is to be found in Pl. XXX, without doubt owed its origin to an actual attempt to reproduce a living flower, while ivy only occurs on a late Græco-Egyptian cylinder, and on a Syro-Hittite cylinder we find a representation of the thistle.

Reeds are found more often than any other tree or plant, alike on cylinder-seals and bas-reliefs. They were in great demand for the construction of huts and light boats, but the clay of their native soil furnished an all-availing and all-abundant material for the building operations of their palaces, temples and houses ; its possibilities were recognized at a very early date, and were made use of accordingly. Stone is practically unknown in the low-lying plain of Babylonia, and when required, it had to be quarried far away in the mountains and transported at great cost and labour, hence it was comparatively seldom used for artistic or decorative effects pure and simple, but was rather employed where the desire for durability rendered it necessary ; for this reason the stone used in Babylonia is generally basalt, diorite, dolerite or some other hard stone of volcanic origin. In Assyria on the other hand, both alabaster and various kinds of limestone were easily procurable, and were used largely for building purposes, while they both, also, adapted themselves readily to the chisel of the sculptor whose duty it was to record the chief events of the king's reign in pictorial form upon the walls of his palace.

Of the cereals, wheat, barley, vetches and millet were the most important, and they all grew in large quantities, while as regards domestic animals—horses, oxen, sheep, pigs, goats, asses and dogs were the most familiar ; upon the bas-reliefs from Kouyunjik, one of the mounds representing the ancient Nineveh (the other being Nebi Yûnus ("Prophet Jonah "), so-called by the natives, owing to their belief that the prophet Jonah was buried there), camels are to be found, while they also form part of the tribute brought by tributary princes to Shalmaneser II King of Assyria 860-825 B.C., and are represented accordingly on the bronze gates from Balâwât and on the so-called Black Obelisk, principally famous for its representation of Jehu and his tribute-bearers. The camels represented here belong to the double-humped Bactrian breed, which have less staying-power than the single-humped dromedaries of Arabia and Africa. In Babylonia at the present day, these last-named are a most important means of locomotion, but in the hilly country of Assyria, they are of less use, owing to their tendency to slip on any but the flattest of grounds. There is apparently only one isolated occurrence of a camel on a cylinder-seal, and that belongs to the Persian period. The Assyrian word used for "camel" is probably of Arabic origin, and Arabia was doubtless the home of the camel. As for horses, oxen, sheep, goats and dogs, they are constantly represented in Assyrian art. The horse being native to Asia, was in all probability domesticated in Mesopotamia earlier than in Egypt ; very early evidence of its existence in Mesopotamia was thought to be afforded by an archaic seal-cylinder, now in the Metropolitan Museum of New York, in which a god is represented driving a four-wheeled chariot, in contrast to the Assyrian war-chariots which were two-wheeled ; the chariot is drawn by an animal of uncertain character, which Ward originally regarded as a horse, but in view of a representation of a bull drawing a chariot, found on an early Assyrian seal which he dates about 2000 B.C., it is clear that the bull was used to draw chariots in early times, and Ward accordingly regards the ambiguous animal alluded to, as also a bull. The Sumerian name for the horse was "the ass of the mountains," an indication that the animal was first known to them in its wild state : we find it figured on one of Nebuchadnezzar I's boundary .stone (*circ.* 1120 B.C.), but it was certainly known in the valley much earlier. The Hyksos, or shepherd-kings from Asia introduced the horse into Egypt about 1700 B.C., while mention is made of horses in a letter from Burraburiash the king of Babylon to Amenhetep, king of Egypt about 1400 B.C.

An extremely early fragment from Nippur (cf. Fig. 25,E) published by Hilprecht and quoted and reproduced by Ward,[1] shows us a horned animal dragging a plough, which Ward thinks may be a gazelle or an antelope ; if the latter be the case, we may perhaps infer that an animal of that species was used for draft purposes before the bull, and certainly before the horse. However that may be, in later days the horse seems to have been reserved for the battlefield and the chase. The Assyrian soldiers both rode them and harnessed them to their war-chariots, and it is worth noticing how much more successful the Assyrian sculptors were in their representations of the horse than the Egyptians. The horses on the bas-reliefs apparently belong to a smaller, shorter and more thick-set breed than Arabs, and the breed is still supposed to be extant in Kurdistan. The Assyrians do not seem to have been in the habit of endowing the horse with wings or with a human head, as they sometimes did the bull and the lion, though some of the Pehlevi[2] seals and rings of later days (A.D. 226-632) show figures of winged horses.

The *Ox* with " long upright and bent horns " seems to have been domesticated from the very earliest period, and it is represented on cylinder-seals which by their inscriptions show that they belong to the early period when the line-writing had not as yet been supplanted by its later off-shoot cuneiform, while on one of these early seals (cf. Fig. 63) the god himself is depicted riding on one of these bulls ; it is however to be observed that the

[1] Ward, *Cylinder-Seals*, p. 30, Fig. 55.
[2] Cf. note on page 86.

bull plays a less conspicuous part in the artistic representations of Mesopotamia than in those of Egypt, where the tombs so often exhibit the daily scenes of agricultural life. Only very rarely is the bull represented on cylinder-seals or sculptures as a sacrificial victim, the best example being afforded by a fragment of the Vulture Stele of Eannatum; the same king informs us elsewhere that he sacrificed bulls to the sun-god in Larsa, and a bull-calf to En-lil, the lord of Nippur, who is better known under the Semitic name of Bêl, a name which however he never bore;[1] if however the bull were used but seldom in sacrificial worship, there is no doubt that he was regarded throughout Mesopotamian history as the embodiment of, and therefore the natural symbol for strength and fertility, while the winged bulls of Sargor (cf. Pl. XXV) are the most familiar and perhaps the most characteristic monuments of Assyrian art.

The *Mule* was used as a beast of burden ; carts were drawn by mules, and women and children were borne by them, while they were used for carrying merchandise, and for menial work of every kind ; they are occasionally seen on Assyrian bas-reliefs and form one of the subjects of Ashur-bani-pal's famous Hunting Scenes, where they are in charge of the king's servants.

The *Sheep* was domesticated from the earliest times, but representations of the goat are more common ; in Fig. 62 we have an extremely archaic seal on which a man is seen driving a goat followed by two sheep. A further example of the goat and sheep is found on the early stone relief seen in Fig. 25, F.

The *Goat* is of frequent occurrence both on seals and also in bas-reliefs. The goat was, as far as we can tell, the most commonly used sacrificial victim, the worshipper often being represented as bringing a goat in his arms. (For an early example of a goat in Babylonian art, cf. the copper goat's head from Fâra, 40, B.) Fig.

---

[1] Cf. Clay, *American Journal of Semitic Languages*, XXIII, p. 269.

C

The beard is sometimes clearly delineated,[1] thereby showing it to be a goat and not an antelope, while both the sheep and goat are well represented on the bronze gate-sheaths from Balâwât. Though the sheep however does not appear to have assumed so important a part as the goat in sacrificial worship, it played a far more conspicuous rôle in augury, and innumerable omens were deduced from an inspection of the various parts of its liver.

The *Ass* was known from the earliest period, both the wild ass, which Ashur-bani-pal seems to have been so fond of hunting (cf. Pl. XX), and also the domesticated ass. Ward has only found one example of its early representation on cylinder-seals, but the god Ningirsu's chariot on the famous Vulture Stele is drawn by an ass, and the fact that Urukagina, one of the kings of the First Dynasty of Lagash, enacted that if a good ass was foaled in the stable of one of the king's subjects, the king could only purchase it by offering a fair price, and that even then he could not compel the owner to part with it, shows that the ass was in common use in his day.

The *Dog* finds a place on some of the earliest seals from Babylonia, and is especially common on those representing the legend of Étana and the Eagle (cf. Fig. 62) : he also appears on the later Babylonian seals, and is of very frequent occurrence in the Assyrian bas-reliefs.

Here they are seen employed in the chase (cf. Pl. XX). The Assyrian hounds apparently resembled mastiffs, and according to Layard the breed is still extant in Tibet though not in Mesopotamia. We have another good reproduction of a dog on a terra-cotta plaque found by Sir H. Rawlinson at Birs-Nimrûd (cf. Fig. 88), while Ashur-bani-pal has left us a number of clay models of his dogs, made in one piece like the colossal bulls, but

[1] Cf. Ward, *Cylinder-Seals*, Fig. 289

rather crude in workmanship. Though we thus know little about the breeds of dogs with which the Assyrians and Babylonians were familiar, we at all events know, that they were acquainted with dogs of various colours, for they derived omens from piebald dogs, yellow dogs, black dogs, white dogs and the rest.

The *Gazelle* was known in Mesopotamia from an early day, and he sometimes appears to take the place of the goat as a victim for sacrifice.

The *Antelope* is often found represented on early cylinder-seals, and apparently it was occasionally yoked to the plough, as may be seen from an early stone relief from Nippur,[1] but it is not always easy to distinguish between the antelope and the goat in Babylonian art.

The *Ibex* is similarly liable to be confused with the mountain sheep, owing to the shape of their horns, but where correctly depicted, it has a beard. A good and very early example of the Ibex is to be found engraved on a fragment of shell belonging to the earliest Sumerian period (cf. Louvre Cat. No. 222).

The *Boar* was not often figured, but was without doubt sufficiently common as it is to-day ; it is found on an extremely archaic seal (cf. Fig. 54), and numbers of little swine are repeated in four registers on a later cylinder-seal, while on other seals, the huntsman is seen spearing a boar, and lastly a sow with her young are represented on one of the wall-reliefs from Sennacherib's palace at Kouyunjik. It is interesting to note that as early as the time of Khammurabi[2] pork was a highly valued food, so much so that it frequently formed part of the temple offerings, and Ungnad calls attention to one case where a certain maleficent person stole one of the temple-pigs and paid a heavy penalty for so doing, while in the official lists of the provisions for the temple, various parts of the pig are specifically enumerated,

[1] Cf. Fig. 25, E.
[2] Cf. Ungnad in *Orient. Lit. XI.*, 1908, *cols.* 533–537.

while from the inspection of pigs favourable and un-
favourable omens were derived.

The *Rabbit* or *Hare* is rarely found in early sculptures or engravings, but it occurs on the later so-called
Syro-Hittite cylinders, and is occasionally portrayed on
the Assyrian bas-reliefs.[1]

The *Oryx*, the *Mountain-Sheep*, the *Stag*, the *Tortoise*,
the *Porcupine*, the *Monkey*, all occur occasionally on
the cylinders, while as regards the monkey, he forms
part of the tribute brought by subject peoples to Shalmaneser II on the Black Obelisk, and is also similarly
depicted on the bas-reliefs which adorned the walls of
Ashur-naṣir-pal's palace at Nimrûd, in both of which
latter, the monkeys represented appear to belong to an
Indian species, and were clearly novelties in the eyes of
the Assyrians, who no doubt valued them accordingly.

There are solitary instances of the *Fox*, the *Frog* and
the *Bear*, but none of the foregoing play what may be
called an important part in the history of the country's
art. The *Lion* and the *Serpent* occupy a prominent position in artistic representations, and were undoubtedly
familiar and formidable entities in real life, while the
majesty of the former and the subtlety of the latter were
alone sufficient to obtain for them a place in the mythological and heraldic symbolism of the dwellers of Mesopotamia. The lion was known everywhere, in highlands
and lowlands alike, while he still haunts the low marsh
country of Babylonia. On the cylinder-seals he generally
appears engaged in deadly combat with Gilgamesh, the
hero of Babylonian folk-lore, or his friend Eabani who
of course on all occasions worsts him; he is figured in
clay and stone from the earliest (cf. Fig. 26, B) to the latest
times, he is embroidered on garments, and decorates
scabbards, while he plays an all-important part in the
heraldic device of the ancient city of Lagash, which is

[1] Cf. Botta, *Nineveh*, II, Plates 108, 110; Layard, Series II,
Plates 9, 32.

composed of an eagle with outspread wings, clutching two lions facing in opposite directions (cf. Fig. 27), doubtless emblematic of the dominion exercised by the king of Lagash over the peoples of the East and West respectively. He enjoys the doubtful honour of being the peculiar object of the Assyrian King's attention in later days, and afforded him the sport which he loved above all others (cf. Pl. XIX) ; individual kings slew great numbers, and Tukulti-Ninib I (1275 B.C.), to take a single example, places it on record that he slew some 920 lions, just as Amenhetep III king of Egypt similarly boasts that he killed 102 lions in the first ten years of his reign. Originally no doubt lions were sufficiently plentiful, but as their numbers were thinned, it became necessary to capture and preserve them in cages till they were required for the royal hunt (cf. Pl. XXVII). The lion is sometimes reproduced in colossal size, and endowed with wings and the head of a man, in which capacity, stationed at the portals of the King's palace, his vocation is to ward off the advances of malevolent and maleficent demons, while at other times, he is less fully equipped, and is provided only with a head, bust and hands of a man. Always a creature of weight in more ways than one, his body is not unfittingly adapted to the requirements of the scales ; a considerable number of bronze lion-weights have come down to us, the workmanship of which was probably Phœnician (as was also the ivory work of the Assyrian empire), while the weight represented by each lion was inscribed in Phœnician characters. Sometimes again the hollow bronze head of a lion formed the ornate fitting of the end of a chariot-pole. As a general rule, the lion emblematized the King's enemies, hence it is that, whenever he is seen engaged in conflict, he is always overpowered either by sheer bodily strength as in the case of Gilgamesh, or transfixed by an arrow, speared, or stabbed as we see him so frequently on the bas-reliefs of Assyrian palaces. But lions were probably domesticated now and again as they are to-day. On Sir Henry Layard's first visit to Hillah, he was presented with two lions by Osman Pasha ; one of these, he tells us, was a well-known frequenter of the bazaars, the butcher-shops of which he was in the habit of regularly looting, but apart from this amiable little vagary, he appears to have been fairly well-behaved. In his description of the animal, Layard says that he was " taller and larger than a St. Bernard dog, and like the lion generally found on the banks of the rivers of Mesopotamia was without the dark and shaggy mane of the African species." He further informs us that he had however, seen lions with a long black mane on the river Karûn, which river flows into the Gulf not far from Mohammerah in the extreme south of Babylonia ; but lions of either class are very rarely seen in Mesopotamia to-day, and these as a rule, only at a distance.

The serpent played a smaller part in Mesopotamian art than the lion, but at least from some points of view, a not less significant one. Two serpents entwined round a pole form the centre of the device engraved on the famous cup (cf. Fig. 90) dedicated by Gudea, patesi or priest-king of Lagash about 2450 B.C., to his god Ningishzida, who was apparently emblematized by serpents, and on either side of the entwined reptiles, are two winged and serpent-headed monsters, while in a few cylinder-seals of the older period, we find a bearded god whose body consists of a serpent's coil. In this connection we may compare the device on a cylinder-seal of the same Gudea (cf. Fig. 64), where the intermediary god who is introducing the patesi to a seated deity, whom Ward believes with some reason to be Ea, is characterized by serpents rising from his shoulders.

But the most familiar example of the serpent in Babylonian mythological representation is that of the seal on which two beings, perhaps divine, perhaps human, are seated on either side of a tree, and behind one of the two an erect serpent is figured; this seal owes its fame to the opinion held by earlier scholars that this scene represents the pictorial counterpart in Babylonia of the Hebrew tradition of the Fall.

Judging from the representations of snakes found on vases, boundary-stones, cylinder-seals and elsewhere, the snakes prevalent in Mesopotamia at the time when these monuments were prepared, must have been of considerable size, while we know from the literature that some of these snakes were poisonous. The Assyrian kings further make mention of the prevalence of snakes in some of the countries whither they conducted expeditions, or which were subject to them, thus Esarhaddon for example tells us that the land of Bazu swarmed with snakes and scorpions like grasshoppers.

Among other beasts familiar to the inhabitants of Mesopotamia may be mentioned, the *Bison* ("rimu") an animal of the mountains and forests, which plays a conspicuous part in the story of Gilgamesh; the old pictograph for the bison consist of the head of an ox in which were inclosed the three diagonal wedges which together signify "mountain," and thus indicate the place of its origin. Various species of the bovine race have been identified on the cylinder-seals of Babylonia, showing that at the time of the making of the seals, the memory of their existence and probably the actuality of their presence were still felt and known. The *buffalo* which haunts the swamps of Southern Babylonia often occurs on cylinder-seals belonging to the time of Shar-Gâni-sharri and his successors, and is found engraved on fragments of shell belonging to the earliest Sumerian period. Layard tells us that these ugly animals which thrive in the marshes to-day supply the Arabs with large quantities of milk and butter; they are normally managed with ease, but they have a peculiar antipathy to the smell of soap, and in consequence the odour of freshly-washed clothes is apt to irritate them in no small degree. The wild-bull was assiduously hunted by the Sargonid Assyrian kings, among whom we may especially mention Ashur-nasir-pal in this connection. (For a graphic illustration of that king's exploits in the chase cf. Pl. XVI). After the Sargonids, the bull-hunt appears no longer as one of the principal royal sports, possibly owing to the relentlessness with which these animals had been hunted down by the kings of that dynasty. In the jungles, at all events in Layard's day, lions, leopards, lynxes, wild-cats, jackals, hyenas, wolves, deer, porcupines and boars still abounded, while hyenas are sufficiently common to-day.

The *Leopard* is occasionally figured on the more archaic seals, but seldom on those of later date, it is distinguished specifically by its spots ; a good example of the leopard is afforded by an archaic seal much earlier than the time of Shar-Gâni-sharri.[1] It will thus be seen that the artistic and literary bequests of Mesopotamia have aided us in no small degree in our endeavour to get a general idea as to the animal-world of that country in bygone days. Such however has been the case, only to a very limited extent in regard to birds, where colour is a more determining factor in their infinite variations than form and shape : here it was that the Egyptian shone forth in all his native genius, and succeeded in vividly depicting so many different kinds of birds upon the walls of his tombs by the aid of his brush and colours. In Assyria and Babylonia, on the other hand, where the artistic genius of the people can never really be said to have used colours alone as the mode of its expression, the only birds frequently found, are the eagle and the vulture,—the eagle as the emblem of sovereign royalty, the vulture as the ever-ready devourer of the remains of slaughtered foes —though without doubt a great variety of birds haunted the plains and marshes as they do to-day.

[1] Cf. Ward, *Cylinder-Seals*, Fig. 179.

The *Eagle*, the royal bird *par excellence*, is the embodiment of kingly rule in the heraldic arms of Lagash as early as the time of her first dynasty, and by the time of Gudea (2450 b.c.) the double-headed eagle, generally characteristic of Hittite art, has made its appearance. It is upon the eagle's pinions that Etana seeks unsuccessfully to ascend to Heaven, which legend is pictorially represented (cf. Fig. 62) on various archaic seals. In course of time the eagle becomes the aerial support of Ashur, the god from whom Assyria derived its name, and lends its form to the winged disc, which, as M. Heuzey well says, is a " yet more mysterious emblem of divinity " ; the Assyrians further deemed it worthy to receive the honour of being united with the body of a man, the composite creature thus produced being accredited with powers more than those enjoyed by mere men, and apparently partaking of a semi-divine character, while on other occasions we see its wings applied to the human-headed body of a bull (cf. Pl. XXV) or a lion, the combined effect of which must have been such as to stagger the boldest of subterranean demons.

The long and bare-necked *Vulture* is not of frequent occurrence in Mesopotamian art, while on cylinder-seals, it only occurs on those known as Syro-Hittite. The birds of prey from which the " Vulture-stele " derives its name, no doubt are intended to represent vultures ; as also are the birds depicted on the bas-reliefs which adorned the walls of Ashur-bani-pal's palace at Nineveh,[1] for in either case they are busily engaged in carrying off the sharply severed limbs and heads of fallen foes.

The *Ostrich* only appears in Mesopotamian art at a late period, though in Elam rows of ostriches are found depicted on early pottery, closely and inexplicably resembling the familiar ostriches on the pre-dynastic pottery of ancient Egypt. It sometimes however assumes

[1] Cf. No. 43, Nineveh Gallery, British Museum.

a conspicuous position in the embroidery of an Assyrian king's robe and is found also on a chalcedony seal in Paris.[1]

The *Stork*, which in winter time feeds in the Babylonian marshes, occurs on the cylinder-seals, but in some cases it is difficult to determine the bird figured ; the *Crane* and the *Bustard* both appear to be represented, while we have an undoubted instance of the *Swan* in a soft serpentine seal which Ward regards as early Assyrian.[2] The *Cock* is confined or practically confined to cylinder-seals of the Persian period.

Ducks are known to have existed by the discovery of stone and marble weights in the form of ducks, one of which is inscribed with the name of Nabû-shum, and another with that of Erba-Marduk.

Doves were used and appreciated from the earliest times, for Eannatum informs us that he offered four doves in sacrifice to the god Enzu, while *Swallows* and *Ravens* abounded, for in the Deluge-story, both the swallow and raven as well as the dove are sent forth by Sit-napishtim to ascertain how far the waters were abated.[3]

Locusts are found on one or two seals, and also appear as articles of diet on the Assyrian bas-reliefs (cf. Layard, Series II, Pl. 9), where they are seen strung up on a stick, while the scorpion is of frequent occurrence on the cylinder-seals, and is found on some of the earliest.

Fishes figure alike on seals and on palace walls, but their presence generally seems due to the artist's desire to remove all doubt from the spectator's mind with regard to the water, of the success of his reproduction

---

[1] Cf. Perrot and Chipiez, II, p. 153.

[2] Cf. Ward, *Cylinder-Seals*, Fig. 93.

[3] For representations of birds on Assyrian bas-reliefs, cf. Botta, *Nineveh*, II, Plates 108, 109, 110, 111, 112, 113, 114, and Layard, Series II, Plates 9, 32, 40.

of which he is by no means too sanguine. We have one humorous episode in fish-life depicted on the walls of Sennacherib's palace at Kouyunjik, where a crab is seen effectually pressing its nippers into the body of a luckless fish, while it also occurs once on a cylinder-seal.

Fish were undoubtedly used for food from the earliest times ; thus Eannatum records that he presented certain fish as offering to his gods, while one of the reforms introduced by Urukagina, a king of the First Dynasty of Lagash, was the deprivation from office of the extortionate fishery inspectors. The marshes still abound in fish, some of which attain to a considerable size ; they are for the most part barbel or carp, their flesh although coarse affording a regular supply of food to the Arabs.

It was not unnatural or unfitting that in a country which had been created and was yearly being created out of and at the expense of the sea, and in which the principal means of transit were the rivers and the canals, the fish as the lord of the waters should fulfil an important place in the mythological and religious conceptions entertained by the inhabitants of that country : thus it was that the god Ea of Eridu, one of the most famous and most important of the Babylonian gods, and the Oannes of the Greeks, who according to one account was the creator of the world, was represented in the form of a fish.

But it is necessary to avoid falling into the danger of assuming that all the animals, birds, fish and trees, either figured on monuments or mentioned in the literature of antiquity, belonged to the fauna or flora of Mesopotamia at the time when these engravings and sculptures were executed ; the only absolutely certain and equally obvious inference is that the existence of such fauna or flora was known, while the degree of familiarity of the artist with the specimen in question may, with a good deal of reservation and allowance for the crudeness of early art, be inferred from the comparative accuracy with which he has reproduced it,and also the frequency of its occurrence on contemporaneous works of art. With regard to the evidence of the literature, unfortunately in many cases there is some uncertainty as to the identification of the animals and plants alluded to, and furthermore, many of the animals represented pictorially on the monuments or alluded to in the literature form part of the tribute brought by subject states, the precise locality of which, to complicate matters yet further, is often uncertain. Sometimes, as in the case of the horse (cf. p. 15), the early ideographic form of writing teaches us something about the origin of the object mentioned, while the appearance of an animal or tree in early Mesopotamian art, and the existence of the same tree or animal in Mesopotamia to-day is good argument for including it among the ancient fauna and flora of the country. Again with exceptions it may be assumed that animals offered and accepted as tribute by the kings of Babylonia and Assyria were utilized in some way other than merely being afforded accommodation in a zoological gardens, in which connection we may perhaps fairly infer that kings of Assyria who accepted camels from vassal chiefs found use for them as a means of transit, though in the rough country of Assyria itself the camel would not be of great use any more than to-day, owing to the tendency of camels to slip on rough ground, and the consequently practical necessity of confining their use to flat sandy ground, such as is found in Babylonia, where they are seen by the thousand to-day.

(b) SKETCH OF BABYLONIAN AND ASSYRIAN HISTORY

In the early days of Babylonian history, the country was divided up into a number of small principalities or city-states, and the practical realization of the approved truism that "unity is strength" was only attained at a later date. In this respect also, the early history of Babylonian civilization presents a parallel to that of ancient Egypt, where we find the country similarly apportioned out into a series of districts or nomes, which in course of time tended to amalgamate and in fact crystallized into a northern and a southern kingdom. But in Egypt the process of unification was carried a step further, and at about the time of the First Dynasty, the inhabitants of Egypt owed allegiance to one lord and one lord only—the king of the north and the south, his dual sovereignty being emblematized by his assumption of the crown of the north, and the crown of the south.

It is of course impossible to fix the date of the first appearance of the Sumerians in Babylonia, but the sites of their earliest known settlements were all situated in Sumer or Southern Babylonia, their principal cities being Ur, Erech, Nippur, Larsa, Eridu, Lagash and Umma. It is equally impossible to give anything in the nature of a definite date for the occupation of Northern Babylonia or Akkad by the Semites, suffice it to say that at the earliest period of which historical records have been brought to light, there appears to be evidence of the presence of Semites or Akkadians in Akkad alongside of the Sumerians in Sumer. The principal centres of Semitic occupation were the city of Akkad or Agade, Babylon, Borsippa (Birs-Nimrûd), Cutha, Opis, Sippar and Kish.

The city of Kish became an influential factor in Babylonian politics from the most ancient times.

Thus a certain Mesilim, king of Kish, whose inscribed mace-head was discovered at Tellô (Lagash),[1] informs us that he had dedicated the same to the god Ningirsu, during the patesiate of Lugal-shar-engur at Lagash, and that he had further restored the temple of this same god. Nothing further is known regarding

[1] Cf. p. 185.

this patesi of Lagash, but Mesilim reigned at Kish at a very early date, for Entemena of Lagash commences his historical sketch of the relationship which had existed between his own city and that of Umma with the period of Mesilim.

Now the racial origin of Mesilim is a matter of doubt, but there is no doubt as to the Semitic origin of Sharru-Gi, Manishtusu and Urumush, later kings of Kish, whose reigns must be assigned to the pre-Sargonic period, and it is perhaps therefore reasonable to suppose that the earlier Mesilim was also a Semite. If that be the case, the mace-head of this ruler contains evidence that the early Sumerian city of Lagash was at one time under the domination of Semites, and conclusively proves that—so far as documentary evidence is concerned—Sumerians and Semites existed side by side in Babylonia from the earliest period of Mesopotamian civilization.

Some time after, Lagash succeeded in asserting her independence, and many of her subsequent rulers style themselves "kings." The First Dynasty of Lagash which was seemingly founded by Ur-Ninâ established themselves securely for some considerable time, but the reign of Urukagina saw the end of the dynasty, and the capture and sack of the city by Lugal-zaggisi, a ruler of the neighbouring city of Umma.

The limits of Lugal-zaggisi's empire included Ur, Erech, Larsa and Nippur, and he was undoubtedly one of the most powerful rulers of his day. Other pre-Sargonic kings whose power was specifically associated with Erech and Ur, were Lugal-kigub-nidudu and Lugal-kisalsi, but the extent of their sway cannot be estimated with any degree of certainty.

In the time immediately preceding the establishment of the empire of Shar-Gâni-sharri and Narâm-Sin, the rallying point of the Semitic forces of Akkad seems to have been the city of Kish, the conquests of whose three

kings Sharru-Gi Manishtusu and Urumush prepared
the way for their successors at Agade. Thus both
Manishtusu and Urumush seem to have extended their
power southward into the land of Sumer, while both
these kings warred successfully against Elam.

The empire of Shar-Gâni-sharri and Narâm-Sin was
however destined to entirely eclipse that of their forerunners, for it not only embraced Mesopotamia north
and south, but also Syria and Palestine, and was in fact
the first Babylonian empire worthy of the name.

Meanwhile the power of the Sumerians in the south
had received a temporary check, and the patesis of Lagash, and other Sumerian centres at the time, clearly ruled
on sufferance and not on the strength of rights which
they were prepared to assert successfully in the battle-
field.

But on the accession of Gudea about 2450 B.C., the
momentarily smoking flame of Sumerian influence in
Babylonia was kindled anew, and a strong anti-Semitic
wave set in. This wave does not seem to have been
characterized by a series of wars or battles, for the records
of Gudea, the most powerful ruler among the later
patesis of Lagash, seldom refer to anything in the nature
of military achievements, but the extensiveness of his
building operations testifies to the abundance of resources at his command, while the names of the countries
which he laid under contribution for building-materials
conclusively prove that the influence exercised by Lagash during the reign of Gudea was considerable. The
list of the places from which he derived wood and stone
includes the mountains in Arabia and on the Syrian
coast, while he obtained copper from the mines in the
Elamite territory east of the Tigris.

But the importance of Lagash was soon to pass away,
and Ur became the dominating power in Babylonia.
The dynasty of Ur (*circ.* 2400 B.C.), which lasted close on
120 years, was founded by Ur-Engur. He included

the whole of Southern Babylonia within his sphere of influence, while in the north, he has left evidence of his architectural undertakings at Nippur ; hence he styled himself the " King of Sumer and Akkad," but the fact that his son and successor Dungi found it necessary to reduce Babylon indicates that his authority in Akkad was not unquestioned.   Dungi reigned 58 years, during which he reduced the whole of Babylonia beneath his sway, and apparently annexed the greater part of Elam. So firmly had he established his control over Elam, that we find the capital of that country (Susa) still retained by his successors, though frequent expeditions had to be undertaken to maintain the " status quo."

The dynasty of Ur would appear to have been brought to an end by an invasion of Elamites ; at all events Ibi-Sin, the last king of Ur, was carried away by the Elamites, and the rule in Babylonia then passed to the city of Isin.   The dynasty of Isin lasted some 225 years, during which Babylonia enjoyed great prosperity.

In the latter part of the first half of this period the power in Babylonia seems to have passed temporarily into the hands of Gungunu, king of Ur and Larsa, who laid claim to rule over the whole of Sumer and Akkad, but his supremacy was of short duration, and Isin soon recovered her position as the paramount power in Babylonia.

Meanwhile the Semitic element in the north was gradually regaining its ascendency, and finally asserted itself as a concrete fact in the establishment of a dynasty by Sumu-abu, at the city of Babylon itself, about 2000 B.C.

At about this time the Elamites established themselves in Southern Babylonia at Ur and Larsa under Kudur-Mabuk and his sons Arad-Sin and Rîm-Sin, and during the earlier part of the dynasty exercised a suzerainty over the whole of that region.   Subsequently Rîm-Sin met with a severe defeat at the hands of Kham-

murabi, the most illustrious king of the dynasty and
the Amraphel of the Book of Genesis, while he met with
his death at the hands of Samsu-iluna, Khammurabi's
successor. With the death of Rîm-Sin Elamite power
in Babylonia came to an end.

Khammurabi consolidated the power of Babylon, and
extended his influence on all sides, but his chief title to
fame depends upon his codification of Babylonian law.
But Babylon's supremacy in the south was soon to be
successfully challenged by Iluma-ilu who founded a
kingdom on the shores of the Persian Gulf, and inaugurated the so-called " Second Dynasty " of the lists of
the kings.

Iluma-ilu was a contemporary of Samsu-iluna, whose
attacks he twice repelled. Abêshu', the successor of
Samsu-iluna on the throne of Babylon, similarly tried
to reduce the rebellious " Country of the Sea " beneath
his sway, but without success, and from this time on,
Southern Babylonia was ruled over by the kings of the
" Country of the Sea."

But Samsu-iluna had another foe to contend with,
besides the southern rebels, a foe moreover ultimately
destined to subjugate the whole of Babylonia, under
whose rule she was governed for several centuries.

The Kassites were a warlike people whose home lay
on the east of the Tigris, and to the north of Elam, and
they apparently commenced raiding Babylonian territory in the reign of Samsu-iluna, though they do not
seem to have materially affected the Babylonian power.
About a century later however, the dynasty of Babylon
was brought to an end by an invasion of the Hittites of
Cappadocia who sacked the city, destroyed the temple
of the great city-god, Marduk, and carried off his statue
as a trophy. The Hittite conquest must have paved
the way for the invasion of the Kassites who established
themselves securely on the throne of Babylon for a very
long period. At first their sphere of influence would

D

appear to have been confined to the northern half of the plain, but later on they extended their power to the Country of the Sea.

Meanwhile, Assyria in Northern Mesopotamia had emerged as a separate and independent kingdom, and already the signs of her future greatness were visible on the horizon.

The date of the colonization of Assyria is not known, but in any case it must have been before the time of Khammurabi, for the country bore the name of " Assyria " in his time, and was embraced within the limits of his empire.   The struggle for supremacy finally ended in a victory for the northerners who under their king Tukulti-Ninib (*circ.* 1275 B.C.) effected the conquest of Babylonia.   In addition to his title "King of Assyria," Tukulti-Ninib styled himself "King of Karduniash (i.e. Babylon), King of Sumer and Akkad."   From that date down to the destruction of Nineveh (*circ.* 606 B.C.), and the foundation of the short-lived Neo-Babylonian empire by Nabopolassar, Babylonia takes a subsidiary place in the political history of Western Asia.

The immediate successors of Tukulti-Ninib I appear to have been perpetually engaged in war with the Babylonians, who at no period of their history readily submitted to the Assyrian yoke.   Tiglath-Pileser I's accession to the throne about 1100 B.C. inaugurated a new period in the history of Assyrian expansion.   Some of the mountain-tribes who had owed allegiance to former Assyrian monarchs had revolted, and Tiglath-Pileser made it his business to crush them.   The northern Moschians who sixty years previously had been the vassals of Assyria, had under the leadership of five kings invaded the territory of Commagene, but they were effectively reduced by Tiglath-Pileser, and the land of Commagene was conquered " throughout its whole extent."

Various other tribes in the north, of whom the Nairi

would appear to have been the most important, were similarly brought beneath the Assyrian sway.

In a campaign against Babylonia he was also successful for the moment, and effected the reduction of Babylon, Sippar, Opis and other cities in Lower Mesopotamia. But his triumph here was short-lived, and the Assyrians were expelled by Marduk-nadin-akhê, the king of Babylon, who further invaded Assyria, and carried off the statues of some of the Assyrian gods.

Ashur-bêl-kala, the son and successor of Tiglath-Pileser I, retrieved the fortunes of the Assyrian arms in the south, and forced Marduk-shapik-zêrim the successor of Marduk-nadin-akhê to sue for peace.

But after the reigns of Tiglath-Pileser I's two sons, Assyria suffered a severe disaster at the hands of the Hittites, and lost the territory gained by Tiglath-Pileser. Northern Syria which had been compelled to acknowledge the suzerainty of Tiglath-Pileser, now asserted her independence, and for some time remained the mistress of her own destinies.

Thus Assyria for the time being lost her position as a world-power, and it was only in the reign of Tukulti-Ninib II (890–885 B.C.) that her fortunes began to revive. The Nairi were again reduced by this king, and apparently the whole of the valley of the Upper Tigris was once more subjugated. Ashur-nasir-pal (885–860 B.C.) carried on the work of expansion and re-conquest. With the further extension of Assyrian power northwards, the need of a capital occupying a more central position than ancient Ashur was at once realized, and accordingly Ashur-nasir-pal transferred the seat of his government to Calah (Nimrûd) some forty miles north of Ashur.

Nearly 500 years before, Shalmaneser I had laid the foundations of a town at Calah, but the unsettled circumstances of the time had retarded its growth. Ashur-nasir-pal demolished what remained of the old town, and founded a new town on the same site, and for at least a century Calah remained the capital of the empire.

Ashur-naṣir-pal also extended his sphere of influence in a westerly direction and made a triumphal march through Northern Syria, but he appears to have cautiously refrained from coming into collision with the powerful king of Damascus.

Ashur-naṣir-pal's son and successor, Shalmaneser II (860-825) consolidated the work of his father and grandfather and at the same time made fresh conquests himself. His campaigns in the west brought him into contact with the Israelites, and we find Ahab, king of Israel, mentioned as one of the Syrian allies who rebelled against him. Some years later, Shalmaneser became the suzerain of Israel, and received tribute from Jehu, the usurper.

After the reigns of Shalmaneser's immediate successors, the power of Assyria began temporarily to decline, and the subject nations asserted their independence, but in 745 B.C. Tiglath-Pileser III, or Pul as he is called in 2 Kings xv. 19 and elsewhere, ascended the throne, and restored the influence and authority of Assyria in Western Asia. His wars in Syria meant disaster to Israel and the loss of independence to Judah. Ahaz, king of Judah, had sought the help of Tiglath-Pileser against the allied forces of Rezin, king of Damascus, and Pekah, king of Israel. Tiglath-Pileser at once seized this golden opportunity of interfering with the internal affairs of Palestine, defeated Israel and Damascus, and carried the Israelite tribes of Reuben, Gad and the half-tribe of Manasseh into captivity (734 B.C.). Hoshea, assassinator and usurper, purchased the right to the throne of Israel for ten talents of gold and a certain amount of silver, but in the reign of Tiglath-Pileser's successor, Shalmaneser IV (727–722 B.C.) he became involved in an intrigue with Egypt, which led to his deportation to Assyria where he spent the rest of

his days as a prisoner. Meanwhile Samaria, the capital
of his kingdom, was beleaguered, and after a two years'
siege was captured by Sargon, who deported the larger
half of the population into Assyria. Sargon, " the son
of a nobody," i.e. a usurper, was one of the greatest of
the Assyrian kings (722-705 B.C.) and was the first to
come into actual conflict with the Egyptians. Palestine
as a whole showed no alacrity to take up arms against
her powerful overlord, but the Philistine town of Gaza,
in reliance on the support of Egypt, refused to submit.
Hannon the Philistine commander, on failing to repulse
the Assyrian army retreated on Raphia, a town border-
ing on the Egyptian frontier, where he was joined by
Shabê the Egyptian general. At Raphia the opposing
armies joined battle, and after a fierce encounter, the
allies had to retire before the better equipped and more
disciplined army of Sargon. On his return, Sargon
found it necessary to again subdue Babylonia, and he
also carried on war with Elam. He was succeeded by
his son Sennacherib (705-681 B.C.). After having suppressed the revolts which always seem to have signalized
the accession of a new king, Sennacherib invaded Syria,
established his authority over northern Palestine, reduced the rebellious Philistine city of Askelon, and
then proceeded to attack the city of Ekron, to whose
assistance an Egyptian army had rallied. Their combined forces were routed by Sennacherib at Altaku, and
Ekron fell. Judah next occupied his attention ; having
captured numerous small towns and enslaved some
200,000 of the inhabitants, he proceeded to lay siege
to Jerusalem. Hezekiah the king of Judah, withstood
the siege for some time, but pressed by famine, he was
compelled to yield and purchased the safety of his city by
stripping the Temple of its treasures. Sennacherib there-
upon returned to Assyria, but two years after, Hezekiah's repudiation of his suzerainty occasioned another
expedition to Palestine. The Assyrian troops first sta-

tioned themselves at Lachish, whence Sennacherib dispatched a messenger to Hezekiah to demand his instant surrender. Meanwhile Sennacherib marched westward with a view to engaging the Egyptian army lying at Pelusium, one of the frontier towns of Egypt. But a sudden catastrophe—possibly an outbreak of plague—overtook the Assyrian host, and Sennacherib returned to Nineveh. On his arrival home, he found it necessary to once more suppress rebellious Babylon, and to render his work more lasting, he completely destroyed the city (689 B.C.). Towards the end of his reign he conducted a campaign in Cilicia where he defeated the Greeks and is said to have laid the foundations of the city of Tarsus. In 681 B.C. he was murdered by his sons, and the crown eventually settled on the head of Esarhaddon (681–668 B.C.). The most striking event of his reign was the conquest of Lower Egypt (672 B.C.), but towards the end of his reign Tirhakah, the Ethiopian king of Egypt, recaptured Memphis and threatened to put an end to the Assyrian domination ; his subjugation was one of the first acts of Ashur-bani-pal, the successor of Esarhaddon. Judah also became disaffected, but she was speedily reduced to submission and her king Manasseh was removed into captivity.

Ashur-bani-pal succeeded Esarhaddon in 668 B.C. The work of re-establishing the Assyrian power in Egypt occupied some time and was finally accomplished by the capture of Thebes (666 B.C.). Under Ashur-bani-pal Assyria attained the height of her power both at home and abroad, and the limits of her empire were extended further than ever before. After a lengthy war, Elam was subdued, but she subsequently joined Shamash-shum-ukîn, the brother of Ashur-bani-pal, and viceroy of Babylonia, in an organized revolt against Assyria, which resulted in the defeat of Shamash-shum-ukîn, and the ultimate capture and sack of Susa the Elamite capital (*circ.* 640 B.C.).

While Ashur-bani-pal was thus preoccupied with Babylonia and Elam, Lydia on the one hand, and Egypt on the other seized the opportunity to throw off the yoke of their suzerain. Lydia was reduced, but Egypt succeeded in maintaining her independence. Towards the close of Ashur-bani-pal's reign, the wheel of fortune had already begun to turn, and clouds were already gathering on the eastern horizon. The Medes had made an inroad into Assyrian territory before his death in 626 B.C., and a few years after that event, Cyaxares king of the Medes inflicted a defeat on the Assyrian army and laid siege to Nineveh. But the end was temporarily stayed by the advance of the Scythian hordes.

Shortly afterwards Nineveh was again attacked by Cyaxares and Nabopolassar, an Assyrian general in command of Babylonia, and after a two years' siege the city was taken and destroyed (*circ.* 606 B.C.). Assyria now passed under the power of the Medes, and Babylonia fell to Nabopolassar who founded the New or Neo-Babylonian empire. This late Babylonian empire only lasted about seventy years in all. Nabopolassar was succeeded by Nebuchadnezzar, who at the time of his father's death was engaged in a campaign against Necho king of Egypt, upon whom he inflicted a severe defeat at Carchemish. His Palestinian expeditions led to the capture of Jerusalem, and the removal of a large part of the population of Judah into captivity. Both Jehoiakim, and Zedekiah, kings of Judah, strove to throw off the Babylonian yoke but without avail. Nebuchadnezzar's successors did little deserving of narration, and in the reign of Nabonidus, Babylon, which was under the command of Belshazzar, was captured by Cyrus, 539 B.C., and Babylonia passed under the rule of the Persians. She remained under Persian rule until the time of Alexander the Great's ascendency when she became a Greek province.

CHAPTER II—EXCAVATIONS

THE history of the actual excavations properly
commences with the first expedition sent out to
dig, but there is one scholar who, although he did not
excavate on any large scale, was the first to bring cuneiform inscriptions to Europe and on this account deserves special mention.

C. J. Rich, born in 1787 at Dijon, was from the early
age of nine attracted to the study of Oriental languages,
and in course of time made himself master of Hebrew,
Persian, Aramaic and Arabic, while he is said to have
attempted to read Chinese Hieroglyphics at the pheno-
menal age of fourteen. In 1803 he became a Cadet in
the East India Company's service, his military post being
subsequently exchanged for a civil appointment. After
visiting Egypt, Palestine, Asia Minor and other countries, he returned to Bombay, but was, before the age
of twenty-four, appointed the East India Company's
resident at Baghdad. In 1811 he visited the ruins of
Babylon, an account of which is to be found in his
"Memoir on the ruins of Babylon," while his visit to
Nineveh is recorded in his "*Narrative of a Residence
in Koordistan and on the site of ancient Nineveh, with
Journal of a voyage down the Tigris to Baghdad, and an
account of a visit to Shiraz and Persepolis.*" It is moreover to Rich that we owe our first accurate plans of both
Nineveh and Babylon. In the course of his travels,
he made large collections consisting chiefly of Arabic,
Persian, Turkish, Aramaic and Syriac manuscripts, a
number of Greek and oriental coins, and also many
antiquities from Babylon and Nineveh, including the

first cuneiform tablets seen in Europe: his collections were acquired by the Trustees of the British Museum, after his death from cholera in 1820.

But as the pioneer in the actual field of excavation, M. Botta, the French Consul at Mosul, occupied the first place in point of time. In the year 1842, on the advice of Mohl, he began the exploration of the Mound of Kouyunjik, one of the two mounds which mark the site of the city of Nineveh, but meeting with scant success, he transferred his attention in 1843 to the Mound of Khorsabad (the town of Chosroes) some miles north of Mosul, where he laid bare the ruins of a palace which proved to be that of Sargon, king of Assyria (722–705 B.C.) and the father of Sennacherib. In the year 1851 the French Assembly voted the money for an expedition to Babylonia, and also for another expedition to Assyria, the object of which was to complete the excavations which had been commenced with so much promise at Khorsabad : this expedition was directed by Victor Place who at the same time succeeded Botta as French Consular agent at Mosul. During the years 1851–1855 Place completed the excavation of Sargon's palace, and also laid bare the surrounding buildings and rooms, carrying his work right up to the wall of the town ; Khorsabad was found to contain the ruins of a whole fortified town, which had remained entombed for some 2500 years : the town was named Dûr-Sharrukîn after its founder Sargon. The four corners of the city walls were oriented towards the four cardinal points, the walls themselves being pierced by eight enormous gates, each of which was named after an Assyrian deity. The palace had been built on a terraced mound 45 feet high, which was made of crude or unbaked bricks, and was protected by a casing-wall of large square stones. The palace contained wide halls, adorned with sculptures, winged bulls and the like. The floors of the various chambers consisted generally of stamped clay, and were no doubt hidden from view by elaborate rugs, sometimes, however, tiles or blocks of marble concealed the unsightly clay.

The walls were of great thickness, i.e. from $9\frac{1}{2}$ to 16 feet, while in one place they measured as much as $25\frac{1}{2}$ feet. The inner walls of the less important chambers were only covered with a white plaster surrounded by black lines, the so-called women's apartments, on the other hand, being decorated with frescoes and white or black arabesques. Marble statues were unearthed in the harem court, and the remains of a ziggurat or stage-tower—a characteristic feature in Mesopotamian temples—were brought to light. Place's excavations were not so productive of large sculptures and monuments as those of Botta had been, but they were particularly fruitful as regards smaller objects of glass, stone, clay, and metal.

The first Englishman to enter the field was Layard who in 1845, only two years after Botta's first expedition, commenced excavating the ruined mounds of Nimrûd. Nimrûd, which proved to be the ancient Calah, was built on a rectangular plateau just as Khorsabad had been, and the exploration of its site yielded a rich harvest of new materials for the reconstruction of the history of the past. Ashur-nasir-pal, king of Assyria (885-860), following the example of Shalmaneser I (about 1300), removed the seat of government from Ashur forty miles northwards, to Calah, where he built a palace for himself, the excavation of which was one of Layard's greatest triumphs. This palace occupied the north-western portion of the mound and was in part restored by Sargon ; to the north of this palace of Ashur-naṣir-pal lay the site of the temple of Ninib or Adar, the god of war. Shalmaneser II (860–825) the successor of Ashur-naṣir-pal, also built a palace at Calah, on the south-east of that of his predecessor ; this palace, known as the

PLATE II

1. KOUYUNJIK AND NEBI YÛNUS FROM THE NORTH   3. NIMRÛD (CALAH)
2. KOUYUNJIK AND NEBI YÛNUS FROM MOSUL.   4. KHORSABAD

central palace, was almost entirely rebuilt by Tiglath-Pileser III, the Biblical Pul (745–727 B.C.).

At the south-west corner, the palace of Esarhaddon (681–668) was excavated, in the construction of which, that king utilized the materials of the older palaces in the most unscrupulous fashion, but the building was found to have been much damaged by fire. North of Esarhaddon's palace and south of that of Ashur-nasir-pal, lay the comparatively small palace of Adad-nirari III (812–783 B.C.), and in the south-east corner of the parallelogram the insignificant remains of the palace of Ashur-etil-ilâni (about 625) one of the last of Assyria's monarchs were brought to light.

Thus Layard discovered and excavated the remains of some seven royal palaces at Nimrûd ; of these seven that of Ashur-nasir-pal was by far the most important from the archæological and historical standpoint.

Wall bas-reliefs, human-headed winged lions and bulls (cf. Pl. XXV), obelisks, bronze bowls, iron reaping-hooks and spear-heads, carved ivory panels and mirrors, a " silver-plated " sceptre-head, and a variety of bells are a few among the many valuable finds at Nimrûd, each of which makes its contribution, be it small or be it great, to the restoration of a page of human history and cultural evolution.

But undoubtedly the most impressive monuments yielded by Assyrian excavations are the gigantic winged bulls and lions which were stationed at the royal palace gates. The removal of these monsters of oriental antiquity was an even more difficult task than their excavation, and taxed the inventive powers of both French and explorers to the utmost.

Those excavated by the French at Khorsabad were embarked piecemeal for Paris, the parts into which they had been sawn, with a view to facilitating their transit, being fitted together again in the Louvre, the museum which they now adorn. Layard however adopted a different method in effecting the transport of the winged bulls from Nimrûd to London, by means of which he successfully brought them over intact without breaking them up in any way ; the extraordinary difficulties involved in this feat give us a vivid conception of the similar difficulties which the Assyrians must have had to overcome in the removal of these solid stone masses from the quarry to the entrances of the palaces, and in the exact adjustment of them in their specific places. Layard gives us a detailed description[1] of the plan he devised for the removal of some of these unwieldy monsters, of which thirteen pairs had already been discovered. His first efforts were directed towards two of the smaller colossi. The first and greatest problem to be solved was how to lower them without risk of their falling and so being broken. The sculptures were first of all wrapped in mats or felt to mitigate the effect of any misfortune that might befall them, either through the ropes giving way or cutting the soft stone. Heavy wooden rollers had been procured from the mountains; these were placed upon sleepers laid parallel to the sculpture, and it only now remained to lower the winged creature on to the rollers ; this was effected by means of ropes skilfully applied, the descent of the gradually sinking monument being checked by thick beams which supported it in its fall and were gradually withdrawn as the occasion required. As the bull approached the rollers the beams had to be entirely removed, the whole of the weight and strain thus being on the cables and ropes, which stretched until finally they reached breaking point, and the bull fell some four feet or more to the ground, but fortunately without being damaged. A trench of about 200 feet in length, 15 feet wide, and in some places 20 feet deep, having been duly made through which the bull might proceed on the rollers to the edge of the mound—this course was necessary owing

[1] Layard, *Nineveh*, p. 74 ff.

PLATE III

From Layard

EXCAVATIONS AT NIMRÛD (CALAH) IN ASHUR-NASIR-PAL'S PALACE

to the impossibility of lifting such a massive weight—
the giant animal was slowly pulled by a large number
of Arabs to the end of the trench and down the slope
of the mound, where it was lowered on to a specially-
constructed cart, which had been a nine days' wonder
to the natives ever since its appearance. The cart itself
was fitted with two strong axles which had been used
by Botta in the removal of sculptures from Khorsabad.
"Each wheel was formed of three solid pieces, nearly
a foot thick, from the trunk of a mulberry tree, bound
together by iron hoops. Across the axles were laid three
beams, and above them several cross-beams, all of the
same wood. A pole was fixed to one axle to which were
also attached iron rings for ropes to enable men as well
as buffaloes to draw the cart. The wheels were provided
with movable hooks for the same purpose." The mulberry wood used had of course to be procured in the
mountains, there being no wood of the required substance
or size in the Mesopotamian valley. Buffaloes were first
harnessed to the pole, while a number of men tugged
at the ropes attached to the wheels and the movable
hooks, but the buffaloes appear to have soon struck, and
they were consequently taken out, the whole of the work
now being done by three hundred Arabs. At length,
after multitudinous efforts, the bull arrived at the river
where it was landed on a specially-prepared platform
from which it might slide on to a raft. Thus much for
the obstacles to be surmounted in the mere removal of
these enormous blocks of stone by an excavator of the
nineteenth century, from which we may form a small and
very inadequate estimate of the indomitable zeal and in-
vincible energy of the Assyrians some twenty-six or
twenty-seven centuries ago in quarrying, carving, trans-
porting and fixing the guardian genii.

Calah (Nimrûd) was the capital of Assyria for 220
years (885–668), but at the close of that period she had
to yield her pre-eminence to Nineveh, which Sennacherib

rebuilt and which was the capital of the empire from his time till the end of the chapter, i.e. till about 630 B.C. Sennacherib naturally built a palace at his new capital, Nineveh, and the discovery and excavation of this palace are also due to the indefatigable efforts of the late Sir Henry Layard and his assistant Hormuzd Rassam. This palace of Sennacherib occupied the south-west corner of the northern of the two groups of mounds known as Kouyunjik which mark the site of ancient Nineveh, Ashur-bani-pal's (668–626 B.C.) palace being located immediately to the north of it. Unfortunately Sennacherib's palace suffered from fire when the Medes took the city in 606 B.C. in consequence of which most of his wall bas-reliefs are greatly marred. The complete excavation of this palace was the great triumph of Layard's second campaign (1849–1851), and the bas-reliefs taken from the walls of its seventy or more halls and chambers now form, in spite of their comparatively bad state of preservation, one of the most priceless possessions of the British Museum. But one more epoch-making discovery in the annals of Mesopotamian excavations must be attributed to this world-renowned excavator.

One day Layard discovered two chambers connected with each other, and after removing the débris, he found that " to the height of a foot or more from the floor they were entirely filled with cuneiform tablets of baked clay, some entire, but the greater part broken into many fragments."

In point of fact he had chanced upon part of the library of Ashur-bani-pal, one of Assyria's greatest kings; the library appears to have been stored partly in the northern palace, that of Ashur-bani-pal proper, and partly in the south-western palace built by Sennacherib ; it was in the latter that the rooms referred to were found ; the other half of this great library of the later Assyrian kings was subsequently unearthed by Rassam. The contents of these tablets, made of the finest clay and ranging from one to fifteen inches, are as varied as the tablets themselves. Some of them contain historical records, others astronomical reports, or mathematical calculations: there are also letters of a private and public character, but the majority of the tablets deal with astrology and medicine, both of which subjects were intimately connected in the mind of the Babylonian. Prayers, incantations, psalms and religious texts in general, formed a considerable part of this library, and as a large proportion of the " volumes " or tablets are not original works but copies from earlier Babylonian productions, the value of the library, —now known under the name of the "Kouyunjik collection,"—for the study of the religious and mythological conceptions of both the Babylonians and Assyrians is more than can be adequately estimated. Many of the tablets are bilingual, the ideographic Sumerian being provided with an Assyrian interlinear translation, and these, together with other tablets of the collection containing syllabaries in which the Sumerian value, the Assyrian name, and sometimes the Assyrian meaning of different signs are given, have been of the utmost use in the rediscovery of the languages of Mesopotamia. Layard also visited Babylonia, and began to excavate at Babylon and Nippur, but his Babylonian operations were not attended with the extraordinary success of his excavations at Nineveh and Calah.

In 1851 a French expedition was sent out to Babylonia under Fresnel and Jules Oppert: they secured various relics from the ruined mounds of Babylon, among which may be especially mentioned a fine collection of colouredbrick fragments, but unfortunately all was lost through a mishap on the Tigris in 1855.

In 1852 Rassam succeeded Layard in the field, and at once had to contend with difficulties resulting from Rawlinson's concessions to Victor Place, to whom he had transferred the right of excavating what remained to be excavated at Kouyunjik, which from Rassam's point of

view fell within the sphere of British influence, and to
which therefore British excavators had a prior claim. In
1853 Rassam commenced operations at Ḳalat Sherḳât,
but apart from the discovery of two clay prisms inscribed with the annals of Tiglath-Pileser I (1100–1080
B.c.), the ancient Ashur did not yield much fruit on this
occasion. At Calah, the scene of Layard's brilliant triumphs, Rassam discovered Ezida, the temple of Nebo,
the god who vied with Marduk for the first place in the
Babylonian pantheon of later days, and whose name is
commemorated in the names of several of the kings of
the first Babylonian empire, as also in three of those of
the second empire, the most familiar of whom is the
Biblical Nebuchadnezzar ; six large statues of the god
were brought to light, two of which at all events are by
their inscriptions shown to be contemporaneous with the
Assyrian king Adad-nirari III (812–783) ; a stele of
King Shamshi-Adad II (825–812 B.c.), and the remains of
an inscribed obelisk of Ashur-naṣir-pal complete the list
of his principal finds on this site. But his name will be
for ever associated with Kouyunjik ; his first efforts were
productive of no very great results beyond the discovery
of a limestone obelisk of Ashur-naṣir-pal covered with
bas-reliefs, and now in the Assyrian Transept of the British Museum, and a female torso from the palace of Ashur-
bêl-kala, king of Assyria about 1080 B.c. (cf. Pl. XXIV).
Rassam however profited by Victor Place's omission to
make use of the permission accorded to him by Rawlinson to explore the northern part of Kouyunjik, but at
the same time took the precaution of making his initial
operations under the cover of night. His nocturnal
labours were crowned with the greatest success which
the excavators of those days could have—the discovery
of a new palace—and after he was satisfied on this point,
the digging was allowed to proceed during the daytime,
as it is a recognized rule that the discoverer of a new
palace has established his claim to the complete excava-

PLATE IV

Both from Layard

"Fish-god," Kouyunjik   Entrance Passage, Kouyunjik

tion of it, as against the rest of the world. The newly-discovered palace turned out to be that of Ashur-bani-pal, king of Assyria (668–626 B.C.), in whose reign Assyria attained the height of her power both at home and abroad, extending her sway even as far as Thebes, the capital of Upper Egypt, which was taken and sacked by this king in B.C. 666. But Ashur-bani-pal as well as being a great warrior, was also a great huntsman, and the bas-reliefs which he caused to be sculptured upon the walls of his palace at Kouyunjik, in commemoration of his exploits in the chase, are probably the masterpieces of Assyrian art. They thus testify not only to the sportsmanship of this king, but also to the encouragement which he gave to art, while Rassam's further discovery of the other half of Ashur-bani-pal's library has shown that king to have been an even greater patron of literature than there had hitherto been reason to suppose.

In the spring of 1854, funds failed and Rassam was in consequence obliged to return, but shortly afterwards he accepted a political appointment at Aden. The meanwhile, work had already been commenced in Babylonia by W. K. Loftus who carried on small excavations at Warka, the ancient Erech, the ruins of which are the largest in Babylonia, but though many interesting antiquities were unearthed, none of them are of an epoch-making character, the slipper-shaped coffins belonging to the Parthian period, being perhaps the best known. Owing to the fact that Erech has been occupied during the greater part of its history, i.e. some 5000 years, it is not a fruitful mine for early antiquities. Senkereh (Larsa) on the other hand, which has been identified with the Ellasar of Genesis xiv. 1, seems to have remained more or less unoccupied after the Persian period, and hence it is a better site for the exploration and study of the earlier history of Southern Mesopotamia. Inscribed bricks from Senkereh show that Khammurabi (the Amraphel of Genesis xiv. ?), and the

E

most famous king of the first dynasty of Babylon, repaired the ancient temple-tower there, as also did his Neo-Babylonian successor, Nabonidus, some fourteen centuries later, while the famous Nebuchadnezzar of Old Testament fame had also not neglected it in his works of restoration. The lower strata of the mound showed that Ur-Engur, King of Ur, whose reign may probably be assigned to the latter part of the third millennium B.C., had also made his presence felt in this ancient city of Larsa. Subsequently Larsa shared the fate of other early Babylonian cities, and was used as a cemetery : the tablets found near the coffins apparently belong to a much earlier date, and were probably found by the grave-diggers to whom their altered position is to be ascribed. Excavations were also conducted at the same time at Tell Sifr, which resulted in the discovery of about a hundred so-called case-tablets (i.e. tablets protected by a clay cover or envelope), belonging to the time of the first dynasty of Babylon, which in their turn led to the discovery of a hitherto unknown king of this dynasty, Samsu-iluna, the successor of Khammurabi.

When Loftus was excavating at Warka at the beginning of 1854, J. E. Taylor, the Vice-Consul at Basra, undertook excavations on behalf of the British Museum at Mukeyyer, the site of the ancient city of Ur. He commenced operations on what appeared at the time, and what ultimately turned out to be, the principal building of the city, the temple of the Moon-god Sin, in the four corners of which he discovered four clay cylinders, and also another barrel-shaped cylinder the inscription of which is of even greater importance than those of the corner-cylinders. We learn that Ur-Engur, King of Ur, built the temple, that his son Dungi repaired it, and that Nabonidus the last King of Babylon restored it some two thousand years later. These foundation-cylinders of Nabonidus proved of great historical interest, the inscription on each of them concluding with a prayer for

Bêl-shar-uṣur, the King's son and heir, the Belshazzar of Daniel v., who was in command of Babylon at the time of the capture of the city by Cyrus. Taylor also conducted excavations on other Babylonian sites, the most important of which was Abû Shahrein, the ancient Eridu whose god Ea was one of the most illustrious as well as one of the most time-honoured gods in Babylonia. Its ruins are smaller than those of Ur, but they contain the remains of a temple-tower, consisting of two storeys, which Taylor laid bare. From the inscribed bricks recovered, the identification of this site with the ancient Eridu was established.

Towards the end of the year 1854, Sir Henry Rawlinson commenced excavating Birs-Nimrûd, the Borsippa of antiquity ; he commenced digging at the four corners of what ultimately proved to be the famous Ezida, the temple of Nebo, in search of clay cylinders such as had been found at the corners of other Babylonian buildings ; he recovered two such foundation-cylinders which turned out to be duplicates, together with fragmentary parts of other cylinders, all of which had been deposited there by Nebuchadnezzar.

Soon after Rassam's return from Assyria in the year 1854, Loftus entered the service of the Trustees of the British Museum, and was sent out to continue the excavation of Kouyunjik. Loftus ably followed up the work of his predecessor ; new reliefs were brought to light, the most celebrated of which perhaps is that of Ashur-bani-pal and his queen reclining at meat in the garden (cf. Pl. XXI), but again though the spirit was willing, the funds were weak, and Loftus had to abandon all hope of completing the excavation of the palace of Assyria's most famous king.

The abundant harvest, yielded by these numerous excavations in Mesopotamia, and stored away in the Museums, afforded a supply of material copious enough to occupy the intellectual acumen of the savants for some time to come, while the general public whose interest in these archæological expeditions depended on the tangible results forthcoming, were inclined to await the decipherment and publication of the accumulated mass of clay tablets, monuments and stelae already to hand, before furnishing the necessary funds for any fresh expeditions, and it was not till 1873 that George Smith, the able assistant of Sir Henry Rawlinson, whose discovery of the Babylonian account of the Deluge had alike won for him great fame, and also kindled again the enthusiasm of the public in the cause of excavation, was enabled, thanks to the munificence of the proprietors of the "Daily Telegraph," to personally conduct an expedition to Mesopotamia.   In the January of that year Smith set out for Mosul, but on his arrival, he found to his dismay that the requisite firmân had not as yet been granted by the Turkish Government, and he accordingly journeyed southward, examining the ruined mounds of Nimrûd and Ḳalat Sherkat on the way.   In northern Babylonia he spent but a short time which he employed in visiting the sites of Babylon, Borsippa (Birs-Nimrûd) and other ancient ruins, but by the beginning of April, he obtained the necessary permission to excavate in Assyria, and accordingly returned at once to Mosul.   His attention was first of all directed to Nimrûd, the scene of so many of Layard's triumphs, but his predecessors in the field had reaped their harvest to the full, and the gleanings which remained were poor and meagre.

In the following month he transferred the seat of his operations to Kouyunjik, with a view to discovering the remainder of Ashur-bani-pal's library.   The work was far from easy owing to the complete state of confusion in which the ruins then were, partly owing to the work of earlier excavators, partly owing to the builders of the bridge at Mosul who had made use of the remains of

Assyria's ancient buildings for the construction of the bridge, and partly owing to the instability of some of Layard's tunnels, which had the meanwhile collapsed. Here too, the harvest was past and the summer of Assyrian excavations was ended, but the object which the "Daily Telegraph" proprietors had in view was realized in the discovery of another fragment of the Babylonian account of the Deluge, which proved to fill in the chief lacuna in the story. Smith had entertained the hope that this all-important discovery would be an inducement to his financiers to grant an additional sum for the continuation of the work, but they declined. Smith accordingly had reluctantly to set his face westward and return to London, but before the year was out he was on his way back to the Orient, the Trustees of the British Museum having voted £1000 for another expedition thither. He arrived at Mosul on New Year's Day 1874, and recommenced his quest for tablets, but the time at his disposal was short, his firmân expiring in the ensuing March; this notwithstanding, in the three months spent at Kouyunjik on these two expeditions, he brought to light some three thousand tablets dealing with a variety of different subjects, and providing invaluable material for the student of Babylonian and Assyrian astronomy, theology and chronology. To him is due not only the rediscovery of the Babylonian story of the Flood, but also of portions of the Creation legends, and of the Epic of Gilgamesh, the hero of Babylonian folk-lore, while to the student of Old Testament History, his discovery of Sargon's own account of his campaign against the city of Ashdod recorded in the twentieth chapter of Isaiah is of paramount importance. In the spring of 1876 Smith conducted his third and last expedition to Assyria, under the auspices of the British Museum, the value of whose collections he had already so greatly enhanced. But he arrived to find the cholera rampant all over the country, and confusion and disorder reigned everywhere. To excavate under such circumstances was an impossibility, but Smith spared no effort in his futile endeavour to overcome the impossible, boldly facing all dangers and difficulties, but he ultimately succumbed to the disastrous effects of climate and exposure, and died at Aleppo in August 1876, a martyr to the cause of science. George Smith was not only an excavator, but also a scholar, and his scholastic achievements are the more praiseworthy, when it is recollected that he was practically a self-educated man, who by dint of his extraordinary perseverance and indomitable will succeeded where other men of perhaps greater ability failed, and who on that account alone is entitled to the prominent place which he occupies in the annals of Assyriology.

Soon after the death of George Smith in 1876, the Trustees of the British Museum requested Rassam to resume his long-abandoned labours in Assyria, and after some unavoidable delay, operations were commenced in January 1878. The work was greatly facilitated by the presence of Sir Henry Layard as British special representative at Constantinople, for the latter having always been on friendly terms with the Turkish Government, was consequently able to secure concessions which might well have been denied to anyone else. Rassam's marching orders were sufficiently explicit, he was sent out to continue the excavation of Nineveh, but his heart was bent on the discovery of palaces and temples rather than on the comparatively unexciting task of searching for tablets, the importance or non-importance of which could never be determined off-hand, without a detailed study of the contents. His ambition was satisfied shortly after his arrival : a year before his resumption of the work of Assyrian exploration two portions of a bronze door-panel covered with figures and cuneiform characters had been sent to him by a friend, and immediately on his

PLATE V

Déc. en Chald., Plate 53, ii

DOORWAY AT TELLÔ, ERECTED BY GUDEA; ON THE LEFT A LATER
BUILDING OF SELEUCID PERIOD

Déc. en Chald., Plate 54

SOUTH-EASTERN FACADE OF UR-NINÂ'S BUILDING AT TELLÔ

return to Assyria he made enquiries as to where these
pieces of worked metal had been unearthed. He soon discovered that they formed part of a large bronze door-panel
discovered quite accidentally by a peasant in a mound,
some fifteen miles east of Mosul, called Balâwât. Accordingly, his immediate desire was to discover the remainder of this unique monument of ancient metallurgy,
and with that end in view he determined to explore the
Balâwât mound. He discovered that the site had been
used as a cemetery by the inhabitants of the neighbourhood, and was consequently outside the limits of
his firmân, but disregarding the risk of a collision with
the authorities and the still more imminent risk of in-
citing the native population to open resistance, for no
people civilized or uncivilized are in the habit of passively acquiescing in the disinterment of their dead, he
determined to hazard everything in pursuit of his prize.
Success attended his efforts, and very soon after the
cutting of the first trenches, fragments of bronze plates
similar to those which had previously come to light, were
unearthed. In the course of a short time, the remaining
panels were duly restored to the light of day : these
panels had once upon a time decorated the wooden gates
of a large building, to which they were affixed. The
scenes portrayed thereon represent incidents in the life
and campaigns of Shalmaneser II (860-825 B.C.), the
successor of Ashur-naṣir-pal, and the first Assyrian king
who is known to have come into immediate contact with
Israel. In the course of his excavation of the mound, he
came across the ruins of a small temple, and a large
coffer made of marble containing two tablets made of
the same material and bearing inscriptions of Ashur-
nasir-pal. Rassam's work at Kouyunjik and Nimrûd
was also far from fruitless, though Nimrûd certainly
failed to yield a harvest in any way comparable to that of
bygone days, a few bas-reliefs, a number of clay tablets
and some enamelled tiles practically comprising all that

Nimrûd contributed to the study of Assyrian antiquity
on this occasion. So too at Kouyunjik, clay inscriptions
were the chief and indeed practically the only fruits of
the excavations carried on by Rassam during his four
expeditions (1878–1882). The most epoch-making of
these inscriptions consisted in a ten-sided baked clay
prism containing the annals of Ashur-bani-pal, and four
barrel-shaped cylinders inscribed with an account of
Sennacherib's various campaigns. Rassam further attempted the complete exploration of Nebi Yûnus, the
second large mound which marks the site or part of the
site of ancient Nineveh, but he did not meet with the
success which his indefatigable efforts deserved, owing
to the innate factiousness and aptitude for intrigue which
lie dormant in the Oriental breast even at the best of
times, and which on this occasion so far from being dormant, showed themselves in all their pristine vigour, the
result of which was the cessation of Rassam's labours,
and the final dissipation of all his hopes.

Meanwhile excavations were also going on in Babylonia, excavations moreover which were destined to
usher in a new era of Babylonian exploration, and
which proved of incalculable value both to the archæologist, and also to the student of early art. In the
spring of 1877, some few months before Rassam's
return to Assyria after an interval of a quarter of a
century, Ernest de Sarzec, the French Vice-Consul at
Basra, started tentative operations at the ruined mounds
of Tellô, whither his attention had been directed by
J. Asfar, a native Christian, and formerly a dealer in
antiquities. Tellô had already won for itself a name
as a site likely to repay the labour entailed in its
methodical excavation, in consequence of the discovery
of inscribed cones and bricks in its ruins, and needless
to say, it has more than lived up to its early reputation,
for of all the ancient sites of Babylonian civilization,
Tellô has yielded by far the richest harvest of material

for the reconstruction of Sumerian history, and the systematic study of Sumerian art and culture. It would be impossible here to chronicle all the far-reaching results of De Sarzec's immortal work, and we must therefore content ourselves with a notice of the more important of his discoveries. On his very first visit to Telló he was fortunate enough to find a portion of a dolerite statue lying at the foot of one of the mounds, from which he correctly inferred that the statue itself must have originally occupied a position in some large building, the ruins of which he assumed to be lying concealed within the mound in question. He accordingly commenced excavating the mound, and very shortly discovered that it contained a building of no small dimensions, erected upon a large platform of crude, or sun-dried bricks : the objects which he unearthed comprised a large statue of dolerite bearing an inscription of Gudea, priest-king of Lagash about 2450 B.C., inscribed door-sockets, sculptures and vases, copper statuettes of a votive character, and last but most important of all, the first fragments of the Vulture stele of Eannatum, one of the most famous works of early Babylonian art, both in regard to its antiquity and also in regard to the manner in which it illustrates not only the artistic but also the military operations of the Sumerians at this remote period (cf. Pl. XII). In his next two campaigns (1880–81) he systematically excavated the building in the mound generally known as "A," in the course of which he discovered some nine or ten dolerite statues, numerous statuettes, and a stone vase of Narâm-Sin, son of Shar-Gâni-sharri of Agade, who probably lived some few centuries before Gudea. The building itself, which in the main belongs to the Parthian period, but in which part of the old palace of Gudea had been incorporated is briefly discussed on page 149. But as Prof. Hilprecht[1] truly says, the dolerite statues of

[1] Hilprecht, *Explorations*, p. 236.

Gudea "will always remain the principal discovery connected with De Sarzec's name," famous alike for the animation and life with which they are inspired, and also for the skill and dexterity which these early Babylonians display in their treatment of the hardest stones. Among other valuable or rather invaluable finds may be mentioned the well-known silver vase of Entemena (cf. Fig. 45), the carved mace-head of Mesilim, an enormous copper spear-head, and some bas-reliefs of Ur-Ninâ, the founder of the First Dynasty of Lagash. In mound " B," De Sarzec's excavations not only laid bare the building of Ur-Ninâ (cf. Pl. V) but also revealed the remains of a yet earlier structure lying beneath the edifice of this ancient ruler, and resting on a pavement some 16 feet below Ur-Ninâ's platform. Copper statuettes and stone bas-reliefs of a most archaic character were also brought to light on this occasion.

In 1889 De Sarzec left Babylonia, not to return till 1894, when he renewed his excavations in mound "B." Two wells and a watercourse of Eannatum's time were discovered, while among the small relics of this long-forgotten age were various pieces of shell carved with pictures of trees and animals. It would be altogether impossible to over-estimate the debt which both the historian of early Babylonia, and the student of early Mesopotamian art owe to the work of that distinguished excavator; if to Layard, Botta, and Place is due the opening up of the book of Assyria's ancient history, and the breaking of the seals that had kept that book closed for so long a period, to De Sarzec we owe the recovery of an even earlier page in the history of human life and progress. The last quarter of the 19th century which embraced the period of De Sarzec's extraordinary activity in the archæological field (the first of his expeditions being conducted in 1877 and the last in 1900) will remain for all time memorable for the epoch-making discoveries in Babylonia, discoveries which posterity

PLATE VI

Déc. en Chald., Pl. 56, ii

REMAINS OF A STELE IN A BUILDING UNDER THAT OF UR-NINÂ

D c. en Chald., Pl. 57, ii

THE WELL OF EANNATUM

will for ever associate with the name of the illustrious French excavator.

The meanwhile Rassam, had used to the utmost the facilities granted to him under the generous terms of the 1878 firmân, and had covered as much ground and visited as many sites as possible, though whether science would have gained more by the systematic exploration of a few mounds than by the ransacking of many is a question which would probably have to be answered in the affirmative. In 1879, he commenced operations in Babylonia, the ruined mounds of Babylon and Borsippa being the first to receive his attention. On his arrival he found a number of Arabs busily engaged in extracting building material from the Babil mound, and in the course of their digging they came upon four wells, some 140 feet deep, and made of blocks of red granite, each block being about 3 feet high, and fitted to the adjoining block with an extraordinary degree of precision. From the general appearance of the mound as well as from the magnitude of the ruined walls which it covered, Rassam came to the conclusion arrived at by Rich nearly a century before, and accepted by Hilprecht some years later, that to Babil we must look for the world-renowned hanging gardens of Diodorus and Pliny.

Rassam's trenches on the Ḳasr mound were attended with no important results, but his work at the Jumjuma mound in the South,—so called from the name of the modern village now situated there,—yielded a rich harvest of tablets, mostly of a commercial character. Borsippa in like manner responded to the appeal made to it by the spade of Rassam, many tablets being recovered, while a large part of the renowned temple of Ezida, dedicated to the god Nebo, once again saw the light of day : among the smaller relics, the recovery of a bronze step of the famous Nebuchadnezzar is deserving of special mention, and also a baked clay cylinder of the time of Antiochus Soter 270 B.C., the latter being, accord-

ing to Hilprecht, "the last royal document composed in
the Old Babylonian writing and language." But perhaps Rassam's most valuable contribution to Assyriology was the identification of the site of ancient Sippar.
Many unsuccessful attempts had previously been made
to locate this city, so frequently mentioned in the cuneiform inscriptions, and already George Smith had tenta-
tively suggested the mound of Abû Habba, located about
thirty miles north of the City of Babylon, as its possible
site, but to Rassam we owe the actual identification of
the site of this old centre of the worship of Shamash the
Sun-god in the Babylonian plain. The ruins of Abû
Habba are low but extensive, the longest of the ancient
city-walls measuring some 1400 yards, while on the
western side the remains of an old ziggurat, or temple-
tower are still to be seen. Rassam's excavations on this
site were abundantly successful, the most important of
his discoveries in the ancient building with which he
was principally concerned, being the famous stone tablet
of Nabû-aplu-iddina, king of Babylonia, about 870 B.C.
The inscription which records the restoration of the
temple of the Sun-god by that king is surmounted on
the obverse side by a magnificent bas-relief representing
the worship of the Sun-god (cf. Pl. XIV and p. 205). The
recovery of this remarkable tablet, apart from the value
attaching to it as a work of art and a historical document,
meant further the identification of one of the earliest
sites of Mesopotamian civilization, and the rediscovery
of the time-honoured shrine of Shamash. Among the
other inscriptions unearthed on this occasion, the large
clay cylinders of Nabonidus (555–538 B.C.), the last king
of the Neo-Babylonian Dynasty, are of paramount importance. Allusion has already been made to the tradition recorded by Nabonidus on his cylinder regarding
the date of Shar-Gâni-sharri of Agade, and his son
Narâm-Sin, and also to the archæological evidence calculated to diminish the historical value of Nabonidus'

record (cf. p. 5). Rassam reconnoitred many other sites in Babylonia, notably that of Tellô, from which he recovered a few objects, including a number of tablets and two gate-sockets inscribed with the name of Gudea, during his swift and somewhat stealthy visit in the early part of 1879. But the three great triumphs of the excavator whose long career came to its natural end in 1910, were the identification of Sippar's long-forgotten site, the discovery of the bronze gates at Balâwât, and last but far from least, the unearthing of Ashur-bani-pal's northern palace at Nineveh, and the disclosure of the priceless relics of art and literature which it was found to contain.

Meanwhile other nations besides the French and the English were preparing themselves for the work so remarkably commenced, and so full of promise for the future. Germany was slow to move, but thanks to the munificence of Mr. L. Simon, an expedition was sent out to the Orient in the autumn of 1886, under the auspices of the Royal Prussian Museums of Berlin, and under the directorship of B. Moritz, R. Koldewey and L. Meyer. But in spite of the tardiness of German activity in the field of exploration, it must never be forgotten that to Friedrich Delitzsch belongs the unique honour and glory of having placed Assyriology upon a scientific basis, and in a real sense that distinguished scholar may be regarded as the father of that science. At the same time Delitzsch's predecessor Schrader deserves a special mention, as being the first to lecture in Germany on this subject, and to whose lectures Delitzsch and other scholars doubtless owed much. The 1886 expedition commenced operations early in 1887 at the ruins of El-Hibba and Surghul, two mounds situated close to each other to the northeast of Tellô, which resulted in the discovery of buildings innumerable, mostly of a private character ; the small relics yielded by the German excavations on these two sites were for the most part considerably damaged by fire which had played considerable havoc in both places.

But the chief point of interest in regard to the excavations at El-Hibba and Surghul was the discovery of a number of early graves. Many of the bodies had been burnt, from which Koldewey inferred that cremation [1] was one of the ways in which the Sumerians of antiquity disposed of their dead. Many of the inscriptions recovered were published by the lately deceased Dr. Messerschmidt. The tablets in question include texts belonging both to first and second Dynasties of Lagash (Tellô). One of the tablets unearthed at Surghul and written by Gudea, the most famous ruler of the Second Dynasty of Lagash, showed that both El-Hibba and Surghul acknowledged Gudea as their suzerain-overlord.

At about the same time, the excavating spirit in America was also gradually fanning itself into life, and to-day America is doing more archæological work than any other country in the world.

The ancient city of Nippur had long been known as one of the most famous centres of Babylonian religion, and of the worship of the great god Enlil, and it was accordingly to this city that the Americans first directed their attention, and it was here that they made those epoch-making discoveries which have won for them so prominent a place in the history of Mesopotamian excavation, and that in spite of all the controversies which

---

[1] It has been argued that the burnt condition of human remains discovered in Mesopotamia is in all cases to be regarded as the effect of a general conflagration, and that in fact cremation was never practised. But if such be the case, then the pottery buried with the burnt human remains would similarly bear the marks of burning. In many cases the pottery apparently affords no definite evidence for or against the theory, but Dr. Koldewey informs me that the vessels containing the burnt remains of human beings at Surghul, showed no trace of their having been in the fire themselves, so here at all events we have clear and incontrovertible evidence of the practice of cremation in Babylonia.

have arisen out of those discoveries. The Americans
had indeed sent out an expedition to Babylonia as
early as 1884 under the directorship of Dr. W. Hayes
Ward of the New York " Independent," but the object
for which it was sent was general exploration rather than
for actual excavation. The first expedition (1888-89)
to Nippur, which was organized chiefly by Prof. J. P.
Peters, who was supported by Dr. Wm. Pepper, Provost
Harrison, Messrs. E. W. Clay, C. H. Clark, W. W.
Frazier, and others, was chiefly tentative in character,
and served rather to show the magnitude of the work
to be accomplished than to achieve any definite and
practical results. Peters was the director of the first
and second (1889-90) expeditions, while Prof. R. F.
Harper and Prof. H. V. Hilprecht were appointed
Assyriologists to the first expedition, Mr. Field being
the architect. The first expedition was engaged in excavating for two months and nine days, while the second
excavated for three months and eleven days. Dr. Haynes
was the field-director of the third expedition (1893-96),
and remained at the mounds of Nippur for nearly three
years without a break. The fourth expedition (1898-
1900) was conducted by Hilprecht as scientific director,
Haynes as field-director, and Messrs. C. S. Fisher and
H. V. Geere as architects, and during the last campaign
excavations were carried on for some sixteen months,
and led to many important discoveries.

The first expedition, as stated, was of a preparatory
character, and consequently its results cannot be estimated merely by the number of discoveries actually
made. During the short two months in which the excavators continued operations, a large building characterized by enormous buttresses and two round towers
was brought to light. The building—without doubt a
fortress—is of comparatively late date, belonging to
the Parthian period, and was built upon the ancient
temple of Enlil and its staged tower.

Bint-el-Amir, the mound which contained the ruins of this renowned temple, was conical in shape and covered a surface of more than eight acres.[1] A scientific examination of a mound of such gigantic proportions was in itself no light task, while the exploration of the buried temple was a work of pioneering, none of the large Babylonian temples having as yet been completely excavated.

The excavation of this temple proved that the stage-tower " did not occupy the central part of the temple-court," and though it was undoubtedly the most conspicuous feature of the temple-area, it was not actually the temple itself : the latter is to be found in a large building adjacent to the stage-tower. This building is at all events as early as the time of the Shar-Gâni-sharri and his son Narâm-Sin. The stage-tower, which probably never had more than three stages, owed its latest form to Ur-Engur, king of Ur (*circ.* 2400), though Ashur-bani-pal, King of Assyria nearly two thousand years after, had occasion to repair and restore it. The bricks of Ashur-bani-pal, which are intermingled with those of Ur-Engur, bear the stamped inscription, "To Bel, the King of the lands, his King, Ashur-bani-pal, his favourite shepherd, the powerful King, King of the four quarters of the earth, built Ekur, his beloved temple, with baked bricks." Four feet behind the facing-wall of Ur-Engur, large bricks characteristic of Narâm-Sin's time were discovered, while the bricks of which the innermost core of the tower was formed belong to the pre-Sargonic and early Sumerian days.[2]

The extreme antiquity of the lower strata in this mound may be gauged from the fact that Haynes in descending into the pre-Sargonic period below the pavement of Narâm-Sin, penetrated through some thirty feet of ruins before he arrived at the virgin soil.

[1] Cf. Hilprecht, *Explorations*, p. 317.
[2] For description of the ziggurat, cf. p. 133 ff.

PLATE VII

The Ziggurat and Palace of Ashur-Nasir-Pal : Ashur

(By permission of the German Oriental Society)

One of the most interesting discoveries in the early strata was a vaulted drain (cf. Fig. 15 and p. 170) which purports to be the earliest Babylonian arch known, while a large number of terra-cotta pipes as well as a terra-cotta drain were also brought to light. The smaller objects include votive stelæ (cf. Fig. 25), tablets, cylinder-seals and terra-cotta vases (cf. Figs. 92, 93). But a large number of relics contained in the strata above the level of Narâm-Sin were found to be pre-Sargonic in spite of their position in the mound. They included door-sockets, fragments of vases, slabs, statues, and more than fifty brick-stamps, bearing an inscription of Sargon or Narâm-Sin.

But the discovery and partial excavation of the Temple " Library "[1] or "archive " at Nippur have produced the most far-reaching and epoch-making results, for thereby literally thousands of tablets have been unearthed, affording an amount of new material for Assyriological study seldom paralleled in the history of Babylonian exploration.

The greater part of the excavated material[2] is scientific or literary in character. The majority of the tablets are unbaked, and have consequently suffered from the detrimental effects of time, climate and other influences, among which may be particularly mentioned the havoc wrought by the invading Elamites during the third millennium B.C. In consequence of this, the decipherer's task is much more arduous than it would otherwise have been, but in spite of the vandalism of the Elamites and the work of destruction which they sought to, and to some extent did accomplish, the archæologist probably owes the preservation of these tablets to their burial in the ruined débris of which they formed a part. These unbaked clay tablets seem to have been generally arranged

---

[1] Cf. however, Jastrow, *Journal of the American Oriental Society*, vol. XXVII, pp. 147 ff.

[2] Clay, *Records of the Past*, Vol. II, Part II, pp. 47 ff.

F

on shelves made of clay and about $1\frac{1}{2}$ feet wide, while they contain every variety of " literature," treating of astronomy, astrology, mathematics, geography, history, medicine, grammar and religion.   One of the tablets gives us valuable information regarding the temple itself ; the name of the great hall of the temple was E-makh, and though Enlil and his consort were without doubt the principal deities of the place, there were some twenty-four shrines dedicated to other gods, just as was the case in Esagila, the great Temple of Marduk at Babylon, recently excavated by the Deutsche Orient-Gesellschaft.

The late Assyrian, neo - Babylonian and Persian periods are also well represented in the enormous accumulation of cuneiform tablets recovered from this site, among the most interesting of which are the " Murashû Tablets," seven hundred or more of which were unearthed in a ruined building some twenty feet below the surface.   The care with which these tablets had been made, and the numerous seal-impressions which they bore, at once attracted Hilprecht's attention.   They proved to belong to the business archives of Murashû Sons, brokers and bankers at Nippur, who flourished in the time of the Persian kings, Artaxerxes I (464–424 B.C.) and Darius II (423–405 B.C.).   But apart from ordinary banking business, the firm acted as an agent for the Persian kings. Apparently the kings of Persia were in the habit of farming out the taxes like the Roman emperors of later days, and Murashû Sons undertook to levy the king's taxes from their Babylonian subjects in Nippur and elsewhere.   The interest of these tablets is not however confined to the information which they afford us in regard to the mode of conducting business at that period ; but they are of even greater value for the insight which they give us into the ordinary life of the people.

It was during the last expedition that the city-walls

were carefully examined, and also those which enclosed
the temple-area, the name of the former being Nîmit-
Marduk and the name of the latter Imgur-Marduk.
Access to the temple was gained by a gate in the southern
wall, which was at all events as old as the time of Shar-
Gâni-sharri of Agade. The " Abullu Rabu," the great
gate of the city, was situated to the north-east of the
Temple ; its length is 35 feet, by which we know that
that was the thickness of the wall itself, though unfortunately nothing remains of the old city-wall at this
point, the crude bricks of which it was composed having been removed and used for building materials in
the later Nippur structures. The gateway itself consisted of a central road some 13 feet wide used for ordinary traffic, on either side of which was a raised passage for pedestrians, while the whole structure was built
of thumb-marked bricks, and is therefore pre-Sargonic.
Under the central roadway a foundation consisting of
massive blocks of stone laid in bitumen was discovered.
Some distance north of this gate a large part of the old
city wall was discovered, belonging in the main to the
times of Narâm-Sin and Ur-Engur respectively, the
work of the latter king being of course superimposed on
that of Narâm-Sin. Traces of some hundred feet of
the wall of Narâm-Sin are still visible, and also a water-
conduit consisting of baked bricks laid in bitumen. The
wall was rebuilt by Ur-Engur, who adorned its outer
face with a series of panels 11 feet in width, and placed
at intervals of 30 feet, of which some seventeen were
found in their original positions ; the excavators were
unable to ascertain the thickness of the wall, but in one
place it was found preserved to the thickness of over 25
feet. Into the inner face of this later wall were built a
number of small chambers in which were found relics
of varying interest ; a description of the later Parthian
fortress, and of the little Parthian palace discovered on
the other side of the Shatt-en-Nil Canal, would treat

of a period with which this volume does not profess to deal, and the reader must accordingly refer to the standard works of some of the excavators themselves (Peters, Hilprecht or Fisher) for information concerning these later buildings, as also for details regarding all the structures and discoveries at Nippur. Sufficient however has perhaps been recounted to indicate the extraordinary importance with which the American expeditions to Nippur have been fraught, though even to-day we are not in a position to adequately appreciate the full value of the self-sacrificing labours of the excavators, and the ample results with which those labours have been and are daily being attended.

Meanwhile, the Turks themselves, alive to the importance of the monuments and relics recovered from the ruined mounds which ever since Rassam's departure from Baghdad in 1882 had been exploited with considerable success by the agents of antiquity-dealers, determined to send out an expedition of their own. The expedition was placed under the directorship of Father Scheil, a young French Assyriologist, and Bedri Bey, the Ottoman Inspector of Antiquities, who commenced operations in the spring of 1894 at Abû Habba (Sippar), the site which had been the particular hunting ground of the dealers, and which therefore was calculated to be worth scientifically exploring. The most important result of the expedition was the discovery of about seven hundred tablets, mostly letters or contracts belonging to the time of the first Babylonian dynasty, and especially to the reign of Samsu-iluna, the son and successor of Khammurabi. In 1891 Dr. Wallis Budge excavated the neighbouring mound of Dêr and recovered many texts, etc. ; these are now in the British Museum.

On March 26th, 1899, Dr. Koldewey, whose excavations at El-Hibba and Surghul had been more than successful, commenced operations on the Kasr mound at Babylon, the mound which marks the site of the world-famed palace of Nebuchadnezzar.

The German excavations at Babylon undertaken by Koldewey, Meissner, Andrae and M. L. Meyer, have not indeed yielded so rich a harvest as was expected from the important part which that city played in the history of the country, from the time of Khammurabi onwards, for Sennacherib's destruction of the city in 689 B.C. had been carried out with such rigour that little was left to tell the tale of Babylon's greatness before his time, that little consisting chiefly of contract-tablets belonging to the time of the First Dynasty, and a number of pot-burials belonging to a yet earlier period. But however greatly we must regret the dearth of material yielded by Babylon's ruined mounds, for the reconstruction of her earlier history, of the period during which she was at the height of her power,—the period of the great king Nebuchadnezzar (604–561 B.C.)—the German excavations have afforded us much valuable information. The Ḳasr mound which was found to conceal the remains of Nebuchadnezzar's famous palace, the palace in which he lived during the greater part of his reign and the same one in which Alexander the Great died, seems to have been a new suburb of Babylon, and contained nothing earlier than the seventh century. The massive city-wall, which in all was found to be some 136 feet in thickness, was discovered, and the palace of Nebuchadnezzar in part excavated, but the two most important discoveries of the summer of 1899 were a stele of dolerite and a sandstone bas-relief. The stele of dolerite is 4 feet 2 inches high, and on the smooth side of it the figure of a Hittite god is depicted, while the reverse contains a Hittite inscription. The god has his two arms raised and brandishes a trident in one hand, a large hammer in the other, while a sword hangs from his side. A long plait of hair hangs down his back, his headgear being a Phrygian cap, his footwear the pointed shoes so characteristically Hittite, and his tunic, decorated with a fringe, reaches just to the knees. The second discovery consisted in a sandstone slab rather over 4 feet long and about $4\frac{1}{2}$ feet in height, showing in relief a group of figures of which the two most noteworthy are the god Adad, armed with two flashes of lightning in either hand, and the goddess Ishtar.

In the following year Koldewey was able to give more detailed information regarding the general plan and arrangement of Nebuchadnezzar's palace. The palace contained a great number of rooms, arranged around larger central courts. The walls of the various buildings rest upon a massive foundation composed of bricks and fragments. Upon this foundation-platform a rampart-wall running east to west, over 56 feet thick and pierced with a single gateway, was discovered, while at the corner of this wall, another building, older than the wall itself, was brought to light. This building was made of burnt brick and asphalt, the bricks themselves bearing an Aramaic inscription and a walking lion.

On the east front of the Ḳasr in Babylon the paving-stones of the street are made of white limestone, or red and white breccia, but the only part of the street paving found in its original position is the layer of burnt bricks covered with asphalt which served as a foundation for the stone pavement above. The enormous limestone blocks measure over 3 feet square and about $13\frac{1}{2}$ inches thick. On some of these limestone blocks an inscription was found giving Nebuchadnezzar's name, and stating that he had paved the Babel street for the procession of the great lord Marduk with " mountain-stone " slabs. The breccia slabs, none of which have been recovered complete, were apparently of more modest dimensions, being only about 26 inches square and 8 inches thick. There is no doubt that these are the paving-stones wherewith Nebuchadnezzar paved the "Processional street of Marduk" the locus of which is now certain. Breccia had been used for building purposes before the time of Nebuchadnezzar : thus we know that Nabopolassar, the founder of the Neo-Babylonian Dynasty, had used it for paving the processional street, while at the Amran mound a block of breccia was found bearing an inscription of Sennacherib.

The discovery of the processional street of Marduk was of the greatest importance in regard to the topography of ancient Babylon, while the confirmation of the theory held by Delitzsch and others—hitherto based chiefly on inferences drawn from Nebuchadnezzar's texts —in the identification of Marduk's temple, E-sagila, with the old Babylonian building concealed within the Amran mound, during the excavations of May 1900, was of even greater moment.

Koldewey was further fortunate enough to discover a temple erected in honour of the goddess Nin-makh (Great Lady), who was at all events in later times identified with Ishtar.[1] The importance of the discovery lay in the completeness of the building, and not in the magnitude of its dimensions, for it is quite small. During the excavation of this temple a well-preserved Assyrian cylinder was found, on which Ashur-bani-pal records that he has newly built Nin-makh's temple in Babylon, in return for which act of piety he clearly expected a rich reward, for he begs the "sublime Nin-makh to look down compassionately" on his pious deeds, to pronounce his prosperity daily before Bêl and Bêlit, to prescribe a "life of many days as his fate," and to establish his government firmly.

Another interesting discovery was that of a terracotta figure of a naked goddess, doubtless a relic of the Nin-makh-cult (cf. Fig. 86).

[1] For a description of the famous Ishtar-Gate, and for further details regarding Nebuchadnezzar's palace, cf. pp. 136, 137, 149.

The excavations on the Amran hill revealed the presence of buildings prior to the time of Nebuchadnezzar. The upper strata of the mound belong for the most part to the Parthian and Seleucidian times, but at a depth of 68 feet below the surface of the mound, the floor of a Babylonian building was uncovered, and the clay walls of this building, which were over 9 feet thick, were still found in position to a considerable height. The floor itself was made of burnt bricks covered with asphalt, apparently only the bricks in the uppermost layer bearing the impress of Nebuchadnezzar's stamp, in consequence of which it seems probable that the foundation of the building was laid before that king's time. Underneath the lowest flooring a solid foundation of brick some 6½ feet thick was found. On the uppermost flooring various objects of interest were brought to light, including a thin plate of gold, a silver knob, a gold ear-ring, and fragments of engraved shells. But the real importance of the excavations at the Amran mound centres round the discovery of Marduk's famous temple—E-sagila, the meaning of which is "the house of heaven and earth." The temple was founded by King Zabum during the time of the First Dynasty of Babylon (*circ.* 2000 B.C.), the period, that is to say, during which the city of Babylon became the most powerful city-state in Southern Mesopotamia. But the supremacy of Babylon meant the supremacy of Babylon's god, and the prestige to which Marduk attained at this time is shown by his identification with Bêl, the ancient god of Nippur. But some few hundred years afterwards, when the power and influence of Babylon had decreased, and dominion in the Mesopotamian Valley had passed to the more warlike Assyrians in the north, E-sagila and her god suffered with the people of Babylon, the temple being looted and the god Marduk carried off by Tukulti-Ninib, King of Assyria (*circ.* 1275 B.C.) Some six centuries later found the Assyrians still all-powerful, though always engaged in suppressing rebellions among the discontented Babylonian princes, until at last Sennacherib resolved to wipe out Babylon from off the face of the earth. E-sagila shared in the general catastrophe, and but little remains of the early city or of the temple of her time-honoured god, though fortunately various documents, vessels and other relics belonging to the time before Sennacherib escaped that king's fury, and have been recovered recently by the German excavators. Esarhaddon however, the successor of Sennacherib, and one of the most humane of Assyrian monarchs,—which is not perhaps saying a very great deal—made it his special business to rebuild the city of Babylon and the temple of her god, but he did not live to see the realization of his project, and the completion of the work was thus left to Esarhaddon's joint successors, Ashur-bani-pal and Shamash-shum-ukîn. The temple was roofed with cedar and cypress-wood, and was rich with gold, silver and precious stones. When all was finished, Marduk's home-coming was celebrated with great pomp and splendour, Shamash the sun-god, Ea, Marduk's venerable father, Nebo his illustrious son—even Nergal the god of the dead, came to welcome the exiled deity back. But magnificent as was the reconstruction of Marduk's ancient fane by Ashur-bani-pal, Assyria's mightiest king, it was surpassed by that of Babylon's native kings—Nabopolassar (625–604) and his son Nebuchadnezzar. Ashur-bani-pal does not seem to have rebuilt the temple-tower, which Sennacherib had of course destroyed, but Nabopolassar reared once more the lofty stage-tower—the E-temen-an-ki ("house of the foundations of heaven and earth"), and Nebuchadnezzar his son carried on the laudable work. He built the walls of the chamber Ekua of pure gold, while the roof he made of cedar-wood which he covered with gold and precious stones, the sanctuaries of Nebo and Zarpanit being treated in the same luxurious manner, while all the sacrificial vessels seem to have been made of pure gold. Neriglissar (559–556 B.c.) a successor of Nebuchadnezzar further built four gates to this temple, and when the city was finally taken by Cyrus, it will be recalled that that king made obeisance to Marduk, at whose behests he professed to have taken the city—" He (Marduk) sought out a righteous prince, a man after his own heart, whom he might take by the hand; and he called his name Cyrus."

Various graves were discovered in the course of the excavations at Babylon, but mostly of a late date. A very interesting sarcophagus was brought to light in 1910,[1] the "head" end of the terra-cotta cover of which bore in relief the bearded head of a man with long hair, and an Egyptian type of face. Two other sarcophagi were found at the same time, and all of these burials were inside ruined houses.

Of the many other important results attending the labours of Koldewey and his confrères, the discovery of the ancient canal Arakhtu, the tracing of its quay-walls, the excavation of the great wall between the north and south castles, and the clearing of the west wall of the southern citadel, are especially deserving of mention, while for details the reader must refer to the *Mitteilungen Der Deutschen Orient-Gesellschaft*.

But Babylon was not the only site in Lower Mesopotamia to receive the attention of the Germans on this expedition. On June 14th, 1902, Koldewey, Delitzsch and Baumgarten, with a party of labourers, took a boat down the Euphrates, arriving eventually at the ruined mounds of Fâra on the 18th. Digging was commenced in the northern part of the ruin, and it was very soon evident that the whole site is of very ancient date, not even the uppermost strata of the mounds containing anything that can be assigned to a late period. Various implements of bone and stone, including a number of

[1] Cf. *Mitteilungen*, No. 44, p. 11.

stone hatchets, as well as saws and knives made of flint or obsidian, all testified to the antiquity of its occupation, and as nothing was discovered at a greater depth than 6 to 7 feet, Fâra promised at the outset to be one of the most important sites for the study of early Sumerian civilization. The ruined mounds of other long-forgotten cities had indeed yielded relics of the past quite as old as those excavated at Fâra, but in nearly every case the upper strata of such mounds were found to contain the remains of a later date and a more recent occupation ; Fâra however stands unique in this respect, as for some reasons unknown, it appears only to have been occupied in the earliest period of Babylonia's history, during which it undoubtedly " had its day," but has ever since " ceased to be" until the German excavators have at last rescued it from permanent oblivion. Among the smaller objects discovered on this site, was a number of seal-cylinders, the majority of which were made of alabaster, though sometimes of shells, but very rarely of the hard stones so frequently employed in later days. They were found sometimes amid the general débris, sometimes in the tombs ; for the most part they exhibit battle-scenes, the combatants being either men, beasts, or mythical monstrosities, as the case may be. The simpler specimens of the pottery found resemble those unearthed by Koldewey at Surghul, while others were more elaborately decorated. A few tablets were unearthed, mostly round in shape, and all of them inscribed in archaic characters. The citizens of Fâra placed the bodies of their dead either in clay sarcophagi, or else in reed mats. The clay sarcophagi are oval in shape, and about six feet in length ; the sides are perpendicular, and they are closed with a clay cover. The corpse was generally found lying on its side with the legs drawn up embryonic-wise, as was the case in pre-Dynastic Egypt, and one of the hands is holding to the mouth a cup made of stone, shell, copper, or clay, an incidental proof

of the Babylonian's belief in the reality of the life after
death even at this remote period. The tombs of the
better classes contain also the implements, weapons and
ornaments of the deceased. The arms include spears,
poniards and hatchets made of "bronze" (?), the jewelry
taking the form of chains, the beads of which are in the
case of the more wealthy made of lapis lazuli, and agate,
while the poorer folk had to content themselves with
ordinary glass. Bracelets and rings of silver and bronze
were also discovered, together with "bronze" staffs provided with lapis-points at either end. Among the tools
may be enumerated fishing-hooks and hatchets made of
"bronze," while colour-boxes made of alabaster or shell
were usually buried with the corpse, and were therefore
presumably regarded as toilet requisites in the life beyond just as in the life which now is. The colours in most
cases were found well preserved, the principal of which
were black, yellow, red and light green. Many stone vessels of varying sizes and shapes were brought to light,
most of them being made of alabaster, in fact alabaster
was used quite extensively on this site, contrary to the
usage of the Babylonians of later days, who seldom employed the softer stones which their Assyrian neighbours
utilized so frequently and for so many divers purposes.
The excavators report that they were unable to determine whether the sarcophagi or the mat-burials were the
older, both apparently being used synchronously; an
assumption that the sarcophagi were used by the better
classes, the mat-interments by the poorer, would in itself
be sufficiently reasonable, but for the awkward fact that
the mat-graves are as richly provided with the accoutrements, ornaments and implements of the deceased as
are the sarcophagi themselves. Very few sculptures were
found, most of them being on alabaster and showing
considerable skill in their general execution. The early
part of 1903 was signalized by the discovery of a building made of well-baked bricks, in the ruined débris of

which were discovered a large number of well-preserved tablets.

Meanwhile excavations had been carried on at the same time at the mound of Abû Hatab, Koldewey having received a report of the discovery of inscribed bricks on this site. Operations were commenced here on December 24th, 1902, and resulted in the discovery of a number of small buildings, the walls of which were notable for their insubstantiality. Some of the bricks were found to bear an inscription of Bur-Sin, king of Ur (*circ.* 2350 B.C.). But Abû Hatab yielded little of interest to the student of early prehistoric remains. The tombs here consisted for the most part in two large pots " adjusted with their edges in a horizontal position," a form of sarcophagus found also in the early strata at Babylon and Mukeyyer (Ur). The corpse lay either on its back or side, but in both cases it was contracted, this being obviously necessitated by the limitations of the sarcophagus, as was similarly the case in the early pot-burials of ancient Egypt. A vessel of clay or copper was generally found placed near the head of the corpse, doubtless destined to fulfil a purpose similar to that of the drinking cups found in the graves at Fâra.

At about this time Andrae, Koldewey's assistant, completed the excavation of the temple of Nebo at Birs-Nimrûd (Borsippa), whence Nebo paid his yearly visit to Marduk on the first day of the New Year.

Koldewey and Andrae did not however confine their attention to the ruined mounds of Babylonia, but in 1903 commenced excavations at Kalat Sherkat, the site of Ashur, Assyria's ancient capital, and the name of the god from whom Assyria derives her name. As early as 1852 Sir Henry Layard had conducted excavations on this site, the chief tangible result of which was the discovery of Tiglath-Pileser I's clay cylinders, though fragments of bas-reliefs and other inscriptions were also

discovered here both by Layard and Rassam. Shalmaneser I (*circ.* 1300 B.C.) had transferred the seat of his
government from Ashur to Calah, but his successor
Tukulti-Ninib (*circ.* 1275 B.C.) restored the capital of
the empire to Ashur. The mounds which mark the
site of this ancient city are to a great extent of natural
formation (cf. Pl. VIII), thereby differing from most of
the ruined mounds in Mesopotamia, which owe their
existence to artificial formation. From September 1903
to April 1904 operations were of a tentative character
and consisted of trial trenches, but in April 1904 the
Germans commenced excavating the large mound of
mud-brick, the ziggurat, the eastern plateau, and the
large court of Ashur's temple, part of the fortification-
wall also receiving attention, while the main work centred round the palace-buildings of Shalmaneser I (*circ.*
1300 B.C.). The great temple of Ashur, built or restored by Ushpia, an early ruler of the city who ante-
dates Irishum, is situated in the north-east corner, and
it adjoins the palace of Shalmaneser I. The ziggurat or
stage-tower lies to the west-south-west, and the palace
of Ashur-nasir-pal adjoins the temple of Anu and Adad,
which would appear to be the best preserved building in
Ashur. Various other buildings have been discovered,
of which the temple of Nebo and the palace of Tukulti-
Ninib I (*circ.* 1275 B.C.) may be specially mentioned.
Numerous graves were found of various kinds, those
with brick walls being undoubtedly Assyrian. Many
valuable historical inscriptions were found, while the
discovery of a wall-decoration consisting of a series of
rosettes was another interesting result. The so-called
"Mushlala" of Adad-nirari I (*circ.* 1325 B.C.), according
to whom it formed a part of the temple of Ashur, was
found to be identical with that restored by Sennacherib
with " mountain-stone," and afterwards repaired by
Esarhaddon (681–668 B.C.) with " pîlu "-stone. The
foundations of the building situated at the southern

PLATE VIII

INSCRIPTIONS ON CLAY ILLUSTRATING THE SIZES AND SHAPES OF THE
TABLETS ETC. USED BY THE BABYLONIANS AND ASSYRIANS

side of the eastern plateau proved to be of very great depth, while the plan of the building itself is said to closely resemble the early Babylonian type. The temple of Ashur the great lord of Assyria is alluded to by Irishum, king of Assyria (*circ.* 2000 B.C.), by Shamshi-Ad d who calls himself builder of the temple of Ashur, by Adad-nirari and by Shalmaneser I. In Shalmaneser I's reign it was destroyed by fire, and that king undertook its restoration. An inscription of Tiglath-Pileser II informs us that he decorated the temple with enamelled bricks. Some of these inscriptions were found " in situ " thus fixing the precise locus of Ashur's famous shrine. The temple was situated at the extreme north of the city, three of its sides overlooking the open country and the fourth over-towered by the ziggurat. Remains of Shalmaneser's work have been found in the foundation and pavement constructed by that king, and some of the enamelled bricks which decorated the buildings of Sargon have also been recovered, while the pavement of the great court, as well as pieces of enamelled brick and the clay cones of Tiglath-Pileser II have been brought to light. The temple itself was originally high above the level of the street. A second smaller ziggurat was further found, which proved to be a part of the temple of Anu and Adad, and the work of three distinct periods has been traced in this structure.[1] Of interesting relics here unearthed, we may specifically mention a three-pronged thunderbolt of wood sheathed with gold.

The remains of various palaces have been unearthed including those of Adad-nirari and Shalmaneser I, and the royal residence of Tukulti-Ninib has been also excavated. Many tablets were recovered, and a pot containing 113 unbaked clay tablets was also brought to light : the tablets are written in a script characteristic of the time of Tiglath-Pileser I, and are chiefly

[1] For an account of this temple, cf. chapter on Architecture, pp. 141 ff.

concerned with receipts for cattle. Much pottery was unearthed, together with a variety of objects including some Roman imperial coins of the second century. The northern part of the city was that which was favoured by the Assyrian kings, and accordingly contains the remains of several temples and palaces, but the ruins of private houses are perhaps of even greater interest than the palaces of kings and the abodes of the gods. They are small in size, but were evidently carefully drained. Within the houses a number of graves were discovered, apparently belonging to the same period as the houses themselves. In many cases the excavators state that they found clear traces of cremation in the graves. Seven distinctly different kinds of graves were found at Ashur —vaults, clay sarcophagi, baked clay trays placed over the corpse, jars, brick graves, potsherd graves, and earth graves. The vaults[1] are of various shapes and dimensions, are made of burnt brick, and consist generally of a fairly spacious chamber and an entrance shaft. The bodies— always more than one in each vault—lay on the floor in a contracted position, surrounded with drinking vessels of every description, and in all cases there was a small niche for a lamp. The clay sarcophagi show even greater varieties, including jars into which the bodies were pressed, and tubs both high and short into which the corpse was placed in a seated position, while both of these classes comprise many different types.

Another class of jar-burial, known as the " capsule," consisted in two jars drawn over the feet and head respectively and pressed together till they met, thus forming a " capsule." The Brick-graves were practically Brick-sarcophagi, the graves being built coffin-wise, but few of these have been found. The Potsherd graves are so called from the use of potsherds to cover the corpse. Apparently these various methods of burial coexisted at the same time, and they accordingly cannot

[1] Cf. further, pp. 176 ff.

be classified into periods, as is the case to some extent in early Egypt.

Concerning the fortifications of the city, the inscriptions of the various kings who built, repaired, or rebuilt these, afford us a good deal of information, but the excavations themselves have not up to the present told us as much as we could desire. Shalmaneser II's work of restoration on the southern wall has been identified by the clay-cones of that king found in the upper part of the wall, while in some of his inscriptions Shalmaneser calls himself the builder of the "Dûru" itself. The quay-wall built by Adad-nirari I, restored by Adad-nirari II, and later on by Adad-nirari III, has been excavated for nearly 490 yards of its length ; it is built of blocks of limestone and is faced with brick on the river-side, coherency being added to the whole by an ample employment of asphalt and clay-mortar. Part of the city-moat built by Tukulti-Ninib I has also been found, the excavations having further revealed the restoration of the city-wall, for which Ashur-naṣir-pal was probably responsible.

The year 1908 saw the excavation of the temple erected in honour of the god Nebo at Ashur by Sin-shar-ishkun, the last king of Assyria (*circ.* 615 B.C.).[1] The general ground-plan of this late Assyrian temple was found to correspond to that of the Anu-Adad temple, and also to that of the temple built by Sargon at Khorsabad.[2] Numerous stelæ and other monuments of stone were recovered from the ruins of Ashur ; they include a basalt stele of Tukulti-Ninib,[3] a stele of Tiglath-Pileser III, and another of Ashur-resh-ishi II,[4] a limestone stele of Ashur-naṣir-pal, an alabaster stele with the representation of a king adoring a god and goddess, which in some way resembles the Bavian relief of Sennacherib,[5] and fragments of a diorite sculp-

---

[1] Cf. Andrae, *Mitteilungen*, No. 38, pp. 23 ff.
[2] Cf. further pp. 144 ff.   [3] Cf. *Mitteilungen*, No. 42, p. 42.
[4] *Ibidem*, No. 42, p. 35.   [5] *Ibidem*, No. 43, p. 34.

G

ture[1] with small figures recalling the style of art characteristic of the Khammurabi period. The interest of these monuments is chiefly centred in the inscriptions which throw new light upon the number and order of the Assyrian kings.

Meanwhile the Americans, whose excavations in Babylonia had been inaugurated with so much promise, had again taken the field. On Christmas day 1903 an expedition sent out by the Oriental Exploration Fund of the University of Chicago, under the directorship of Professor R. F. Harper (E. J. Banks as field-director) commenced excavations at Bismâya, the name of a group of mounds situated between the Tigris and Euphrates, and due south of Bagdad. The mounds are very extensive, measuring about a mile in length and half a mile in breadth, but their altitude is very low compared with that of other mounds, such as Erech, Nippur (cf. Pl. X) or Borsippa. The temple was the first building at Bismâya to receive attention, partly owing to the fact that it happened to be concealed beneath one of the loftiest of the Bismâyan mounds, and partly because the general shape of the mound suggested the possible existence of a stage-tower beneath its ruined débris. Trenches dug on all sides of the mound towards the centre soon revealed the lower storey of one of these temple towers, the second storey of which had disappeared, though some of the burnt bricks which formed its outer casing were found lying about. The surviving lower stage consisted in crude bricks and clay, but was provided with a facing of burnt brick some four feet thick. Many of these casing bricks were inscribed with the name of Dungi, king of Ur (*circ.* 2400 B.C.). Beneath the bricks of Dungi was found another layer of burnt bricks, some of which bore the name of Ur-Engur, Dungi's immediate predecessor on the throne of Ur. Of small objects unearthed, the three most in-

[1] Cf. *Mitteilungen*, No. 44, p. 34.

teresting were a thin strip of gold found about two feet below the baked bricks of Dungi, and bearing the name of the renowned Nârâm-Sin, the son of Shar-Gâni-sharri of Agade, and the second was a small white marble statuette found at no great distance from the strip of gold, and conforming to the style of art characteristic of the age of Narêm-Sin, while the third was another marble statue belonging to the earliest Sumerian period, and closely resembling those excavated in the lowest strata at Tellô (Lagash). This statue (cf. Fig. 32) is probably unique as a statue in the round belonging to so early a period, and is especially noticeable for the fact that the arms are in this case entirely free from the body, and carved altogether in the round.

Just below the place where the gold of Narâm-Sin was recovered, large bricks about 18 inches square and belonging to the age of Shar-Gâni-sharri were found, while numerous inscriptions of this same king were forthcoming from some of the other mounds at Bismâya. Beneath the large Sargonic bricks there was a layer of thin oblong and finger-marked bricks, while lower still, some five feet below the surface, small plano-convex bricks set in bitumen were brought to light.

A great number of vase fragments made of marble, porphyry, granite, alabaster and onyx, together with innumerable objects made of ivory, mother of pearl, metal and stone were found round about the temple tower.

In regard to the temple itself, an entrance was discovered on the south-east side, the principal remaining features of which were the marble gate-socket supported on two slabs of pink marble. At the south corner, an oval-shaped room was brought to light, which was once covered with a dome-shaped roof. But the base of the temple tower had depths even below the stratum containing the small plano-convex bricks, which yet remained to be fathomed.

Some sixteen or seventeen feet below the surface a

large metal spike (cf. Fig. 40) terminating in a lion's head was recovered, while much lower still, about thirty-nine to forty feet below the level of the mound a number of fragments of wheel-made black pottery were revealed. The date of this wheel-made pottery is of course unknown, but judging from the depth at which it was found, Dr. Banks, the Field-director of the expedition, suggests a date of 10,000 B.C. In the same year (1903) in which these successful excavations were being carried on at Bismâya, Nineveh, the ruined mounds of which once-famous city had already yielded such a rich harvest to the great pioneers in the field of Mesopotamian exploration, received further attention at the hands of the Trustees of the British Museum, who sent out an expedition under Messrs. L. W. King and R. C. Thompson, with a view to the further excavation of the Kouyunjik mound. The principal result of the excavations carried on there between the years 1903 and 1905 was the discovery of the site of Nabû's temple, which had however been so ruthlessly destroyed —presumably by the Elamites—that no complete plan of the temple could be made.

Meanwhile the excavations at Tellô (Lagash) which had been brought suddenly to an end by the death of the brilliant French excavator (M. de Sarzec) in May, 1901, were resumed in January, 1903, under the directorship of Captain Gaston Cros. The principal fresh discovery made was a massive fortification wall built by Gudea (circ. 2450 B.C.). It is about thirty-two and a half feet thick, and in places is still in position to the height of twenty-six feet. Captain Cros also excavated a large rectangular building, and brought to light various objects of interest, including implements of flint and copper, together with a brick-stamp of Narâm-Sin, which latter may be regarded as evidence that building operations were carried on in Lagash by a Semitic king of Agade during the period of Semitic supremacy.

CHAPTER III—DECIPHERMENT OF THE CUNEIFORM INSCRIPTIONS

THE first person to bring reports of cuneiform inscriptions to Europe was Pietro della Valle, an Italian belonging to a Roman family of noble birth. In the years 1614–26 he made a journey to Turkey, Egypt, Palestine, Persia and India, and published an account of his travels in 1650, but the first communication of his discovery of cuneiform inscriptions at Persepolis was contained in a letter written from Shiraz and dated October 21st, 1621. Josafat Barbaro at the end of the fifteenth century had already taken notice of the strange signs found on the monuments at Persepolis, but Pietro della Valle was the first to suspect that the inscriptions were something more than mere decorative incisions on the rock. But though Pietro della Valle had made copies of a few of the inscriptions on the walls of the ruined palaces of Persepolis as early as 1621, to Chardin (1674) belongs the honour of making the first copy of a complete cuneiform inscription, the so-called " Window-Inscription," the shortest of the trilingual Achaemenian inscriptions, and his copy is to be found in the account of his travels (published 1711). This same inscription was copied in 1694 by Kampfer, who also copied the Babylonian text of the "H" inscription found at Persepolis, and who was the first to adopt the term " cuneiform." In the work which he published in 1712 he discusses whether the unknown script is alphabetic, syllabic, or ideographic, and decides in favour of the last. In 1701, the Dutchman De Bruin commenced his travels :

he devoted the year 1704 to an examination of the ruins at Persepolis and ten years later he published two new trilingual inscriptions in addition to an Old Persian and a Babylonian inscription, but to copy was one thing and to decipher was quite another, and well nigh a century elapsed before any real progress was made towards the unravelling of these cryptic signs, and the reconstruction of the languages which they embodied. In 1762 the inscription on the Vase of Xerxes found by Count Caylus was published, and a quadrilingual inscription of this king was published the same year. In 1765 Carsten Niebuhr, a Dane, copied several Achaemenian inscriptions at Persepolis, and pointed out that the first of the three columns on each of the trilingual inscriptions that had been found, contained only forty-two varieties of cuneiform characters from which he surmised rightly that the system in the first column was neither ideographic (each sign representing a word), nor syllabic (each sign representing a syllable), but alphabetic. From 1798 onwards, Tychsen and Münter, also a Dane, carried on the work begun by Niebuhr, and published their results in 1802. Münter had correctly guessed that the ubiquitous diagonal wedge ◁ served to separate the words from each other, and one word which occurred at the beginning of each inscription, he rightly adjudged to be the word for " king." In the meantime the Zend[1] language of the later Zoroastrian faith had been rediscovered, and with the aid of it de Sacy had been able to decipher the Pehlevi[2] inscriptions. Now only the older

---

[1] The Zend-Avesta is practically the equivalent of the Bible and prayer-book of the Zoroastrians. The Zoroastrian faith flourished as early as the sixth century B.C., and probably became the religion of the later Achaemenian kings.

[2] The Pehlevi language and literature belongs to the middle Persian period, i.e. from the third to the ninth century or so A.D. The language is related to old Persian on the one hand, and to modern Persian on the other. The Zend as it were bridged over the gulf between modern

Persian inscriptions of the Achaemenian kings awaited interpretation. In 1802 G. Friedrich Grotefend, of Hanover, a schoolmaster by profession, entered the field, and by the following process of reasoning he became the pioneer discoverer of part of the Persian cuneiform alphabet, and the first decipherer of a complete cuneiform inscription. Old writers had provided him with the all-important information that the palaces of Persepolis, amid the ruins of which so many of these cuneiform inscriptions had been found, were built by the Achaemenian kings. The Pehlevi inscriptions moreover, which had also been found on this site and had been deciphered by de Sacy, led him to expect that the cuneiform inscriptions would contain something analogous. Grotefend had already satisfied himself that the inscriptions read from left to right, and selecting two short inscriptions, one engraved on a gate-post of a building on the second palace-terrace, and the other engraved on the wall of a building on the third palace-terrace at Persepolis, he commenced his successful investigations. Both inscriptions contained the group of signs which Münter had already rightly inferred represented "king," though what was the Persian for "king" remained as yet unknown, the only difference being that in Inscription I "king" was preceded by group of signs which may be conveniently designated "X," while in Inscription II "king" is preceded by a group of signs which may be called "Y," and that moreover in Inscription II "X" and the word for "king" following it occurred after the "Y" + "king." In I on the other hand "X" + "king" was followed by another group of signs which may be labelled "Z," without however the usual accompanying "king."

Thus I reads "X"+king.........."Z"..........
And II reads "Y"+king..........."X"+king.

and ancient Persian, and was of the greatest assistance in the decipherment of the old Persian language as found in the cuneiform inscriptions.

From this, Grotefend concluded that the groups of
signs " X " " Y " and " Z " represented proper names,
and that as " X " and " Y " were accompanied by
" king," they must be king's names, and lastly Achaemenian kings' names, for ancient writers stated that
these palaces at Persepolis were built by Achaemenian
kings, and furthermore their position suggested that
these proper names must stand in genealogical relation to each other. In I " X " must be the son
of " Z," and in II " Y " must be the son of " X " ;
" X " and " Y " are accompanied with the sign for
" king," " Z " is not, therefore " Z " the father of " X "
is not a king, and consequently " X " is presumably the
founder of the dynasty. But apart from this hypothesis,
some of the names of the five kings composing the (fortunately) short Achaemenian Dynasty—Cyrus, Cambyses, Darius, Xerxes and Artaxerxes—were at once ruled
out of court : thus Cyrus and Cambyses were out of the
question, for " X " and " Y " did not commence with the
same cuneiform letter (it must be remembered that it
had already been rightly assumed that the system was an
alphabetic one), and moreover Cyrus' father and son
were both named Cambyses, and accordingly if " X "
were Cyrus then " Y " and " Z " should be the same,
which they are not. Cyrus and Artaxerxes were likewise disqualified, as there was no such discrepancy in
the length of the words, there thus remained only Darius
and Xerxes to be considered, and as " X's " father " Z "
is not called king, and it is further known that Hystaspes the father of Darius is not styled " king " by
the classical writers, " X " was rightly assumed to be
Darius. Having ascertained the oldest forms of the
names of the Achaemenian kings in question from the
classical writers, and Hebrew and Persian literature, he
applied these forms to the groups of cuneiform signs
which he had been led to believe they represented, and
he found the respective groups contained the same

number of individual signs as the proper names in question contained letters, and for

" X " he accordingly read—D A R – – U SH = Darius
" Z " he read—G O SH T A S P = Hystaspes
± the Zend form of the name.

But " Y," which on his hypothesis should be Xerxes, was not quite so easy to explain. He already knew the values of four or five of the seven signs composing group " Y," and these known values occurred in the order he expected, but the first and third signs in the group remained to be dealt with. Grotefend observed that the first sign was the same as the first sign of the group correctly guessed by Münter to represent " king " : he ascertained that the Greek letter " x " was transliterated in the Zend by " kh," and rightly inferred that the Greek " x " commencing the proper name Xerxes would be similarly transliterated by " kh " in old Persian, in other words that the first sign in the group should be read " Kh." The result of Grotefend's investigations was the discovery of the correct values for eight letters in the Persian cuneiform alphabet, the letter "a " having been already rightly read by Tychsen and Münter. His method of decipherment was proved to be correct by the quadrilingual vase-inscription already alluded to. The first version of this latter inscription is written in Egyptian hieroglyphics and was deciphered by Champollion as the name of Xerxes. The other three versions are written in cuneiform characters, the first of which, the old Persian, gave precisely the same group of signs as that which Grotefend read as Xerxes on the inscription from Persepolis. As Sayce[1] well says, the decipherment of cuneiform and all the far-reaching consequences resultant from it, depended upon a successful guess, but a guess made " in accordance with scientific method," and it was upon Grotefend's discovery that all

[1] *Archæology of the Cuneiform Inscriptions*, p. 8.

subsequent attempts to decipher cuneiform—Persian, Median, or Assyrian—were based. But unfortunately, though Grotefend had thus given the clue, and scented the track for all future scholars, his own ignorance of eastern languages prevented him from reaping himself the full harvest of his brilliant commencement, and the work so nobly begun was not completed till a later day.

The next great step forward was taken by the French scholar Emile Burnouf in 1836 ; he discovered that one inscription contained a list of the satrapies, and as the names of the satrapies where known from the Greek writers he was able on the partial knowledge of the alphabet already attained, to fit in the names to the cuneiform signs, and as a result he produced an alphabet of thirty letters mostly correct. About the same time Lassen assigned the correct values to almost all the letters in the alphabet, and further demonstrated that the language of the inscriptions was akin to the language of the Zend and also to the Sanskrit, though identical with neither.

Meanwhile Rawlinson had entered the field, and being attached to the British Mission in Persia, he had opportunities which others lacked, his position making it possible for him to copy and on a subsequent occasion take squeezes[1] of the inscription on the sacred rock of Behistun, which is filled with proper names. The French traveller Otter was apparently the first European to draw attention to the inscribed rock of Behistun, about the year 1734, and it is also mentioned by Oliver, but the earliest reference to it is contained in the History of Diodorus Siculus who flourished in the first century A.D. Kinneir who saw it in 1810 states that it is clear that the figures portrayed there are of the same age and character as those from Persepolis. In 1818 Porter

---

[1] Squeezes are made by means of a series of layers of thick paper, which has been moistened, the impression being gained by applying the substance thus formed to the inscription and beating it in with a brush.

made a sketch of the figures, but did not attempt to copy the inscription in spite of the experience he had gained in copying the inscription at Persepolis. The copying of it was no easy task, for Rawlinson had to be lowered in a basket from the top, the ladders which he had with him not being long enough to reach the upper part of the inscription from below. He sent his copy[1] to Edwin Norris, the secretary of the Royal Asiatic Society, who carefully revised it, and in 1849 an analysis and commentary on the text was published. With Rawlinson and Norris must be mentioned the Irish clergyman Hincks, who with his unrivalled genius in the decipherment of inscriptions was the first to discover that the alphabet was not a true one, but that a vowel-sound was attached to each of the consonants ; and also Beer Holtzman and Westergaard, all of whom contributed to the work of investigation and made discoveries in regard to both the grammar and lexicon. Rawlinson cannot indeed claim to have actually discovered the first clue which led to the decipherment of cuneiform, but his translation of the Behistun inscription was unquestionably the most valuable contribution ever made towards the unravelling of the old Persian language. His work was moreover at first quite independent of Grotefend's, and without any assistance from the latter he had deciphered the names of Cyrus, Hystaspes and Darius on the inscriptions from Elvend and Hamadan as early as 1835. Thus the efforts of half a century resulted at length in the discovery of a new alphabet and the resurrection of an old language. The Persian texts on the inscriptions were accompanied by two other texts, which as Grotefend divined must have been the two other principal languages used in the Persian Empire. The third text

[1] A partial duplicate of this inscription on the Behistun Rock is inscribed on a dolerite block discovered by the German excavators at Babylon ; it contains many interesting additions.

closely resembling the inscriptions on bricks and cylinder seals found in Babylon was naturally and correctly assumed to be Assyrian.[1] The decipherment of this third transcript was fraught with difficulties of every description ; there was such an endless variety of signs of a simple and complex order, and there was nothing whatever to indicate where a word or a sentence started or finished, and further the characters on the monuments from Persepolis differed very considerably from those found on the Babylonian monuments, which also varied among themselves very greatly. On the seal-cylinders they were especially complicated, and it was almost impossible to see any resemblance whatever between the characters on the latter and those of the Persepolitan inscriptions.

But light was to come from another quarter : in 1842 Botta, French Consul at Mosul, began excavating on the site of Nineveh, but not meeting with success he transferred his operations to Khorsabad further north, and there excavated a large place which subsequently turned out to be that of Sargon. In 1845 Layard entered the field, and carried on most successful excavations at Nimrûd (the ancient Calah) and then at Kouyunjik, one of the mounds which represents the site of Nineveh.

Botta published the inscriptions he had found in 1846–50, and also classified the signs, which numbered 642, while he further demonstrated the identity of the cuneiform system of the Nineveh inscriptions with that of the third column on the Persepolitan monuments, but it was reserved for the incomparable Hincks to discover the fact that the Assyrian cuneiform system was syllabic and not alphabetic like the Persian.

[1] The term "Assyrian" is used, as a large part of the earlier Babylonian literature comes down to us through Assyrian hands, being copied and as it were republished by Assyrian scribes. Assyrian and Babylonian were different dialects of the same language ; similarly Assyrian and Babylonian cuneiform exhibit great differences in style, Babylonian being more cursive and generally therefore more difficult to read.

The proper names in the Persian columns gave the first clue to the decipherment of the Assyrian columns. The values thus obtained for some of the Assyrian signs made it possible to read many of the words, their meanings being determined by a comparison with the Persian columns. It was then seen that Assyrian was a Semitic language and resembled Hebrew in particular ; this was proved conclusively by De Saulcy in 1849. In 1850 Rawlinson submitted a translation of the inscription on the Black obelisk of Shalmaneser II to the Royal Asiatic Society, a translation which was in the main correct, and in the following year he published the text and translation of the Assyrian transcript on the Behistun inscription, and announced two facts, one already known, namely that the Assyrian signs can be used ideographically, i.e. to denote an object or idea, as well as to represent merely a syllable, the other fact was that the characters were polyphonous, i.e. could represent more than one syllable each : this was again proved to demonstration by the redoubtable Hincks. Both facts alike argued that the cursive Assyrian cuneiform had its origin in picture writing, for in the latest times when cuneiform was as it were fully stereotyped, the signs were still used alone singly to represent an object or an idea, and also the polyphonous character of the individual signs testified to the same origin, for example the picture of an arm would signify not merely an " arm" but also " strength," " might," " grasp," etc., and thus though the sign would—at least originally—only have one general idea attached to it, it would have quite a number of phonetic values : these phonetic values would in the first be inseparably connected with the root *idea*, but in time when the sign had become cursive and developed and no longer resembled the original picture, the various phonetic values of the sign would not necessarily have anything whatever to do with the original root idea.

For example, a character with the *meaning* and *phonetic* value of the word " *win*," would in later times come to represent the syllable " *win* " quite apart from the basis meaning of the word win, thus the sign could be used to represent the first syllable in the word *win-ter*.

In 1857 the Royal Asiatic Society proposed to test the reliability of the translations put forward by scholars of the Assyrian inscriptions in the following manner : some eight hundred lines of cuneiform writing contained on clay cylinders found by Layard at Ḳalat Sherḳat, the ancient Ashur, were to be independently translated by any scholars who were prepared to accept the proposal ; the translations were to be sent under seal to the society's secretary, and were to be opened together and examined before a commission on a set day. Rawlinson, Fox Talbot, Hincks and Oppert entered the lists, and on May 25th their respective products were opened and compared. The great similarity which they all displayed afforded conclusive proof as to the correctness of the method of decipherment, and demonstrated finally that the investigations carried on, together with the results of those investigations, had not been mere speculative guesses, but were based on sound scientific principles.

Many other scholars deserve our gratitude for the share they took in the decipherment of the cuneiform inscriptions, of whom one may perhaps specially name Westergaarde, Löwenstern, De Saulcy and Longperier, but for an account of the particular achievements of each, the reader must refer to general works on the subject.[1]

[1] Cf. A. J. Booth, *Trilingual Inscriptions;* Rogers, *History*, pp. 175 ff.; Sayce, *Archæology of the Cuneiform Inscriptions*, pp. 1–35 ; Harper, *Biblical World*, XVI, pp. 294–7, 371–3 (a short and concise summary).

CHAPTER IV—CUNEIFORM INSCRIPTIONS

ALL alphabets and all modes of writing have their ultimate origin in pictures or hieroglyphs, and the cuneiform script offers no exception to this universal rule. When the early pictorial symbols are used to indicate objects and ideas other than the particular object of which the symbol is a representation the accuracy or inaccuracy of the picture becomes a matter of small importance, and an inevitable tendency to sketch the picture in the most speedy manner possible ends finally in the evolution of a purely cursive script. In Mesopotamia this course of development—or deterioration—was hastened by the nature of the material used in later times for all ordinary writing purposes, i.e. the all-abundant clay of the valley, it being impossible to draw the lines and curves necessary for the production of pictures on so plastic a substance as clay. The shape assumed by the signs forming the characters was due to the same cause, the point at which the stylus first comes in contact with the soft clay being unavoidably thicker than the remainder of the stroke which automatically tapers off into the form of a wedge. But so forcible is the influence of habit and so strong the imitative tendency, that we find the cuneiform characters which owed their wedge-shaped formation entirely and solely to the adoption of clay as a writing material, faithfully and slavishly copied on the colossal stone bulls, stelæ and wall-reliefs of later Assyrian kings.

The early decipherers of cuneiform had no specific knowledge of its pictographic origin, for all the inscriptions at that time discovered showed the same stereo-

95

typed and cursive script, but since their day a vast number of archaic inscriptions have been brought to light which prove conclusively that cuneiform as such was no invention of either Semites or Sumerians, but was simply the last stage in the process of degeneration to which the early pictures of the pre-Semitic Sumerians were subject. In the following illustrations (Figs. 1 and 2) we have a number of characters taken from actual inscriptions and arranged in order of evolution so to speak,[1] the sign in the left-hand column containing the most archaic form of the sign as yet discovered, the signs in the right-hand column showing the gradual transition to cursive cuneiform, while the last sign in the column is the ordinary late Assyrian ideograph. Thus in "A" we have the crude picture of a man recumbent, and one can follow the course of its development or deterioration from the various forms it has assumed on monuments and bricks arranged in order of sequence. Given the ordinary cuneiform sign for "man" by itself, it would be quite impossible to conjecture that it originated in the picture of a man at all. Below ("B") we have the old Sumerian hieroglyph for "king," consisting in a man lying down, surmounted by either a crown or an umbrella as part of the insignia of royalty. In "C" we have the picture of a man's head in recumbent posture, the lips being represented by two slanting lines, while the series of characters in the centre illustrates the various forms the sign has assumed on the bricks and monuments, and the arrangement shows the process whereby the original hieroglyph gradually discarded all trace of its pictorial origin, and became a cursive stereotyped sign the principal value of which is "mouth." Below we have another rude picture of a man's head, but on this occasion he wears a beard, which would suggest a full-grown man ; hence the meaning of the

[1] For references to texts in which these signs occur, cf. G. A. Barton in Harper's *Old Testament and Semitic Studies*, Vol. II, pp. 241 ff.

Assyrian ideograph is "strength," "be strong," or "protection." In figure "E" there is a representation of a

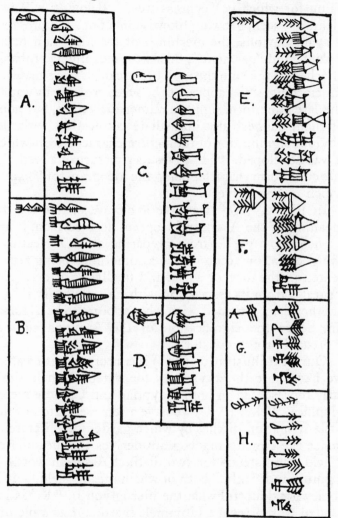

FIG. 1.—From Harper's *Old Testament and Semitic Studies*, Vol. II, pp. 241 ff.—*By permission.*

potted plant: this sign, instead of becoming simpler as it makes each progressive step towards cuneiform, becomes paradoxically more complex, until it finally subsides and assumes its normal cursive form, the principal value for which is " cypress-tree." Below (" F ") two plants are seen, growing likewise in a pot : the progress is again obvious, the meanings of the ideogram being "plant" and "garment"; this latter meaning is probably attached to the sign through the use of flax as a material for clothing. "G" appears to be a tree growing by water ; the late cuneiform sign has numerous values, but none of them suggest any immediate connection with the obvious signification of the picture-character from which it was developed. "H" gives us a picture of a reed, the late cuneiform character being the ideogram for "kanu" which means a " reed."

In Fig. 2, " Q " we have a picture of a fish ; the meaning of the Assyrian ideogram derived from it are a " fish," to " peel" (from preparing a fish for eating), the god Ea, on account of his sometimes being represented in the form of a fish, and finally a " prince," and "great" from its association with Ea. Below (" R ") is another fish, provided with what appears to be a dorsal fin, hence the signification of the Assyrian sign is " broad " or a " monster."

Our next illustration ("I") is concerned with water : we have here the wavy lines for water which is similarly represented in both Egyptian and Chinese hieroglyphics. Below (" J") we have a representation of the little irrigation ditches by which gardens are watered : hence the cuneiform ideogram derives the meaning of " field " and stands for two distinct Assyrian words— "ginu " and "iklu," both of which mean " field." It is somewhat doubtful what the hieroglyph in " K " is intended to represent : Hommel regarded it as a picture of a leathern bottle which would not unnaturally suggest the meaning " desert "; Barton, on the other hand, with perhaps greater probability regards it as a rude outline of the Euphrates valley, with its two rivers and

its " occasional sections of irrigated and so fertile land,"
indicated by the cross-lines, and he rightly says that

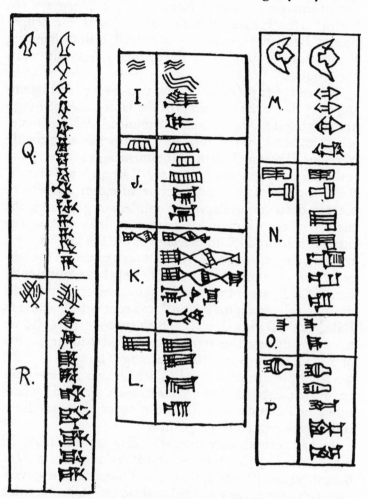

FIG. 2.—From Harper's *Old Testament and Semitic Studies*, Vol. II,
pp. 241 ff.—*By permission.*

this would account for the meanings " plain " and
"lands," and by an extension " desert," " elevated
country," and last of all " back." In " L " we see the

picture of a house, which however hardly corresponds with our conception of what a house should be : the cuneiform sign derived from it is the ideogram for "bitu" (the Hebrew "Beth" occurring in the proper names Bethlehem, "house of bread," Bethshemesh, "house of the sun," etc.), the ordinary Assyrian word for "house."

The next figure ("M") shows us a covered and steaming pot; hence the meanings of the later cuneiform sign are to "burst forth," "exult," "rejoice." "N" is somewhat doubtful, but it probably represents a "priestly garment," inasmuch as the cuneiform sign derived from it is the Assyrian ideogram for "šangu" a "priest." "O" is apparently a rude picture of either a crown or a ceremonial umbrella, as the emblem of greatness, the picture of the Assyrian king attended by a slave whose office it is to hold an umbrella over the head of his royal master being, through its frequent occurrence on the bas-reliefs which adorned the walls of the palaces, sufficiently familiar. However that may be, the cuneiform sign is the ordinary ideogram for "rabu" (the root which occurs in Rabshakeh, Rabsaris, etc.), which means "great"; we have already seen this sign compounded with the picture of a man, the two together meaning "king." In "P" we see a picture of a bowl in which two tinder-sticks have been inserted with a view to their ignition by friction; hence is derived the meaning of the cuneiform sign developed from it,—"fire."

As has been already indicated, clay was the material mostly used by the Assyrian and Babylonian scribes for the purposes of writing; but stone was also extensively used from the earliest to the latest times. Stone obelisks, colossal statues of bulls and lions, and last but far from least the bas-reliefs which decorated the walls of the royal palaces were generally covered with an inscription, the wedges sometimes measuring as much as two inches. In writing on sculpture the carved figures were completely ignored, the inscription being chiselled regardlessly through every detail of the carving. Stone was however sometimes used solely and exclusively as the material medium for perpetuating a legal agreement, or immortalizing the work of some self-satisfied grandee, and tablets of limestone or alabaster exist in large numbers, good examples of which are those of Rîm-Sin and Sin-Gamil, rulers of the ancient city of Larsa.

Boundary-stones or land-marks form another interesting class of inscribed stone objects. The texts refer to land-tenure and property conveyancing, while the upper part of most of these boulder-shaped monuments is sculptured in relief with mythological emblems. They belong almost exclusively to the Kassite period. Sometimes a plan of the field seems to have been chiselled on the stone which marked its boundary. A good example of such a boundary-stone is that of Nebuchadnezzar I, which was discovered at Nippur and is published by W. J. Hinke ;[1] a further point of interest about this stone is that it is inscribed with a hymn to Enlil, the god of Nippur.

But neither the Babylonians nor the Assyrians confined themselves exclusively to the use of clay and calcareous stone as the material whereon to write their inscriptions. Sometimes the hardest volcanic rocks were employed for the purpose, doubtless in consideration of their durability and power of resisting the devastating influences of time and climate. Thus in the course of the German excavations at Babylon a plate of dolerite measuring about a foot and a half square and bearing an inscription of Adad-nirari the son of Ashur-dan was discovered. So too Dungi and Bur-Sin, kings of Ur (*circ.* 2350 B.C.), have left us inscriptions chiselled on hard diorite, the inscriptions themselves being of a votive

[1] Cf. *Babylonian Expedition of the University of Pennsylvania IV, Series D,* for this Babylonian boundary-stone and for a full discussion of the subject generally.

character, while a club-button made of the same material
and bearing an inscription of ten lines was found at
Babylon. The various statues and stelæ made of these
hard igneous stones and found both in Assyria and Babylonia, though more frequently in the mother country,
practically always bear an inscription. A good example
of an Assyrian inscription on basalt is that found on the
basalt statue of Shalmaneser II (860–825 B.C.), which
was brought to light in the course of the recent excavations conducted by the Deutsche Orient-Gesellschaft at
Ashur. Again the numerous stone gate-sockets discovered in the ruins of early buildings in Babylonia are
nearly all inscribed with the name and titles of the person
who erected the building, and sometimes the original
inscription has been erased or obliterated to make room
for the inscription of a later ruler, who knowing full well
the difficulty of procuring stone in the low-lying country
of Babylonia, was not so short-sighted as to cast away
the gate-sockets of his vanquished predecessor, but on
the contrary utilized them for his own new building.
Thus for example the gate-socket of Lugal-kigub-nidudu, an early king of Sumer, was subsequently used by
Shar-Gâni-sharri, king of Akkad, in the construction of
his temple at Nippur.

But sometimes stones of comparative rarity, such as
lapis lazuli, were employed as a material whereon to
engrave inscriptions : thus a tablet made of that material and dedicated by Lugal-tarsi, an early king of
Kish, to the god Anu and the goddess Ninni, is preserved in the British Museum, and in the course of
the recent excavations at Babylon two bars of lapis
lazuli with reliefs and both bearing cuneiform inscriptions were discovered. One of these showed the picture of a god standing up, surmounted with a feather
crown, and holding the symbol of lightning in each
hand, while his dress is decorated with three shields,
and a cuneiform inscription of five lines is further added ;

on the other, a god in similar posture and dress but holding a staff and ring on his breast and grasping the tail of a double-horned dragon in his right hand is portrayed : the god's girdle is decorated with figures, while on one of the three shields adorning the raiment, horses are depicted, and there is an accompanying inscription of eight lines.

Metal in like manner was not exempt from being drawn into the service, the metals mostly employed being bronze and copper. Thus the female statuettes from Tellô all bear an inscription, Elamite or Babylonian as the case may be, the general purport of which is that the statuette is dedicated with a view to the preservation of the life of the donor : so too the colossal copper lance-head discovered on the same site bears a royal inscription, while the famous bronze gate-sheaths from Balâwât belonging to the time of Shalmaneser II, are perhaps the most familiar instance of cuneiform inscriptions engraved on bronze. Many bronze tablets of the Assyrian period have been found, and the well-known bronze doorstep of Nebuchadnezzar II provides us with another excellent example of an inscription engraved on metal. Moreover the more precious metals such as silver and gold were occasionally inscribed. Inscriptions on gold are very rare, but by no means unknown. M. de Sarzec for example found a plate of gold bearing a cuneiform inscription at Tellô, and a strip of gold bearing the name of the illustrious Narâm-Sin of Agade was brought to light in the course of the American excavations at Bismâya.

But the inscribed clay tablets, countless in number and infinitely various in size, shape and contents, far outweigh in importance all other kinds of cuneiform inscriptions in existence. A detailed treatment of the latter would far exceed the necessary limits of this little volume, but a few words may be said regarding the main classes of tablets discovered. Their size and shape are sometimes indicative of the period to which they belong, sometimes of the subject-matter with which they deal. A very early type is represented by those found below the level of Ur-Ninâ's building at Tellô; the tablets in question which have not been baked in an oven, and are round in form, deal with the sale and purchase of land. Similar round tablets were found by the German excavators at Fâra, which were however baked and not sun-dried. The same rounded baked clay tablets were evidently in vogue at the time of Bur-Sin, for several have been brought to light which are dated in his reign, and contain details regarding certain landed property. But the commonest type of clay tablet is that characterized by its rectangular shape, sometimes square, but more frequently oblong, and varying greatly in size. The tablets in the Kouyunjik collection, which represents the largest, and in one sense the only Assyrian library as yet discovered, vary from one to fifteen inches in length when complete, many of them being made from the very finest clay. The writing is sometimes exceedingly minute, though marvellously clear and sharp, and is more or less stereotyped in character. Astrology, astronomy, history, mythology, magic, medicine, mathematics, prayers, hymns, lists of gods, omens, lexicography and grammar are all well represented in this famous library. Many of the texts are copies of older Babylonian literature made by Ashur-bani-pal's scribes, and stored away in the royal archives. Some of the texts are bilingual, the top line containing the Sumerian ideographic version, and the lower line giving the Assyrian translation, and these bilingual inscriptions together with the syllabaries have enabled scholars to unravel and elucidate at all events to some extent the old Sumerian language.

By the year 1873 all scholars were agreed that the cuneiform script was not invented by the Semitic Babylonians, but by a people who spoke an agglutinative as opposed to an inflexional language, a language which was therefore, at least in this respect, akin to the Tartar languages. In the following year however Joseph Halévy, the famous French Semitist, started a theory which denied the existence of a Sumerian language altogether, and explained the ideographic texts in the bilingual inscriptions already alluded to, as a secret writing intelligible only to the priests ; but primâ facie the theory lacked probability and even plausibility. Halévy, it is true, propounded his theory at a time when the study of Sumerian was in its infancy, though it can hardly be said to have grown out of its childhood even at the present day, but this notwithstanding, it would be indeed singular if the priests took the precaution to enshrine their secret lore in cryptic language, and then frustrated themselves by subscribing an Assyrian translation. Moreover many of the Sumerian inscriptions treat of such very ordinary matters, that it is extremely difficult to see how it could have been necessary to employ a cryptic language to conceal them. A more ready explanation is to be found in the theory accepted by the majority of scholars to-day,—that the Sumerian language existed side by side with Semitic Babylonian, and was used much as Latin is to-day.

One class of tablet especially easily distinguishable by its shape and size is that comprising legal contracts for the exchange of land, cattle and property of every description. They are small in size, oblong in shape, both sides being slightly concave, and the whole not unlike a small narrow pillow in general appearance. Many of these contract tablets were enclosed in clay envelopes to ensure their preservation. When a contract was effected by the Babylonians, the contracting parties had recourse to a legal or priestly official, and the terms of the agreement were set forth on a clay tablet which was deposited either in the temple or the record chamber : it was furthermore protected by a clay envelope upon which the terms inscribed on the contract tablet were copied in duplicate; thus every precaution was taken to secure the preservation of the original document. Sometimes the text on the envelope varies somewhat from that contained in the document itself, and in such cases the envelopes therefore have more than a purely archaic interest, and are of actual linguistic value. One or two copies were made of the contract and were kept by either or both of the contracting parties. The deed was subscribed by the witnesses, one of whom was the scribe who drew up the document and sealed it. The seal was generally affixed by rolling a small cylinder seal over the tablet while still moist, though sometimes a three-sided clay cone received the impress of the seal, and this cone was attached to the tablet by means of a reed inserted in the apex of the cone, the other end of the reed being joined to the tablet by a piece of moist clay. Many of these contract "case" tablets belong to the times of Khammurabi, the most celebrated king of the First Dynasty of Babylon (circ. 1900 b.c.). Some of the envelopes of these tablets bear the impression of a cylinder-seal, a good example of which is found on a tablet recording the sale of a piece of land by Sin-eribam and his brother to Sin-ikisham (Brit. Mus. No. 92649). The clay of this class of tablet is generally somewhat dark in colour, and the characters are often difficult to read.

The later, or Neo-Babylonian legal and commercial documents show greater variation in size and shape than those belonging to the time of the First Dynasty of Babylon. They are generally oblong, but on the smaller tablets the text is generally written in such a manner that each line extends over the length of the tablet instead of over its breadth. The larger legal documents of this period are sometimes inscribed on tablets of quite exceptional thickness, their general size and shape being not unlike that of an old Latin prayer-book.

PLATE IX

THE RUINED MOUNDS OF NIPPUR

COURT OF THE MEN FROM THE NORTH-EAST: NIPPUR

(Both from C. S. Fisher's "Excavations at Nippur," by permission)

But contracts were not the only kind of inscription protected by a clay envelope or "case"; letters and despatches sometimes shared the same consideration. Like contracts, letters were inscribed on small oblong tablets, such as might be easily transmitted through the Babylonian and Assyrian post, that is to say carried by the messenger whose duty it was to convey the letter to its destination. As might be expected, the envelope in this case bore the name of the person to whom the letter was addressed, and occasionally also that of the sender, just as the envelopes of letters are sometimes initialled to-day. Many of these letters are of a royal character, and emanate from kings and princes. Quite a number of letters and despatches from the early kings of Babylon to their officials and governors have come down to us. They treat of divers subjects: in one Khammurabi writes to Sin-Idinnam commanding him to send forty-seven shepherds to Babylon in order that they may give an account to the king of the flocks under their care (Brit. Mus. No. 23122). In another letter the king writes to the same prince with instructions to arrest three officials and despatch them to Babylon, while in yet another Khammurabi writes to Sin-Idinnam with orders to restore a certain baker to his former position. Some of Sin-Idinnam's official correspondence has also been preserved. In one communication he directs a legal officer to summon a certain man to appear in court (Brit. Mus. No. 12868). Sin-Idinnam's duties were clearly very varied and must have been sufficiently arduous. In one of these despatches Khammurabi orders Sin-Idinnam to cut down some "Abba" trees required by smelters of metal (Brit. Mus. No. 26234). In another he commands the same personage to see to the mustering of crews for transport-barges (Brit. Mus. No. 27288). Others contain instructions to attend to the repair of the banks of the Euphrates at various points. But his duties were not exclusively civil ; judicial affairs fell to his charge also ; thus it is that to him the king writes regarding a dispute between a landlord and his tenant concerning the payment of rent for land, while he is perpetually receiving orders to arrest delinquent officials and other misconducted persons. In one letter (Brit. Mus. No. 12827) Khammurabi directs Sin-Idinnam to postpone the date of a certain trial, owing to the presence of the plaintiff, one Ili-Ippalzam, in the city of Ur at a certain festival.

Elsewhere (Brit. Mus. No. 12841) Khammurabi issues a report to the same overburdened official to the effect that certain persons have cancelled a deed of mortgage, and commands the instant presence of Enubi-Marduk, who received their lands on mortgage, in Babylon. Many of the letters of these early kings of Babylon embody the royal wishes regarding the date of sheep-shearing, or the reaping of corn, as well as instructions concerning the irrigation canals.

In one letter, Samsu-iluna (Brit. Mus. No. 27269) instructs Sin-Idinnam and the judges of Sippar to prohibit certain fishermen from fishing in forbidden waters ; at other times the same judges are directed to send a particular case for trial in the capital (cf. Brit. Mus. No. 27266). Another collection of letters written in cuneiform and on clay tablets are the famous Tell el-Amarna Letters,—generally of somewhat larger size and less distinctly oblong than the ordinary Babylonian despatches. The majority of them are rectangular, though a few are oval. Some are convex on both sides, some are flat on both sides, while others are plano-convex or pillow-shaped. These tablets were discovered at Tell el-Amarna in Egypt ; they represent nearly all that remains of the official and diplomatic correspondence which passed between the Pharaohs Amenhetep III and Amenhetep IV of the Eighteenth Dynasty (i.e. they belong to the fourteenth or fifteenth century B.C.), and their various officials and vassals in Palestine. Some of the tablets found at Tell el-Amarna are inscribed with letters from the King of Babylon, from the King of Mitani, from the King of Alashiya, and other royal potentates, but as they are mostly of Palestinian and Egyptian interest, a detailed consideration of them would be out of place in this volume.

Among the larger rectangular clay tablets in existence are those containing syllabaries. Owing to the deterioration and simplification which the cuneiform characters underwent in the course of ages, the Assyrian scribes found it necessary to make lists of the early Babylonian characters adding what they believed to be the later Assyrian equivalents. Most of these syllabaries consist of three columns; in the middle column the Assyrian sign to be explained is given, on the left the Sumerian value of the same, and in the right-hand column either the Assyrian name for the sign, or else the Assyrian meaning, and occasionally both. These syllabaries are obviously of immense importance in the reconstruction of the old Sumerian language.

Other tablets of abnormally large size are those dealing with astrology, magic and medicine : the two latter subjects are inextricably confused owing to the fact that they went hand in hand with each other ; the medicine was prescribed and administered, but the medicine alone was by no means sufficient to cure the patient, that could only be effected by the potent spell of the magician.

But the largest clay tablets emanate from Babylonia and contain lists of accounts mostly concerning grain, cattle, asses, lambs, sheep. Some of these tablets are perfectly square, and measure as much as a foot each way, while nearly all of them are more square than oblong: the clay of which they are made is of fine quality, and the Babylonian characters with which they are inscribed are singularly clear. Most of them may be assigned to the second half of the third millennium B.C., and many of them are specifically dated in the reign of Dungi, king of Ur about 2500 B.C. But as already mentioned, tablets were not always rectangular ; sometimes they assumed a circular form. Tablets of this kind are usually inscribed in the Sumerian language, and contain lists of landed estates and fields, with information regarding their size, their capacity for producing crops and other details. Many of these circular tablets are dated, the year deriving its name after some noteworthy event, as was the regular mode of dating in the early days of Babylonian civilization. Thus many of these lists are dated "in the year after that in which the land of Khukhnuri was laid waste," and were drawn up in the reign of Bur-Sin and other kings of Ur, i.e. during the second half of the third millennium B.C.

The clay of which these tablets are made is of the finest, while the writing is exceedingly clear ; they vary from about two to six inches in diameter, and are oval on one side and more or less flat on the other.

Other large rectangular tablets are inscribed with lists of the principal events in different kings' reigns and are obviously of immense importance for the reconstruction of Babylonian and Assyrian history. One of the tablets belonging to this class (Brit. Mus. No. 92702) gives us a list of the chief events, after which the various years of Sumu-abu, Sumu-la-ilu, Zabum, Apil-Sin, Sin-muballit, Khammurabi and Samsu-iluna, kings of the first dynasty of Babylon (about the end of the third and beginning of the second millennium B.C.) were named. Another of the same class (Brit. Mus. No. 92502) gives us a list of the leading events which took place in Babylonia and Assyria from the third year of Nabonassar, king of Babylon 744 B.C., and the first year of Shamash-shum-ukîn, the contemporary of Ashur-bani-pal (668 B.C.). One of the most interesting events here alluded to is the assassination of Sennacherib by his son on the 20th day of the month Tebet, and in the 23rd year of his reign. Among other historical documents of primary importance, a tablet generally known as "the Synchronous History" must be placed in the first rank. This document is an agreement drawn up about the time of Ashur-bani-pal, and it had as its object the settlement of boundary-disputes between Babylonia and Assyria, while its historical value lies largely in the short notices of the various conflicts and alliances between the two countries from about 1600–800 B.C. One other large rectangular tablet (K. 3751) of exceptional interest alike to the historian and the Biblical student, is the document in which Tiglath-Pileser III, king of Assyria 745–727 B.C., gives us an account of his building operations and conquests, and mentions "Ahaz, King of Judah" as one of his tributary princes. This tablet must have been very large when complete, for what remains of it measures nine inches by seven and a half. The largest tablet in the Kouyunjik collection is not however historical in character, but contains a list of the names and titles of various gods, and in its present fragmentary state measures fifteen inches in length.

Other cuneiform inscriptions were written on pieces of clay shaped like cones. Most of these terra-cotta cones date from the time of the dynasty of Ur, i.e. the latter half of the third millennium B.C. Two good examples of this kind of cuneiform inscription bear the name of Sin-gashid, king of Erech, and record the dedication of a temple to the god Lugal-banda and the goddess Ninsun, and give the price of wool, grain, oil and copper during the reign of Sin-gashid (Brit. Mus. 91, 150). Another baked clay cone is inscribed with the name of Sin-idinnam, king of Larsa about 2300 B.C., and likewise records the dedication of a temple—in this case that of the Sun-god, Larsa being one of the principal centres of the worship of the Sun-god. But the conquering Elamites, who imitated their subjugated enemies, the Babylonians, in so many ways, also adopted the

practice of writing cuneiform inscriptions on clay cones ;
for an example of an Elamite cone we may compare
Brit. Mus. 91, 149, which bears the name of Kudur-
Mabug. But the habit of writing inscriptions on clay
cones did not cease at this period, at least not perma-
nently, for a similar cone exists bearing the name of the
Neo-Babylonian king Nabopolassar (625–604 B.C.), and
like the older cones recording the dedication of a temple,
this time the temple of Marduk at Babylon. (Brit.
Mus. No. 91,090.)

But Babylonian and Assyrian inscriptions on clay were
not always in the form of rectangular or circular tablets ;
frequently they assumed the form of large hexagonal,
octagonal, or decagonal prisms, or in the case of Babylonia of barrel-shaped cylinders. It was customary to
place these large clay memorials in the four corners of
the foundation of a building in Babylonia and Assyria,
a good example of which practice was found at Mukeyyer (Ur): the cylinders from Ur had been deposited at
the four angles of the foundation of the temple of Sin,
the Moon-god, by Nabonidus, and they record the rebuilding of the temple by Nabonidus (555–538 B.C.) on
the site of the ancient temple erected by Ur-Engur and
his son Dungi, about 2400 B.C. The text finds a fitting
conclusion in a prayer to the god whose fane he is re-
storing, on behalf of his eldest son Bal-shar-uṣur, the
Biblical Belshazzar. Three octagonal prisms of baked
clay give us an account of the campaigns and building
operations of Tiglath-Pileser I, king of Assyria about
1100 B.C. (Brit. Mus. 91033–91035). Another prism is
inscribed with an account of the expeditions of Sargon,
king of Assyria 721–705 B.C. (Brit. Mus. No. 22505),
while the fragments of an octagonal prism of the same
king, and also preserved in the British Museum, (K. 1668,
etc.) are of peculiar interest in that they give Sargon's
own account of his campaign against the Philistine city
of Ashdod, which is referred to in Isaiah xx. 1. Judah is

mentioned as one of the allies of Ashdod, but the Assyrians were ultimately successful in reducing the rebellious city. Sargon's successor, Sennacherib (705–681 B.C.), similarly caused his military achievements to be recorded on large clay prisms, and the most interesting document of his reign is preserved on the six sides of a hexagonal prism now in the British Museum (91032). It records the defeat of Merodach-Baladan, king of Babylon, and the subjugation of various other peoples, but the particular interest attaching to this cylinder lies in the allusions to the Palestinian campaign of 2 Kings xviii. Sennacherib states that he severely punished the rebellious people of Ekron and restored the banished Padî to his throne ; he then proceeded to attack Hezekiah in Jerusalem " his royal city " ; he laid siege to Jerusalem, and shut Hezekiah up like a bird in a cage, but in spite of this demonstration, he was clearly unable to open the cage and seize the bird. However, Hezekiah seems to have been duly impressed, and he hastened to buy off Sennacherib with gifts and tribute—" thirty talents of gold, eight hundred talents of silver, precious stones, eye paint . . . ivory couches and thrones, hides and tusks, precious woods and divers objects," together with his daughters, his women - folk and male and female musicians—apparently being the price.

Another interesting octagonal prism of this same king has been recently acquired by the British Museum (No. 103,000). It contains information regarding two campaigns not recorded elsewhere. The first of these, which took place in 698 B.C., was undertaken to suppress a revolt in Cilicia ; the campaign was completely successful and the Assyrian power was entirely restored in those regions. It is interesting to note that the city of Tarsus was one of those which Sennacherib sacked on this occasion. The second campaign took place three years later in 695 B.C., and resulted in the siege and capture of a certain city called Til-Garimum in the land of Tubal,

I

which lay to the north-east of Cilicia. We are also furnished with an account of the rebuilding and fortification of Nineveh by Sennacherib, which contains valuable information regarding the inner and outer wall of the city, and the positions and names of the fifteen gates. It is dated in the eponymy[1] of Ilu-Ittia, the Assyrian governor of Damascus. This cylinder was apparently buried as a foundation memorial in the structure of one of the city gates referred to in the text.

Esarhaddon, Sennacherib's son and successor, has likewise left us a number of hexagonal prisms of historic importance. One of the principal events narrated on Esarhaddon's cylinders is the siege and capture of Sidon and the subjugation of the surrounding country. Ashurbani-pal, Esarhaddon's famous son and successor, has left us a number of cylinders and prisms, but by far the most important is that upon which an account of the principal events of the early part of his reign is inscribed (Brit. Mus., No. 91,026). We have here a record of his first and second Egyptian campaigns, of the defeat he inflicted upon Tirhakah, the Ethiopian king of Egypt, and the sack of Thebes, the capital of the country. The capture of Tyre is also narrated and the campaign against Te-Umman, king of Elam, whom Ashur-bani-pal slew and whose severed head is seen hanging from a tree in the bas-relief in which Ashur-bani-pal and his wife are reclining at meat in their garden. There is also an account of the siege and capture of Babylon, whose king Shamash-shum-ukîn had thrown off the suzerainty of Assyria; the conquest of Arabia is recorded as well as the final triumph of the Assyrian arms over Elam, and the text concludes with an account of Ashur-bani-pal's building operations.

---

[1] An eponym was an official of high rank—sometimes the king himself—who held office for a year, and whose name was used to date all documents drawn up in that year. He corresponded to the Roman consul and the Athenian archon.

We have already alluded to a clay cylinder belonging to the Neo-Babylonian king Nabonidus, while another cylinder of the same king, which has been discussed elsewhere (cf. p. 7), is equally notable, as a complete system of chronology has been based upon its contents. Nebuchadnezzar II, king of Babylon 604–561 B.C., and belonging to the same dynasty has likewise left us a number of barrel-shaped cylinders, the inscriptions upon which are chiefly concerned with a recital of his building achievements, while to the cylinder of Cyrus the Persian conqueror of Babylonia (538 B.C.) reference has been made elsewhere (cf. p. 74). But the practice of writing cuneiform inscriptions on baked clay cylinders did not even come to an end with the Persian kings of Babylonia, for we have a cylinder (Brit. Mus. 36277) bearing an inscription in archaic Babylonian characters, of Antiochus Soter, king of Babylonia about 280 B.C.; it records the restoration of the temples E-Sagil, and E-zida in Babylon and Borsippa in the year 270 B.C., and concludes with a prayer to the god Nebo on behalf of Antiochus, his son Seleucus and his wife.

But besides rectangular, round, barrel-shaped, cylindrical and cone-shaped clay inscriptions, yet other varieties exist. Among these a four-sided block of clay forming an elongated kind of cube, the height of which is $9\frac{1}{2}$ inches and the breadth of each of its four sides $3\frac{3}{4}$ inches (Brit. Mus. No. 92611), deserves a mention; its date is about 2100 B.C., and it is inscribed with lists of the names of fish, birds, plants, stones and garments.

Another unique object is a clay model of an ox-hoof (Brit. Mus. No. R. 620), inscribed with forecasts. A somewhat similar object is found in a clay model of a sheep's liver, also preserved in the British Museum (No. 92,668); the inscription which it bears is magical in character, and the object was probably used for divination purposes. Other tablets, though not being moulded in the form of a sheep's liver, bear the incised outlines of different parts of the liver. Hepatoscopy, or the practice of deriving omens from the shape, size, or condition of the liver, was one of the most popular forms of magic among the Babylonians and Assyrians.

Plans of cities seem to have sometimes been drawn on clay tablets, a good example of which is afforded by a tablet discovered at Nippur, and incised with a plan of that city, a plan which in spite of its antiquity seems to have helped the work of the excavators in no small degree. Another example is the British Museum fragment (No. 35385), on which a plan of part of the city of Babylon is still to be seen. Sometimes the plan was merely that of an estate (cf. Brit. Mus. No. 31483), but in one instance at all events, the world itself is the subject (Brit. Mus. No. 92687), the most interesting feature of which from the geographical point of view is the world-encircling ocean—the Babylonians believing the earth to be surrounded by and apparently supported on water : the earth itself was supposed to resemble an inverted saucer in shape, while the heavens bore the same shape, the only difference being that they were obviously more extensive, and the lower edges rested on the earth itself, while the edge of the earth rested upon the ocean.

Sometimes amulets were made of clay, a good example of which is Brit. Mus. No. 85–4–8, 1 ; it is shaped like a cylinder-seal, and is inscribed with an incantation for Shamash-Killâni.

Other inscribed clay objects are those known as astrolabæ or instruments for making astrological calculations.

Labels again were made of clay : two small clay labels (Brit. Mus. K. 1400, K. 1539) give us the titles of two series of astrological and omen tablets; while another (K. 3787) gives us the name of Khipa, a female slave ; it is dated in the 11th year of Marduk-aplu-iddina, i.e. *circ.* 710 B.C. There are miscellaneous clay objects which do not properly come under the heading of terra-cotta figures or clay bas-reliefs, and therefore may be mentioned here. Sometimes clay squeezes or impressions were made of early inscriptions; an excellent example of such squeezes was acquired some years ago by the University of Pennsylvania (cf. Fig. 3);[1] it is a squeeze made

FIG. 3.   FIG. 4. (Brit. Mus., 103040.)

by a Neo-Babylonian scribe of the sixth century B.C. of an inscription belonging to Shar-Gâni-sharri, king of Akkad. The characters of course are raised in relief and read backwards. Allusion is elsewhere made to the clay

FIG. 5. (Brit. Mus., 91102.)

brick-stamps with which Babylonian kings were in the habit of inscribing their building bricks: an interesting specimen of a clay brick-stamp is seen in Fig. 4. It is a fragment of a stamp belonging to Narâm-Sin, the son of

[1] Cf. Hilprecht, *Explorations*, p. 517.

Shar-Gâni-sharri. The characters here are of course in relief and reversed as in the case of a seal. Another clay object of exceptional interest is seen in Fig. 5 ; it is a clay covering made by order of Nabopolassar, king of Babylon 625–604 B.C., for the preservation of the stone tablet of his predecessor Nabû-aplu-iddina (*circ*. 870 B.C.). It was presumably during the course of his work at the restoration of the temple of the Sun-god at Sippar that he alighted upon this early tablet. The clay cover bears an inscription of Nabopolassar on the reverse side and records the various offerings he deposited at the shrine of the Sun-god. The cover itself was found in a baked clay box, also preserved in the British Museum, and probably belonging to the same reign. Clay was further employed by the sculptor for tentative sketches, and by the stone-inscriber for rough drafts. Thus the sculptor to whom we are indebted for the portrayal of Ashur-bani-pal, king of Assyria, spearing a lion, sketched out his picture in clay preparatory to chiselling it on slabs of stone, and his original sketch is still extant (cf. Brit. Mus. 93011), while we can still see two rough drafts on clay of epigraphs inscribed on Ashur-bani-pal's bas-reliefs (cf. Brit. Mus. Sm. 1350 and K. 4453 + K. 4515).

CHAPTER V—ARCHITECTURE

THE architecture of a country is determined very largely by the materials with which nature has endowed that country; it is also influenced by the configuration of the country itself as well as by the climate whose effects it is the builder's object to either regulate or counteract. The physical characteristics of the Mesopotamian Valley as also the climatic conditions which prevail there have already been under consideration, but it will not perhaps be unfitting to devote a few pages to a review of the materials which were used for building operations, before we proceed to discuss the ruins of the buildings themselves.

It has been already stated, that practically no stone at all is to be found in the low-lying and marshy country of Babylonia, hence it never assumed an important place in Babylonian architecture; any stone required, had to be quarried far away in the mountains and transported at great labour, in consequence of which it was only employed for exceptional purposes and in cases where the desire for permanent durability rendered it necessary. Accordingly the stone used was generally diorite, basalt, or some other hard stone of volcanic origin, contrasting strikingly with the softer stone utilized so freely by the Assyrians. Assyria on the other hand was more fortunate in this respect and afforded a very fair supply of limestone and alabaster which were used extensively by her sculptors and builders, though the clay so easily procurable all over the valley was the one indispensable element in the erection of temples, palaces, or houses in both countries. The supply of wood again was extremely scanty not only in Babylonia but also in Assyria, and any wood used for columns, lintels or thresholds was generally brought from Lebanon, Amanus, or some other distant place.

We thus see that the art of brick-building was almost forced upon the dwellers of Mesopotamia from the very necessity of the case.

The clay used for the purpose was by no means uniform either as regards its colour, or as regards its quality. Sometimes it is of a light yellow colour, sometimes it is almost black, while the clay from which other bricks are made is of a reddish hue. Those made of light yellow clay are the best from the point of view of durability. The bricks further vary both in size and shape according to the period to which they belong, so that it is often possible to provisionally assign a date to a building or the remains of a building by an examination of the style of brick employed. The type of brick characteristic of the early periods of Sumerian history is that known as the plano-convex[1] type ; thus the kiln-burnt bricks of which the storehouse of Ur-Ninâ, the first king of Lagash, was composed, are oblong and plano-convex, while each of them also bears the impression of a thumb-mark on the convex side.

But a yet earlier form of brick[2] was found in the building underneath Ur-Ninâ's storehouse : the bricks of which this building was composed were indeed plano-convex like those of Ur-Ninâ, but they were smaller, had no thumb- or finger-marks and were also unfortunately uninscribed.

At Muḳeyyer (Ur) Taylor came across a pavement

---

[1] A "plano-convex" brick is a brick which is flat on one side and convex or oval on the other, its general appearance resembling an oblong cake, or a small pillow.

[2] Cf. De Sarzec et Heuzey, *Une Villa Royale Chaldéenne*, p. 47.

made of plano-convex bricks, the antiquity of which was attested alike by the appearance of this type of brick and also by the depth below the surface at which the platform was found. This excavator discovered similar bricks at Abû Shahrein (Eridu), a further corroboration of the traditional antiquity of Ea's once famous city. The excavations at other early sites have also yielded the same results ; at Fâra (Shuruppak) the traditional scene of the Deluge, as well as at Yôkha, Bismâya, and in the pre-Sargonic strata at Nippur, the same style of bricks has been found.

But with the expansion of the Semites, culminating in the establishment of the empire of Shar-Gâni-sharri and his son Narâm-Sin, the comparatively small, oblong and plano-convex brick fell into disuse, and gave way to a large square brick. Immediately beneath the crude-brick platform of Ur-Engur (*circ.* 2400 B.C.) at Nippur, part of the earlier work of Narâm-Sin and Shar-Gâni-sharri was uncovered, the bricks used being no longer plano-convex and oblong, but flat and square, and measuring 20 × 20 × 3½ inches ; they are made of clay mixed with straw, and are at the same time well-dried and very hard ; this type of brick was employed in all the buildings of these two kings.

The next period in the history of Babylonian brick-making is that belonging to the times of the second dynasty of Lagash and the first dynasty of Ur (i.e. *circ.* 2450 B.C.). The type of brick characteristic of this age resembles that of the preceding in regard to shape but not in regard to size. The bricks of Ur-Engur, king of Ur, and of Gudea, the most renowned ruler of the second dynasty of Lagash (*circ.* 2450 B.C.) are square like those of their Semitic predecessors, Shar-Gâni-sharri and Narâm-Sin, but very much smaller, measuring a little over 12 × 12 inches, and this small square brick remained in use, with occasional slight variations, till the close of Mesopotamian history. The transition from the large brick used by the kings of Agade to the small brick in qnestion was doubtless effected only gradually, for the bricks of Urbau, ruler of Lagash some time before Gudea, are larger than those of the latter king, but after the time of Gudea and Ur-Engur, the shape and size of the bricks became more or less stereotyped. The bricks of Ur-Engur himself vary somewhat from those of Gudea, thus the solid mass underlying the temple-tower at Nippur, which was constructed by Ur-Engur, is composed of bricks measuring only $9 \times 6 \times 3$ inches, the arms of the causeway on the other hand are built of larger bricks measuring $14 \times 14 \times 6$ inches. Kiln-burnt bricks were always used for the important parts of the building in Babylonia, the crude sun-dried bricks which as a rule formed the core of the terraced platforms, being revetted with a wall of burnt brick, or sometimes, in the case of Assyria with a supporting wall of stone. The reason of course for this lay in the inability of sun-dried bricks to resist damp, and their corresponding tendency to disintegrate. The bricks were as a rule carried on to the ground as soon as they were fairly dry and firm, and were laid while still soft.

Generally speaking the bricks bear the name of the king who caused the structure to be made, thus the majority of the bricks of Nebuchadnezzar, king of Babylon (604–561 B.C.) are inscribed :—" Nebuchadnezzar, King of Babylon, restorer of the pyramid and tower, eldest son of Nabopolassar, King of Babylon, am I." It is interesting to note that though the tiles on the western side of Nebuchadnezzar's palace at Babylon bear the ordinary stamp of that king, those on the eastern side are stamped with a lion and an Aramaic inscription. Koldewey indeed says that there is no doubt that this part of the building was also erected by Nebuchadnezzar, as wall-tiles bearing the regular palace-inscription of the king have been found there. Prof. Euting however, from the forms of the Aramaic characters, would assign these Aramaic-inscribed bricks to the middle of the seventh century, i.e. about 650 B.C. None of the bricks found on the Kasr mound bear the stamp of any Assyrian kings, the latter apparently only having left their marks on the floor-bricks of E-sagila, the temple of Marduk. The characters were generally impressed with a stamp, though on both Assyrian and Babylonian bricks the inscription was sometimes engraved by hand. The stamps used were made of terracotta ; a well-preserved specimen of a terra-cotta brick-stamp is that of Narâm-Sin referred to above (cf. Fig. 4), while a terra-cotta brick-stamp of Shar-Gâni-sharri, the father of Narâm-Sin, was discovered at Nippur, and one of the minor results of the expedition to Bismâya, directed by Harper, was the discovery of a number of clay brick-stamps. Many Assyrian and Babylonian bricks are glazed or enamelled and coloured in the most ornate fashion, and with the most striking pictures and designs, but an examination of these will naturally find its place in the chapter devoted to " Painting."

Sometimes the architects of Babylonia contrived to adapt the clay employed in their building operations to decorative devices. Such was the case at Warka (Erech) where Loftus discovered a wall some thirty feet long, composed entirely of clay cones fixed in a cement made of mud and straw, and laid horizontally with their bases outwards. Some of these cones had been coloured red or black and were arranged to form various geometrical designs. They were sometimes inscribed, sometimes not. But clay cones were apparently not the only kind of cone used for architectural decoration, for in the course of his excavations at Abû Shahrein, Taylor[1] discovered cones of limestone and marble, some of which had a " rim round the edge filled with copper"; these cones vary from four to ten inches in length, their diameter measuring from one to three inches.

[1] Cf. Loftus, *Travels*, p. 189.

MORTAR

The layers and courses of clay bricks of which the buildings in Mesopotamia were for the most part composed, were cemented together by mud in the earliest times ; this clay-mud is generally distinguishable from the bricks which it unites by the difference of its colour. Mud-mortar has been found on some of the earliest sites and in some of the most ancient buildings, while in Assyria it appears to have been the regular form of cement used at all times. In the city of Babylon, strange to say, clay mortar appears to have been used instead of lime or asphalt in the late buildings of Sassanidian times. This mud-mortar consisted of clay mixed with water and perhaps a little straw, as was the case in the cone-wall at Warka,[1] while sometimes reeds embedded in clay were laid between the bricks, as was the case at both Warka and Hammam, but at an extremely remote period the Babylonian architect began to avail himself of the rich supply of bitumen gratuitously yielded by the soil of his native land, for the purpose in question.

The most famous bituminous springs in Mesopotamia were those at Hit on the Euphrates. Their fame had reached Egypt as early as the time of the eighteenth dynasty, for Thothmes III brought bitumen thence to Egypt. Herodotus a millennium later—about 450 B.C. —alludes to Hit as famous for her bitumen, and subsequent writers make similar mention of the springs there. A good example of the early use of bitumen in Babylonia was found at Abû Shahrein, the site of ancient Eridu, where a very early building was excavated by Taylor, the antiquity of which was proved by the pre-Sargonic plano-convex bricks used in its construction, and these bricks were all laid in bitumen ; the same was

[1] Loftus, *Travels*, p. 187.

found to be the case in a building composed of finger-marked bricks at Ur (Mukeyyer), all of which were embedded in bitumen.

The platform upon which Ur-Ninâ's storehouse at Tellô was erected consisted of three layers of plano-convex and finger-marked bricks, all set in bitumen, while in the building underneath that of Ur-Ninâ, bitumen was also freely used.[1]

In like manner at Nippur, the finger-marked bricks of which the city-gate was constructed were laid in bitumen, though the bricks composing the early arch found on this site were set in mud, probably an indication that at the time when the arch was built bitumen was not used ; around the base of Ur-Engur's ziggurat on the other hand there was a coating of bitumen, while the crude brick altar found by Haynes in the lowest stratum at Nippur had a rim of bitumen ; but in later times it was supplemented by the more tenacious lime-mortar, though only partially was this the case, for even as late as Nebuchadnezzar's time (604–561 B.C.) its practical utility as a preventive against the destructive forces of rain were still recognized, the burnt brick retaining walls of his palace at Babylon being actually laid in bitumen. In like manner the bricks composing the old fortification wall, are rendered adhesive by means of a lavish prodigality of asphalt, so adhesive in fact, that it is often very difficult to separate them. Fortunately the side bearing the stamped inscription has its face downwards and therefore is not in immediate contact with the asphalt from which it is separated by the layer of reeds or clay already alluded to.

In the later buildings at Babylon, however, lime-mortar is also used, the transition period being marked by the employment of both in one and the same building, and in point of fact Koldewey found that in the case

[1] Cf. Heuzey, *Une Villa Royale*, p. 48.

of one of the walls of a building of Nebuchadnezzar, one half of the wall was cemented together by means of asphalt, while in the other half lime-mortar alone was used. But in the new castle which Nebuchadnezzar built for himself on the Kasr, the very finest materials were employed, the bricks being of a pale yellow colour and extremely hard, contrasting with the bricks used in his earlier buildings, which are of a reddish-brown colour and less durable, while in this new structure, pure white lime-mortar alone is used. Lime-mortar, as well as mud-cement and bitumen, was employed at Nippur, as also at Birs-Nimrûd (Borsippa), and the mortar used has such adhesive properties that the bricks can only be separated by breaking them, while at Mukeyyer (Ur) a mortar composed of a mixture of lime and ashes was employed.

In Assyria on the other hand, mortar seems to have been used more sparingly; when stone was employed as a building material, generally speaking no cement of any kind was used, the stones being carefully dressed so as to permit of no interstices, as for example was found to be the case with the stone retaining-wall round the ziggurat at Nimrûd; when ordinary crude bricks were employed, they were laid in a sufficient state of moisture to render them adhesive; while when burnt brick was the material in question, the mortar adopted was a mixture of clay and water. Bitumen however was by no means unknown in Assyria, but it was used chiefly under pavements or the limestone floors of sewers, to prevent leakage or infiltration.

STONE

The use of stone in Babylonia, as a building accessory, although seldom as a fundamental material, dates from the most ancient Sumerian times. A very early example of the use of stone for definitely architectural purposes in Babylonia is afforded by the pavement upon which a building at Lagash, found under the structure of Ur-Ninâ, was erected. The pavement[1] consists of slabs of limestone, three or four feet long, one and a half to two feet broad, and about six inches thick. The door-sockets, again, of some of the earliest rulers of Lagash have been brought to light, among which may be mentioned those of the illustrious Eannatum and Entemena, all being made of marble or some other hard stone, while in Eridu, one of the most ancient sites of civilization in the Euphrates Valley, stone seems to have been quite extensively used. The terraced artificial platform upon which the temple and city of Eridu were built was buttressed by a wall of sandstone, and the staircase which led up to the first stage of the ziggurat was made of polished marble slabs, which are now lying about casually on the mound ; pieces of agate and alabaster were discovered, and granite was also employed there. Stone gate-sockets have been similarly found at Nippur and in the ruins of other early cities of Babylonia, while both the Semite Narâm-Sin, and the Sumerian Gudea a little later, brought heavy blocks of diorite from Magan, or Sinai, though apparently for sculptural rather than for architectural purposes.

In the Neo-Babylonian era stone was employed to a greater extent : the procession pavement of the god Marduk at Babylon, discovered recently by the Germans, was formed of slabs of limestone, bearing an inscription of Nebuchadnezzar, while Herodotus tells us that the bridge which then united the two banks of the Euphrates was made of " very large stones,"[2] and according to the classical writers, Strabo and Diodorus, the famous hanging gardens of Babylon, which Koldewey would locate to the east of the palace, were supported by stone architraves. But the stone used only for excep-

---

[1] Heuzey, Une Villa Royale, pp. 47, 48.

[2] In the northern fortification wall, and according to Koldewey, there only on the Kasr, great building blocks of limestone were also discovered.

tional purposes in Babylonia, was re-used time and again, the ruins being regarded as a quarry, and consequently the stone has for the most part disappeared entirely.

In Assyria, on the other hand, stone was easily procurable and therefore readily used, though not to the extent one would expect, the reason being that the Assyrian was not an inventor but an imitator of his predecessor, the Babylonian, who afforded him little or no example in the working of stone. Accordingly even in Assyria, stone was for the most part used only for pavements, plinths and the lining of walls : at times however it was also used for the retaining walls which enclosed an artificial mound. The blocks of stone used for this latter purpose were sometimes of colossal size, measuring even as much as $6 \times 6 \times 9$ feet and weighing some tons. The principal kinds of stone employed by the Assyrian architects were limestone, of varying degrees of hardness, and alabaster, which latter is often found in Assyria itself a little below the surface of the soil. Alabaster is a sulphate of chalk, it is grey in colour, soft, and admits of a high polish, but it is brittle and deteriorates in course of time. At Nimrûd (Calah) some of the drainage channels were covered with large slabs of limestone, and the ziggurat of Nimrûd, of which only one storey remains, was faced with a massive stone revetment wall, while occasionally stone columns appear to have been used, and one part of a column composed of carved limestone, some forty inches high and including both the capital and the upper part of the shaft in one piece has been actually discovered. Layard further found four bases of columns made of limestone, on the northern side of Sennacherib's palace at Nineveh (cf. Fig. 14). Sometimes the lintels of doors were made of stone ; one such stone lintel was found by George Smith at the entrance to the hall in Sennacherib's palace, while the sill or threshold generally, or at all events very frequently, consisted of alabaster or limestone. Similarly the floors of the more important rooms were formed of limestone-slabs.

The harder stones were notwithstanding sometimes employed in Assyria just as limestone was occasionally used in Babylonia, but as a general rule, in either case for sculptural rather than building purposes. The well-known black obelisk of Shalmaneser II (860–825 B.C.) already alluded to, was supposed to afford a good example of the use of volcanic stones in the northern country, but the material of which it is made is probably alabaster. A basalt statue of this same king was however brought to light by the German excavations at Ashur some few years ago, while the capital of a column found on the same site, belonging possibly to the time of Tiglath-Pileser I, gives us an illustration of the use of hard stones for purely architectural purposes by the Assyrians. It is uncertain from what quarter they obtained these harder stones, but basalt and other igneous rocks may be quarried in the valleys of the streams that poured their waters into the Tigris and Euphrates, and in the valley of the Khabour Layard informs us that he discovered many extinct volcanoes.

WOOD

Assyria afforded a better supply of wood than Babylonia, the latter country being as poor in wood as it is in stone. The only trees from which beams sufficiently long to be of any use could be obtained, were the poplar and the palm tree. Wood being more perishable than either clay or stone, we naturally do not expect to find the same amount of material evidence of its usage ; sufficient however has survived the ravages of time to establish the certainty of its usage in Mesopotamia as a building material from the earliest to the latest times. Thus for example at Nippur, Peters found charred beams of palm-wood which evidently had at one time formed the roof of the corridor in which it was discovered ;

K

pieces of tamarisk were in like manner found upon the brick threshold of a doorway, which probably represented all that remained of the doors and door-posts. Similarly at Lagash not far from Ur-Ninâ's storehouse were found the charred remains of pillars made of cedarwood, which doubtless at one time supported a portico made of the same material, while Ur-Ninâ himself records that he fetched wood from the mountains, as did his descendants of later days. In like manner the roof of a temple erected by Enannatum I a successor of Ur-Ninâ was constructed of cedar-wood. So too at Mukeyyer (Ur), large quantities of charred wood were discovered,[1] while at Abû Shahrein (Eridu), the casement wall of the ziggurat is studded with square holes—three inches square, which are filled with wood.[2] After the establishment of Babylonian sovereignty over the land of Amurru, (i.e. Syria and Palestine) by Shar-Gâni-sharri and Narâm-Sin, the kings of Babylonia regularly obtained cedar-wood from the Lebanon, as did the early kings of Egypt. In a room at Nippur used apparently for storing unbaked tablets in the time of Gimil-Sin (c. 2400 B.C.) wooden shelves had seemingly been used for the purpose, while the roof of the famous castle at Babylon, rebuilt by Nebuchadnezzar, was made of cedarwood, as also were the doors, and the portal-like entrance of one of the buildings at Babylon excavated by Koldewey was roofed throughout with a ceiling of timber.

Of the use of wood in Assyria, the wall reliefs would alone afford ample evidence, for parts of some of the structures there encountered could only possibly have been made of wood. Shalmaneser II (860–825 B.C.) in commemorating his reconstruction of the temple of Anu and Adad at Ashur, says that he roofed it over with beams of cedar, and those of the larger rooms of the palaces which were not vaulted must have

[1] J. R. A. S., 1855, p. 266.   [2] *Ibidem*, p. 407.

been roofed with wood, because there is no evidence of the existence of slabs of stone of sufficient size to have effected the purpose, and large flat brick roofs would be out of the question. In like manner Tiglath-Pileser III states that he made a palace of cedar-wood[1] while Esarhaddon says that the doors of one of the palaces which he erected for himself were made of cypress-wood and were covered with silver and copper,[2] while in another passage he states that in his building operations at Babylon he used oaks, terebinths and palms. At Khorsabad, Place further found fragments of cedar-beams which had been clearly used for architectural purposes, and probably formed part of the lintels of the doorways in which they were found; so too Layard in the course of his excavations found the charred remains of wood together with a beam of cedar-wood, all of which are now in the British Museum. The scantiness of the remains of wood thus used is adequately accounted for by the destructibility of that material.

METAL

Metal can hardly be said to have been used for purely architectural purposes at all, and when employed seems rather to have been added for the adornment of the more conspicuous parts of the building, than used as an integral part of the structure. There are, however, one or two exceptions to this generalization. The sills were sometimes made of metal in the more luxurious buildings, and a bronze sill measuring $60 \times 20 \times 3\frac{1}{2}$ inches, with an inscription of Nebuchadnezzar has actually come to light, and is now in the British Museum, while another object of a singularly unique character, consisting of a bronze gate-socket set in lead, has similarly found its way to that famous institution. Herodotus furthermore tells us in his account of Babylon that the walls had a hundred gates " all of bronze ; their jambs and lintels were

[1] Cf. Harper, *Assyrian and Babylonian Literature*, p. 57.   [2] *Ibid.*, p. 87.

of the same material." Some of the bas-reliefs also exhibit structures, parts of which must seemingly have been made of metal : the royal pavilion carved on the tablet from Abû Habba (Sippar) for example (cf. Pl. XIV) is provided with a curved back wall which at the same time is bent right over so as to form a roof ; this wall and roof may indeed have been constructed of wood, but metal would clearly have adapted itself the more easily to such a form. Of other minor building materials, such as tools, and nails which played a subsidiary part in Mesopotamian architecture, we know comparatively little, though a number of nails have been recovered from different sites.

TEMPLES

It would be quite impossible to give an account of all the temples and palaces in Mesopotamia, excavated during the last sixty years, we must therefore confine ourselves to a brief description of a few of the better explored buildings, which may with reserve be regarded as typical. The temples have not weathered the deteriorating effects of time and climate so well as the palaces, the reason for which is to be found in the fact that, generally speaking, the object of the temple-builder was so far as possible to erect a structure whose top should metaphorically " reach unto heaven," whereas the culminating glory of palaces lay not in the height to which they were reared but in the extent of ground which they covered.

As to the general plan of Sumerian temples we are still in a state of ignorance, for on the earliest sites of Babylonian occupation, few important buildings have been unearthed. The best preserved and most thoroughly explored temple in Southern Babylonia is that of Enlil at Nippur. A Babylonian plan of this once famous shrine, drawn on a clay tablet and probably belonging to the first half of the second millennium B.C. was dis-

PLATE X

WATER CONDUIT OF UR-ENGUR : NIPPUR
(From C. S. Fisher's " Excavations at Nippur," by permission)

covered by Haynes in the course of his excavations, and has been of no small assistance in determining the general character of this Babylonian temple in its later reconstructed state, while it may be in reality a copy of an earlier plan,[1] as it accords so well with the general conclusions to be drawn as to the configuration of the temple in the time of Shar-Gâni-sharri and Nâram-Sin, both of whom, and especially the latter, did much in the way of repairing this ancient fane.

The most prominent feature in connection with the temple of Nippur as revealed by the excavations, is the ziggurat, or stage-tower erected by Ur-Engur, king of Ur (*circ.* 2400 B.C.). The ruined mounds of Nuffar, or Niffer (cf. Pl. X), are situated on the eastern side of the Shatt-en-Nîl canal which at one time formed a line of communication between the Persian Gulf and the city of Babylon. The mounds in question, the principal of which marks the site of Ur-Engur's ziggurat, were excavated by Peters, Harper, Haynes and Hilprecht, under the auspices of the University of Pennsylvania, between the years 1889 and 1900. The tower surmounts an artificial platform measuring roughly 192 × 127 feet, and in accordance with the usual Babylonian principle of orientation, has its four corners facing the cardinal points of the compass. The ziggurat apparently only had three stages in contradistinction to the seven-staged tower characteristic of the Babylonian and Assyrian temples of later days, though Gudea's temple of E-pa erected in honour of his god Ningirsu was seven-zoned, which probably means that it was a seven-staged tower. The ziggurat at Mukeyyer[2] (Ur) excavated by Taylor similarly appears to have been three-storied, or possibly only two-storied. The lower storey, protected with a wall of burnt brick four feet in thickness, was further strengthened with buttresses,

[1] Cf. King, *Sumer and Akkad*, p. 88.
[2] Cf. Taylor in J. R. A. S., 1855, pp. 261 ff.

though it should be mentioned that the so-called " buttresses of the stage towers of Babylonia and Assyria are in the majority of cases water-conduits for draining the upper platforms. The second storey, the base of which is connected with the lower storey by means of a staircase three yards broad, is composed of bricks entirely different to those of the lower storey, those of the lower storey being $11\frac{1}{4} \times 11\frac{1}{4} \times 2\frac{1}{4}$ inches, and bearing a small stamp $3\frac{1}{4}$ inches square, while those of the second are $13 \times 13 \times 3$ inches, the stamp measuring 8×4 inches. The bricks of the first storey were laid in bitumen, while those of the second—the bricks on the northern side being excepted—are set in a mortar consisting of lime and ashes. The ascent to the summit of the second storey was effected by means of an inclined pathway : from which facts it would appear that the two stories were not built at the same time. The ziggurat at Abû Shahrein,[1] also excavated by Taylor, is about seventy feet high, and like that at Mukeyyer is cased with a wall of burnt brick. Here, too, the top of the first storey is reached by means of a staircase, fifteen feet broad, access to the summit of the second storey being gained by an inclined road as at Mukeyyer.

The approach to En-lil's ziggurat at Nippur is on the south-east side, and is marked by two walls of burnt brick, some ten or more feet high and over fifty-two feet long, a space of about twenty-three feet separating the two walls from each other, while the causeway itself which led up to the ziggurat was formed of crude bricks. The whole of the temple enclosure was surrounded by a massive wall, and some thirty courses of the bricks which composed it, still remain. Below the crude-brick platform upon which the tower was erected, another pavement of much finer construction, made of large well-burnt bricks nearly all of which were inscribed with

[1] Cf. J. R. A. S., 1855, pp. 405 ff.

the stamps of Shar-Gâni-sharri or Narâm-Sin, was discovered. Directly to the south-east of the ziggurat, a large chamber about thirty-six feet long, over eleven feet wide and some eight feet high was found, the floor of which rested on the platform of Narâm-Sin. The inscribed bricks proved that this chamber, like the ziggurat itself was built by Ur-Engur. Immediately below it, a second chamber of the same kind was discovered, in which was found a brick stamp of Shar-Gâni-sharri: around the walls of this chamber ran a narrow shelf on which some tablets are said to have been found. Haynes excavated right down to the virgin-soil, and states that he discovered at least two temples below the pavement of Narâm-Sin; in the lowest stratum an altar of crude brick measuring 13 × 8 feet is said to have been found, on which there was a large deposit of white ashes. Around the "altar" there was a low wall surrounding the sacred enclosure, on the outside of which two clay vases some twenty-five inches high, and decorated with a rope-pattern were brought to light. On the south-east of the "altar" is a crude-brick platform nearly twenty-three feet square and over nine and a half feet thick. Around the base of this, Haynes informs us that he found a number of water-vents, while beneath this solid mass, he found a drain running underneath the platform, in the roof of which a true key-stone arch was discovered. This arch was found about twenty-three feet below the pavement of Ur-Engur and more than fourteen and a half feet below the platform of Narâm-Sin. Unfortunately the lowest strata in the mound have been so much disturbed, and the buildings so ruthlessly pillaged, that it is impossible to dogmatize about the dates of all that the excavations have revealed.

With regard to the ziggurat itself, the lowest of its three stages would appear to have been some twenty and a half feet high: the slope of the sides upwards is about one in four, and the second terrace is set back some thirteen and a half feet from the surface of the one below. The lower terrace is protected with burnt brick on the south-east side, while on all the other sides the foundation is of burnt brick, four courses high and eight courses wide, surmounted by crude bricks covered with a plaster consisting of clay and chopped straw, which helped to preserve the crude brickwork. In the centre of each of these three sides there was a water-conduit by which the upper parts of the ziggurat were drained (cf. Pl. XI); the conduit was made of burnt bricks, and was ten and a half feet in depth and three and a half feet span. Around the base of the ziggurat, was a coating of bitumen which sloped outwards, with gutters to drain off the water, and thus preserve the crude bricks from dissolution.

From this brief description of the architectural remains discovered at Nippur, it will be seen at once, that, though the information afforded is of supreme importance and of the utmost value, we are still at a loss as to the general appearance of an early Babylonian temple, the temple-tower of the later Ur-Engur of course being excepted. A restoration of the temple as it probably appeared in the days of Ur-Engur has been made by Hilprecht and Fisher, and is reproduced by their kind permission in Fig. 6.

Of the temple erected by Gudea to the honour and glory of his god Ningirsu, we know comparatively little beyond what he tells us, but from his account, it was evidently very elaborate, for it contained chambers for the priests, treasure-houses, granaries, and enclosures for the various sacrificial victims. In later times there appear to have been two general types of temple in vogue in Babylonia, the one having a staged tower as its characteristic feature, the other being distinguished by its absence. Of the latter type, we have a good example in the temple of Nin-makh at Babylon, excavated by the

Deutsche Orient-Gesellschaft. The goddess Nin-makh had been venerated as early as the first dynasty of Lagash, for in Entemena's time temples were already erected in her honour. Her temple at Babylon was made chiefly of sun-dried bricks, the four corners being oriented towards the four points of the compass as usual : it comprised a courtyard, as well as a number of rooms some of which were painted, and traces of white decora-

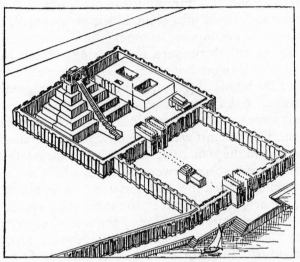

FIG. 6.—Restoration of the Temple at Nippur. (After Hilprecht and Fisher.)

tion were still visible. Apparently a vestibule led into a courtyard or hall, around which were situated various rooms and halls, and into which they also opened. The inner courtyard offers a point of contrast with the Assyrian temple at Nimrûd, which has no such interior hall. Near the ruins of this temple was the famous Ishtar-gate, the sides of which were formed of massive walls which were found still preserved to the height of thirty-nine feet. These walls were decorated with reliefs on enamelled bricks representing animals of both normal and abnormal character. There were apparently at least eleven rows of these reliefs portraying bulls or dragons one above the other.

But of all Babylonian temples, that of E-temen-an-ki built by Nebuchadnezzar king of Babylon upon the site of an ancient shrine, is by far the most famous. This temple is called by Herodotus (I, 181) the temple of Belus, and it was undoubtedly a very magnificent building both in point of size as well as in point of splendour. Herodotus in his description states that it was formed of a solid block of masonry, upon which was superimposed another block of smaller size, and so on till there were finally eight blocks in all, the first or lowest however, was simply the foundation of the whole ziggurat, and is not to be regarded as a " stage " at all ; it was accordingly a perfect seven-staged tower, the topmost block of which supported a shrine. The summit was reached by means of an ascent going round the structure. According to the late George Smith, whose estimates were based on a Babylonian description contained in a tablet at one time in his possession, the height was 300 feet, the sides of its square base being of the same dimensions ; the second storey measured 260 feet square and its height was 60 feet. The third, fourth and fifth storeys were each 20 feet high, and measured 200, 170 and 140 feet square respectively. The variation in height of the different stages forms a point of contrast with the regularity exhibited by the ziggurat at Khorsabad, of which the remains of four stages are still to be seen. Concerning the sixth stage the Babylonian tablet was apparently silent, while the top storey supporting the sanctuary of the god was stated to have measured 80 × 70 feet, and to have been 50 feet high. The seven stages without doubt at one time shone with the seven planetary colours, as was the case with the seven-staged tower at Khorsabad, on the lower remaining stages of which the colours were still found, the order of the colours being, white for the lowest stage,

PLATE XI

EXCAVATIONS IN THE TEMPLE COURT: NIPPUR

(From C. S. Fisher's " Excavations at Nippur," by permission)

black for the next, while the succeeding storeys were painted blue, yellow, silver, and gold. The ziggurat was surrounded by an enclosure, some 400 yards square, the ingress and egress to which was by means of bronze gates. A double-winged building on the west, presumably the shrine of the god, contained a couch of gold and a throne with steps also of gold, while the temple further contained an image of the god himself, made of solid gold. The Babylonian account informs us that the temple comprised two oblong courts, one within the other, the building as a whole consisting in a series of sanctuaries, although of course the most conspicuous and therefore perhaps the most important element in its composition, was the ziggurat.

But Nebuchadnezzar's building operations were not confined to the erection of a temple in honour of Belus : he rebuilt or restored the great walls of the city of Babylon, Imgur-Bel and Nimitti-Bel, he constructed temples for Shamash the Sun-god at Sippar and Larsa, both of which cities had been ancient centres of the cult of this god, while in Babylon he erected a temple to the goddess Nin-makh. At Borsippa (Birs-Nimrûd), he bestowed much attention and care upon the ancient shrine of Nebo, and his work on this site has been identified by some scholars with the magnificent temple described above, to which Herodotus refers at such length, though as Hommel and Pinches both point out, the distance of Borsippa from Babylon is rather against the identification. On the other hand at Borsippa there are the remains of what once may well have been the magnificent temple in question, while at the city of Babylon itself no such remains are to be seen ; and in regard to the objection raised to the identification of these remains with the famous temple of Belus on the ground that Borsippa was too far distant, it must be recollected that we do not really know how far the city extended, whether in fact it may not have even included Borsippa within its boundaries, for, according to Herodotus, the circuit of the city measured some fifty-six miles. Nebuchadnezzar's own account of his architectural achievements is inscribed on a number of barrel-shaped clay cylinders and on the well-known East India House Inscription.

The Assyrian temples seem for the most part to have conformed to the same general type as that prevalent in Babylonia. One of the earliest explored, and at present perhaps the most famous, is that excavated by Layard at Nimrûd (Calah).[1] It consisted in an outer courtyard, from which the worshipper entered into a vestibule measuring 46 feet by 19 feet,[2] beyond which there was a side chamber and a hall 47 feet long and 31 feet broad, ending in a recess paved with a huge alabaster slab, 21 feet long, 16 feet 7 inches broad and 1 foot 1 inch thick, in which was probably set the image of the god ; many stone slabs of a religious character were found within, while upon the stone pavement a history of the reign of Ashur-naṣir-pal was inscribed. The main entrance was decorated and protected with winged human-headed lions 16½ feet high and 15 feet long, whose rôle of guardianship at the portals of the king's palace is thus exchanged for a yet higher and more exalted position of trust, while the entrance into the side room was covered with reliefs portraying the god in the act of expelling a malicious demon. The side entrance was thirty feet to the right of the main entrance, and the chamber into which it led was connected by two corridors with the vestibule and the main hall. It was to the right of this smaller entrance that the famous arch-topped monolith of Ashur-naṣir-pal was discovered (cf. Pl. III). A short distance from the building just described, and on the very edge of the artificial plat-

[1] Cf. however Andrae, *Der Anu-Adad Tempel*, p. 80.
[2] Cf. Pinches, Hastings Dict., Religion and Morals, "Architecture," *Perrot and Chipiez*, II, p. 393 ; Layard, *Discoveries*, pp. 348 ff.

form, another temple was discovered. The entrance was guarded by two colossal lions (cf. Pl. XXVI), 8 feet high and 13 feet long, and the gateway which was about 8 feet wide was paved with one inscribed slab. In front of the lions were two altars similar to the altar in the Khorsabad relief reproduced in Fig. 14, C. The gateway led into a room 57 feet long and 25 feet broad, ending in a recess paved with an enormous alabaster slab inscribed on both sides and measuring $19\frac{1}{2}$ feet by 12 feet. It was in this temple that the statue of Ashur-nasir-pal was discovered (cf. Pl. XXIV).

The resemblance which the staged towers of Mesopotamia bear to the pyramids of Egypt naturally led to an interrogation as to whether they resembled them also in regard to the use to which they were put. Accordingly Layard endeavoured to answer the question, which had already been categorically answered by Ctesias and Ovid, by making cuttings in a ziggurat at Nimrûd with a view to ascertaining whether they contained voids in which the bodies of kings or heroes might have at one time been deposited, whether in fact the ziggurats were primarily tombs like the pyramids of Mişraim. The possibility of such being the case was proved by the discovery of a vault, on a level with the platform itself, measuring 100 feet in length, 6 feet in breadth and 12 feet in height, though if this had actually been the last resting-place of a departed king, it had been completely rifled. Of the ziggurat in question, but one storey remained, protected by a massive facing of stone, and about twenty feet high ; the stones seem to have been laid together without any mortar, as was so often the case in Assyrian masonry.

Another excellent example of an Assyrian temple is the Anu-Adad temple at Ashur, recently excavated by the Deutsche Orient Gesellschaft. The code of Khammurabi shows that this city was in existence at all events as early as his time, and the German excavations have proved that it did not lose its importance when the seat of government was removed thence to Calah (Nimrûd) about 1300 B.C., but on the contrary continued to be a royal city and maintained its importance till the seventh century B.C., and possibly later.

The temple of Anu-Adad was founded by Ashur-resh-ishi (*circ.* 1140 B.C.). It consisted of a rectangular terrace to which access was gained by a doorway flanked by towers : beneath the terrace there were a number of rooms. The two temple-towers were separated from each other by a long passage, on each side of which were four small rooms surrounding a large chamber in the middle, which may well have been the sanctuary. One of these large chambers was dedicated to Anu, and the other to Adad. The two temple-towers were according to Andrae four-staged ziggurats, and no doubt upon the topmost storey there was a shrine, as in the temple of Belus at Babylon. Many of the bricks composing the towers were inscribed as was nearly always the case. Tiglath-Pileser I (1100 B.C.) the son and successor of Ashur-resh-ishi had occasion to repair or rebuild this temple, and he records that he raised its towers to heaven and made firm its battlements with baked brick.[1] His account reads as follows :—

"In the beginning of my government Anu and Adad, "the great gods, my lords, who love my priestly dig-"nity, demanded of me the restoration of this their "sacred dwelling. I made bricks, and I cleared the "ground, until I reached the artificial flat terrace upon "which the old temple had been built. I laid its founda-"tion upon the solid rock and incased the whole place "with brick like a fireplace, overlaid on it a layer of "fifty bricks in depth, and built upon this the founda-"tions of the Temple of Anu and Adad of large square "stones. I built it from foundation to roof larger and "grander than before, and erected also two great tem-

[1] Cf. Harper, *Assyrian and Babylonian Literature*, pp. 25, 26.

" ple towers, fitting ornaments of their great divinities.
" The splendid temple, a brilliant and magnificent dwell-
" ing, the habitation of their joys, the house for their
" delight, shining as bright as the stars on heaven's firma-
" ment and richly decorated with ornaments through the
" skill of my artists, I planned, devised and thought out,
" built and completed. I made its interior brilliant like
" the dome of the heavens ; decorated its walls, like the
" splendour of the rising stars, and made it grand with re-
" splendent brilliancy. I reared its temple towers to heaven
" and completed its roof with burned brick ; located
" therein the upper terrace containing the chambers of
" their great divinities ; and led into its interior Anu
" and Adad, the great gods, and made them dwell in
" this their lofty home, thus gladdening the heart of
" their great divinities. I also cleared the site of the
" treasure-house of Adad, my lord, which the same
" Shamshi-Adad, priest of Ashur, son of Ishme-Dagan,
" likewise priest of Ashur, had built and which had
" fallen into decay and ruins, and rebuilt it from founda-
" tion to roof with burned brick, making it more beauti-
" ful and much firmer than before. I slaughtered clean
" animals therein as a sacrifice to Adad, my lord."

This same king, with the prescience characteristic of
Assyrian monarchs, prays that, in the event of the
building falling into disrepair, a future king may restore them, and he further begs that such king may
anoint his own inscribed tablets and his foundation-
cylinders with oil. His prayer was justified by after
events, for in Shalmaneser II's (860–825 B.C.) time, the
temple had already suffered from the effects of time and
climate, and that king consequently rebuilt it throughout. Shalmaneser's reconstruction was not so aspiring
in its dimensions as that of Ashur-resh-ishi, the original founder of the temple. He erected two temple-
towers (cf. Fig. 7) parallel to those of his predecessor,
differing however from those of Ashur-resh-ishi, ac-

cording to Andrae, in being panelled instead of plain, as was the case with the ziggurat (the so-called " Observatory") at Khorsabad and the ziggurat of Belus at Babylon. But Shalmaneser was not the last king to whom was accorded the privilege of repairing this ancient fane: Sargon (722–705 B.C.) the successor of Shalmaneser IV, and the immediate predecessor of Sennacherib, also found occasion to devote himself to this work of piety, and in the court-yard of Shalmaneser II, the pavement-tiles nearly all bear the name of Sargon, a permanent testimony to his sense of religious

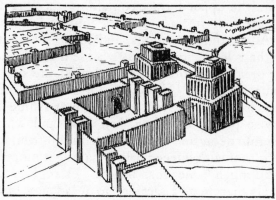

FIG. 7. (After Andrae, *Der Anu-Adad Tempel*, *Tafel IX*.)

obligation in this matter. The unique feature about this temple is its double ownership.

Another temple recently excavated at Ashur by Koldewey and Andrae, is the temple erected by Sin-sharishkun in honour of the god Nebo. Sin-shar-ishkun was the last king of Assyria and reigned about 615 B.C. This temple, which comprised a considerable number of rooms of various shapes and sizes, was separated into two main divisions, both of which consisted in a group of apartments leading into a main court, the two courts being connected with each other. Access to the temple from outside was gained through a door and vestibule leading into the northern court, though possibly the southern court with which the latter is connected at one time had a similar entrance.

The southern court measures over ninety feet in length and about thirty-seven feet in breadth, and is surrounded by rooms on its southern, eastern and northern sides, while on the northern side it is connected with the northern court. But it is on the western side of this southern court that the main temple rooms are located. Thanks to the excellent state of preservation in which the brickwork foundation of the walls was found, the excavators were able to determine the ground-plan of two parallel series of rooms, to each of which access from the court was gained by an entrance-gate provided with a tower; both the northern and southern series of rooms contained first of all a broad room which communicated with a long room, at the extreme end of which was a recess for the statue of the god. The recess at the end of the long room in the northern series is so well preserved that the general plan of its reconstruction is quite certain. The limestone paved pedestal in the recess was ascended by a small double flight of low steps, the steps being similarly paved with limestone and numbering four. All these rooms including the southern and western corridors and the southern court were paved with brickwork, some of the bricks bearing the building inscription of Sin-shar-ish-kun, and the bricks in both the southern and the northern broad rooms were inscribed " temple of Nebo," thereby proving that this whole part of the building belonged to the temple of that god, and that his temple was thus double in character.

Sin-shar-ishkun had evidently not been above utilizing the building materials of his predecessors, for one of the door-sockets bears the name of Ashur-nasir-pal, while among other inscribed objects discovered were fragments of hollow terra-cotta cylinders and prisms as well as clay cones bearing an inscription of Sin-shar-ishkun. The ground-plan of the southern division of this temple

L

of Nebo corresponds in all essential particulars to that of the normal Assyrian temple, of which the outstanding characteristics—apart from the ziggurat—were the broad-room, the hall with a recess for the god's statue, a group of surrounding rooms and a corridor.

The most famous temple at Ashur was that of the god Ashur himself, but unfortunately it is badly preserved, and is consequently of less archæological importance than the Anu-Adad temple or the temple of Nebo. One point of interest about the ancient temple of Ashur, is that the rooms appear to have been broad rather than long. In the oldest part of the building, an alabaster block[1] bearing an inscription of twenty-four lines written in archaic characters was discovered. The characters somewhat resemble those found in Irishum's inscriptions and are similar to the characters used in early Babylonian inscriptions, while like them, they read longitudinally and not laterally, but the lines run from left to right instead of from right to left, and in this they resemble a few inscriptions found at Tellô.[2] This alabaster block is possibly the oldest Assyrian inscription as yet brought to light. In the fore-court of this same temple, some fragments of a diorite sculpture with small figures similar to those of the Khammurabi period were found.

The best-preserved ziggurat in Mesopotamia is that which was discovered at Khorsabad ; four stages of this tower still remain, and the colours with which they were painted are yet visible. It is in close proximity to though not in immediate connection with the group of buildings formerly regarded as the harem of the palace, but recently shown by Koldewey[3] to be in reality a group of temples (cf. Fig. 24 B). The argument upon which the harem-theory was based was the fact that this block of

---

[1] Cf. *Mitteilungen*, No. 44, p. 30.
[2] Cf. *Découvertes*, Pl. 22 bis, Figs. 2*b*, 3*b*.
[3] Cf. Andrae, *Der Auu-Adad Tempel*, p. 80.

buildings is separate from the palace, but this argument could be used with even greater force in support of the temple theory, while its proximity to the ziggurat, and the general correspondence in form and shape of the several buildings which it comprises, to the normal Assyrian temple as revealed by the excavations, makes Koldewey's contention a practical certainty. Furthermore, though the ziggurat, as is the case at Borsippa, is not connected with the theoretical " temple-complex," there seems to be no doubt they belong to each other as there is no room elsewhere in the neighbourhood for a temple proper, and the adjacent parts of the palace were certainly used for secular and not religious purposes. The block would appear to contain three temples the entrance to each of which was through a central court ; the temples consisted in a broad-room or vestibule, a long-room or hall at the end of which was another room—presumably the sanctuary where the statue of the god was enshrined. The entrance to the sanctuary from the hall was through a broad opening and up some stairs.

In addition to these salient parts of the building there were various subordinate rooms, which in one temple flanked the right side, in another the left, and in the third both sides of the main hall, these rooms being connected in one case with the broad-room, the hall and the sanctuary, in the second with the hall and sanctuary, and in the third with the hall only. Sometimes they further have surrounding corridors ; it will be thus seen that though they show considerable variation among themselves, they exhibit the same general type, a type totally different from that to which the Assyrian palaces and houses conform, the general shape of which was broad rather than long.

But in spite of the general similarity of Assyrian temples, the earlier buildings differ from those of later date in at least one important respect ; in the former the sanctuary is simply a deep niche in the back wall of the main long-room or hall, while in the later temples of Sargon, the niche has been developed into a special sanctuary chamber.

It has been already demonstrated that the ziggurats in Mesopotamia did not by any means all conform to the same plan ; not only did the number of their stages vary however, but occasionally their shape also. As a rule they were square, or at all events rectangular, but the ziggurat excavated at El Hibba by the Deutsche Orient Gesellschaft proved to be an exception to this general rule. The tower in question is circular in form, and comprises two stages ; it is not built on an artificial mound, but on the natural soil, and is still standing to the height of twenty-four feet. The diameter of the first storey [1] is over four hundred feet, while that of the upper storey is only a little over three hundred feet. The last-named is protected with a casement-wall of burnt bricks laid in bitumen, and the upper surfaces of both stories were coated with the same material in order to protect them from the disintegrating effects of the rain. The structure was drained by means of canals made of burnt bricks, which served the further purpose of strengthening the lower storey, and acted in fact as a buttress. A number of clay cones or nails were found on the surface of the upper storey, similar to those found at the foot of the Nippur ziggurat, but none of them apparently bore any inscription.

PALACES

Other buildings in Babylonia of a more secular character have been preserved in a more satisfactory state than those specifically dedicated to the gods, but the royal palaces themselves have for the most part undergone such a course of reconstruction that it is very difficult to determine the precise form which the original

[1] Hilprecht, *Explorations*, p. 286.

building assumed. Ur-Ninâ has bequeathed to us the remains of an elaborate building which he erected at his royal city Lagash, but it appears to be a storehouse rather than an integral part of a palace ; Urbau and Gudea some centuries later have also left unmistakable signs of their building activity at this famous city of the past. In the course of the excavation of a large palace in one of the ruined mounds of Tellô, many bricks inscribed with the name of Gudea were found, and this discovery not unnaturally led to the hasty conclusion that this elaborate building so wonderfully preserved, was actually the royal residence of this long deceased ruler, but a closer investigation revealed the presence of other bricks bearing the name of one, Hadadnadinakhe, in both Greek and Aramæan characters, thereby proving conclusively that the building in question belonged to the Parthian period and could not be assigned to a date earlier than the latter half of the second century B.C. The bricks belonging to Gudea's early building had been reused as material for this later structure, a practice to which recourse was frequently had in Mesopotamia. Parts however of Gudea's early building were actually incorporated in the Parthian palace, the best preserved of which are a gateway (cf. Pl. V) and a portion of a tower, while underneath one corner of the palace, part of a wall erected by Ur-bau, one of Gudea's immediate predecessors, was discovered.

Another palace of great fame was that of Nebuchadnezzar at Babylon, known as the El-Kasr (cf. p. 69). This palace has been excavated by Koldewey and Andrae. The outer wall was made of bricks stamped with the name of Nebuchadnezzar, and was some $23\frac{1}{2}$ feet thick, the inner wall also made of brick being over 44 feet thick, while the space between the two walls, nearly 70 feet, was filled in with sand and other material, the total thickness thus being nearly $136\frac{1}{2}$ feet. The burnt bricks of which the retaining walls were composed were laid in asphalt and are so compactly joined that it is impossible to separate them into their layers. The Kasr mound, which represents a new suburb of the city of Babylon itself, has revealed nothing earlier than the seventh century. Ashur-bani-pal (668–626 B.C.) built a temple here which has been duly excavated, but Nebuchadnezzar's palace is the principal building which has been discovered on this famous site. Before the time of Nebuchadnezzar there had seemingly been a palace here, which had undergone a course of reconstruction at the hands of Nabopolassar (625–604 B.C.) the founder of the Neo-Babylonian dynasty, but it subsequently suffered grievously from an inundation of the Euphrates, and was accordingly repaired and enlarged by Nebuchadnezzar who rebuilt it with burnt brick ; so enduring was his work that the lower portions of it have remained in position till our own day.

The interior of the palace consisted in a great number of rooms arranged around courtyards. The large hall, situated on the south of the main court, had a niche in its southern wall and was further provided with three doors in its northern wall, where traces were also to be found of what may have been at one time a colonnade. The roof of the palace was made of cedar-wood, as were also the doors, which latter were covered with bronze, just as was the case with the famous gates at Balâwât (cf. Fig. 43). The thresholds were made of the same metal, as also were the steps in the temple E-zida at Borsippa, one of which has come down to us and bears this king's name, while gold, silver and precious stones of various kinds were used with an unsparing prodigality in the decoration of the royal residence.

Nebuchadnezzar further erected another building on the northern side of the wall, which was apparently a fortress, and was connected with the palace. According to the India House Inscription, and the statement of Berosus the Babylonian historian (about 300 B.C.) whose history unfortunately is lost, but from which extracts have been handed down to us by Josephus, this building was completed in the incredibly short period of fifteen days.

Assyrian palaces are however in a better state of preservation than those of Babylonia, and afford more material for the study of Mesopotamian architecture. First and foremost of these must be mentioned that built by Sargon (722–705 B.C.) at Khorsabad (cf. Fig. 8). The palace

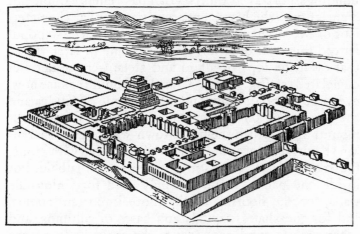

FIG. 8.—Restoration of " Sargon's Palace " at Khorsabad.   (After Place.)

in question was built upon an artificial mound, like most of the important edifices in Babylonia and Assyria, these mounds serving a more practical purpose in Southern Mesopotamia, as by their means the buildings themselves were thus elevated beyond the reach of the waters of the inundating Euphrates. The mounds, sometimes formed of a mass of crude brick, sometimes of sand, gravel and other material, were kept together and protected by a casement wall of either burnt brick or stone. The revetment-walls at Khorsabad, which were formed of blocks of stone weighing sometimes as much as twenty-three tons and measuring 6 × 6 × 9 feet, gradually become thinner towards the top. The inner face of this stone wall in immediate contact with the crude brick mass, was left rough, which added to the general coherency of the whole. The total height of the wall at Khorsabad was some 60 feet, the foundations measuring 9 feet, and the retaining wall 46 feet, a parapet of 5 feet making up the total of 60 feet. When the roof was flat, it seems to have generally been surmounted by a parapet the top of which was crenelated. Nearly all the buildings portrayed on Assyrian bas-reliefs exhibit this crenelation, which was apparently a peculiar characteristic of Mesopotamian architecture, and indeed so popular did this style of arrangement become in later times, that even the tops of altars and stelæ were sometimes crenelated (cf. Fig. 14, C). Crenelated buildings are however not found in Babylonia till the time of Gudea and the dynasty of Ur (circ. 2450 B.C.). The foundation-mound upon which the brick town-wall of Dûr-sharrukîn (Khorsabad) was built was similarly faced with stone, the mound itself consisting of stones and rubble, but inside the palace, stone was only used for lining the walls, for the flooring of the more important rooms, and for the shafts, capitals and bases of columns, and other architectural accessories, the main body of the edifice being built entirely of brick. The outer walls of buildings were as a rule fortified with " buttresses," made of stronger and more durable material than the walls themselves, while apparently the only foundations were the artificial mounds upon which the buildings were constructed. Unfortunately but little is known as to the internal arrangements of the buildings, and we are in considerable doubt even regarding the manner in which the various rooms were roofed.

The rooms in Sargon's palace are nearly all rectangular in shape, sometimes square, but generally very long in proportion to their breadth. The walls of the rooms were phenomenally thick and vary from twelve to twenty-eight feet. The roofs of these long chambers must have either been vaulted, or else constructed of timber-beams, though the former would have been the more serviceable in a climate characterized by extreme heat on the one hand and extreme cold on the other, for the thick vaulting would alike avert the scorching rays of the summer's sun and the penetrating cold of a rigorous winter, while the discovery of an enormous quantity of broken bricks, débris and rubble, and the corresponding absence of any trace of wood in the excavated rooms supports the theory that the roofs were made of clay rather than of wood ; and lastly, the only wood easily procurable would seemingly have been quite inadequate to support the strain of a superimposed flat roof of mud. Victor Place furthermore actually discovered the remains of vaults which had collapsed, while the extensive use of the arch both in the city walls of Khorsabad as well as in the drainage of the palace furnishes an additional argument and increases the probability of the theory yet the more. The disappearance of any trace of wood in the rooms themselves might have been explained by the frailty and non-enduring character of that material, but near the doorways, which obviously could not have been formed of clay, or stone, fragments of wood as well as door panels are said to have been found, and without doubt, had the ceilings of the rooms been made of wood also, similar evidence of the fact would be forthcoming. Place further alludes to the discovery of rollers made of limestone in some of the chambers : these rollers may have been used to flatten and solidify the pisé-roofs after a downpour of rain, and thereby been the means of preventing the dissolution and general collapse of this integral part of the structure. But these clay roofs however unsatisfactory they may have been in days gone by from the architectural standpoint, have proved of incalculable value to the archæologist of to-day, for to the softness of the material of which they were composed is due the perfect preservation of the sculptures and statues which they were destined to entomb for so long a period.

As already mentioned, the partition-walls of the rooms exhibit the same extraordinary solidity noticeable, alike in the outer walls of the palace and in those of the city, the thinnest being some ten feet thick. The massiveness of these partition walls bears out the theory that the roofs were not formed of wooden beams but of clay vaulting, and is thus an additional piece of evidence to that afforded by the absence of any trace of wood in the chambers themselves on the one hand and the discovery of fragments of wood in the doorways on the other ; for the only available explanation and general *raison d'être* of such thick interior walls is that vaulted roofs made of soft clay could only be supported by walls of more than ordinary solidity. Doubtless the vaulted roofing was also a determining factor in the shape and general contour which the rooms assumed, and it is to the dearth of wood suitable for building purposes, and the consequent use of clay for roofing as well as for other parts of the structure that we are to ascribe the narrowness of most of the chambers, which in truth resemble galleries more than halls or rooms.

It must not however be supposed that all the rooms in Sargon's palace or in the palaces of other Assyrian kings were one and all shaped like passages, or that they were one and all roofed with barrel-shaped vaults. Square rooms were discovered in the palace which we are discussing, some of which were of no mean dimensions and measured forty-eight feet each way ; these clearly could not have been covered with barrel vaulting, while the difficulty of procuring timber of sufficient length would make itself felt more in the case of a large square chamber, than in an elongated gallery. The problem therefore resolves itself into an inquiry as to what other modes of roofing were adopted by the Assyrians apart from roofs made of wooden beams which were apparently only used in exceptional cases, and barrel vaults, which would have been out of the question in these large square chambers. It is here that the bas-reliefs adorning the walls of the royal palaces come to our aid. On one of these reliefs from Kouyunjik (cf. Fig. 9) are portrayed a number of buildings surmounted by domes of varying shapes and sizes, which prove conclusively that the Assyrians of Sen-

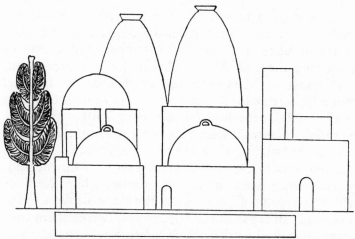

FIG. 9.—From an Assyrian Bas-relief. (After Layard, Ser. 2, Pl. 17.)

nacherib's time had evolved the art of constructing domed roofs, or perhaps we should say borrowed the art from their mother-country, as the principle of the domed roof seems to have been known in Babylonia in the pre-Sargonic times, for the American excavations at Bismâya having disclosed an oval-shaped room of the Sumerian period, provided with a domed roof of which the larger portions still remained, and without doubt the square chambers in Sargon's palace at Khorsabad as well as those in the palaces of other Assyrian kings were roofed in this way. The buildings on the right (cf. Fig. 9) have flat roofs, while those on the left have either hemispherical cupolas, or conical-shaped domes; most of the doors are rectangular in shape, two of them however are arched like the famous gates at Khorsabad. These rounded roofs are to be seen all over the East even at the present day, so persistent is the influence of custom and habit when both are but the offspring of the natural environment of climate and owe their very origin to the great mother of invention.

PRIVATE HOUSES

Of the arrangement of private houses in Babylonia we know comparatively little. Taylor excavated a small house of uncertain date at Muḳeyyer, and a plan of some chambers at Abû Shahrein was also made out. The house at Muḳeyyer was erected on an artificial mound of crude brick upon which a pavement of burnt brick was laid, the house itself being built of the same material. The walls were very irregular, but the general plan of the building seems to have been cruciform. The outer layer of bricks was apparently set in bitumen, mud-mortar being used for the remainder, while the floor which was made of burnt brick like the walls, was laid in bitumen. In regard to the doorways, two of them consisted in arched vaults, the arch being semicircular and made of wedge-shaped bricks, and the charred remains of wooden rafters or beams were found within. The outside of the house was decorated with perpendicular grooves, or "stepped recesses,"[1] and many of the bricks were coated with enamel or gypsum, and were inscribed.

The external decoration of a building at Warka (Erech) excavated by Loftus consisted on the other hand of series of coloured clay cones[2] embedded in mud or plaster and arranged in various patterns, with their circular bases outwards. The patterns were mostly triangular, striped, diamond-shaped, or zigzags, and the wall

---

[1] Loftus, *Chaldæa and Susiana*, p. 133; J. R. A. S., XV, pp. 265, 266.   [2] Loftus, pp. 187 ff.

of which they formed a part measured thirty feet in length. The flat part of this wall projected one foot nine inches beyond the semicircular half columns which occurred at intervals as in the Wuswas façade.

The rooms excavated at Abû Shahrein were built of crude brick, the walls being covered with a plaster on the inside and painted. In one of these chambers the walls were decorated with white, black, and red bands, about three inches broad, while in another there was a crude red picture of a man holding a bird on his wrist, and a smaller figure standing close by.

The buildings uncovered by the German excavations at Fâra appear to be chiefly characterized by the feebleness of the walls and the elaboration of the drainage system. The general plan of these brick buildings consisted in a central court surrounded by chambers of very small dimensions. Private houses, like palaces, were often occupied over and over again : thus at Nippur some of the houses excavated by Haynes had been occupied at least three times over, while in one of them three distinctly different doorways were visible, the lowest and therefore the earliest being roofed by a segmental arch. But other buildings of quite a different shape and character were found both at Surghul and Fâra ; these buildings are not rectangular but circular in form, and measure from six and a half to sixteen feet across. These rotundas, which are particularly numerous at Fâra, were surmounted by arched vaults, and one of them was found to contain four skulls. For what these circular structures were used it is difficult to say. We know something about the ordinary houses of later times from the classical writers : Herodotus for example informs us that the houses were generally lofty, having three or even four stories (Herod. I, 180), while Strabo tells us that the roofs of the houses were vaulted. The latter writer informs us that the pillars of the house—when such existed—consisted in the trunks of palm trees, around which wisps of rushes were entwined, the whole being thus coated with some kind of plaster and then painted (Strab. XVI, I, 85).

Of the private houses in Assyria we are little better informed than of those in Babylonia. The German excavations at Ḳalat Sherḳat (Ashur) have however thrown some light on the subject. The foundation-walls of the houses discovered on this site showed that they conformed in general plan to that of the old Babylonian house as illustrated at Fâra. The foundations themselves present some novel varieties to the student of Mesopotamian architecture ; the foundation-walls referred to were sunk down through the amassed débris with which the plateau had been covered, to the rock bottom ; and these walls were covered with a layer of stones, upon which the actual walls of the building were superimposed. One of the houses in question measured roughly 86 × 61 feet, and is rectangular in shape. As at Fâra the rooms surround a central court. On the south side of the building two narrow corridors run east and west, and are traceable in the foundations, access to the court being gained only by passing through the outer corridor and turning two corners.

In the débris beneath this house were found various graves of the capsule type.[1]

The drains of the early Babylonians were either made of bricks, or else of baked clay rings. Of the larger type of drain or water conduit generally used to drain the upper stages of ziggurats, we have a good example in Pl. XI. Similar drains were discovered by Loftus at Erech, though he mistook them for supporting buttresses,[2] to which they bear a striking resemblance. In the temple court at Nippur numerous drains of the second class were discovered. These were constructed of terra-cotta rings set one on the top of the other, and sometimes

[1] Cf. p. 80.   [2] Cf. Hilprecht, *Explorations*, p. 372.

provided with a bell-shaped top, while occasionally it was surmounted by a terra-cotta floor,[1] as in Fig. 10. The average diameter of the rings composing this drain was two feet and three-quarters, and it descended some six and a half feet. At Bismâya a drain consisting of round tiles about eight inches in diameter was discovered, while similar drains made of terra-cotta rings superimposed one on the top of the other were discovered by Taylor at Mukeyyer (Ur). Frequently these shafts were double as in the illustration (Fig. 11). The rings com-

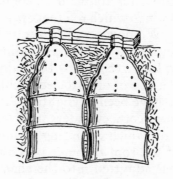

FIG. 10. (After Hilprecht.)   FIG. 11. (After Taylor.)

posing this drain were two feet in diameter and about a foot and a half broad, and in some instances they were cemented together by means of a thin layer of bitumen. " For about a foot right round these drain-pipes and throughout their whole length, were pieces of broken pottery, the more effectually to drain the mound."[2] Over the mouth of the top ring, which is of a different shape to the others, were layers of perforated bricks leading up to the top of the mound. Sometimes these drains consist of as many as forty of these rings. Numerous drains made of both bricks and tiles were dis-

[1] *Ibidem*, p. 402.
[2] Cf. Taylor, *Journal of the Royal Asiatic Society*, 1853, p. 269.

covered at Bismâya, while the drainage system at Fâra and other early Babylonian sites seems to have been very extensive. The main drains in Babylonia and Assyria frequently assumed the form of vaulted aqueducts. Concerning the drainage of the inner rooms, the palace of Sargon at Khorsabad is our best source of information. Nearly all of the rooms were drained by a hole cut in a stone in the centre of the floor towards which the brick floor gradually sloped ; the water passed through the hole into a circular brick conduit, which descended into a horizontal drain connected with the main vaulted drain to which reference will be made later on (cf. p. 174).

Windows, which to our idea form one of the most important parts of a building, were apparently taken into little account by the Babylonians and Assyrians. In the case of one-storied buildings the only windows seem to have been skylights. At all events Place discovered terra-cotta cylinders in several of the rooms at Khorsabad, which according to him, must have formed a part of the roof through which air and a modicum of light was admitted into the chamber. The buildings represented on the bas-reliefs are indeed provided with small openings, but these appear to be embrasures rather than windows properly so-called. But in any case, even if windows were cut in the walls, the extreme thickness of the latter would have excluded nearly all light.

THE COLUMN

The column never seems to have occupied a prominent position in the history of Mesopotamian architecture, a fact which was again due to the dearth of stone and wood ; there is however sufficient evidence to prove that it was certainly not unknown, though it was not very frequently employed. In modern architecture the column forms the main support of arches, but in Babylonian and Assyrian architecture the archivolts and pendentives of the arch are generally supported by thick walls ; this fact is testified to alike by the remains of ancient buildings and also by the figured representations of such buildings found on the bas-reliefs.

Probably the best examples of an early Babylonian column are those discovered by De Sarzec at Tellô in 1881, though strictly speaking they are not columns, but piers formed by the union of four circular columns (cf. Fig. 12). The piers are composed of circular, semi-circular, or triangular bricks, which bear an inscription, from which we gather that the new construction of which they presumably formed a part was largely made of cedarwood, a statement confirmed by the discovery of fragments of this wood amid the ruins.

FIG. 12. (Cf. *Déc. en Chald.*, Pl. 53, 2.)

Evidence of the very early use of the column on the same site was forthcoming in the discovery of a series of eight brick bases, situated some thirteen feet from the ancient building of Ur-Ninâ, the charred remains of pillars of cedar-wood by which these bases were once surmounted being still visible. Probably the most familiar example of the use of the column in Babylonia, afforded by the excavations, is that of the Court of columns at Nippur (cf. Pl. X). This court is over forty-eight feet square; its floor consists of a thick pavement made of unburnt bricks, and is over six feet in depth ; around three of the sides of this square, Peters tells us, ran a kind of edging formed by a double row of burnt bricks, out of which arose four brick columns, round in shape, but rest-

M

ing on square brick pillars which descended some three feet or so below the surface; the fourth side was without doubt similarly occupied with columns, but nearly every trace of even the foundations of them has been washed away owing to the slope of the hill. On the other sides of the platform the columns remain standing to a height of about three feet; they appear to have tapered upwards, the diameter at the base being just over three feet. They were built of bricks especially made for the purpose: these bricks, in shape, are segments of circles, the apexes of which are truncated, and the hollow thus left in the centre of the circle compounded of these deformed segments was filled in with fragments of bricks. The segmentary bricks are well baked though somewhat brittle, and they were laid in mortar. According to Peters, these columns were carefully dressed with a sharp instrument, to remove any irregular projections there might be owing to the mal-formation of any of the component bricks. The columns are moreover not arranged with mathematical accuracy, being only roughly equidistant from one another. The corner-columns differ from the others in being half-round and half-square. Peters dates this colonnade in the second millennium and assigns it to the Cassite period. Hilprecht however believes it to be a product of the Parthian times, and dates it about 300 B.C.

But yet other columns were found at Nippur, some rectangular and oblong in shape, others assuming an oval form, both kinds however being made of brick like the columns in the court. In one room in a building close to the court, two columns were found built into the wall, and two more round columns on square bases, the latter being composed of four courses of bricks, and resting on a foundation of mud-brick. The circumference of these round columns is over twelve feet. On the south-east of the court the remains of another pair of round columns of gigantic size were discovered; the base of one of these was found still in its original position, while the remains of the shafts lay strewn about promiscuously. The diameter of these columns at the base must have been between six and seven feet, that is to say more than double the size of the columns in the court itself.

Tellô and Nippur are however not the only sites which have yielded evidence of the use of the column in the Babylonia of antiquity. Loftus in his excavations at the Wuswas mound at Warka (Erech) came across the remains of seven half-columns repeated seven times,[1] and used for the decoration of a façade; these half-columns were made of semicircular bricks. There is no trace of capital, base, cornice or any of the features which columns generally exhibit, they therefore occupy an early place in the development of columnar architecture, and Loftus assigns the building in which they were discovered to the second millennium b.c.,—not later than 1500 b.c. The excavations at Abû Adham, a mound situated near Tellô, revealed a building with brick columns exactly like those found by Peters at Nippur, while at Abû Shahrein (Eridu) Taylor discovered the remains of a column[2] consisting, in contradistinction to those mentioned above, of "slabs of sandstone twenty inches square and four inches thick, which disposed in a circular form, and joined together by lime, formed the chief material; between each layer were cylindrical pieces of marble, and the whole had a thick coating of lime; successive layers of which, mixed with small stone and pebbles, were laid on till it had attained the desired size and thickness. Its base was shaped like a bowl, and rested upon a layer of sun-dried bricks, under which again was fine sand." No doubt the column was used in Babylonia more frequently than might be inferred from the paucity of the cases in which the excavations have actually produced tangible evidence of its employment, and the fact

[1] Loftus, *Travels*, pp. 174 ff.
[2] Cf. *Journal of the Royal Asiatic Society*, 1855, p. 406.

that Nebuchadnezzar represented columns with great voluted capitals on coloured tiles in the Kasr shows that they must have been a comparatively familiar architectural feature in his day, in spite of the fact that, as Koldewey points out, their pictorial representation on coloured tiles was probably an artistic substitute for the real things, for which there was apparently neither place nor use, as in every place where one might expect them, simple doors are found ; two column-shafts consisting in palm-trunks, sunk into the ground and surrounded at the foot, by a circular brick walling strengthened with asphalt and lime, were however actually found in one of the courts, but Koldewey assigns the restored building of which they form a part to the Persian period.   In the Amran[1] mound at Babylon Koldewey discovered the truncated remains of twenty-two brick columns, which evidently formed part of a columned building, but the date of this building seems to be uncertain.

It is here however that the bas-reliefs come to our aid; in Pl. XIV we have a reproduction of the famous Sun-god Tablet which was made by Nabû-aplu-iddina, king of Babylonia in the first half of the ninth century B.C., in which there is a shrine, the roof of which is supported by a column in the form of a palm-trunk which was probably overlaid with plates of metal, for plain unadorned wood would hardly be suitable for the shrine of Shamash, and moreover the capital and base, both of which are much the same, could only have assumed this form in metal, the one material that would easily adapt itself to such motifs. Similarly the curved back wall and roof were probably made of metal, for wood of the kind procurable in Babylonia would not readily bend in this manner.   But this notwithstanding, the column always appears to have occupied a subordinate position in Babylonian architecture.

Such also appears to have been the case in Assyria :

[1] Cf. *Mitteilungen*, No. 43, p. 7.

there too the excavations have done little in the way of recovering the actual columns used by the Assyrian monarchs, and for our knowledge of the general form and appearance of Assyrian columns we are in the main dependent on the information afforded us by the wall bas-reliefs. Another source of great fruitfulness would be the series of ivories found in the north-west palace of Nimrûd (Calah), but as these are the work of either Egyptian or Phœnician artists, the columns therein repre-sented can hardly be regarded as illustrations of Assyrian columns.

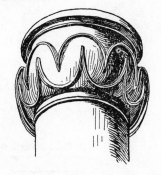

FIG. 13, *a*.—Capital of large Column.　　FIG. 13, *b*.—Capital of small Column.
(Place, *Nineve*, Pl. 35.)　　　　　　　　　(Brit. Mus.)

Of remains of actual columns, the best-preserved is probably that discovered by Victor Place at Khorsabad; it comprises the capital and a portion of the shaft (cf. Fig. 13, *a*) both in one piece; it is made of limestone, and the surviving fragment is some forty inches high. The decoration of the capital proper is a variety of the volute, a device which probably originated in a more or less accurate imitation of the horns of the goat, and which is a characteristic feature of Babylonian and Assyrian decoration.

Sometimes columns represented on the bas-reliefs are actually surmounted by goats (cf. Fig. 14, G) but more often, the horn-shaped volutes (cf. Fig. 14, F) are the only artistic elements borrowed by the Assyrians from the animal world, in the formation of their column capitals. A variety of the same design is seen on the four circu-

FIG. 14.—A, cf. Layard *Discoveries*, p. 590.
B, cf. Layard, *Mon. Ser.* I, Pl. 95.
C, cf. Botta, *Ruines de Ninive*, II, p. 114.
D, E, Bas-reliefs from Kouyunjik.

lar limestone pedestals discovered by Layard at Nineveh[1] (cf. Fig. 14, A) which doubtless at one time supported wooden pillars ; the diameter of these bases varied from eleven and a half inches in the narrowest to two feet seven inches in the broadest part.

[1] Cf. Layard, *Discoveries*, p. 590 ; Dieulafoy, *L'Art Antique*, V, pp. 57 ff.; *Perrot and Chipiez*, p. 214.

Sometimes the backs of lions (cf. Fig. 14, E), sphinxes or other composite monsters formed the bases of columns, and two such bases in the form of winged sphinxes were found by Layard in the south-west palace at Nimrûd, but they were in such a state of decay that they crumbled soon after excavation, though not before Layard was able to take a sketch of one of them (cf. Fig. 14, B).

An interesting example of a capital of a column is the small stone capital preserved in the British Museum (cf. Fig. 13,*b*). It probably formed the upper part of one of the diminutive columns adorning a balustrade, and doubtless when complete was a more or less faithful miniature replica of the full-sized capital discovered by Place (Fig. 13, *a*).

Until recently, owing to the fact that the columns portrayed on Assyrian bas-reliefs, and also the scant remains of actual columns which had been recovered, yielded no examples of shafts other than round,[1] or possibly square (cf. Fig. 14, C) it was thought that polygonal-shafted columns were unknown, but the German excavations at Ashur have brought to light a capital of a column made of black basalt,[2] together with a portion of the shaft which is sixteen-sided, and probably belongs to about the time of Tiglath-Pileser I (1100 B.C.).

This column at one time bore an inscription, but unfortunately it is worn away. The remains of another polygonal-shaped basalt column [3] was discovered on the same site. It is eight-sided, and bears an inscription of Shamhsi-Adad, the son of Tiglath-Pileser I.

Two interesting column-bases made of limestone were also discovered at Ashur,[4] under the brick-pavement of a late Assyrian dwelling-house. One of these con-

---

[1] Place discovered an eight-sided column at Karambs, but it apparently belonged to the Parthian period (Place, *Nineveh*, II, pp. 169 ff.).
[2] Cf. *Mitteilungen*, No. 40, p. 25.   [3] Cf. *Ibid.*, No. 40, p. 24.
[4] Cf. *Ibid.*, No. 42, p. 40.

sists in a plinth, a torus and a thin over-plate, all made in one piece, while in the other case a part of the shaft is preserved with the torus.

Judging from the bas-reliefs the corner columns of a building were generally more massive than those which were intermediate (cf. Fig. 14, C, D), a circumstance which added not only to the stability of the building itself, but also to the elegance of its appearance. But in both Babylonia and Assyria the column was used more often as an adornment to the façades of buildings than as an actual support for the structure itself. As we have so little positive evidence of the use of stone columns in Mesopotamia, it seems probable that as a rule columns were made of wood or bricks, the disappearance of almost all trace of which would be adequately accounted for by the natural destructibility of such materials, though the disappearance of stone columns, for such were clearly used, at all events sometimes, might be readily explained on the supposition that they had been subsequently used as rollers or for some other purpose.

THE ARCH

It has been truly said that the arch was first invented by people whose building materials were of a small size, and however open to objection this generalization may be, it is certainly true in the case of Babylonian architecture, and also in a somewhat lesser degree in that of the later Assyrian architecture. Strabo informs us that " all the houses in Babylonia were vaulted "—διὰ τήν ἀξυλίαν—" because of the dearth of wood," XVI, 1, 5— but however reliable or unreliable his statement may be, the dearth of wood and stone in the alluvial plain of Lower Mesopotamia of necessity taxed the inventive powers of the Babylonian architect to the utmost, when he was confronted with the problem of roofing the buildings he had erected, and the various rooms which they were destined to contain. But his genius seems to have arisen to the occasion, and evolved the principle of the arch as the best, and indeed the only means of coping with an otherwise insurmountable difficulty, for the construction of flat roofs depended on the existence of slabs of stones or timber-beams, alike large in size and durable, but both stone and wood of the kind wanted were not to be found in Babylonia, and the architect would clearly be unable to fetch wood or stone from the distant mountains for the purpose of roofing the chambers of an ordinary house. His inventive faculties were thus stimulated by the urgency of the case, and the result produced by these combined factors is to be seen in the early appearance of the arch, crude indeed as regards its structure, but none the less involving the same principles upon which all arches are built.

The early arches in the tomb-passages in Egypt are supposed to owe their origin to the removal of the lower part of the buttress-walls erected to keep the side walls of the passages from collapsing : such buttress-walls would of course fulfil their function in preventing the side walls from falling in, but they would frustrate their own ends by completely blocking the passage, thus rendering it perfectly useless. Accordingly the lower portion of the buttress-wall was removed, the upper part being allowed to remain, and forming in fact a rudimentary arch, and it is possible that the Babylonian arch owes its origin to like fortuitous circumstances. It is perhaps more probable, however, that the origin of the arch-shaped structure, if not the discovery of the principle of the arch, is to be traced to the peculiar form assumed by the native reed-huts, which doubtless bore a close resemblance to those commonly used in the Euphrates valley to-day. This view is advocated by Heuzey, and is the one which Hilprecht is disposed to favour.

Most of the ancient buildings of Babylonia have succumbed to the concurrent ravages of time and climate, and have consequently bequeathed to us very little material for the study of Babylonian architecture ; the roofs of buildings, and of the chambers comprised therein, have long since ceased to be, and we can thus only theorize as to the general mode of roofing adopted, but the drains and aqueducts constructed beneath the buildings have luckily survived to tell their tale, and we owe

Fig. 15.—Early T-shaped Arch   Fig. 16.—Arch at Tellô.
at Nippur.   (Cf. *Déc. en Chald.*, Pl. 57 (bis), 1.)
(Cf. Hilprecht, *Explorations*, p. 399.)

our knowledge of the early existence of the arch in Babylonia chiefly to these comparatively insignificant remains.

One of the most ancient arches as yet discovered is that which was brought to light during the course of the excavations carried on by Peters, Harper, Haynes and Hilprecht at the ancient city of Nippur (cf. Fig. 15). It was found at a great depth below the surface of the mound, being more than twenty-two and a half feet below the pavement of Ur-Engur (*circ.* 2400 B.C.), and fourteen feet below that of Narâm-Sin (*circ.* 2700 B.C.); it is a true

key-stone arch pointed in shape, made of well-burnt
plano-convex bricks, and measuring a little over two feet
in height and having a span of about one foot eight
inches, while its length is about three feet, but it seems
probable that originally the tunnel was vaulted throughout. The irregularity of its construction somewhat
diminishes the significance that it would otherwise have,
but it is of supreme interest as testifying to the fact
that the principle of the arch was known at this very
remote period, however crude the embodiment of that
principle may happen to be. The plano-convex bricks
composing this arch measure $12 \times 6 \times 2\frac{1}{2}$ inches and bear
the impress of finger-marks on their convex side, a
characteristic feature of pre-Sargonic bricks at Nippur,
Tellô and elsewhere, while the clay from which the bricks
are made is of a light yellow colour. The tunnel itself
seems to have been "a protecting structure for a drain,"[1]
rather than a drain itself, for below the pavement two
terra-cotta pipes were discovered, the existence of which
can only be explained on this hypothesis. At the top
of the arch were found the remains of another terra-
cotta pipe, the object of which must have been to drain
off the percolating rain-water, and thus prevent it penetrating through and disintegrating the vaulted structure
below. The T-shaped centre-piece, which was similarly
made of plano-convex bricks, doubtless served the purpose of keeping the sides of the arch from falling in.
Haynes further informs us that in one of the private
houses at Nippur which had been occupied at least three
times, the earliest of the three doorways traceable in the
ruins, consisted in a segmental arch.

Another very early arch was discovered by M. De
Sarzec at Tellô, close to the building of Ur-Ninâ (cf.
Fig. 16), having much the same shape as the Nippur
arch illustrated in Fig. 15 and doubtless used for a
similar purpose, while vaulted passages of which the arch

[1] Cf. Hilprecht, *Explorations*, pp. 397 ff.

was semicircular, were discovered by Taylor[1] in his excavations at Muḳeyyer (Ur), as early as 1855.

Again the German excavations at Fâra (Shuruppak) in 1902 and 1903 revealed a number of circular rooms, each of which was roofed by means of an arch formed by overlapping bricks placed horizontally, somewhat after the fashion of the later corbelled arch at Nippur seen in Fig. 17, to which Hilprecht assigns a provisional date of 2500 B.c. We know that the dome was invented in Babylonia at a very early date, thanks to Dr. Banks' discovery at Bismâya of an oval-shaped room in the vicinity of the temple, the lower parts of the domed roof of which were found still in place. Its antiquity is attested by the date of the temple itself which would appear to have belonged to the pre-Sargonic period, as the ziggurat was faced with the plano-convex bricks characteristic of that period, and the pottery furnace, not far distant, was composed of bricks of the same kind.

In later times the arch was doubtless used more frequently in Babylonia. A good example of a late Babylonian arch was discovered by the German excavators on the Ḳasr at Babylon; the arch in question (cf. Fig. 18) which is Roman in character, forms the roofing of a lofty gate cut in the fortification wall. Koldewey[2] is of opinion that the wall in which this arched gate occurs, is a good deal older than the Nebuchadnezzar period.

But Assyria, the more or less faithful imitator of Babylonia in all matters great or small, is also known to have employed the arch as an architectural device, though, as in Babylonia, most of the Assyrian arches which the excavations have brought to light are connected with the drainage system with which all the principal buildings were provided. The best examples of an Assyrian arch of ordinary dimensions are those found at Khorsabad, the gateways of which town were

[1] Cf. J. R. A. S., 1855, p. 266.
[2] Cf. *Mitteilungen*, No. 8, p. 4.

roofed with semicircular vaults. One of these gateways was pulled down by Place in order to make a close examination of its construction. The height from the pavement to the top of the arch was found to be twenty-four and a half feet, the width being a little over fourteen feet. The arch was made of crude bricks, all of which were of the same size, and had the same shape, the bricks being cemented together with soft clay. The vault itself had long since become disintegrated, but the ma-

Fig. 17.—Corbelled Arch at Nippur.   Fig. 18.—Arch at Babylon.
(Cf. Hilprecht, *Explorations*, p. 420.)   (Cf. *Mitteil.*, 8, *Abb.* 1.)

terials of which it was made were discovered in the ruins. Of the brilliantly painted friezes which adorned these rounded openings (cf. Pl. XXX), something will be said in the chapter on Painting.

But in regard to the study of what may be called the arch-principle, the subterranean channels which formed part of the system of drainage employed by the Assyrians are of greater importance. These aqueducts are found in all the palaces, both at Nimrûd and Kouyunjik, but Khorsabad furnished the best preserved examples, and therefore afforded the most valuable material for the careful examination of this architectural contrivance. At

Khorsabad, Place discovered several arched drains of different shapes, some of them being round, others elliptical, while others again were pointed, but apparently in every case the stones or bricks were set at an angle, so that each course had the support of the course

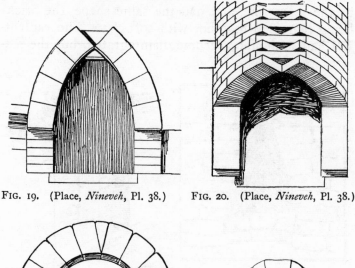

FIG. 19.   (Place, *Nineveh*, Pl. 38.)   FIG. 20.   (Place, *Nineveh*, Pl. 38.)

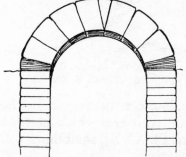

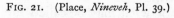

FIG. 21.   (Place, *Nineveh*, Pl. 39.)   FIG. 22.   (Place, *Nineveh*, Pl. 39.)

preceding it, and thus the pressure on the centre of the arch was reduced to the minimum. In the case of the pointed arched aqueducts found by Place, the arches in question are no true keystone arches, indeed they have no keystones of any kind as will be seen in Figs. 19, 20; this arched drain measures four feet eight inches from the ground to the centre of the vault, its width is about three feet nine inches, while its original length is unfortunately not known, though Place succeeded in tracing it for some two hundred and twenty feet. The floor was made of large slabs of limestone set in asphalt, while the ends of the stone-slabs extended beyond the walls of the vault on either side. The rounded type of arch is seen in Fig. 21 ; it is semicircular in shape and is formed of three voussoirs on each side, which together with the key, thus make seven in all, but owing to some miscalculation, the keystone appears to have been too small, in consequence of which there was a gap between it and the top voussoir on the right, which was filled in by means of a stone wedge which can be seen in the figure. Its width and height vary at different points, in some places it is said to be wide enough for two men to walk abreast in it.[1] The floor was composed of slabs of limestone which were laid in asphalt just like the floor of the pointed arch described above. An elliptical-shaped arch, also found at Khorsabad, is illustrated in Fig. 22 : it is formed of eight voussoirs and a keystone, the gap on either side of which is filled in by means of two stone wedges. The failure to make the keystones sufficiently large, and the consequent necessity for these supplementary wedges may be due to the architects not having allowed for the shrinkage of the bricks.

In regard to the arched structures at Nimrûd (Calah) Layard says he found a vaulted room and more than one arch. He tells us that " the arch was constructed upon the well-known principle of vaulted roofs, the bricks being placed sideways, one against the other, and having been probably sustained by a framework until the vault was completed." Knowledge of the principle of dome-shaped roofs in Assyria as well as in the mother-country, is evidenced both by the discovery of rooms whose dimensions would have rendered any other mode

[1] Cf. *Perrot and Chipiez*, p. 231.

of roofing impossible, and also by the representations on Assyrian bas-reliefs, as we have already seen.[1]

The arch-principle is further embodied in some of the Babylonian and Assyrian graves, and as there is no other opportunity of discussing the burial-places of the Babylonians and Assyrians in this volume, it may be permissible to give here a brief and general description of one or two of the best preserved of these burial-vaults. At Muḳeyyer (Ur) Taylor found a number of arched vaults (cf. Fig. 24) which in most cases measured about 5 feet in height, and 3 feet 7 inches in breadth, while they

FIG. 23. (After Andrae.)   FIG. 24. (After Taylor.)

were about 7 feet long at the bottom and 5 feet long at the top. The arch is formed by successive layers of overlapping bricks. It is interesting to compare the burial vaults discovered by Andrae at Kalat Sherḳat (Ashur), one of the best preserved of which is seen in Fig. 23.[2] This vault was discovered about 16 feet below the level of the floor of a Parthian door in the neighbourhood, and over 13 feet below a later Assyrian pavement. At the time of its construction the vault would appear to have been about 9 feet beneath the surface of the soil.

[1] Cf. Fig. 9.   [2] Cf. Andrae, *Mitteilungen*, No. 27, pp. 29–32.

The perpendicular walls forming the sides of the lower part of the tomb are set upon a brick pavement, the bricks being about 10½ inches square and nearly 2½ inches thick. The height of these perpendicular walls is approximately 30½ inches and the layers of bricks which each contains number 13. The vault itself, which of course commences where the perpendicular walls cease, is more or less oval in shape, has a span of 5 feet 2 inches, and is 2 feet 11 inches high, the total height of the tomb from the floor to the top of the arch thus being nearly 5½ feet. The arch, upon the construction of which much care had evidently been bestowed, was formed of forty-six courses of quasi-wedge-shaped bricks, each resembling a truncated segment of a circle. The interstices between the courses were filled in with stones, broken pieces of clay and clay mortar. The outside of the vault was coated with clay, but the inside was left plain. The walls at either end incline inwards, while they are built separately from the arch and are also rather higher. Access to the tomb from outside is gained by a slanting and somewhat winding entrance-shaft built close to the western wall, in which there is a small arched opening. The threshold of this opening, which was filled in with loosely laid bricks, lies 23¼ inches above the floor of the tomb. In the eastern wall the usual recess was found, the floor of which was some 35 inches above the floor of the burial chamber. This recess was about 19 inches in height and 13 inches in breadth, while the depth of the recess was greater than that of the wall, and it was therefore necessary to build another wall on the outside to close it up. In the recess of another double grave found by Andrae on the same site, a clay lamp was found, but this was not the case here ; possibly there was at one time a lamp in the recess of this tomb, its disappearance being due to the disintegration to which the long infiltration of damp subjects all articles of unburnt clay. The entrance-shaft

N

was 39 inches square, while its bottom was level with the threshold of the small opening in the western wall ; 4 feet 2 inches above this floor was a second floor made of gypsum blocks which were supported by the walls of the shaft. The interstices between these blocks were filled in with stones and pieces of clay, while the upper part of the shaft (i.e. the part above these blocks), the walls of which had only half the thickness of the walls below, was similarly filled in right up to the surface level. The uppermost part of the shaft had been disturbed by a later building. In the vault, Andrae found three skeletons, one of which apparently belonged to a man, and the other two to women. The arms of these skeletons were at right angles to the bodies, and the legs were contracted and apart, while the man lies on his right side and the two women on their left. Traces of a decayed whitish material were found in the tomb, which Andrae believes to be the remains of graveclothes. Bone needles and pottery had also been deposited with the corpses. The most interesting articles of pottery were three wide-necked bottles, two of which were decorated with dark horizontal lines, while the neck of the third was adorned with white painting on a dark ground, a technique well known in early Assyrian times. What were the contents of the vessels we do not know ; rams' bones were found near the door as well as elsewhere, and without doubt these vessels once contained meat offerings and drink offerings for the dead. There was evidence for at least three different periods of occupation in the strata above the grave, two of which belonged to the Assyrian era and one to the Parthian times.

The vaulted graves at Ashur do not however all belong to the same time ; some of them may be assigned to the early Assyrian period, while others were built at a later date. One of these later brick burial-vaults was excavated and carefully examined by Andrae in the spring of 1909.[1] The construction of this vault apparently involved the demolishment of an earlier Assyrian building. The bricks of which the vault was composed in some cases bore the inscription of Tukulti-Ninib I, but in spite of this fact, the grave itself was not built till a later date. Access to the vault was gained by means of an entrance-shaft the lower end of which was connected by means of a passage with the door of the burial-chamber. A few inches above the ruined débris of the entrance-shaft the remains of a Parthian building were discovered. The passage was entirely destroyed, though the shape of the displaced bricks led to the conclusion that it was roofed by a barrel-vault. The arched door into the grave-room which measures nearly 4 feet in height and has a span of about $22\frac{1}{2}$ inches is composed of very small bricks $6\frac{1}{2} \times 2\frac{1}{8}$ inches. It is built into one of the small walls of the grave-room, and the threshold is made of bricks like its other parts.

The bricks composing the barrel-vaulted roof of the grave-room are $11\frac{3}{4}$ inches square and $2\frac{3}{8}$ inches thick. At the other end of the burial-chamber is a small arched door leading into another room, also barrel-vaulted. This latter room which measures nearly 5 feet in length, and $35\frac{1}{2}$ inches in breadth, is built with less care and regularity than the main burial-chamber. The side-walls of the annexed room are $5\frac{1}{8}$ inches thick, but the thickness of the back wall is only 2 inches. The threshold of the entrance-door to the main burial-chamber is $20\frac{3}{4}$ inches lower than the pavement of the entrance-shaft, and nearly 19 inches above the floor of the burial-chamber. Asphalt and plaster were both used extensively in the interior.

North-east of the entrance-door, there was a lamp-niche, 3 feet $11\frac{1}{4}$ inches above the floor, and measuring $12\frac{1}{2} \times 13\frac{3}{4}$ inches in size, and $12\frac{1}{2}$ inches in depth. In this niche, three terra-cotta pots were discovered, and

[1] Cf. *Mitteilungen*, No. 40, p. 29.

Andrae thinks that these pots were probably used as lamps. The burial-chamber contained two bath-shaped sarcophagi, one of which measured 6 feet 7½ inches in length, 28 inches in breadth and 18⅛ inches in height, while the other was just over 6 feet 6 inches long, 31 inches wide, and 17 inches deep. The lids of both these sarcophagi were slightly arched and were tightly cemented. The top end of one of the covers bore the rough outline of two flowers.

Upon the brick floor of the annex was the extended skeleton of a man, while in one of the sarcophagi four skulls and three skeletons were found. Two of the skeletons belonged to men, but the third and best-preserved was that of a woman, while the skeleton to which the fourth skull belonged was not found. The funeral furniture was of the ordinary type and consisted chiefly in terra-cotta dishes and vases, copper bangles and glass beads.

Fig. 24 A.—Ziggurat on an Assyrian Bas-relief.

Fig. 24 B.—Actual remains of Ziggurat at Khorsabad. (After Place.)

CHAPTER VI—SCULPTURE

A CHAPTER on Sculpture naturally divides itself into two parts, the one dealing with those works which are wrought in the round, and the other with those fashioned in relief, or by incision, upon a flat surface. It was in the latter department that both the Babylonians and Assyrians excelled, and their chefs-d'œuvres belong to the bas-relief order. It is accordingly not unfitting that a consideration of their bas-reliefs should precede a treatment of their works in the round.

BAS-RELIEFS

The bas-relief was the favourite, and undoubtedly the most successful expression of the artistic genius of both Babylonians and Assyrians from the earliest to the latest times. Their first efforts in this direction were crude indeed, but this is a fault incidental to the beginnings of any art. One of the most ancient bas-reliefs yielded by Babylonian excavations is reproduced in Fig. 25, A. We have here a representation of a man apparently engaged in some act of worship, or in the performance of some unknown ceremony. His large, almond-shaped eyes are portrayed full face, his aquiline nose stands forth in an altogether aggressive fashion, his long hair hangs down his back, while a fillet surrounds his head, from which two long feathers emanate ; these feathers sometimes adorn the heads of Asiatic princes represented on early Egyptian monuments. His otherwise nude bust is to some extent relieved by the presence of a somewhat lengthy beard, and his clothing consists in the characteristically Sumerian square shawl arranged skirt-wise.

FIG. 25.

A, Musée du Louvre.　(Cf. Cat., p. 77, No. 1 ; *Déc. en Chald.*, Pl. 1 (bis).)
B, C, Musée du Louvre.　(Cf. Cat., pp. 87, 89, No. 5 ; *Déc. en Chald.*, Pl. 1 (bis,
　　D. (From Hilprecht, *Explorations*, p. 475.)　　　　　　　　[tert).)
E, F. (From *Old Bab. Inscr.*, II, Pl. XVI.)

With his left hand he grasps one of the three sacred poles before which he stands : the poles are surmounted by a knob, more or less identical in shape with the early Babylonian mace-heads. The inscription, written in very archaic line characters, which still preserve in part, traces of their pictorial origin, contains a list of offerings and also a mention of the god Ningirsu and of his temple E-ninnû. This most ancient sculpture was found by De Sarzec on the site of the earliest buildings at Tellô. It is made of white limestone and is about seven inches in height.

Two of the fragments of another very archaic bas-relief found in the same neighbourhood are seen in Figs. 25, B, C. In all the faces portrayed in these two fragments we observe the same prominent nose, and the same large, lozenge-shaped eyes already alluded to, but in other respects they differ from the type illustrated in Fig. 25, A. The most striking and probably the most consequential individual in the present group occupies the left end of Fig. 25, B. His importance is evidenced by the excessive length of his long hair, and by the hooked sceptre which he carries on his shoulder, probably in token of his royal attributes. In his left hand he holds what appears to be a fillet, which he is presenting to the trusty warrior who stands before him, lance in hand. On the other fragment (Fig. 25, C) we have two other types represented, one characterized by the luxuriancy of his hair and the profusion of his beard, the other being distinguished by the complete absence of hair from both the head and face. In both cases they are clad after the same fashion, their one and only garment consisting in a short skirt, the lower portion of which is represented in a most archaic fashion by a series of tongue-shaped strips, and the upper portions of which are inscribed in archaic line characters, while their hands are clasped across their breast in an attitude of submissive if not subservient obedience. The why and the where-

fore of the absence of hair from the head and face of one
of these figures is of course unknown, but M. Heuzey
suggests with some plausibility that the figure is thus
represented in virtue of his sacerdotal character. Both
of these fragments once formed part of a round socket
which probably served to support a votive stave or
weapon ; they are made of hard limestone, and were
found amid the débris of a building belonging to the
time before Ur-Ninâ.

In Fig. 25, F, we have a reproduction of an early limestone votive tablet from Nippur,[1] in the upper register
of which a naked and clean-shaven worshipper is offering a libation to a seated and bearded god, the whole
being represented in duplicate. Below, a goat and a
sheep are followed by two men, one of whom bears a
vessel on his head and the other holds a stick in his right
hand, while both are clad in the ordinary Sumerian skirt.
Another interesting votive-tablet (cf. Fig. 25, E) from
Nippur shows us a similar scene—a naked worshipper
standing before a seated god is offering a libation, the
god being reversed on the left, but the unique interest
attaching to this fragment is in the ploughing-scene
represented below ; we see a man ploughing with a
horned animal, probably a gazelle or an antelope, which
appears to indicate that this archaic fragment dates from
a period when neither the ox nor the ass were used as
beasts of labour, while a third[2] bas-relief (cf. Fig. 25, D),
also religious in character and emanating from the same
site shows a seated goddess accompanied by a bird, while
a burning altar, and a lighted candlestick stand before
her. She holds a pointed cup in her right hand and behind her we see a long-bearded priest leading a clean-
shaven worshipper who carries a goat in his right arm,
into the presence of the goddess.

[1] Cf. Hilprecht, *Babylonian Expedition of the University of Pennsylvania*, Vol. I, part ii, Pl. XVI.
[2] Hilprecht, *Explorations*, pp. 474, 475.

The extraordinary popularity of what may be termed
the bas-relief mode of sculpture among the Sumerians
is strikingly illustrated by its employment in the decoration of mace-heads and other objects ; in Fig. 26, B we
have a large mace-head made of hard white limestone,
seven and a half inches in height, and having a diameter of little over six inches. The scheme of decoration
takes the form of a procession of lions, six in number,
all following in the same direction, and each burying

FIG. 26.—Musée du Louvre. (Cat. pp. 81, 96; *Déc. en Chald.*, Pl. 1 tert, 2 bis.)

his teeth in the back of the lion going before. The
bodies of the lions are portrayed side-wise, but the colos-
sal-eyed heads are seen full face. These lions are, despite
their crudeness, already surprisingly true to life ; the
top of the mace-head (A) is not left unadorned, but has
been made good use of by the sculptor who has carved
the heraldic lion-headed eagle of Lagash upon its smooth
surface. It bears an inscription of Mesilim, king of
Kish, who is known from another inscription to have
flourished and ruled over the country some time before
the foundation of the first dynasty of Lagash by Ur-
Ninâ, in the neighbourhood of whose building this mace-

head was actually found, though at a slightly lower level.

We now come to the time of Ur-Ninâ, the most interesting of whose monuments, at least from the pictorial point of view, is the sculpture reproduced in Fig. 26. This relief, which is divided into two registers, introduces us to Ur-Ninâ, his family and his courtiers. The king himself is of colossal size, indicative doubtless of his colossal power ; in the upper register he is portrayed standing, his left hand on his nude bust as in the lower register, while with his right hand he is balancing a basket, which, as M. Heuzey has pointed out, probably contains the clay and foundation brick for the temple of Ningirsu, rather than offerings for the god. This view is further supported by the inscription written alongside the figure of the basket carrier, the first line of which contains a mention of the temple of Ningirsu. Ur-Ninâ is thus represented as the servant of his god, and the honour attaching to the menial task in which he is engaged may be judged by the fact that he alone is apparently accounted worthy, his sons and followers merely standing by, their hands clasped in a reverential attitude. Below, the king is seen in a more comfortable and homely pose, though here too he would seem to be attending to his religious duties ; he is raising his cup either to drink to the honour of the gods, or else to offer a libation, but in either case the task must have been less arduous and possibly more pleasant than that which occupies him in the upper register. With one exception all the heads and faces are devoid of hair, and all are clad in the Sumerian short woollen skirt, though the king's skirt is more flounced than those of his courtiers, as becomes royalty. The type of vesture met with here, as well as on the Vulture Stele and on so many of the early Sumerian sculptures, was called "Kaunakes." The figure immediately in front of the standing king in the upper register is distinguished from

PLATE XII

Musée du Louvre: Déc. en Chald., Pl. 3, ii

PORTION OF THE VULTURE-STELE OF EANNATUM, PATESI OF LAGASH

the others not only by being taller, and wearing a skirt resembling the king's garment, but also by having long hair. Opinion differs as to whether we are to see in this figure the daughter of the king, or whether, on the contrary, we have here a portrait of the king's eldest son, as both Heuzey and Radau think, and in support of their view, the improbability of assigning such a leading part to a woman at this period has been aptly urged ; the dress differs from that of Ur-Ninâ in being suspended over the left shoulder, and in this respect recalls Eannatum's mantle on the Vulture Stele (cf. Pl. XII). The round or square hole in the centre of many of these early plaques was without doubt destined to serve as a socket for some votive stave or weapon, and the plaques pierced with such holes must accordingly have been laid in a horizontal and not in a vertical position. Ur-Ninâ was succeeded by Akurgal, who in turn gave place to Eannatum, whose famous Stele of Victory we now come to consider.

This monument was unfortunately not found intact and complete, but six fragments, some small, others comparatively large, but all full of interest, were unearthed at Tellô by M. de Sarzec. The scenes depicted and the events portrayed on the surviving fragments of this renowned stele, are instructive both from a religious as well as from a historical point of view. In Pl. XII we have a reproduction of perhaps the most interesting of these fragments. The scene here is divided into two registers, in both of which the troops of Eannatum are seen engaged on active service. The king leads the vanguard in person and on foot ; above his head the title "Conqueror for the god Ningirsu" is inscribed. His apparel consists in the "kaunakes" skirt, to which allusion has already been made, while over it is a mantle suspended over the left shoulder and passing under the right arm. His head is protected by a helmet, pointed at the top like those of his warriors, but differing from theirs in being furnished with ear-pieces ; his long hair for the most part hangs down his back, some of it however is gathered up and bound by a fillet at the back of his head. In his right hand he holds what purports to be a species of boomerang.

His troops are drawn up in a wedge-shaped formation, and if this representation is intentional, it is a surprising testimony to the skill in military tactics to which the Sumerians had attained at this extremely early date, but it may on the other hand be merely due to ignorance of perspective on the part of the artist. Their offensive weapons consist of lances some six or eight feet in length, while for defence they hold large rectangular shields which cover the whole of their bodies from neck to ankle. Were there any doubt as to the fortunes of this army of Eannatum, it would be immediately dispelled by a glance at the feet of the troops engaged, who are ruthlessly trampling on the prostrate bodies of their vanquished foes.

Below we have another battle-scene : the king again leads his troops to action, but here he is mounted in his chariot, his dress is identical with that worn by him in the upper half of this relief, and in his right hand he grasps a boomerang similar to the one with which he is armed above, but in his left hand he poises a long stave, the end of which is unfortunately not visible owing to the poor preservation of this part of the sculpture, but without doubt the point of this formidable weapon was once in immediate contact with the shaven head of a conquered enemy, while before him there is a quiver packed with arrows.

His followers in this instance are armed with a long lance and a battleaxe, but are protected by no shields, though their heads are covered with the same conical-shaped helmets, and they are clad in the familiar "kaunakes" skirts. Perhaps we are to see in these troops a detachment of the king's personal bodyguard. What

FIG. 27.—Musée du Louvre.

A, B. (Cf. Cat., pp. 105, 107.)
C. (Cf. Cat., p. 123 ; *Déc. en Chald.*, Plate 5, bis.)

strikes one at once about this sculpture is the extraordinary disparity between the crudeness of the art on the one hand, and the elaborate equipment and arrangement of Eannatum's army on the other, from which it is clear that the energy of the Sumerians at this time was spent in the battlefield rather than in the pursuit of the peaceful arts.

Another fragment of this remarkable sculpture is reproduced in Fig. 27, A. We have here a veritable heap of corpses piled on top of each other. They are entirely naked, and their heads are shaven in apparent contradistinction to the troops of Eannatum. The bodies are extended and are arranged so that the head of each lies in contiguity with the feet of his next door neighbour; two figures clad in short archaically-fringed skirts are ascending this heap by means of a rope; the free hand of each is engaged in balancing a basket on the head which may contain offerings for the fallen, but more probably earth wherewith to bury their corpses. It is a matter of dispute as to whether these superimposed corpses represent the fallen warriors of Eannatum's army, or the smitten foes of Lagash; but the fact that the bodies are naked, and the further fact that in none of the Babylonian or Assyrian battle-scenes is there a single example of a warrior of the victor's army being represented as killed, and lastly the improbability of the artist having accentuated the losses of Eannatum in such a conspicuous manner, and especially upon a stele of victory, all militate against the former and for the latter view. In that case we have a striking testimony to the clemency exhibited by the Sumerians of the earliest times, the enemy being apparently allowed sometimes the privilege of burying their dead.

In Figure 27 B we have another fragment of this unique specimen of Sumerian art. The representative of Lagash is here portrayed on a colossal scale; his head has a profusion of hair, and from his face hangs a long streaked beard similar to that worn by Gilgamesh on the cylinder-seals. Possibly, as Heuzey suggests, this figure is a representation of that hero of Babylonian folk-lore, but it is probably a picture of the god Ningirsu himself. In any case, it can hardly be Eannatum, as the latter is on this same stele portrayed clean shaven. This colossal figure grasps in his left hand the heraldic arms of Lagash, while in his right hand he holds a round-headed mace similar to that seen in other early bas-reliefs. Before him lie a number of prisoners confined in a net or a cage (cf. Hab. I. 15); one of these unhappy victims has thrust his head through the meshes of his prison with a view to evading the next blow, but this laudable attempt does not seem to have met with the success which it deserved, for the head of the mace is seen in immediate contact with that of the individual in question. All the figures here portrayed, whether belonging to Eannatum's army, or to that of the enemy, exhibit the same type of face, the most distinguishing characteristics of which are the large almond-shaped eyes and the aquiline nose. The stele is known as the "Vulture Stele" and derives its name from another fragment on which are portrayed a number of vultures making off with the heads, and sharply severed limbs of the slain. Eannatum, whose victories are here depicted, was succeeded by Enannatum, and after him Entemena, the nephew of Eannatum ascended the throne. Unfortunately the artistic relics of his time are few in number, but those that have survived are peculiarly interesting. In a subsequent chapter (cf. Fig. 45) we shall devote some space to an examination of the silver vase of this ancient ruler, but here (cf. Fig 27, C) we have a specimen of the sculpture of his reign.

This little sculptured block, which is made of a mixture of clay and bitumen, and in appearance resembles black stone, was found in the neighbourhood of a building composed of bricks bearing the name of Entemena.

In the upper register we see the heraldic device of the city of Lagash—a lion-headed eagle grasping two lions facing in opposite directions, doubtless indicative of the power exercised by Lagash over the peoples of Sumer and Akkad. We have already seen it on the Vulture Stele, and it occurs also on the yet earlier monuments of Ur-Ninâ, but a comparison of the royal arms as here represented with the device on the Vulture Stele (cf. Fig. 27, B) shows a marked advancement from the artistic point of view. The eagle is still sufficiently stereotyped, and the extraordinary amount of detail with which the artist has treated his subject has had the undesirable effect of making it even more formal than it would otherwise be, but the lions are much more animated and vigorous in conception than in the earlier sculptures. Instead of walking along in an impassive, lifeless manner, they literally writhe under the grip of their victorious foe, whose wings they seek to gnaw with their teeth. Below, we have a representation of a crouching calf or heifer, one of whose front legs is raised as though about to leap up. As Heuzey says, the pose of this animal is wonderfully natural, and must have been studied from nature ; it at once recalls the procession of animals engraved on the silver vase of Entemena (cf. Fig. 45). No doubt the animal here portrayed is a sacrificial victim. To the right of the central hole found so frequently in these early sculptures, stands the worshipper, of gigantic size, holding a staff in his left hand. He is clean shaven, and is nude down to the waist, from which hangs the usual kaunakes skirt. The lower part of this little block is decorated with the scroll design so frequently encountered on cylinder-seals. The size of its reproduction here however is entirely out of proportion to the rest of the sculpture, and it may therefore in this case represent a skein of wool as another form of offering. The mention of the priest Dudu, whose name also occurs on the

PLATE XIII

STELE OF VICTORY OF NARÂM-SIN

silver vase of Entemena, removes any uncertainty there might be as to the period to which we should assign this little block, though a judgment based on an examination of the style of art here exhibited would have independently placed it in the same category as the silver vase of Entemena. The line-characters in which the inscription is written are more developed than those found on the monuments of Ur-Ninâ and Eannatum, many of them already betraying the wedge-shaped formation characteristic of the writing called " cuneiform."

Sufficient perhaps has been said to give a general idea of the artistic merits or demerits of the old Sumerian bas-reliefs of the first dynasty of Lagash. The next Babylonian school of art which specifically compels both attention and admiration is that to which the era of the kings of Akkad or Agade gave birth. From some points of view Mesopotamian art reached her climax at this period ; neither before nor after was the same success in the reproduction of human figures attained, and the sculptures belonging to this period are in some ways unique in the history of oriental art. The most famous of these monuments of Babylonian genius is reproduced in Pl. XIII. This stele, which was found at Susa in the course of M. G. de Morgan's epoch-making excavations on that site, was fashioned to commemorate some notable victory achieved by Narâm-Sin of Agade. The king is seen in the act of ascending a high mountain ; behind him march his trusty warriors armed with spears or lances, and apparently carrying standards. The king himself is armed with a bow and arrow, and also a battle-axe, while his head is protected by a horned helmet ; before him crouches one of the enemy, into whose neck an arrow has sunk deep, while another grasps the broken end of a spear. The figure of the king is full of vitality and animation, and offers a very striking contrast to the lifeless conventionalism characteristic of the older Babylonian and the later Assyrian representations of human

o

beings. The whole scene is alive with action, and the effect is not marred by any undue disproportion between the figure of the king and those of his followers. Above

Fig. 28.—A. (Hilprecht, *Old Bab. Inscr.*, II, p. 63, No. 120.) B, C, D, E, F, Musée du Louvre. (Cf. Cat., pp. 131, 133, 139, 151, 147; *Déc. en Chald.*, Plates 5, 22, 23, 24.)

the king's head are the remains of an inscription by Narâm-Sin, but upon the cone intended to represent the mountain which the king is scaling, is an inscription occupying seven lines and bearing the name of Shutruk-Nakhkhunte, king of Elam, which seems to indicate that the stele had been captured by the Elamites and carried off to Susa as a trophy. An interesting basalt bas-relief of this same king was discovered near Diarbekr (cf. Fig. 28 "A"). Narâm-Sin is standing on the right of the inscription, clad in a kind of plaid and wearing a conical hat. His beard is long and pointed, while bracelets encircle his wrists, and he carries a short staff in each hand.

The remains (cf. Fig. 28 " B," " C ") of another very interesting stele belonging to about the same epoch or a little earlier, and military in character, were discovered by De Sarzec at Tellô. In the top register of fragment " B " three warriors are seen proceeding in file, two of whom are archers and carry quivers which are decorated with large leaves, while a leg is all that remains of the third. In the second register an archer is seen in the act of drawing his bow ; his attitude is fixed and steady, and his bow is bent to the utmost, while his quiver hangs over his shoulder; before him a smitten foe lies prostrate on his back, and in contradistinction to his van-quisher who is clad in a long tunic, is entirely naked, while his right hand is raised in supplication. We next come to another warrior clad in a short fringed skirt and wearing a conical helmet : with his left hand he is seizing the beard of an enemy, who is also naked like his prostrate brother in the same register, and his right hand is raised, about to bring down his knotted club upon the face of his defeated prisoner. Below, is the figure of another warrior armed with a long pike. In "C" we have another fragment of this interesting sculp-ture, in the top register of which two warriors are seen marching in file ; the one behind is carrying a battle-axe at the trail. In the register below, a warrior clad in a short skirt and wearing a helmet is engaged with a prostrate enemy ; one of his feet is firmly planted in the unfortunate man's stomach, and with his right hand he is further punishing him with the aid of his knotted club. Behind these two figures we have another like scene represented ; here the all-powerful warrior is armed with a long lance, which he is carrying at the port ; with his right arm he is marching along a prisoner much shorter than himself, whose arms are bound behind his back ; the prisoner is naked, like most of the defeated enemies of Sumer and Akkad as portrayed by the sculptor. All that remains of the third register is the head and the upper part of the bow of an archer.

Apart from the spirit which animates these little figures, the chief point of interest in connection with them lies in the general scheme of artistic representation here adopted. No longer is the conquering army portrayed *en masse* as on the Vulture Stele of Eannatum, but the idea conveyed and the event commemorated are precisely the same in either case. The all-prevailing idea is that of victory, only the picture of a phalanx of armed troops trampling the nude bodies of their foes beneath their feet, has given place to a series of selected incidents of individual combat, represented after the Homeric fashion. This sculpture clearly belongs to the same school as Narâm-Sin's stele of Victory, which, however, it probably somewhat antedates, as the cuneiform signs found on the second fragment are of a more archaic character than those used on the monuments of Shar-Gâni-sharri and Narâm-Sin. The little that remains of the inscription is of considerable interest as it contains a mention of the city of Agade, the centre of the Semitic Empire established by the two last-named kings.

We must now pass from the epoch of the Semitic kings of Agade or Akkad, to the later period of Sumerian civilization, the age in which Ur-Engur and Dungi, kings of Ur, and Ur-Bau and Gudea, rulers of Lagash, lived and reigned. We are unable to assign a definite date to any of these rulers, but they probably flourished somewhere about the middle of the third millennium B.C. One of the most interesting bas-reliefs belonging to this time is reproduced in Fig. 28, " D." We have here a representation of a god seated on a throne. He wears a long square beard, and his head is surmounted by the horned cap emblematic of divinity ; his mantle covers nearly the whole of his body, the right arm alone being excepted. The head, which in its contour and general appearance recalls the heads of the Assyrian winged human-headed lions and bulls of some fifteen or sixteen centuries later (cf. Plate XXV), is like them, depicted full face, the seated body being sculptured in profile ; in his left hand the god holds a sceptre, the end of which is fashioned like a leaf. In Fig. 28, " E," we have a reproduction of what is probably the largest fragment of an early Babylonian bas-relief in existence. It was excavated at Tellô and measures about four feet in length. The upper part of the relief is occupied with a procession of four figures apparently engaged in the service of the gods, while below, a seated figure is seen playing an elaborate instrument of eleven strings, the lower part of the frame of which is decorated with a horned head and the figure of a bull. This relief would appear to have formed part of a stone socket.

As might be expected, the material used for most of the Babylonian as well as the later Assyrian bas-reliefs was a species of limestone and alabaster, as this kind of stone lends itself readily to the impress of the chisel, but the harder stones were also sometimes utilized for the purpose.[1] Thus in Fig. 28, F, we have a sketch of what remains of a black steatite relief belonging to this period. The fragmentary inscription gives us the name of the goddess Ningal, who is here portrayed in a singularly attractive manner, and with an extraordinary amount of detail. An elaborate robe covers the whole of her body, and a necklace adorns her throat ; her hair hangs over her shoulders, while the crown of her head is encircled by a fillet. The general technique of this little sculpture is surprising in its fidelity to nature ; the attitude of the

[1] Cf. also above, Fig. 28, A.

goddess, her body half turned and her left arm resting negligently on the back of her chair is life-like, and the face itself is not without a beauty of its own. The difficulty involved in the portrayal of a human eye in profile, so painfully manifest on the Vulture Stele and other earlier Sumerian monuments, where the eye is portrayed full-face, the rest of the head being done in profile, has here been surmounted, and we have before us a perfectly naturally conceived and executed face and head.

Some few centuries after the time of Gudea the city of Babylon became the centre of the chief power in Southern Mesopotamia. Unfortunately the excavations have not yielded us a rich harvest for the study of the artistic development of sculpture during this period, but the material at hand would tend to show that there was far less development in the interval between the later dynasty of Lagash, the age in which Gudea lived, and the establishment of the first Semitic dynasty of the city of Babylon, than there was in the period separating the first dynasty of Lagash from the epoch of Sargon and Narâm-Sin, the Semitic kings of Agade.

In Pl. XIV we have a reproduction of the sculptured stele of black basalt upon which is inscribed the world-renowned legal code of Khammurabi, the most illustrious king of this first dynasty of Babylon. The king is seen standing in reverential attitude before the Sun-god Shamash, from whom he is receiving the laws inscribed below. The king wears a long robe reaching down to his ankles, but leaving his right arm, which is raised in adoration, untrammelled by the folds of his mantle. The seated deity likewise has a long beard, but his high horned cap differentiates him at once from his adoring servant, while from his shoulders tongues of fire are seen shooting forth, doubtless representing the rays of the sun. In his right hand he holds the ring and staff emblematic of dominion and power. He is similarly represented in Nabû-aplu-iddina's tablet (cf. Pl. XIV)

PLATE XIV

THE SUN-GOD TABLET

STELE ENGRAVED WITH KHAMMURABI'S
CODE OF LAWS

and also on two contemporaneous stelæ in the Louvre,
in one of which he is in a standing position. Beneath
his feet are the mountains portrayed in miniature. The
laws enacted on this stele, which is now one of the treasures of the Louvre, number about two hundred and
eighty, and deal with all kinds of subjects. It was set
up in E-sagila, the temple of the chief god Marduk in
Babylon, so that every aggrieved party at law could go
and consult it. Like so many of the monuments of Babylonian antiquity, this stele was captured by the Elamites
and removed to Susa, where it remained until the French
excavations on that site brought it once more to light.

As we have already seen[1] the dynasty to which Khammurabi belonged was brought to an end some time later
by an invasion of the Hittites, a powerful mountainous
people whose home lay in Cappadocia. A century or so
afterwards, i.e. about 1800 B.C., another mountainous
nation known as the Kassites swept down from their
strongholds in the Elamite territory on the east of the
Tigris into the defenceless Babylonian plain, where they
established and maintained their supremacy for a long
time to come. Unfortunately the artistic relics of the
Kassite period are few, and for the most part unimpor-
tant. Meanwhile, however, the Assyrians in the north
had asserted their independence, and ultimately (i.e.
about 1275 B.C.) succeeded in reducing Babylonia and
establishing their sway over the whole of Mesopotamia.
In spite of this fact, we have practically no specimen of
the sculptor's art during the long interval separating the
fall of the First Dynasty of Babylon and the ninth century B.C., and it is not till the time of Ashur-naṣir-pal,
king of Assyria, and Nabû-aplu-iddina, king of Babylon,
that we are able again to study in detail the work of the
sculptor in the Tigro-Euphratian valley. To the former
king we are indebted for a large series of bas-reliefs
taken from the walls of his palace at Nimrûd (Calah),

[1] Cf. above, p. 33.

while to the latter we owe one of the most interesting and instructive Babylonian bas-reliefs in existence (cf. Pl. XIV).

One of the earliest specimens of Assyrian bas-relief as yet discovered is that which was found by Taylor at a village called Korkhar, situated some fifty miles north of Diarbekr. The relief in question was sculptured on the natural rock, which had been smoothed for the purpose by order of Tiglath-Pileser I (circ. 1100 B.C.).[1] The king is represented in a standing posture, his right arm is extended and he is pointing with his forefinger, while in his left hand he holds a mace ; the king's figure and general appearance are already quite stereotyped, and show no more originality or vigour than the representations of the later Assyrian kings. This same monarch has further left us the upper part of an obelisk erected to commemorate his feats in the chase, on one side of which there is a small relief in which Tiglath-Pileser is seen receiving the submission of various vassal-chiefs, while above their heads are the emblems of certain deities, the most interesting of which is the winged human-headed disc of Ashur, the patron god of Assyria. But these reliefs, interesting as they are, afford us little material upon which to form an estimate of the sculptural ability of the Assyrians at this period; the chief inference which they permit us to draw is that Assyrian art seems to have neither advanced nor declined appreciably, during the interval of two hundred or more years which lapsed between the time of Tiglath-Pileser and Ashur-nasir-pal. The latter king succeeded his father Tukulti-Ninib II as king of Assyria (885 B.C.). Tukulti-Ninib had largely restored the fallen fortunes of the northern country, thus paving the way for the successes of future reigns, but Ashur-nasir-pal extended the power of Assyria in

---

[1] For a rough sketch, cf. Rawlinson, *The Five Great Monarchies*, II, 79.

every direction, as well as consolidating her rule over
the districts reduced by his father. It is accordingly by
no means unnatural that he should have desired to commemorate and perpetuate the record of his triumphs in
pictorial fashion upon the walls of his palace at Nimrûd,
and it is with his reign that the history of Assyrian bas-
reliefs really commences, so far as our present material
goes.

Assyria was in some ways the natural home of the bas-
relief, for she contained a plentiful supply of alabaster
and limestone, the softness of which facilitated the
work of the artist and reduced his difficulties to a
minimum : Babylonia on the other hand yielded practically no stone, and all that was used had to be
quarried at a distance and transported at great cost and
labour, and that fact makes the early efforts of the
Babylonians in this direction all the more praise-wor-
thy, and the proficiency to which those efforts gave
birth, as seen for example in Narâm-Sin's stele of
Victory, the more astonishing. But this notwithstanding, the bas-relief was more highly developed in the
northern country, where it played an all-important part
in the artistic life of the people. The general object
of these bas-reliefs was to commemorate the king's
victories over his enemies and his conquests in the
chase, rather than to produce a purely æsthetic effect.
In other words they are pictorial records rather than
artistic products, and that fact is further borne witness
to by the cuneiform texts with which they are generally inscribed. At the same time however, they afford
material for the study of Assyrian sculpture. The art
of sculpture in Assyria suffered all the drawbacks which
befall every art once it becomes professionalized; it lacks
spontaneity which is the very connotation of art, it is
made to order, and therefore it inevitably knows no
freedom but is the dull slave of conventionalism. But
in spite of all this, the bas-reliefs of Ashur-nasir-pal

and his successors, hampered as they are by those universal enemies of human art, professionalism and conventionalism, still enshrine, or imprison if you will, the artistic genius of the people, and on this account, if for no other, are deserving of careful attention.

The reliefs which covered the walls of the palace of Ashur-nasir-pal at Nimrûd (Calah) consist either of single figures of gigantic size, or else in a series of small scenes divided into two friezes by cuneiform inscriptions. In Pl. XV we see Ashur-nasir-pal followed by a winged mythological being; both are engaged in the performance of a religious ceremony, the king with the bow and the arrow which he holds in his hands, the attendant with the cone which he holds up in his right hand. The semi-divine character of the winged creature is evidenced by his head-gear which consists of the horned cap, but the faces of both figures are more or less identical, a lamentable characteristic of all Assyrian portrayals of human or semi-humanly conceived beings. The chief peculiarities of this type of face are the large eyes, the curved nose, and the profusion of hair on both head and face. Both figures are clad in a long robe and deeply fringed mantle which extend to the feet. The footwear consists of sandals fastened by thongs passing over the instep and round the big toe. The muscular arms of both are adorned with bracelets, the pattern of the decoration on which is a replica of the ubiquitous rosette so characteristic of Assyrian art. The king's head-gear consists of a helmet from which two tails hang, and in its appearance generally, is not unlike a bishop's mitre. Both king and divine attendant carry what appear to be two daggers tucked into their waistbands. The muscularity noticeable in the arms is yet more aggressive in the left leg of the mythological being, which, unlike that of the king, is left exposed. This grotesquely realized conception of strength is but the decadent descendant of the naturally ex-

PLATE XV

BAS-RELIEF OF ASHUR-NASIR-PAL

pressed vigour so noticeable in the statues of Gudea. And here may be mentioned one characteristic peculiarity of Assyrian sculpture ; it will be observed that a long cuneiform inscription is chiselled right across the relief, pursuing the even or uneven tenor of its way quite recklessly through wings, garments, bodies and hands, and there is no obstacle which it fails to overcome, not even excepting the deep fringe on the mantles.

The subjects of the smaller reliefs of Ashur-naṣir-pal are many and various, though they all revolve round one of two themes, the battle-field or the chase. In one, Ashur-naṣir-pal has alighted from his chariot and is receiving the submission of the enemy ; in another we see a number of fugitives swimming to a fortress on inflated skins. Here we see tributary chiefs bringing offerings to lay them at the feet of their imperious lord, while further on we see the bowmen of Ashur-naṣir-pal mounted in their chariots and discharging arrows against the enemy. In one relief the king himself is seen erect in his chariot with his bow fully drawn ; elsewhere Ashur-naṣir-pal is represented in the act of crossing a river ; the king has not however dismounted from his chariot, but is being rowed over, chariot and all.

One of the most luminous of these small bas-reliefs is reproduced in Pl. XVI(2). Ashur-naṣir-pal and his army are storming a beleaguered city ; the walls of the city are crenelated after the regular Mesopotamian fashion. Immediately before the walls the movable tower resting on six small wheels and containing the battering ram is stationed, the efficacy of which may be judged from the bricks falling from the battered walls. Mounted on the top of the tower is an archer with bow bent, whose person is protected by another warrior bearing a shield. The king is portrayed behind the movable tower in the act of drawing his bow ; his head-gear differs from that of the warriors, who wear a conical helmet. In Pl. XVI(3), we see the warriors of Ashur-naṣir-pal returning victorious from the battle-field. On the right of the picture are two three-horse chariots, both of which carry standard-bearers ; above them we see a vulture making off with his prey, which in this instance consists in a human head, and in front are the infantry who appear to be gloating over the gory heads of their smitten adversaries, while to add to the ghastliness of the scene two musicians are playing on stringed instruments.

Ashur-nasir-pal was however quite as proud of his victories in the chase as he was of his conquests in the battle-field, as is attested by the numerous hunting scenes which he caused to be carved in relief on his palace walls. In Pl. XVI (4) we see Ashur-nasir-pal, erect in his chariot, in the act of dispatching a lion by the aid of his bow and arrow. The lion is treated with considerable boldness, and the skill of the artist in the portrayal of animal life —or death, as here—when compared with the stereo-typed lifelessness of the king, is sufficiently striking. But Assyrian art does not reach its climax here, as we shall see when we come to consider the lions on Ashur-bani-pal's bas-reliefs; the latter show a certain delicacy in the handling, and an intuition into all those infinite subtleties and varying nuances which are the hall-mark of life, animal or human as the case may be, and which apparently are not felt or at all events not successfully realized in the earlier works. The portrayal of the lion here is strong and life-like, but the spectator can never get away from the consciousness of the fact that it is a pic-torial representation ; he can never abandon the thought of the sculptor and the excellence of his art, or lose himself, be it only for a moment, in the reality itself. But in the reliefs of Ashur-bani-pal, one can for a brief space forget the artist and his work, and see the lion itself; one can catch a faint note of his dying gasp as he lies there motionless, his body transfixed with arrows, and it is in the effacement of the artist and the material which he uses that art attains the zenith of her power.

PLATE XVI

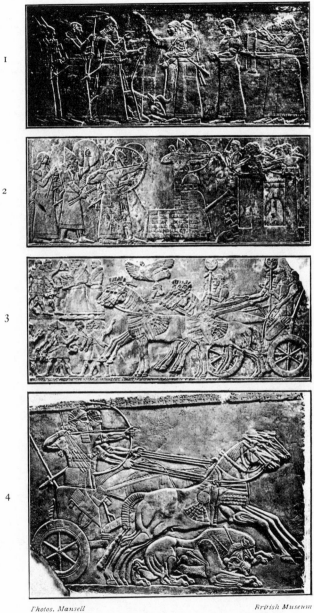

BAS-RELIEFS OF ASHUR-NAṢIR-PAL
1. LIBATION OVER A DEAD BULL   3. RETURN FROM BATTLE
2. SIEGE OF A CITY   4. LION HUNT

But Ashur-nasir-pal's love for sport did not deter
him from his religious obligations, on the contrary he
appears to have attributed his triumphs in the chase to
his god, for on his return he offers a libation over the
body of the lion or bull which providence has delivered
into his hand (cf. Pl. XVI (1)). The cup he holds in his
hand resembles the top of a champagne glass, while his
left hand is leaning on a bow in the usual characteristic
manner. Before him is an officer, evidently of high
rank, for his dress is an exact replica of the king's, but
his head is bare and his hands are clasped in a defer-
ential manner. By the side of this high official is an
attendant or eunuch with a fly-flap, while behind him
is another attendant, and last of all are two musicians
playing stringed instruments. On the other side of
the picture, immediately behind the king is an attendant with a ceremonial umbrella, followed by two servants with bows on their shoulders.

Although Ashur - nasir - pal's contemporary Nabû -
aplu-iddina king of Babylon has left us but few memorials of his reign, we are nevertheless indebted to
him for one unique specimen of Mesopotamian sculpture (cf. Pl. XIV). Reference has already been made
to this tablet on account of the light which it throws
on certain architectural problems, it now remains for
us to consider it as a work of art and an historical
monument. The text records the restoration of the
temple of Shamash by two kings called Simmash-
shipak and Eulmash - shakin - shum, both of whose
reigns took place some time in the eleventh century
B.C. It then proceeds to describe the condition into
which the temple, its ornaments and accessories subsequently fell ; the shrine of the god had been denuded
of its treasures which had been misappropriated in one
way or another ; the sculptures which adorned the
walls and the image of the deity himself had suffered
violence at the hands of the godless. All this Nabû-

aplu-iddina set about to rectify ; he restored the glory which the fane had enjoyed in early days, in particular he enriched the time-honoured statue of the god with gold and lapis lazuli, he re-established the temple worship in all its former pomp and splendour, and took vengeance upon the enemies of Shamash and the king who had perpetrated this sacrilegious outrage. The king himself celebrated the occasion of the temple's re-dedication by a munificent supply of offerings, and issued detailed regulations as to the ceremonial vestments of the priests, and the days upon which in each case they were to be worn in future. In the scene above, Shamash is portrayed enthroned in his shrine at Sippar, holding a disc and rod in his right hand; the sides of the throne are sculptured with mythological beings, whose rôle seems to be to support the throne, while above and in front of the god's head are three astrological emblems. The roof and supporting pillar of the shrine itself have been discussed elsewhere (cf. p. 164): two divine beings are stationed on the top of the shrine ; they hold in their hands two taut ropes which are attached to a large disc, emblematic of the sun, placed on an altar immediately in front of the shrine, and by means of which the disc is kept in position. Approaching the altar and advancing towards the shrine are seen three worshippers, the first of whom is the high-priest of Shamash, who is introducing the king into the presence of the divine symbol in a manner so frequently seen on Babylonian cylinder-seals, while last of all comes a goddess. One of the interesting points about this little sculptured tablet is that though it was made by a ninth century king of Babylon the style of art to which it conforms would indicate that it is not an original work of Nabû-apluiddina, but a copy of a much older archetype. The headdress of the god for example is characterized by four tiers of horns, and is practically identical with that found even as early as the time of Gudea, the later Assyrian divine

PLATE XVII

Photo. Mansell   *British Museum*

SIEGE OF A CITY BY BATTERING-RAM AND ARCHERS
(Reign of Tiglath-Pileser III)

head-dress on the other hand generally having but two or three horns on either side : Shamash here too holds the disc and rod in his hand in precisely the same manner as he is represented doing on the famous stele of Khammurabi (cf. Pl. XIV) ; his long beard is likewise depicted in much the same way as it is there. In short, there seems little doubt that the original of this ninth century product must be sought for somewhere about the commencement of the second millennium B.C. Another particularly interesting feature about the discovery of this sculpture was the simultaneous discovery of two clay coverings for it. One of these was found to be broken, and was probably made by Nabû-aplu-iddina himself, but the other bears an inscription of Nabopolassar, king of Babylon from 625–604 B.C. During the two centuries which had elapsed between the time of Nabû-aplu-iddina and the reign of Nabopolassar, the oft-restored temple had again fallen into disrepair, and it fell to the lot of the last-named king to once more restore the time-honoured fane ; he too, like his predecessor two hundred years before, made " offerings rich and rare" to the immortal Shamash. The object of these clay coverings was of course to preserve the sculpture from damage (cf. Fig. 5).

To return to Assyria, Ashur-nasir-pal was succeeded by his son Shalmaneser II : we unfortunately possess but few bas-reliefs belonging to the time of this king, the best-known being those sculptured on the Black Obelisk ; these reliefs have been illustrated and dealt with in detail in so many works, owing chiefly to the historic importance of the inscription on this monument, that it seems hardly necessary nor desirable to discuss them here. Shalmaneser's immediate successors have left us few memorials of themselves, artistic or otherwise, and after their reigns a general decadence seems to have set in, from which Assyria did not recover till the reign of Tiglath-Pileser III, or Pul as he is called in 2 Kings xv. 19 and elsewhere. This king restored the fortunes of the empire, and extended his power on every side, and happily for our subject he has immortalized his exploits in picture-fashion on hard stone, as well as in writing on clay cylinders and tablets, though unfortunately the bas-reliefs of this king which have survived are few in number. One of the best preserved is that in which Tiglath-Pileser III is seen conducting a siege (cf. Pl. XVII). The details of this sculpture vividly recall the words Isaiah is reported to have used in his endeavour to rally the failing courage of Hezekiah, king of Judah, who was inclined to surrender himself and his city to Sennacherib—" Thus saith the Lord concerning the King of Assyria, he shall not come into this city, nor shoot an arrow there, nor come before it with shields nor cast a bank against it." All the means of attack here mentioned are represented in our bas-relief. The warriors have their bows bent, and doubtless have already dispatched many an arrow with deadly effect : their persons are protected by large wicker shields which cover the whole of their bodies. The " bank " in this case has clearly been " cast against " the besieged city, and the purpose that the " bank " was destined to serve is at once manifest. It consisted in an artificial mound up which the movable tower containing the battering-ram was advanced. On the top of the wall of the besieged city, a man is seen with hands outstretched suing for mercy. The defeat of the enemy and the reduction of their city is signalized in a highly realistic fashion ; beneath the " bank " some of the vanquished are seen prostrate and naked, while above, on a level with the top of the wall a number of captives, also naked, are impaled on stakes. The inscription refers to the various articles of tribute brought by conquered peoples, but is not possessed of any especial interest.

Tiglath-Pileser III was succeeded by Shalmaneser IV,

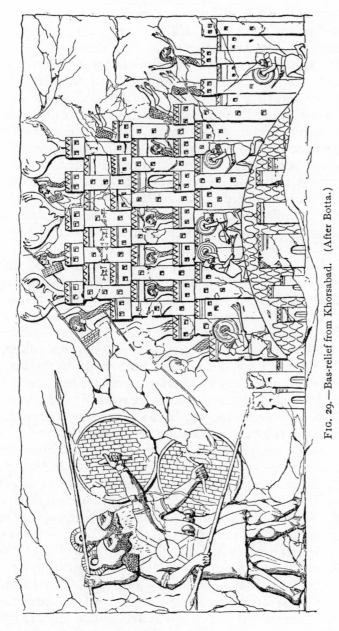

FIG. 29.—Bas-relief from Khorsabad. (After Botta.)

P

the most noteworthy event of whose reign was the siege of Samaria ; the city held out two years, and fell in 722 B.C., after Shalmaneser had been dethroned by Sargon the usurper. Sargon reigned some eighteen years and achieved many victories, the most momentous of which was that gained over the united Egyptians and Philistines at Raphia, near the Egyptian frontier. His sculptural bequests are many, and they comprise the gigantic winged human-headed bulls and lions which are in some ways the most impressive and the most characteristic specimens of oriental art. These winged monsters are neither bas-reliefs, nor are they perfect round sculptures, but a mixture of the two, and will accordingly receive consideration in the second half of this chapter.

But the palace erected by Sargon at Khorsabad, which was excavated by Botta more than half a century ago has yielded a rich harvest of bas-reliefs pure and simple, one of which is reproduced in Fig. 29. The scene is a familiar one in Assyrian sculpture ; a fortress is being attacked, of course successfully, by Assyrian soldiers. The fortress appears to have been built on the top of a height, doubtless with a view to rendering it the more impregnable. It consists of three rows of towers, superimposed one on the top of the other, the largest row being at the base and the smallest at the top, the general contour not being unlike that of a ziggurat with its receding stages. One wing of the fortress is protected by two towers, with which it is connected by means of a wall, while the other wing apparently extends right down the slope of the height. Access to the fortress is gained by arched doorways, one of the many incidental proofs of the frequency with which the arch was used in Assyrian architecture. A number of small rectangular houses lie at the foot of the hill, the doorways of which are arched like those of the flanking towers, while in both cases the doors or gates themselves are double-leaved. The windows, or embrasures, which are very numerous, are all square, and the battlements are crenelated as usual. Three pairs of colossal horns crown the fortress, which Botta is inclined to think may be actual horns, the disproportion of their size being of course no argument against that view, for disproportion is a characteristic of early oriental art. In such case they could be only emblematic, and presumably indicative of strength, but it seems infinitely more probable that the horns represent the sculptor's attempt to portray flames of fire, which are thus seen leaping up from the fired fortress. Some of the besieged are suing for mercy with outstretched hands, while others are evidently determined to fight to the last : they are armed with long spears and rectangular shields, while their backs are covered with the skins of animals. The enemy are literally at the gate, and it is impossible to tell when they will effect an entrance. Three of them are attempting to undermine the wall by means of long-handled prongs, two more are at work with their short swords, while to the left are two Assyrian spearmen of superhuman size, whose symbolic presence at once removes even the faintest shadow of doubt there might be as to the issue of the conflict. The attack is a strenuous one, as a mere walkover would bring no glory to the Assyrian arms, but at the same time, in spite of the severity of the battle raging round the fortress, the irresistible might of the Assyrian colossus is grimly suggested by the two giant warriors. The artistic treatment of the two heroes deserves some notice ; the aggressive muscularity so characteristic of Assyrian representations of kings and warriors is not indeed altogether wanting in the legs, but the arms are wholly free from this all but universal defect, while the pose of both arms and legs is exceptionally natural and singularly true to life. They are armed with spears of the same type as those used by the beleaguered army, but their shields are round in contradistinction to the oblong shields of the enemy, and they are girded with short swords. Their clothing and helmets are of a frequently recurring type, while both of them wear armlets and one of them wears a plain bracelet on his left wrist.

Sargon was succeeded in 705 B.C. by his famous son Sennacherib, the principal event of whose reign was probably the destruction of Babylon in 689 B.C. But the name of Sennacherib is famous rather on account of his close relations with the kingdom of Judah, and the unsuccessful siege of Jerusalem during the reign of Hezekiah, than for the conquests which he made, considerable as they were. The excavation of his palace at Nineveh has led to the discovery of a large number of bas-reliefs, many of which had been fractured as well as damaged by fire when the city was sacked by the combined forces of the Medes and the Babylonians about 609 B.C. For the most part they illustrate the campaigns undertaken by Sennacherib. What is noticeable at once in the bas-reliefs of this king is their complexity, as contrasted with the simplicity of those of Ashur-naṣir-pal. We have already observed that entire scenes are sometimes portrayed upon the bas-reliefs of the last-named monarch, though more often the relief is monopolized by two or three large and striking figures, one of which generally represents the king, but by Sennacherib's time what had hitherto been the exception now becomes the rule, and the bas-reliefs of this king are practically all scenic in their effect and most elaborate in their composition. This exaggerated complexity is due not so much to the variety of subjects treated in each relief, as to the ignorance of perspective on the part of the artist, for the treatment of even a limited number of subjects or objects within the scope of a single picture demands that these objects be seen and represented in perspective, and if that demand is not met, confusion worse confounded is the inevitable result of the artist's abortive attempt. This confusion is seen to perfection, if the "*oxymoron*" may be allowed, in the reliefs which adorned the palace walls of Sennacherib king of Assyria. A portion of one of the most instructive of these sculptured slabs is reproduced in Fig. 30.

The scene is one of great interest, not merely for the student of Assyrian art, but for the light which it throws

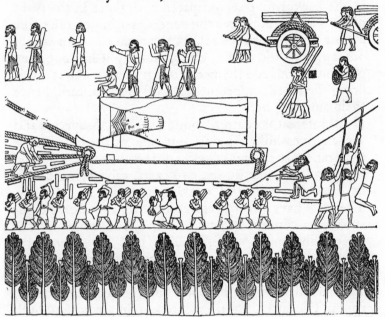

FIG. 30.—Bas-relief of Sennacherib. (After Layard.)

upon the mechanical resources of which the Assyrians of that day availed themselves, resources which the very existence of the gigantic human-headed bulls and lions presupposes, but which are here illustrated in a specific manner by Sennacherib's sculptors. The safe transport of a gigantic mass of solid stone was no easy matter even for the excavator of the nineteenth century,[1] how much greater the difficulties to be surmounted by a people whose mechanical knowledge was some two and a half

[1] Cf. p. 45.

millenniayounger! Inthe artistictreatment ofthis sculpture there are of course obvious defects. There is the
usual ignorance of perspective on the part of the sculptor, though this is less pronounced than elsewhere ; the
trees in the foreground and background are arranged in
lines in a somewhat conventional manner, though the
intentional or accidental diminution of size in the trees
in the background as compared with those in the front
of the sculpture, makes the general setting of the scene
appear much more true in its arrangement than would
otherwise be the case. Unfortunately it has not been
possible to include the back row of trees without sacri-
ficing the more important parts of the sculpture, hence
their omission here.

All interest is centred round the bull, Assyrians and
war-captives alike having but one work and that is
the transport of this awe-inspiring monster. In the
right-hand corner we see two carts, each being drawn
by two prisoners and containing ropes and timber.
The carts have two wheels, each wheel containing eight
spokes in contradistinction to the four spokes of the
early Babylonian wheels. The bull has been carefully laid on its side upon a sledge which is shaped
like a boat in the front. Both ends of the sledge
are pierced with round holes for the reception of the
ropes. The latter, tightly secured to the sledge and bull,
are about to be pulled by a number of prisoners who
succeed under the gentle stimulus of the taskmaster's
lash in gradually moving the colossal monster. Before
starting, however, it was seemingly necessary to give the
sledge some assistance by means of a huge lever, one end
of which is placed under the stern while to the other end
three ropes are attached, by means of which a number
of workmen are doing their utmost to move the lever
on its fulcrum. To gain a greater leverage one of the
workmen is engaged in inserting a wedge between the
upper surface of the fulcrum and the under side of the

lever, while the movement of the sledge is further facilitated by means of rollers which workmen are seen busily
putting in position. Upon the top of the recumbent bull
kneels the foreman engineer giving the signal for each
successive and united effort to the men on the towing-
ropes. The presence of three soldiers was apparently
necessary to enforce the admonitions of the foreman—

FIG. 31.—Sennacherib at Lachish. (After Layard.)

an early example of the invocation of the military to support civil authority. Below in the foreground, a number
of captives are seen carrying rollers to be set down as the
bull advances. They are accompanied by taskmasters who
appear to have been wholly devoid of any sense of mercy.

But the best known, because from certain points of
view the most interesting, bas-relief from Sennacherib's
palace at Kouyunjik is that in which Sennacherib is seen
receiving the submission of the conquered inhabitants of
Lachish (Tell el-Ḥesy) (cf. Fig. 31). The king is seated

on a throne of great magnificence, and his feet repose on a high footstool. The side of the throne is divided into three registers, each of which is occupied by a row of men with arms upstretched to support the bar above: the bars themselves are decorated with various geometrical devices, while the throne stands upon four large cone-shaped feet. The king's robes are as elaborate as his throne, both mantle and tunic being richly embroidered and fringed with tassels, while his head-gear consists in a kind of mitre, apparently the usual state head-gear of Assyrian monarchs. Behind him are two attendants, probably eunuchs, each holding a fly-flap in his right hand and a bandlet in his left; their dress consists in a long robe reaching down to the ankle and tied round the waist with a girdle, while a variegated sash passing from the left shoulder across the chest relieves the monotony of the comparatively inornate costume. Their hair is long, and the ends are curled as in the other figures here represented, but they are beardless and hatless. Behind these two attendants is the royal pavilion, the roof-canvas of which is apparently raised either for ventilation or to keep off the sun. The king with a bow in his left hand and an arrow in his right, is listening to his chief officers who are reporting the incidents of the siege of Lachish. The personage who leads the procession carries no arms, but has his head bared and is clad more sumptuously than the attendant officers, as befitteth the king's vizier; the warriors are armed with maces, short swords, bows and arrows, or spears as the case may be. At a respectful distance from the royal throne three representatives of the conquered inhabitants of the city are making their obeisance before the king, one of them literally grovelling on all fours. The prisoners have a thick, though not a long, crop of hair, while their beards are also thick and short, in contradistinction to those of the Assyrians. Their dress consists of a perfectly plain, short-sleeved tunic reaching from neck to ankle, while their feet are unshod. The dress of the Assyrian warriors will be considered in a subsequent chapter (Chap. XIII). The scene of this somewhat dramatic spectacle is outside the captured city, under the grateful shade of vines and fig-trees, while mountains covered with trees form a fitting background to the picture. The purport of the four-lined cuneiform inscription in front of the king is that Sennacherib, king of hosts, king of Assyria, sat upon his throne of state, and the spoil of the city of Lachish passed before him. But magnificent as is the throne upon which Sennacherib is here seated, it must have been far surpassed in splendour by his royal throne at Nineveh ; the latter was apparently made of rock crystal, some of the fragments of which are still preserved.

Sennacherib was succeeded after some intestine feuds by his son Esarhaddon ; Esarhaddon carried on the traditions of his predecessors in warring against Phœnicia, and reducing Babylonia, but the distinguishing feature of his reign was the occupation of Lower Egypt by the Assyrians in 672 B.c. Unfortunately we have very few sculptural monuments of this king, though it must not be assumed from this that he was a whit less proud of his feats than his father, but his reign has practically no interest for the student of art and affords us little material for the pursuit of our present subject. This remark, however, is very far from applying to Ashur-bani-pal, his all-glorious son, whose triumphs in the field of art were as great in their way as those achieved in the battle-field. Ashur-bani-pal came to the throne in 668 B.c. and ruled some forty-two years, during which he raised the power of Assyria to a point never reached before and never reached again. The more noteworthy events of Ashur-bani-pal's reign as well as the consequential effects of his taste for literature have been treated of elsewhere ; suffice it to say here that this outburst of military, intellectual and artistic activity was but the supreme effort of an empire whose strength was exhausted and whose vitality was impaired, and even before the death of Ashur-bani-pal the meteoric splendour of her glory had begun to pale. It was as it were the final sickness of an aged man who had weathered many storms and whose recuperative power had hitherto risen to every occasion, at last however the final crisis comes and all is over. But that golden era of Assyrian art, so brief and short-lived, has nevertheless been immortalized by the artists of that day in those stone slabs which now form one of the most precious possessions of the British Museum.

Ashur-bani-pal's exploits in the hunting field have been already referred to, and it is these that he chose to record pictorially upon his palace-walls rather than his victories on the field of battle, and it is to this choice that we owe those masterpieces of animal representation, which otherwise might never have been crystallized into concrete and permanent results.

A large number of these bas-reliefs are concerned with lion-hunting; from Pl. XVIII it would appear that lions sometimes suffered themselves to become domesticated; we here see a lion and lioness, the one standing, the other lying carelessly stretched at its ease upon the ground, in a kind of garden, the cultivated character of which is manifest from the presence of a vine. The lion stands before the crouching lioness with head and forepaws outstretched, in a manner well-illustrative of that dignity and majesty which is always and has always been associated with the king of animals. Unfortunately most of the head and the entire hindquarters of the lion are missing, but sufficient remains of the animal for us to imagine the rest without much risk of our imagination leading us astray.

But the animals which were the victims of the royal sport must clearly have been wild; sometimes they admitted of being hunted in their natural state, but in Ashur-bani-pal's time it was evidently necessary to capture them beforehand and keep them in cages till

PLATE XVIII

Photo. Mansell

British Museum

ASHUR-BANI-PAL'S HUNTING SCENES: LION AND LIONESS IN A PARK OR GARDEN

PLATE XIX

Photos. Mansell   *British Museum*

ASHUR-BANI-PAL'S HUNTING SCENES

required for the hunt. In Pl. XIX we see one such captive specimen emerging from his temporary prison at the instance of the attendant who has pulled up the wicker gate of the cage. The lion's satisfaction at his release is shown by the alacrity with which he sallies forth, little conscious of the doom in front of him. Though the end seems always to have been the same, the method by which the end was accomplished varied from time to time. Thus on one occasion the king is seen thrusting his long-shafted spear into the lion's back, himself securely mounted in his chariot ; at another time he is on foot, and is almost playfully stabbing the lion in the neck with his dagger, but the more usual way—no doubt, because the safest—of dispatching big game, and lions in particular, seems to have been by means of the bow and arrow which could be brought into play at a respectful distance. In Pl. XIX we see a number of lions thus transfixed; their various positions, some of which are sublimely natural, while others appear rather imaginative, all speak eloquently and in moving terms of that common tragedy to which all the animal world, whether human or bestial must some day become victims,—the tragedy of death. One lion is seen transfixed by four arrows, two of which are deeply lodged in the lion's neck, a third in the centre of the head, and the last in the middle of the back. The lion is prostrate, his four legs dragging helplessly behind and underneath his massive body, while his face bespeaks the death-agony in which he lies convulsed. Above, on the left, another animal has been incapacitated, if not mortally wounded, by two arrow wounds, one in the neck and the other in the back, while a little lower down to the right, a lioness smitten through the lungs has rolled over helplessly on her back. At the bottom of this unique scene we have another lion transfixed by some five arrows, most of which are lodged in or about the animal's head ; like the lioness he has sunk over on his back, his limbs being contorted almost beyond recognition. To the left we have the full hindquarters of a lion who is springing up in a frenzy of rage excited by an arrow-wound in the back. Last of all in the bottom left-hand corner another lion is seen in the act of expiring as the result of his wounds. But whatever end befell the unfortunate lion, he seems to have been attended with ceremonial rites at the last, his body was conveyed home by three or four male servants, and stretched upon the ground, after which the king himself pours a libation over the silent, motionless animal, whose grandeur in death is only surpassed by his energy in life (cf. Pl. XX).

The large majority of the visitors to the Assyrian Saloon in the British Museum, where these masterpieces of animal reproduction are arranged, have never witnessed a lion hunt in real life, but none can go away without having an ineffaceable impression left on his mind of the grimness of such a scene, of which the reality is here so graphically portrayed. Lion-hunting was doubtless the favourite sport of the Assyrian kings, but other game also engaged the royal patronage, notably deer, wild asses and bulls. Ashur-naṣir-pal has left us a sculpture in which he is represented hunting wild bulls from his chariot, and in Pl. XX we have a bas-relief from Ashur-bani-pal's palace on which a wild-ass hunt is seen in full progress. In the upper part of the scene a wild-ass lies helpless on his back, pierced by three arrows, while a fourth arrow is on the wing, though swiftly nearing its appointed goal. To the right we see another ass rushing away in hot haste before the double onslaught of dogs and arrows. To the left two dogs resembling mastiffs are busily engaged in checking the headlong course of a wild ass whose flight has already been retarded by the arrow which has pierced his forequarters. Below, a hound of the type already alluded to is in mad pursuit of a young foal. The foal is preceded

PLATE XX

ASHUR-BANI-PAL'S HUNTING SCENES : HUNTING WILD ASSES WITH DOGS

Photos. Mansell *British Museum*

ASHUR-BANI-PAL POURING OUT A LIBATION OVER DEAD LIONS

by a full-grown ass who is turning its head solicitously,
possibly in anxiety for its own safety, possibly for that of
the young foal behind. The manner in which this latter
action has been portrayed by the artist is surprising in its
fidelity to nature and its artistic merits. To enable the
reader to form a fair and correct estimate of the genius
of the Assyrians in the art of animal representation it
would be necessary to give reproductions of the whole
series of Ashur-bani-pal's hunting scenes, but it is hoped
that sufficient has here been shown to demonstrate their
extraordinary ability in this direction.

Not only however are we indebted to Ashur-bani-pal
for the animal masterpieces of Assyrian art, but also for
one of the few scenes which give us a glimpse into the
private and non-official life of the king (cf. Pl. XXI). The
king is reclining on a magnificently carved couch, while
his queen sits bolt upright on a chair immediately opposite; the chair is as elaborate in its way as the couch, as
is also the stool upon which her feet repose. In spite of
the tropical appearance of the garden in which the feast
is spread, the king is covered with a rug, while the queen
is clad in richly-woven robes which look anything but
cool. A table is set by the side of the couch and in front
of the queen's chair, upon which are laid the royal dain-
ties. Both their majesties are about to quaff the ambro-
sial nectar with which their low but capacious cups are
without doubt filled, but the scene of their banquet is in
itself an appetizer: the thick palm trees, the rich clusters
of grapes, and the hovering birds all adding a stimulus
to the royal digestive faculties. Behind the king stand
two attendants with fly-flappers, and another richly
carved table upon which the royal weapons are laid.
The queen is similarly protected by fly-flappers, behind the bearers of which are other servants laden with
oriental luxuries, while in the distance the musicians are
playing their voluptuous eastern melodies. The instruments are stringed, as are most of the musical instru-

ments portrayed on Babylonian and Assyrian bas-reliefs, though tambourines, double-pipes, cymbals, drums and trumpets were also apparently known.[1] In spite however of all these intoxicating influences, there remained one other item in the programme—an item which doubtless had the most stimulating effect of all upon the appetite of the great king, i.e. the head of Te-umman of Elam, which hangs from a tree in the king's immediate line of vision, and no doubt was a most gratifying spectacle to his majesty.

With Ashur-bani-pal Assyrian art as well as her literature reached its climax ; with him the limits of the empire were extended further than ever before ; but after his reign no slow decadence, but a swift collapse set in which was alike tragic in its significance and momentous in its consequences. It is however not altogether unfitting, either in the case of empires, or in that of individuals, that when the climax is reached, and the highest possibilities are realized, life should not be prolonged for retrogressive purposes, and Assyria was in a large degree saved from this misfortune. The memory of her greatness and of her wide influence was in no way marred by a long period of decline, her time was up and her end came, but the reason was to be found rather in those indomitable circumstances of fate and external environment than in a radical and internal demoralization. We have no reliefs of the Neo-Babylonian period worth recording, with the exception of the coloured clay reliefs which we shall consider in the chapter on painting.

SCULPTURE IN THE ROUND

For the study of early Sumerian sculpture in the round, we unfortunately have not much material at hand. As has been already stated, both the Babylonians and Assyrians excelled in bas-relief work rather than in full rounded sculpture, and what they excelled in, that

[1] Cf. Rawlinson, *Five Monarchies*, pp. 151–62.

PLATE XXI

ASHUR-BANI-PAL RECLINING AT MEAT

Photos. Mansell   *British Museum*

MUSICIANS AND ATTENDANTS

they practised most ; in spite of this fact however, both peoples were alive to the superiority of sculpture in the round, but the difficulties involved in producing work of this kind prevented such work being undertaken save for exceptional purposes, hence they never attained a very high degree of excellence in this department of art. Of the earlier Sumerian period we have hardly any complete statues, and the paucity of such makes those that have survived the more valuable. One of the most interesting of these is that of Esar king of Adab (Bismâya), which was discovered during the course of the American excavations on that site,[1] and is now preserved in the Imperial Ottoman Museum, Constantinople (cf. Fig. 32). It is made of marble and weighs two hundred pounds. In height it measures just under thirty-five inches, the circumference of the skirt being close upon thirty-two inches. The latter is heavily plaited and is a replica of the garment in which the Sumerians portrayed on the earliest monuments are always clad. The type of face in like

FIG. 32. (*A. J. S. L.*, XXI, pp. 59, ff.)

manner attests its great antiquity ; the bald head, the aquiline nose forming a straight line with the forehead, the triangular eye-sockets which were at one time inlaid with ivory, all being characteristic features of the most ancient Sumerian attempts at human portraiture. The king bears an inscription upon his right shoulder written in a very archaic and semi-pictorial script, from which we learn the name of the king, and also of the city over

[1] Cf. E. J. Banks, *Scientific American*, Aug. 19, 1905, p. 137 ; *American Journal of Semitic Languages*, XXI, p. 59.

which he ruled. It was discovered at a great depth below the surface of the mound, among the ruins of a temple constructed of the small plano-convex bricks character-istic of the pre-Ur-Ninâ buildings. A particularly in-teresting feature about this unique monument is that the arms are free from the body, whereas in nearly all Mesopotamian statues they are joined up to the sides. The hands are clasped in front as is the case in so many

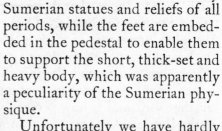

Sumerian statues and reliefs of all periods, while the feet are embed-ded in the pedestal to enable them to support the short, thick-set and heavy body, which was apparently a peculiarity of the Sumerian phy-sique.

Unfortunately we have hardly any complete figures of early Su-merian women, the little stone statuette in Fig. 33 gives us how-ever some idea of the appearance and dress of women in early Baby-lonia. Her features conform to the usual Sumerian type, while her long hair is tied with a fillet which

FIG. 33. (*Déc. en Chald.*, Pl. I, *ter.* No. 3.) surrounds her head and gathers up her flowing tresses at the back.

But the three archaic stone heads (cf. Pl. XXII) which were unearthed at Tellô enable us to form a somewhat more complete estimate of the artistic ability of the sculptors of that age in regard to the portrayal of the human face and head. The head on the right closely resembles the central one, both of which exhibit a more advanced style of art than that exhibited in the head on the left, which is, however, the most interesting of the three. It was discovered on the other side of the Shatt-el-Hai, the canal which connects the Tigris with the Euphrates; unlike the others, the aquiline nose is per-

PLATE XXII

Photo. Mansell   *British Museum*

LIMESTONE FIGURE OF AN EARLY SUMERIAN

Musée du Louvre : Déc. en Chald. Pl. 6, 1-3

ARCHAIC LIMESTONE HEADS

fectly preserved, the eyes are as usual large and shaped like almonds, and were doubtless at one time inlaid with shell and coloured, while the lips betray a suppressed smile ; the type of face is exactly the same as that seen on the Vulture Stele, though the details are of course more precise, as might be expected from a work in the round.

In Fig. 34, A, we have an alabaster head of an early

FIG. 34.—A. (Louvre, Cat., p. 217 ; *Déc. en Chald.*, Pl. 6, Fig. 3.)
  B. (*Comptes Rendus*, 1907, p. 398; *Délég. en Perse Mém.*, X, Pl. 1.)
  C. (Louvre, Cat., p. 227 ; *Déc. en Chald.*, Pl. 8 (bis), 4.)

Sumerian woman ; the face belongs to the same type as that to which the male heads in Pl. XXII conform. The ears, so prominent in the case of the clean-shaven male heads, are here entirely concealed by the tresses of hair which hang in thick horizontally streaked lines about her forehead, head and neck. The hair is kept in its place by means of a fillet fastened at the back. The large eye-holes must have at one time been inlaid, probably with lapis lazuli in the case of a woman as here. The eye-brows are sculptures in relief, and not incised as is the case in other early Sumerian sculptures.

Q

Other early specimens of Babylonian sculpture are to be found in the various statues of Manishtusu discovered during the course of the excavations carried on by the French Mission to Susa, one of which is reproduced in Fig. 34, B. Manishtusu was a Semitic king of Kish and probably reigned about 2700 B.C.; the statue here shown is consequently one of the earliest examples of Semitic sculpture in the round as yet known, and according to De Morgan[1] is the most ancient work of art as yet discovered on the old Persian sites. Even at this early date we see traces of that Semitic conventionalism so prevalent in the later Assyrian era. The square face, the large eyes, the coiffure and the long symmetrically arranged beard here seen, all being prominent features in Assyrian representations of kings and potentates. The pupils of the eyes were black and were fixed in their sockets by means of bitumen, as was frequently the case in these early sculptures. The statue is made of alabaster, and the inscription on the back is written in archaic line characters.

This age was followed by a period during which the sculptor's art gradually made itself master of the means at its disposal. This transition period is well illustrated by an alabaster statuette of a seated woman reproduced in Fig. 34, C. The advance which the configuration of her face shows on the archaic head in Fig. 34, A, is at once obvious : the stereotyped eyes have become less exaggerated and more natural, the lips are more womanly, the nose less obtrusive. Her long hair hangs naturally and loosely down her back, while a thick fillet encircles her head. Her long robe covers the whole of her body from neck to ankle, and she holds in her hands a round-shaped vase which probably contains a libation for the gods. This little statuette is just over seven inches high.

But it was not till the middle of the third millennium B.C. i.e. the age of Gudea, patesi of Lagash, that sculpture

[1] *Comptes rendus,* 1907, p. 399.

in the round assumed a prominent part in the artistic life of the people, and it was not till then that the sculptor seems to have regularly aspired to reproducing human figures at quasi-life size, fashioning them at the same time out of the hardest volcanic rocks. In Pl. XXIII, A, B we have reproductions of two of the decapitated statues found by De Sarzec at Tellô. Eight of these statues, some of which are in a standing posture, while others are seated, bear inscriptions of Gudea, patesi of Lagash ; one of the remaining two being inscribed with the name of his predecessor, Ur-Bau. The majority of these statues are under life-size, but the dimensions of one of them at least considerably exceed those of an ordinary man. The statue here represented (Pl. XXIII, A) is the most artistically conceived of the series; it possesses both grace and force, and shows very little trace of the conventionalism so noticeable in later Assyrian sculptures, the feet being the only inanimate and truly conventional part of the production. The arms are strong and sinewy, but the muscles are perfectly naturally executed, and contrast very favourably with the exaggerated muscles of the royal statues of Assyria. The hands are folded in token of submission to the goddess Nin-harsag, to whom this statue was seemingly dedicated. Among the epithets applied to this goddess here, are " Lady of the Mountains," "protectress of the town and mother of its inhabitants," and lastly, " mother of the gods." This statue is made of green diorite and is just over four feet high.

In Pl. XXIII, B we have another statue of Gudea, this time seated. The chief peculiarity about this and its companion statue, both of which are in the Louvre, lies in the flat tablet which each of them carries on their knees. On one of these tablets a regular plan of Gudea's buildings has been engraved, showing various doors, crenelated towers, and so forth, together with the carpenter's rule and stylus, which are similarly engraved on the knee-tablet of the statue reproduced here.

The most striking feature in the sculpture itself is the boldness with which the nude limbs are carved, and the nervous vitality with which they abound. This is especially noticeable in the treatment of the right arm and shoulder, which the arrangement of the mantle leaves exposed. The cartouche on the shoulder contains the name and titles of Gudea. The lengthy inscription below records that this statue has been dedicated to the goddess Gatumdug, who is styled " the mother of Shir-purla " (=Lagash), it then treats of the various rites and ceremonies with which the building of the temple of this goddess was accompanied. This statue, like the standing one in Pl. XXIII A, is made of diorite. Several of the heads belonging to these statues have been brought to light, one of which is seen in Pl. XXIII, C. The head which is decked with a variegated turban is again remarkable for its strength and the boldness with which it is executed ; the eyes are large and wide open, a noticeable characteristic in all Mesopotamian art, whether early or late; the eyebrows are heavy, and the chin firm, while the jaws are thick-set and make the general contour of the face square. The absence of due proportion in all these early Babylonian sculptures is at once manifest : they one and all have a more or less squat appearance, the breadth being always too great proportionally for the height, while the head is too large for the body and the latter is too thin from back to front. But when all the failings incidental to the products of an inexperienced art are duly taken into consideration, there is a certain fidelity to nature, and consequently a degree of life observable in the crudest of these early Babylonian sculptures which at once raises them to a higher level than the Assyrian statues to which they unconsciously gave birth. The accentuation of the strong lines and curves of the earlier sculptures in the later products of Assyrian times, has merely led to exaggeration, and the effect is inevitably stereotyped and unnatural.

PLATE XXIII

A, B. DIORITE STATUES OF GUDEA, PATESI OF LAGASH
C. DIORITE HEAD OF GUDEA
D. UPPER PART OF A DIORITE STATUETTE OF A WOMAN
   (GUDEA PERIOD)

In Pl. XXIII, D, however, we have the upper part of a diorite figure of a woman belonging to about the same period as Gudea, which has to a great extent lost the heavy and massive appearance so noticeable in the statues of the patesi, and possesses both grace and beauty. The dress will be considered in a subsequent chapter, and it will be sufficient to here call attention to the singularly natural manner in which the folds of the garment are represented. During the interval between the epoch associated with the name of Gudea and that rendered illustrious by Ashur-naṣir-pal and the Assyrian kings, the practice of sculpturing in the round appears to have fallen largely into desuetude, if we may judge from the extreme paucity of the material that has come down to us, and it is not till the time of the Assyrian Empire that we are able again to make a detailed study of the sculptor's art in Mesopotamia.

One of the earliest examples of Assyrian sculpture in the round is reproduced in Pl. XXIV, B. It is a torso of a female figure, who bears upon her back an inscription of Ashur-bel-kala, king of Assyria, whose reign may be assigned to the first half of the eleventh century B.C. It was discovered at Kouyunjik, and is now in the British Museum. The size is somewhat below that of life ; but in spite of the fact that the proportions are bad, the body between the legs and arms being too short, this sculpture, when compared with the generality of Assyrian attempts to reproduce human beings, is at once striking for the natural manner in which the artist's conception of feminine beauty is realized, and as such is entirely unique in the realm of Assyrian sculpture.

The remains of another very early Assyrian sculpture[1] in the round were discovered in the course of the German excavations at Ashur. Unfortunately the head, hands and feet of this statue are missing, but the small part of the head which is preserved, though having an

[1] Cf. *Mitteilungen*, No. 29.

abundance of hair shows no trace of the elaborate curls of later days, the beard being represented by a series of twelve or more corrugated strands, thereby recalling the Babylonian statues of the Khammurabi period. The clothing consists of a close-fitting garment made of a simple fine-textured material, and is decorated with a fringe.

Of Assyrian royal statues that of Ashur-naṣir-pal (cf. Pl. XXIV, C) is the best preserved and the most successful. It is made of hard limestone, and measures three feet four inches in height ; it was found in a broken condition along with the limestone pedestal upon which it once stood, and it now stands upon the same original pedestal in the Nimrûd Gallery of the British Museum. The total height of the statue with the pedestal is five feet eleven and a half inches. Fortunately none of the fragments of the figure were missing, and consequently it was possible to restore the statue so perfectly as to render it one of the finest Assyrian statues in existence. The king stands there, the very incarnation of impassive dignity and imperturbable majesty, and it is strange how impressive the motionless can at times be. It would perhaps be hardly true to employ such words as " life " or " animation " in attempting to describe this sculpture, but it possesses something even higher than external vigour and vitality, it has a force, an indescribable " reserve of strength," which the absence of anything like aggressive activity only serves to enhance. The king is clad in long and elaborately made robes which reach down to his toes. The beard and hair, both of which are rich and profuse, are curled with much care and precision. The king holds in his right hand a sickle-shaped object, which is presumably meant to be a sceptre, while in his left he holds a mace with a tassel at the lower end. His left arm is concealed by the fold of his outer mantle, but the right is bare with the exception of a wrist-bracelet. The type of face bears all the acknowledged

PLATE XXIV

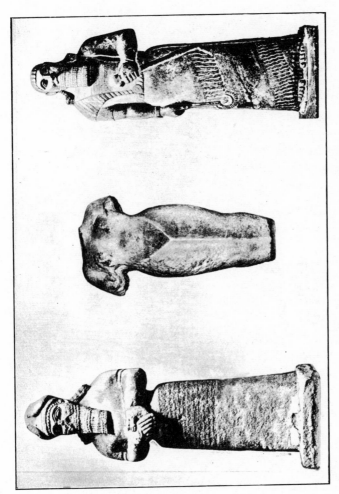

STATUE OF NEBO TORSO OF A WOMAN STATUE OF ASHUR-NASIR-PAL.

(From Dieulafoy, " L'Art Antique de la Perse," Vol. 3. Pl. 12)

Assyrian characteristics; large, wide-open eyes, a curved nose, and the wealth of hair to which we have just referred. The proportions are fairly accurate, though the depth or thickness of the body from back to front is as

FIG. 35.—Shalmaneser II. (British Museum.)

usual, not sufficiently great. The king has an inscription carved upon his breast, the text of which, after having given the name and genealogy of Ashur-naṣir-pal, goes on to recount the triumphant achievements of the king in the extension of his dominion over the whole country between the river Tigris and Lebanon, and concludes by stating that he has made all the countries from the rising of the sun to the setting of the sun to submit to his feet.

Ashur-naṣir-pal's son and successor, Shalmaneser II, has bequeathed to us one of the comparatively few examples of an Assyrian seated figure sculptured in the round (cf. Fig. 35). The decapitated figure, which is a representation of Shalmaneser II himself, is made of black basalt, and it was discovered at Ḳalat Sherḳat (Ashur). The inscription on the throne, which is partially effaced, gives the name and titles of the king, enumerates his various conquests in Babylonia, and also contains an allusion to the statue itself. It is interesting to compare this figure with the seated and likewise decapitated figures of Gudea a millennium or so earlier (cf. Pl. XXIII, B). Both are made of a hard volcanic stone, and the garment in which each of these Eastern rulers is clad reaches down to the ankles, though the end of Shalmaneser's skirt is however decorated with a fringe, while Gudea's is quite plain. Both figures are seated on a simple kind of throne such as is very frequently encountered on cylinder-seals, but there are certain striking points of difference between the two statues. The Sumerian Gudea has no beard, while the Semitic king of Assyria has a long square beard, and Gudea's arms are moreover clasped in a reverential attitude across his breast, while Shalmaneser's arms are apparently resting easily upon his lap. The feet which in each case rest upon a plinth, are well portrayed in both figures, though what advantage there is is clearly on the side of the earlier Babylonian sculpture.

Another good example of Mesopotamian sculpture in the round at about this time is afforded by the two statues of the god Nebo which were excavated by Rassam in the ruined temple of Adar at Nimrûd, one of which is reproduced in Plate XXIV, A. They were made by a certain governor of the city of Calah (Nimrûd), and were dedicated to the god in the hope of thereby ensuring length of days to Adad-nirari III, king of Assyria from 812–783 B.C., the queen Sammuramat, and incidentally to himself also. The mention of Sammuramat is interesting as she is supposed to be the original of the Semiramis of later Greek and Roman writers. The god is apparelled in a simple robe confined at the waist, the arms being left uncovered and free. He wears both a moustache and a beard, the latter being curled and waved, as is also the long hair of his head. The horned cap of the gods furnishes his natural head-gear, and his wrists are encircled with the rosette-patterned bracelets in which both kings and gods seem to have delighted, while his hands are clasped upon his breast. The inscription chiselled all round the lower part of his robe, is chiefly concerned with a rehearsal of all the wonderful attributes and gracious deeds of Nebo, and ends with an exhortation to all future generations to put their trust in Nebo, and not in any other god.

But neither the Babylonian nor the Assyrian sculptors confined their attention to human beings, any more than did the bas-relief artists. They also attempted the reproduction of animals, mythical or real as the case may be, with varying degrees of success. The animal that seems to have more or less monopolized their artistic capacity in this direction was the lion. We have already seen the important part played by the lion in the heraldic arms of Lagash, in the coloured decoration of walls, and in the bas-reliefs which adorned the interiors of Assyrian palaces, as well as in the decoration of various objects such as mace-heads and stone bowls, and we are accordingly not surprised to find examples of the lion realized in hard stone and worked in the round. The early specimens are for the most part small, and as a rule only the heads are preserved. The dates of most of these heads are uncertain as there is generally no inscription, but fortunately there are some exceptions. Like the majority of the earlier specimens of Sumerian art, they nearly all come from Tellô and were excavated by M. De Sarzec. One of the best preserved is reproduced in Fig. 36, A. Only one side of the lion's head has survived, but it is sufficient to demonstrate the success with which the Sumerian sculptor treated his sub-

FIG. 36.—A (*Déc. en Chald.*, Plate 24, 1); B, C (after Heuzey).

ject. The arrogance and impassive majesty of the lion are here realized more impressively than is the case with the lions of many a European artist ; this notwithstanding, the spirit of conventionalism has already crept in as a thief, though it has as yet only made its presence felt in the hem of the garment so to speak. The head itself is entirely unmarred by any deteriorating influence, but the treatment of the mane is in a measure the victim of the force of habit, which, in spite of the common saying that it is " second nature," is as a matter of fact as unnatural as it can be in its effect upon art. It is formed somewhat after the pattern of the " *kaunakes* " material used in the manufacture of early Sumerian garments.

The remains of another stone lion bearing an inscription of Gudea, from which we gather that the lion in question formed part of the decoration of the door through which access was gained to the sanctuary of the goddess Gatumdug were recovered from the same site. This lion [1] shows still further the subtle influence of conventionalism in the manner in which the hair on the lower part of the belly is portrayed, a series of triangles, such as is often seen in the figures of lions on the cylinder-seals, representing a fringe of long hair. Many of the lion-heads discovered at Tellô were provided with holes for the insertion of a peg, and probably served for lower supports of the back of thrones. One of these lion-heads is of especial interest as it bears the name of Ur-Ninâ, the founder of the first dynasty of Lagash,[2] while a second mentions *Magan*, the uncertain district whence the Babylonians procured their stone. Another early animal sculpture of some considerable interest was discovered by Captain Cros at Tellô in 1904 (cf. Fig. 36, B). It represents a recumbent dog—apparently of the mastiff breed, and identical in species with those figured on Ashur-bani-pal's bas-reliefs : the length of the dog is only about four inches, its height just under three and a half inches, and it is two inches thick, but the interest attaching to it lies in the fact that it bears an inscription of one Sumu-la-ilu, a king of Ur who probably reigned towards the close of the third millennium B.c., but of whom little else is known, and whose name had not even been heard of before the discovery of this little black stone dog. The material used for this sculpture is steatite, and the dog's back is pierced with a hole which served as a stand for a cylindrical steatite vase.

[1] Cf. *Découvertes*, Pl. 24, Fig. 2.
[2] *Revue Archéologique*, 189 ı, I, 108.

The hole and the vase are apparently of later date than the dog itself.[1]

Another very interesting example of early Babylonian sculpture in the round is that of a small human-headed bull[2] (cf. Fig. 36, C) now preserved in the Louvre. It is, as it were, the archetype or prototype of those winged human-headed bulls and lions placed at the entrances of palaces to guard against maleficent demons. The pose of the bull is one that is entirely natural, and recalls the semi-recumbent calves on Entemena's silver vase (cf. Figure 45), but the body of the animal lacks the intense realism of the earlier animal representations. He wears a long vertically streaked beard, which is flanked on either side by plaits of hair, and his head is surmounted by a cap with four pairs of horns.

In the centre of his back there is a hole which doubtless once served as a socket for some votive object or figure as seems so frequently to have been the case ; but the particular interest of this little sculpture lies in the shell inlay work on the back. The figure itself is made of black steatite, the inlay work consisting of yellow shell, and we have as a result a somewhat grotesquely marked bull. Sometimes animals were carved in wood, a good example of which is the little wooden lion in the Louvre, but the remains of Babylonian or Assyrian wood-carving are far too scanty to enable us to undertake a study of their work in this direction.

In later times sculpture in the round, which had never been popular with the artists of Mesopotamia owing to the obvious difficulty of procuring the necessary material in the first instance, and in the second to the nature of the work itself and the obstacles which had to be surmounted in the realization of that work, went almost entirely out of fashion. There remain, however,

---

[1] Cf. Heuzey, in *Mon. Mem. Acad. Insc. Fondation Piot*, XII, pp. 19–28, and *C. R. Acad. Inser.*, 1905, p. 75.

[2] Cf. *Mon. Piot.*, t. VII, Pl. 1, Fig. 1, and *Louvre Cat.*, p. 324.

PLATE XXV

British Museum

WINGED MAN-HEADED BULL

Photos, Mansell

WINGED MAN-HEADED LION

a few examples of sculptured animals to be considered, among the first and foremost of which are those colossal human-headed winged-bulls and lions which guarded the entrances of the palaces of Ashur-nasir-pal and Sargon (cf. Pl. XXV). They are, it is true, neither bas-reliefs nor round sculptures, but a combination of the two, whereby the artist has endeavoured to create a perfectly natural and complete effect from every point of vision, and his efforts have met with the success which they deserved. The means he has employed to produce this satisfactory result is the provision of each of these extraordinary monsters with a fifth leg, though all these winged monsters were not so provided, the principal exceptions being the four-legged bulls in Sennacherib's palace at Kouyunjik. The difficulty with which the artist found himself encountered, and which was obviated by the above-mentioned device, lay in the inability of four legs of natural proportions to support a stone body of the gigantic size demanded by the architectural requirements for which these creatures were destined to be used. In short, a pure round sculpture of a lion or bull of the portentous size desired was a literal impossibility, and relief accordingly had to come into play, it being merely a question of how far the relief should be low or high, and the higher it was the more it of course approximated to the round, and realized what was presumably the artist's real intention. The creation of a satisfactory front view of these animals involved no difficulty, for the visibility of the two front legs was all that was necessary, and the drawback of the space between the legs being occupied with the solid mass of stone which supported the animal and out of which it was sculptured in high relief, was comparatively slight and negligible. But the satisfactory portrayal of the animal from the side aspect was fraught with much greater difficulty. Normally the two near legs of a quadruped viewed from the side, by no means exclude the two legs on the off-side from one's vision. The artist was clearly conscious of the difficulty which here confronted him and he has devised an ingenious means, indeed the only means under the circumstances for surmounting this inherent difficulty. He has provided the lion or the bull, as the case may be, with a fifth leg with the satisfactory result that viewed from either standpoint the animal's action or inaction is conceived in a perfectly natural fashion. From the front the winged monster is seen in a stationary attitude, his two fore legs firmly planted together on the ground, while from the side, on the other hand, the animal is walking along in an entirely normal and lifelike manner. These winged monsters were placed on either side of the portals of the king's palace and they helped to support the palace walls. But the object which they were supposed to serve, and the duties which they were expected to perform, were not of the purely architectural or even of the decorative order, their vocation, though embracing all these minor functions, involved the fulfilment of yet higher obligations, for they were destined to ward off the attacks of malicious spirits from the nether world. Esarhaddon, king of Assyria from 681–668 B.C. specifically states for what purpose these " shedi " or " lamassi "—the Assyrian names for these semi-mythical monsters—were created and made, for example, in one passage—to quote the translation given by Perrot and Chipiez (p. 266)—Esarhaddon says that " the *shedi* and *lamassi* are propitious, are the guardians of my royal promenade and the rejoicers of my heart, may they ever watch over the palace and never quit its walls," and again in another passage he says, " I caused doors to be made in cypress, which has a good smell, and I had them adorned with gold and silver and fixed in the doorways. Right and left of these doorways I caused *shedi* and *lamassi* of stone to be set up, they are placed there to repulse the wicked." The front parts of these monsters always projected beyond the general

PLATE XXVI

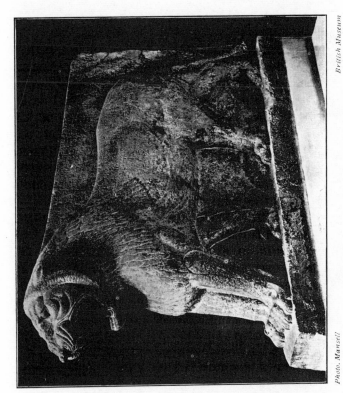

STONE LION OF ASHUR-NAṢIR-PAL

line of the wall, the human head and the chest at all events being outside the arch which these animals supported.

Sometimes the winged human-headed monster is flanked by a mythical creature with wings, holding a basket in his left hand, and a cone in his right (cf. Pl. XXV), at other times he stands in isolated glory alone. The head is of the familiar type to which one-half of the Assyrian representations of men so rigidly conform, the type characterized by a beard, the other type being beardless : all the royalty and nobility seem to have worn beards, and, according to the Assyrian sculptors, to have had precisely the same features, the numerous beardless figures portrayed on the bas-reliefs representing the humbler classes, and no doubt in some instances eunuchs. The head of this winged colossus is surmounted by a lofty head-dress richly decorated with rosettes, and furnished with two pairs of horns, the ever-present mark of sacro-sanctity. The hair and beard are profuse in their luxuriance, and elaborate in their dressing, while the tail is treated with the like punctilious care. Two enormous wings cover the back, extending their overshadowing protection some way beyond it. The relief in which the body and specifically the legs are raised is very high, and they stand out almost in the round. Many of these gigantic stone animals have been found at Nimrûd, Khorsabad, the capital of Sargon, and Nineveh.

But although the Assyrians show a marked predilection for mythical monsters in their large sculptural achievements in the round or semi-round, they showed themselves capable of conceiving and admirably realizing animals of the normal order ; one of the best examples of an Assyrian carved animal is the colossal lion of Ashur-nasir-pal (cf. Pl. XXVI), which is now in the British Museum and once formed part of an entrance to a building. This lion is about eight feet high and thirteen feet long, and bears an inscription like many of the winged human-headed bulls and lions. The lion also has five legs like so many of the latter. The head is carved with great boldness and vigour, although it is a little conventional. The jaws are extended, the upper lip and nostrils being drawn up, and even an unimaginative person may well fancy he can hear a deep roar proceeding from that fierce, wide-opened mouth. His neck is covered with a thick mane and ruffles of stiff hair. To obtain the best view of the sculpture, the view, that is to say, in which the spectator will accord the full measure, or even an over-measure, of justice to the skill of the artist, one must make one's point of observation on the side. The front aspect is disappointing, as the lion is too thin for its length and height, and is consequently deficient not only in artistic merit, but also in the dignified majesty of which he has ever been the symbolic incarnation. But in spite of these obvious drawbacks, the work as a whole compels admiration and inevitably arrests the attention, for it possesses the " one thing needful "—life. A comparison between the lion's head, and that of any of the winged human-headed monsters, at once demonstrates the point to which allusion has so frequently been made, the genius which the Assyrians at all times and all periods show in the delineation of animals, and the contrasting laboriousness with which all their representations of human faces are invariably marked. But there is at least one general remark which may fairly be made of Assyrian sculpture, a remark applicable both to human as well as animal sculptures, and that is that whether the subject be natural or mythical, human or bestial, the artist's product is never without force and never lacks impressiveness, a quality which in our own day is generally made conspicuous by its absence. Other interesting animal-sculptures have been found in Lower Mesopotamia, the most famous of which is the immense black basalt lion on the Ḳasr mound at Babylon (cf. Pl. XXVII).

PLATE XXVII

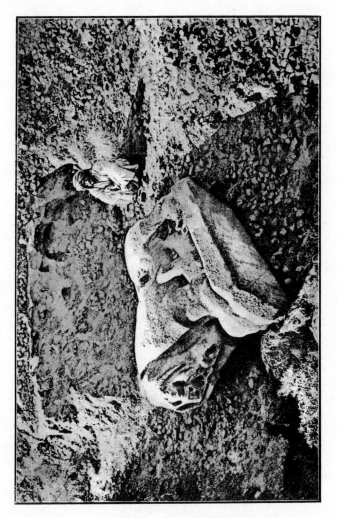

THE KASR LION

(From Dieulafoy, "L'Art Antique de la Perse," Vol 3. Pl. 13)

It consists of a lion towering over a nude human being lying on the ground, the whole piece being made of basalt. The remains of another stone lion of large proportions were discovered in the course of the recent German excavations at Babylon.; thirty fragments of the dolerite of which it was composed have been recovered including a portion of one of the claws, which measures over three inches in length, and proves that the lion must have been of abnormal size, while its general form and appearance would seem to indicate a great age.

It is indeed well for us that the æsthetic genius of the Babylonians and Assyrians should have found expression in durable stone rather than in some other more perishable material; the difficulties involved in sculpture are admittedly sufficiently great, and we owe a debt of gratitude to the perseverance and determination of those ancient peoples, which led them to conquer and mould for the ultimatization of their ideas, a material which a less determined and a less persevering nation might well have shrunk from attacking.

R

CHAPTER VII—METALLURGY

I N the art of working metals the Babylonians showed
no small degree of proficiency : evidence has already
been given of the way in which metal was made to contribute her share to the perfected work of the architect,
as also of its employment as a material whereon the
scribe might engrave his comparatively imperishable
memorials, but the part which it played in the history
of the country's art, as well as in the growth of her civilization, remains to be considered. The metals which appear to have been most in use among the dwellers in
Mesopotamia are copper and bronze. As in every other
country, before metal became known and utilized in the
Euphrates valley, stone was employed as the material for
making knives, axes, and implements of every kind.
Various flints were found by Taylor at Abû Shahrein
(Eridu).[1] At Fâra (Shuruppak) also, numerous flint
knives and saws, together with some hatchets and tools
made of the same material, were discovered by the German excavators, and tools made of bone were further
found on the same site. But the copper age commenced at a very early period in the history of Babylonian civilization, at a time previous to the appearance
of cuneiform, and while even the earlier picture-signs
were still untrammelled by the stereotyped formalism of
later days, copper had already been adapted to the needs
and requirements of humanity.[2]

At Ur (Muḳeyyer) Taylor discovered a large copper spear-head and two arrow-heads made of the same

---

[1] Cf. *Journal of the Royal Asiatic Society*, XV, p. 410.
[2] Cf. Sayce, *Archæology of the Cuneiform Inscriptions*, p. 58.

metal, while in the early strata at Tellô, M. De Sarzec discovered a copper blade some thirty-one and a half inches in length, and belonging to a votive-lance ; unfortunately the name of the king by whom it was dedicated is lost owing to the oxydization of the metal, but the title "King of Kish" is still clearly legible, Kish being one of the most ancient sites of Euphratean civilization (cf. Fig. 37, A). The tang of the blade is pierced with four holes, and one of the flat surfaces of the blade itself is engraved with the figure of a lion, crude indeed, but spirited. This unique object was found at a great depth, and only six inches above the stratum in which the

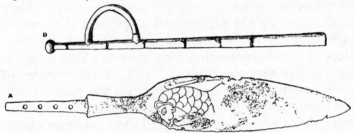

FIG. 37.—A (Cat., p. 367 ; *Déc. en Chald.*, Pl. 5 tert. Musée du Louvre.)
B (Heuzey, *Une Villa Royale*, Fig. 19.)

architectural remains of Ur-Ninâ were buried. Not far distant, De Sarzec discovered an immense hollow pipe of beaten copper (cf. Fig. 37, B) over ten feet long and having a diameter of four inches ; a number of copper nails by means of which this long tube was fastened to a wooden pole being also found. The pipe itself tapers upwards and the top of it is crowned with a hollow ball of hardened bitumen, a little below which there is a large semicircular handle, or what purports to be a handle, consisting in a hollow tube and likewise made of copper. The use to which this strange implement was put is unknown, but it is exactly reproduced on some of the early cylinder-seals as well as on the well-known vase of Gudea. Various suggestions have been made as to the purpose which it served ; one theory is that it is a chariot pole, another that it is a part of a standard, but the former is ruled out of court by the position which it occupies on the seals and on the aforementioned vase. The latter, however, may be near the truth.

Among the earliest specimens of Babylonian metallurgy may be mentioned a number of very small copper representations of animals in a crouching attitude, and all apparently belonging to the domestic order, though in some cases they are so covered with vert-de-gris that it is difficult to determine with precision what animals they are intended to represent. They are probably to be regarded as sacrificial offerings to the gods, being in fact economical substitutes for actual victims. They were found by De Sarzec in the lowest and therefore earliest strata of the ruined mounds of Tellô. Another class of metal objects to which we must also assign a date earlier than the time of Ur-Ninâ, the founder of the first dynasty of Lagash, comprises a number of copper statuettes, all much the same in shape, contour and style, though not in size. They all show a woman's bust, her hands clasped across her chest, and her hair hanging about her neck like a heavy wig, while the waviness of the hair is indicated by strongly-marked horizontal lines (cf. Figure 38, C). The style at once recalls the figures on the crude bas-reliefs belonging to the same period. A further peculiarity of these little figures is the manner in which they all terminate in the point of a nail, by means of which they were destined to be fixed in the ground with a view to deterring the advance of demons from the nether world.

So too Ur-Ninâ employed copper extensively as the material for his votive statuettes. A number of these statuettes were found at Tellô by De Sarzec; they all exhibit much the same characteristics as the earlier figures referred to above, and represent a woman whose hands are clasped across her breast, and whose hair hangs down her back in strongly marked perpendicular streaks,

while the body similarly finds its termination in a nail-point destined to be stuck in the ground (cf. Fig. 38, A).
But the chief pointwhich distinguishes Ur-Ninâ's statuettes from those belonging to the earlier period lies in the additional rôle which they were expected to play; not only were they protective amulets, but they were also required to carry stone tablets on their heads. To enable

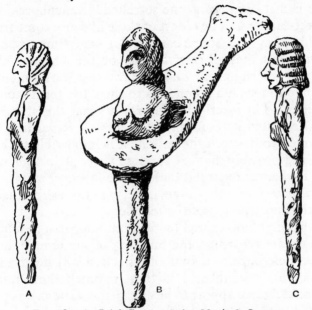

FIG. 38.—A, C (cf. Cat., p. 295).   Musée du Louvre.
B (cf. *Déc. en Chald.*, Pl. 2 tert., No. 3).

them to bear their burden the more easily, they were fixed into a kind of flat ring, the end of which was made to resemble the tail of a bird, which thus assisted the head in its otherwise arduous task (cf. Fig. 38, B). Five of these little figures still carried on their heads a thick tablet of greyish stone, convex on the uppermost side, like the bricks of this same king. They were generally found buried in hollows about twenty-eight inches in breadth, length, and height, and walled in with bricks and bitumen. Later on in the dynasty the practice of providing these statuettes with bird-tailed rings to assist in supporting the inscribed stone tablet appears to have fallen into disuse ; at all events the statuettes of Entemena, the fourth successor of Ur-Ninâ, show no such rings ; the alabaster tablets are simply bored with holes, into which the head of the statuette was firmly inserted.

Another class of copper statuettes of somewhat later date is that comprising the so-called " Kanephores " or basket-carriers. The oldest of these likewise come from Tellô: they are sometimes male, sometimes female figures, but they all carry baskets on their heads. One of them is seen in Fig. 39, B. In this case the garment is arranged in such a manner as to show the formation of the legs. The inscription informs us that this statuette was dedicated by Gudea to Nin-girsu. Regarding the assumed contents of the baskets it is impossible to dogmatize : possibly they are supposed to contain offerings, but De Sarzec regarded these figures as representations of the patesi himself, conveying clay in the sacred basket for the construction of the temple.

The directions issued by the god Nin-girsu to Gudea in a dream regarding the building of his temple, have direct reference to a symbolical action which certainly has a close resemblance to that in which ·these Kanephorous figures appear to be engaged. Gudea was presented with a sacred brick on a cushion, which, after the performance of various rites and ceremonies, he placed upon his head and carried to the temple—an outward and visible sign of his obedience to the divine will and of his determination to restore the time-honoured fane of his god. But whatever the correct interpretation of these Kanephorous figures be, they certainly recall the task in which Ur-Ninâ is engaged on the famous bas-relief in which he is portrayed surrounded by his family and the court (cf. Fig. 26).

Another of the same class of figures and also reproduced in Heuzey and De Sarsec's monumental work, bears an inscription of Dungi, king of Ur (*circ.* 2500 B.C.), but the lower limbs instead of being modelled out, are in the form of a cone ; the other statuette illustrated on the same plate[1] is on the contrary very carefully

FIG. 39.—A, B, C (cf. Cat., pp. 315, 307, 301 ; Nos. 164, 158, 146).
Musée du Louvre.

modelled, and is clad in a short garment reaching to the knees, but unfortunately bears no inscription.

Some centuries later the Elamite conquerors, Kudur-Mabug and his son Rîm-Sin, who established their supremacy over the whole of Sumer and Akkad and

[1] Cf. *Découvertes*, Pl. 28, Figs. 1 and 2.

maintained their position till Khammurabi, the then king of Babylon, defeated Rîm-Sin in his thirty-first year, caused their names to be inscribed on similar statuettes (cf. Fig. 39, A).

The figure here reproduced is that of a woman ; her garment, which is of the nature of a skirt, allows us no view of the feet, and itself tapers downwards and recalls the earlier nail-pointed statuettes. The nudity of the bust, and the absence of hair on the head, are indications that the woman in question is a slave, and her vocation was probably to assist in the building of the temples of the gods. In style this figure is more boldly executed than the earlier statuette of Gudea seen in Fig. 39, B. It bears an inscription in which mention is made of Kudur-Mabug and his son Rîm-Sin.

Sometimes male Kanephores occur, a good example of which is preserved in the British Museum ; it came from Tellô like so many of these early works of art. Another excellent specimen was presented some few years ago to the Berlin Museum ; it is rather more than ten inches in height, and bears a very clearly written Sumerian inscription ; the names of Kudur-Mabug and Rîm-Sin occur, and the statuette was dedicated "for the preservation of life," as was always the case with these votive-figures.

Another interesting class of copper figures was further discovered by De Sarsec at Tellô : it consisted in a number of small statuettes most of which were dedicated by the patesi Gudea ; each is in a kneeling posture and holds a cone between his hands, while the head-dress consists in the horned cap characteristic of all Mesopotamian deities, whether early or late. These little figures are about eight or nine inches high. The cones are inscribed with a votive inscription, and the cones themselves must probably be regarded as religious symbols. Cones made of clay or stone belonging to this period are common enough, their occurrence however in copper and in immediate contact with the statue of a human being is very rare. A plain long copper cone measuring 1 foot 1½ inches in length, and bearing an archaic inscription, is now preserved in the British Museum, this is however an exception, metal cones being, on their rare occurrence in Babylonian art, in nearly all cases associated with human or quasi-divine figures.

One of the best and also earliest examples of these copper cone-statuettes is that of Ur-bau (*circ.* 2500 B.C.) patesi of Lagash, now preserved in the Louvre, and reproduced in figure 39, C. This figure was found enclosed in a clay vase in the bottom of which three holes had been bored, and it was accompanied by a fine white marble tablet, the inscription upon which is a kind of résumé of the text found on the statue of this patesi. The god is kneeling on one knee, and his hands are fixed firmly on an elongated cone which resembles the nail-pointed terminations of the earlier figures. The head-dress consists in the horned cap. The features are full of expression and force in spite of their heaviness, and the statuette as a whole shows a great advance on the artistic products of the time of the first dynasty of Lagash, and also compares very favourably with the later work of Gudea's time.

Among other early copper objects of interest we may especially mention two bulls' heads the casting of which is not solid, as is the case with all the figures hitherto referred to, but hollow, and a curious vase, all found together at Tellô in the stratum immediately above that representing the age of U r-Ninâ.[1] The bulls' heads (cf. Fig. 40, A) are practically identical in type though not in size; the horns are long and the muzzle short, but notwithstanding their crudeness are full of vitality, and are not without a charm of their own. The larger of the two, which is seen in Fig. 40, A, has its eyes inlaid with mother-of-pearl, while the pupils of the eyes are made

[1] Cf. Hilprecht, *Explorations*, p. 539.

of lapis lazuli ; it is some seven and a half inches high (including the horns), the smaller head being only five and a half inches in height.

At Fâra an exquisite head of a Markhur goat was discovered (cf. Fig. 40, B); the head itself is made of copper, but the eyes were made of shell, the white of them being represented by white shell, and the pupils by dark

FIG. 40.—A, C, D (Musée du Louvre) Cat., pp. 318, 310, 324.
B (from Hilprecht, *Explorations*, p. 540).
E (from Harper, *A. J. S. L.*, XX, p. 266).

brown. Between the eyes there is a three-cornered ornament of mother-of-pearl inlaid with white and brown shells. The gazelle's neck is hollow, and its head was attached to a wooden body overlaid with copper.

Another interesting representation of the animal world in metal, has been bequeathed to us by Dungi, king of Ur, and consists in a bull reclining on the top of a long nail (cf. Fig. 40, C). The bull recalls the sacrificial animal portrayed on the little sculptured block reproduced in Fig. 27. The horns are short as there, but the thick neck and inflated throat at once give us the idea of a bellowing bull, the attitude being wonderfully natural, and the whole work full of vigour and animation. It is about twenty-six inches in height.

In Fig. 40, D[1] we have an illustration of another little metal bull, the metal in this case being bronze—an indication of a somewhat later date—and the posture a standing one. The place of its discovery is uncertain, but as M. Heuzey says, it shows no trace of hard Assyrian conventionalism, but on the contrary has all the characteristics proper to early Babylonian art. The bull, which is twelve inches in height and thirteen inches in length, stands on a narrow plinth to the bottom of which a nail was apparently fixed, recalling the nail-pointed statuettes from Tellô. The particular interest of this little figure lies in the fact that it is inlaid with silver, the object of which was clearly to represent the markings of a certain breed of bulls. The eyes were once inlaid with this metal, and the thin plates of silver with which the body of the animal was inlaid are still in place. This little figure thus proves that the Babylonians had not only acquired the art of inlaying objects made of stone, but also those that were made of metal.

Among other early Babylonian representations of animals in metal, may be mentioned a "bronze lion-headed object" (cf. Fig. 40, E) discovered at Bismâya.[2] The spike itself, apart from the lion, measures nineteen inches. As it was found over eight feet below a platform of plano-convex bricks, its antiquity must be very great, and in the light of subsequent research it may probably be assumed that it is bronze only in appearance, like so many of the products of early Sumerian metallurgy, any alloy there may be in the copper being at this date accidental and not intentional. The lion is crude, but the artist's

---

[1] Cf. *Louvre Cat.*, No. 173; and *Mon. Piot.*, t. VII, Pl. I, Fig. 1.

[2] Cf. Harper, *American Journal of Semitic Languages*, XX, pp. 266, 267.

inexperience has not prevented him from producing an animal both natural in its pose, and therefore artistic in its effects.

Various other objects and weapons made of copper have been discovered at Nippur, Fâra, Tell Sifr, and other Babylonian sites, and they include hammers, knives, daggers, hatchets, fetters, mirrors, fish-hooks, net-weights, spear-heads, vases, dishes and caldrons, the weapons sometimes having rivets for wooden handles, which have long since perished.[1]

The moulds in which all these copper objects, both hollow and solid, were cast were probably made of clay, though in later times stone was frequently used as a material for making moulds for metal-casting, and various examples of such moulds made of steatite, wherein were cast ear-rings and other articles of jewellery, are now in the British Museum, while at the same late period bronze itself seems to have been employed, and bronze moulds for arrow-heads are still extant. But there is no evidence for the use of either stone or metal moulds among the Sumerians, and it is to their use of clay moulds that we must doubtless ascribe, at least in part, the extraordinary animation which these early Babylonian figures exhibit, for obviously the fashioning of the head of a bull or of a human being in clay would be a comparatively easy work to chiselling it in stone, and the work would consequently lack the heavy laboriousness which is so often the outstanding characteristic of early stone sculptures. The copper remains of this age are far from being as ample as one might wish, but many weapons, tools and other objects which must undoubtedly have been made of metal, and therefore probably of copper at this time, are portrayed on some of the earliest Babylonian reliefs and seals, and give us some idea of the extensive use which the Babylonians

[1] Cf. King, *Sumer and Akkad*, p. 26 ; and Hilprecht, *Explorations*, p. 156.

of this remote period must have made of metal, and of the numerous purposes for which they employed it. Sometimes it would appear that instead of fashioning the required objects by means of moulds, they relied entirely on the hammer : evidence of this was forthcoming by the discovery of a portion of the horn of an ox by De Sarzec at Telló. Unfortunately no other part of the animal to which this horn belonged was brought to light, but the horn is life-size and well made. The core consisted of wood upon which the copper plates were fixed by means of small nails.

The exact time when the Mesopotamians acquired and practised the art of adding a percentage of tin to the copper, thereby making it bronze—a metal possessed of greater strength than copper—is not known, but a judgment based on the evidence afforded by the cases which have been actually chemically analysed, would indicate that the artificial combination of copper and tin was not known till the Assyrian era, and that any percentage of tin or antimony found in the copper objects of earlier date is a natural and not an artificial alloy. It is however worthy of note that apparently as early as the time of Bur-Sin, king of Ur (circ. 2400 B.C.), the art of mixing metals was not unknown. At all events a copper statuette of the Kanephorous order, and bearing an inscription of this king, contains an alloy of lead, the percentage of lead being as much as eighteen per cent. But with the rise of Assyrian power, bronze gradually supplanted copper ; copper was indeed still used, and Esarhaddon, for example, informs us that he made the doors of one of the palaces which he erected for himself, of cypress wood, and that he further overlaid them with silver and copper; it was also used for subordinate purposes, as for example in the manufacture of colour,[1] but it ceased to occupy an important place in the life of the people, though of course as the principal contributor to the artificially-

[1] Layard, *Discoveries*, p. 357.

composed bronze it was still used extensively, though in a less conspicuous manner.

A good example of the use of bronze in the early Assyrian period is to be found in a scimitar (cf. Fig. 41, A) bearing an inscription of Adad-nirari I, king of Assyria about 1325 B.C. The whole length of the sword is just over twenty-one inches, the length of the blade being sixteen inches, and that of the hilt about five, while its width varies from just over one to just under two inches. The sword was evidently a ceremonial one, and possibly was at one time placed in the hand of a god's statue;

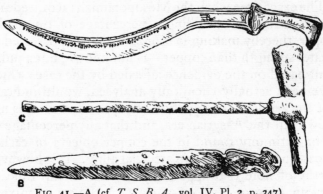

FIG. 41.—A (cf. *T. S. B. A.*, vol. IV, Pl. 2, p. 347).
B (cf. Andrae, *Der Anu-Adad Tempel*, p. 53).

its hilt was apparently jewelled and inlaid with ivory,[1] and it resembles that found by Macalister at Gezer in Southern Palestine. It is interesting to compare the scimitar of Adad-nirari with the sword found by Andrae at Ashur (cf. Fig. 41, B) from which it differs entirely in character and design, the latter being perfectly straight. Another interesting discovery made by Andrae on the same site is a bronze axe (cf. Fig. 41, C), which is quite modern in its appearance, and is not unlike a short-handled ice-axe.

Many other weapons, implements, dishes, bowls and

[1] Cf. Boscawen, *Transactions of the Society of Biblical Archæology*, 1876, p. 347.

PLATE XXVIII

British Museum

BRONZE OBJECTS, FROM NIMRÛD

Photo. Mansell

rings of bronze were discovered at Nineveh, Nimrûd and elsewhere. In Plate XXVIII, we have a bronze ox-hoof, which apparently formed the leg of a throne, —and two other bronze fittings of a throne. Below are two of the bronze lion-weights from Nimrûd. Many of these weights are inscribed in cuneiform with the names of the kings in whose reigns they were made, e.g. Tiglath-Pileser, Shalmaneser IV and Sennacherib, the amounts they weighed being inscribed in Phœnician. They were possibly made by Phœnician immigrants. The specific gravity required in the case of each weight was normally arrived at by chiselling pieces off the base, but in one case, the gravity had to be increased and not diminished, and this was effected by filling the hollow body of the lion with lead, until it weighed the necessary amount. Immediately above the head of the larger of the two lions here represented, we see the bronze head of a Babylonian demon.

Assyrian bronze generally contains one part of tin to ten of copper, but in the case of the bronze bells found by Layard at Nimrûd (one of which is reproduced in Plate XXVIII), it was found by analysis that the percentage of tin was about fourteen. This was doubtless to make their ring more resonant. The bells in question vary in size, the largest being about three and a quarter inches in height and two and a quarter in diameter,[1] while the smallest is one and three-quarter inches high and one and a quarter inches in diameter. The clappers of these bells are made of iron.

But the bronze dishes from Nimrûd show the Assyrian metal-engravers' work perhaps at its highest, and offer more material for the study of that branch of Assyrian metallurgy than any other class of objects. The general style of decoration to which they conform is that determined by concentric circles cutting up the upper surface of the dish into so many registers, though sometimes nearly

[1] Layard, *Discoveries*, p. 177.

the whole of the field is occupied with one scene. The figures portrayed frequently exhibit a very strong Egyptian influence, and are sometimes entirely Egyptian in design.

In Plate XXIX we have a reproduction of one of the best preserved of these bronze dishes found by Layard at Nimrûd. The griffins which occupy the principal place in the scheme of decoration are entirely Egyptian in conception, while they further wear on their heads the familiar double crown of Upper and Lower Egypt. The front left hoof of each griffin rests in an almost parental fashion upon the head of a child, who is also clearly Egyptian. Both before, between and behind the griffins, tapering columns such as are frequently found in Egyptian architecture are observable, and in the centre of the space separating the back of one griffin from the back of the nearest animal in the adjoining group, there is a more substantial pillar, the capital of which is shaped to represent a winged scarab. The animals are all beaten out in relief, but the finely chased circles of fleurettes which form the sole decoration of the centre, are the work of the engraver.

In Fig. 42 on the other hand we have a dish also made of bronze, and found on the same site as the one described above, but it betrays not the slightest trace of Egyptian influence. The motif is one frequently employed in Mesopotamia ; the decoration of circular objects by consecutive chains of animals following each other round in a circle was no invention of the Assyrians, for it may be traced back to the earliest Sumerian times. It occurs on the famous silver vase of Entemena (cf. Fig. 45) as well as on the stone mace-head of Mesilim (cf. Fig. 26), which is decorated with a group of wonderfully life-like lions pursuing each other round the mace. In the innermost circle, a troop of gazelles, such as are often seen depicted on cylinder-seals (cf. Fig. 51), march along in file ; the middle resister forms the circus for a variety of animals

PLATE XXIX

Photo, Mansell BRONZE BOWL, FROM NIMRÛD *British Museum*

all marching in the same direction as the gazelles. A bull, a winged griffin, an ibex and a gazelle, are followed by two bulls who are being attacked by lions, and a griffin, a bull, and a gazelle, who are all respectively being attacked

FIG. 42. (After Layard.)

by leopards. In the outermost zone there is a stately procession of realistically conceived bulls marching in the opposite direction to the animals parading in the two inner circles, and thus relieving the otherwise aggressive monotony of the decorations. The preservation of the handle by which it was held or suspended is an additional

S

point of interest. Unfortunately these platters bear no cuneiform inscriptions, though a few of them contain an inscription written in Phœnician characters on the reverse, which is probably an indication that they were fashioned by Phœnician artists, if they were not actually made in Phœnicia itself. As has been already stated, some of the dishes under consideration are clearly Assyrian in art and conception, while others are as certainly Egyptian, but notwithstanding this fact, there is evidence to show that those betokening the greatest Egyptian influence did not originate in Egypt, and were probably not the work of Egyptian artists. One of these dishes for example is decorated with a circle of cartouches containing Egyptian hieroglyphs: but the hieroglyphs are placed together quite haphazard, they mean nothing, and this fact alone would suggest that the artist, whoever he was, was not an Egyptian but a plagiarist.

The varying and distinct styles of art to which the decorations of these different dishes conform, are illustrated again in an equally conspicuous manner in the carved ivories, which were discovered on the same site and in the same palace.

As has been already seen, engraving was not the only manner in which the Assyrians utilized metal for artistic and pictorial purposes ; they also learned to excel in metal repoussé work, a process whereby the figures are beaten out in relief on the reverse, though they are sometimes finished off with a graver on the right side. The bronze gate-bands discovered by Rassam at Balâwât are by far the largest and most important monument of this branch of Assyrian metallurgy. Balâwât is situated about fifteen miles south-east of Nineveh, and on this site Rassam discovered the remains of four pairs of large folding-doors. Of two pairs of these doors the cedar-wood backing still remained, but all that remained of the other two were the bronze bands which were nailed on to the doors themselves for decorative purposes. These bands were fashioned and affixed to the wooden doors by Shalmaneser II, king of Assyria from 860 to 825 B.C. The largest of these doors was nearly twenty-two feet in height, six feet in width and three inches thick. Each of these doors was attached to a rounded post, the diameter of which was about eighteen inches, and the foot of

FIG. 43.—Bronze gate-band from Balâwât. (British Museum.)

which was covered with bronze with a view to facilitating its revolution in the stone gate-socket which was destined to hold it and the affixed door.

In Fig. 43 we have a reproduction of a portion of one of these bands. In the upper register we have a procession of foot-soldiers armed with maces, swords, bows and quivers, and also a charioteer, all in attendance on the king, who goes before ; in the lower register a number of chariots are seen crossing a river by means of a bridge of boats. The whole is beaten out in relief on the reverse, with the exception of fine lines representing the horses' trappings or the decoration of garments. Strange to say, the reins of the chariot horses on these gate-sheaths are sometimes raised in relief by the repoussé method, sometimes on the other hand they are incised. At the top and bottom of each register a row of the ubiquitous rosettes are introduced as a deco-

FIG. 44.—Bronze gate-band from Balâwât. (British Museum.)

rative accessory, and the nails which fastened the metal bands to the woodwork transfixed the rosettes. In Fig. 44 we have another scene in which is represented the capture of a certain city called Dabigu. The centre of the upper register is occupied with a representation of the Assyrian camp, within which the king is seen seated before the royal pavilion and attended by two eunuchs, while behind the camp there is another band of eunuchs, and in front to the right of the register there is a detachment of bowmen. Below, the assault of the city "by the assault of engines and the attack of foot soldiers and mines and breaches"[1] is vividly represented. The city itself has apparently an outer and an inner wall, both of which are crenelated as usual. The outer wall has an arched gate to the left, while within the city there are various conical shaped objects which recall the domed and conical roofs seen in Fig. 9. Three archers are defending the inner wall of the city, while only one archer and another warrior remain at their posts on the outer wall, the lower part of which appears to be speedily succumbing to the irresistible attack of the battering-ram. The latter has six wheels and seems to bear a kind of platform on which some Assyrian soldiers have taken their stand and from which they are discharging their unerring shafts ; behind are a troop of archers actively engaged though very passively portrayed, as is always the case with Assyrian representations of human beings.[2]

In the recent excavations conducted by the Deutsche Orient-Gesellschaft at Ashur, bronze plates for overlaying and decorating doors, precisely similar to those found by Rassam at Balâwât, were brought to light.

But bronze found its natural sphere of use in the necessities of daily life, and afforded a first-class material wherefrom to fashion knives, tools, swords, and implements of all kinds ; many of these have been brought to light by Layard and other excavators, while without doubt the innumerable spears, swords, shields and arrows depicted on the Assyrian bas-reliefs were made of this metal. It was used also in the manufacture of personal ornaments, such as finger rings and bracelets. Bronze was similarly used in Babylonia during the Neo-

---

[1] Cf. the Taylor Cylinder of Sennacherib.

[2] For an admirable reproduction of the best half of the Balâwât Gates, a good introduction, and translation of text, cf. Birch and Pinches, *The Bronze Ornaments of the Palace Gates of Balâwât*. Cf. also Delitzsch, *Beiträge zur Assyriologie*.

Babylonian dynasty, and was employed for building as well as for other purposes; doorsteps were sometimes made of bronze, and one such bronze step bearing an inscription of Nebuchadnezzar II (cf. above, p. 131) is preserved in the British Museum. It is interesting to note the discovery of similar bronze doorsteps by the French excavators at Susa, especially bearing in mind the close relationship which existed between the two countries and peoples throughout their history, though unfortunately Mesopotamia has at present offered no parallel to the life-size statue in bronze of Napir-asu, the wife of Untash-gal king of Elam about 1600 b.c. A small bronze plaque bearing in relief the four-winged demon of the south-west winds was discovered by Layard, and is now preserved in the British Museum (No. 86262), while a statuette of the same picturesque creature and made of the same material now adorns the galleries of the Louvre. The demon in question is of a highly composite character like so many of the Babylonian and Assyrian genii. His body resembles that of a dog, his arms find their natural or unnatural termination in lion's claws, his head is a caricature of a human skeleton, which is in its turn crowned with the horns of a goat, his tail is that of a scorpion, and his back is protected with four huge wings, which in their extended position form a grim and fitting background to the whole. But this demon, hideous as it is, was constructed for distinctly beneficent purposes, and was used as a talisman. One perhaps might not have at once conjectured that this fascinating personage was really the embodiment of the south-west wind, but fortunately he bears an inscription on his back which removes all doubt on the point. He was destined to be suspended from the door or window of a house in order to scare away any spirits of evil or doubtful intentions. The figure is unnatural in its conception, but it is grimly realistic and full of life, if not life-like, and in some ways recalls the hideous wicker-work and feather-covered war-gods of the Hawaiians.

Gold has not been found as frequently as one could wish in the course of Babylonian and Assyrian excavations; doubtless this is in part due to the depredations of booty-hunters, but it is nevertheless an indication that it was only used for exceptional purposes as is indeed the case with us to-day. It was regularly used for commercial transactions; a good example of its use in this connection is afforded by a tablet belonging to the Kassite period, the text of which is to be found in Vol. XIV (40) of the University of Pennsylvania's publication.[1] A woman agrees to adopt a girl, tend her during life, and after death offer libations of water for the repose of her soul, and as consideration she receives the sum of seven shekels of gold. One of the earliest pieces of gold actually discovered in Babylonia is the narrow strip inscribed with the name of Narâm-Sin of Agade, to which we have already had occasion to allude (cf. p. 103).

But gold was also employed for decorative purposes ; at Abû Shahrein (Eridu) for example, Taylor found various fragments of gold on the base of the second storey of the ziggurat,—apparently the remains of the ornamentation of the sanctuary which doubtless crowned the tower ; gold-headed nails and fragments of gold leaf were also found on the same site. In the course of the recent excavations at Ashur, a representation of lightning in gold, about a foot and a half in length, which doubtless was once in the grasp of the hand of a life-size statue of Adad, the storm-god, was brought to light. The handle was made of wood, but was covered with a thin sheath of pure gold. The three-pronged end, of which only two remain, was welded to this covering. The whole is said to weigh about 290 grains, 250 of which represent the weight

[1] For translation, cf. Ungnad, *Or. Lit.*, IX (1906), 534–8.

of the gold. At Babylon, the most famous of all the cities in the Euphrates valley, gold was employed with great prodigality. As early as the first dynasty of Babylon it was used in the service of the gods, and Sumu-la-ilu, the second king of this dynasty, built a throne of gold and silver for the great lord Marduk,[1] while the statues of the gods themselves were frequently made wholly or in part of pure gold ; thus for example Nabû-aplu-iddina, king of Babylon *circ.* 870 B.C., tells us that he carefully prepared the image of Shamash, the Sun-god, with pure gold and lapis lazuli, while the famous statue of Marduk of Babylon would also appear to have been made of pure gold.

The temple of E-sagil erected at Babylon in honour of this same god was covered with gold, silver and precious stones by Ashur-bani-pal,[2] king of Assyria from 668 to 626 B.C. Yet later Nebuchadnezzar added his contribution to the great work of restoration ; he built a certain magnificent chamber called Ekua, the walls of which he made of pure gold, and the cedar-wood roof of which he also covered with the same precious metal, while he similarly decorated the cedar-wood roof of Nabû's shrine with gold. Gold was further used for personal adornment ; in the Amran mound at Babylon, which represents the site of the world-renowned E-sagil, a gold ear-ring was found upon a platform composed of bricks bearing the name of Nebuchadnezzar, and therefore possibly belonging to his time, while a plate of gold was also found in the same neighbourhood, and rings of gold are perpetually mentioned in Babylonian and Assyrian literature.

Many golden face-masks, ear-rings, necklaces and other pieces of jewellery have been found in Babylonia, but for the most part their date is uncertain, the only certainty about them being their comparative lateness :

[1] Cf. Delitzsch, *Records of the Past*, 1903, pp. 323 ff.
[2] Cf. Harper, *Assyrian and Babylonian Literature*, p. 129.

they may probably be assigned to the Sassanidian period, and consequently their treatment will be outside the scope of the present volume.

Silver was also used for much the same purposes as those for which gold was employed. The finest and at the same time the earliest specimen of the Babylonian silversmith's art has been bequeathed to us by Entemena, one of the more famous rulers of the first dynasty of Lagash, and takes the form of a magnificent silver vase. This renowned vase (cf. Fig. 45) is some twenty-eight inches in height, and rests upon a copper base seven inches high, while the largest diameter is eighteen inches. The copper base is supported by four feet resembling the paws of lions, and on the centre of the vase just above two of these feet, is engraved the lion-headed eagle with outstretched wings whose two claws firmly grip the backs of two lions facing in opposite directions, a motif frequently found on the works of art belonging to the period of the first dynasty

Fig. 45.—(Cf. Cat., p. 372; *Déc. en Chald.*, Pl. 43.)
(Museo de Louvre.)

of Lagash, and representing the heraldic arms of that ancient city. Above the other two feet of the base the motif is slightly varied, the two lions being exchanged in one case for two deer, in the other for two goats. Each lion is engaged in putting its teeth into the mouth of the deer or the goat of the adjoining group, the whole thus forming a continuous chain admirably suited for the decoration of a circular vase. The lion-headed eagles and their submissive animals, are separated from the upper and lower portions of the vase by means of a double fish-bone line ; upon the upper part of the vase are seven heifers all facing in the same direction, and all in a semi-reclining attitude, one of their fore-legs being raised preparatory to standing up ; these heifers are marvellously life-like and true to nature, and already we seem to see in them the forerunners of those masterpieces of Assyrian art which adorned the palace walls of Ashur-bani-pal. This scene of country life was evidently very popular at this period, it occurs on the little sculptured block seen in Fig. 27, as well as elsewhere. But success in the reproduction of animal life at this epoch seems to have been largely conditioned by the artist's abstention from trying to depict the animals full-face ; when he aspires to the latter the result is amazingly stereotyped and formal, and a comparison between the lion-headed eagles and the lions on the one hand, and these spirited heifers, at once reveals the contrast, as well as the cause of the contrast. The artist himself was evidently conscious of his failure, for he has striven, but it must be admitted without much success, to impart life to his lions and lion-headed eagles by elaborating the wings of the one and the mane of the other by means of an altogether extravagant amount of detailed attention. The inscription round the neck informs us that this vase was dedicated by Entemena, the fourth successor of Ur-Ninâ, to the god Nin-girsu in his temple Eninnu, during the priesthood of one Dudu, whose name also occurs on the little sculptured block (cf. Fig. 27), thus proving the contemporaneity, which the style of art to which the decorations on both conform would have independently led us to infer.

But silver sometimes played a subsidiary, though nevertheless from the artistic point of view an essential part in the decoration of metal figures : a good example of the latter is afforded by a bronze figure of a bull, already referred to (cf. Fig. 40, D).

It is somewhat uncertain whence they obtained their silver ; in a letter of Lu-enna to Enitarzi, a ruler who apparently flourished shortly after the first dynasty of Lagash, silver is mentioned as forming part of the booty taken from Elam, and in later times it was one of the principal items of tribute exacted by the Assyrian kings from their vassal princes, and as such, is frequently mentioned on the Black Obelisk of Shalmaneser II. The excavations have yielded very few relics made of this material, the reason again being probably due to the predatory raids of booty-hunters. Of smaller objects belonging to the Assyrian period may be mentioned a silver bell with a bronze clapper, a silver ring set with a garnet, and a silver bracelet, all in the British Museum, but the dates of these are unfortunately quite uncertain. That it was used extensively, however, is shown not only by the important place which it occupies in the tribute brought by subject tribes and peoples, but also by the allusions made to this metal in the royal inscriptions. Thus Esarhaddon informs us that he covered the doors of one of his palaces with this precious metal. Idols were also sometimes made of silver as well as of gold, to both of which classes Tiglath-Pileser I makes allusion in one of his inscriptions.[1]

With two of the so-called " baser metals " we have already had occasion to deal at some length, owing to the important part they played in the civilization of the Babylonians and Assyrians, but we have tangible as well as linguistic evidence of their acquaintance with and utilization of other metals as well as gold, silver, copper and bronze. It has been shown that lead was sometimes used as an alloy, but it was sometimes used in its unmixed state ; a very interesting example of its use in this latter condition is to be found in a gate-socket now preserved in the British Museum. The socket it-

[1] Harper, *Assyrian and Babylonian Literature*, p. 14.

self is made of bronze, but it is set in solid lead. The date of this unique object is uncertain, but it may probably be assigned to the Assyrian era. Few leaden objects have as yet been yielded by the excavations, though it is frequently mentioned as forming part of the tribute of subject peoples, and we know that it was used in the manufacture of colours, as well as being placed inside the hollow lion-weights found at Nimrûd to add the specific gravity required. In Egypt lead would appear to have been known and used at a very early period, judging from the little statuette in the British Museum, which apparently dates from about the time of the First Dynasty, and is said to be made of solid lead.

Iron was first known to the Babylonians in its meteoric state, for its designation is AN-BAR, which signifies "stone of heaven." Allusions to objects made of this metal are very frequent in the inscriptions of Assyrian kings. Tiglath-Pileser I for example makes reference to a certain lance of iron, and Shalmaneser II to the point of an iron dagger, while both the latter king and Adadnirari III mention iron as forming part of the tribute they received from their vassal-kings. A century later Tiglath-Pileser III records that he put iron chains upon a certain Zaquriu and his followers, while a hundred years after, Ashur-bani-pal refers to an iron dagger overlaid with gold.[1]

Place found a number of iron axe-heads, knives and other implements at Khorsabad, while Layard discovered a bracelet, a lock-plate, some spear-heads, two reaping-hooks, rings and staples, axe-heads, arrow-heads, finger-rings and a part of a helmet, all made of iron, in the north-west palace at Nimrûd. An interesting specimen of oriental ironwork was found at Babylon by the German excavators in the shape of an iron rod beautifully decorated with a series of polished ornaments, and possibly formed part of a royal throne. Lastly many of

---

[1] Cf. Harper, *Assyrian and Babylonian Literature*, pp. 54, 99.

the Assyrian bronze bells already alluded to have tongues made of iron.

Iron was apparently not known or at all events not used in Mesopotamia as early as it was in Egypt. Evidence of its use in the early dynastic period was afforded by Maspero's discovery of this metal in a fifth dynasty pyramid in 1882, and Petrie discovered a piece of worked iron in sixth dynasty deposits, while in the year 1837 iron was discovered in the Great Pyramid of Gizeh.

Sufficient will have been said to indicate the important part played by metal in the history of both the Babylonians and Assyrians ; not only was it used as a commercial medium of exchange, it was also adapted to the innumerable requirements of humanity ; implements, weapons, vases, personal decorations were all easily realized in this pliable and at the same time durable substance, while the artistic genius of the Mesopotamian population which finds its most perfect expression in the sculptured bas-reliefs of early and late date, was entirely dependent on the forging of metal tools and implements for the purpose.

CHAPTER VIII—PAINTING

" PAINTING" in the ordinary sense of the word
to-day, was an art never practised by the dwellers
in Mesopotamia : like all Orientals both the Babylonians
and Assyrians were fond of gay colours, and they grati-
fied their taste for such in various ways, but as a rule no
attempt was made to faithfully represent the objects of
nature through the medium of the brush and the employment of colours alone, and the colours which they used
on their sculptured reliefs, their stuccoed walls, or their
enamelled bricks, were very frequently entirely impossible from the naturalistic standpoint. Thus the lion of
brilliant yellow hue (cf. frontispiece), the commonest of
all pictorial representations in Babylonia, has no counterpart whatever in real life ; the effect is pleasing, it catches
the eye, it awakens a sense of appreciation in the spectator, but this is due to the general cheerfulness of the
colours themselves, certainly not to their fidelity to
nature.

The lion itself bears no comparison with the Babylonian lion represented in Fig. 46. The action is the
same in either case—both lions are proceeding with sure
and deliberate step, roaring as they go, but there is a vast
difference between the artistic merits of each. The Assyrian lion is not indeed entirely lifeless, but it lacks the
freedom and spontaneity which characterize the highest
forms of art ; the body is also somewhat heavy and clumsy
compared with the lion of Ishtar's Gate.

The colours chiefly employed in Babylonian and Assyrian paintings are blue, yellow and white, while green
red and black are of comparatively rare occurrence. The

background of the picture is generally a shade of royal blue, the figures, usually animals, being of a brilliant yellow. In Babylonia, the demand for colours in architectural decoration was naturally more pressing than in Assyria, for in the latter country, where alabaster and limestone were easily procurable, the adornment of the interiors of buildings fell to the sculptor, but in the southern country the dearth of stone at once precluded the possibility of covering the walls even of the palaces with the sculptured bas-reliefs so dear to the heart of apparently all Assyrian monarchs. Thus it was that colour was largely made to take the place of sculpture in Babylonian decoration, the sculptor's chisel being exchanged for the painter's brush, though in Assyria sometimes the art of the sculptor and painter were both invoked to beautify the walls of the king's palace, for in some of the halls in the royal residence of Sargon at Khorsabad the sculptured reliefs on the lower part of the walls were painted;[1] while Layard, after describing some of the wall-reliefs found in the north-west palace at Nimrûd, says:[2] "On all these figures paint could be faintly distinguished, particularly on the hair, beard, eyes and sandals," which rather suggests that the earlier Assyrian sculptures were only partially coloured. Some of the sculptured bas-reliefs from Ashur-naṣir-pal's palace at Nimrûd still bear traces of colour, the sandals of many of the figures even now showing the faded red and black paint which at one time covered the soles and upper parts of the sandals respectively, while in one case Ashur-naṣir-pal's bow still retains traces of red paint. At Khorsabad, on the other hand, colour was used more generally, the raiment and head-gear of the king as well as the harness of the horses, the chariots and the trees, being all painted. Layard says that he was unable to ascertain whether the ground as well as the figures, or parts of the figures, were

[1] Cf. Perrot and Chipiez, p. 277.
[2] Layard, Nineveh I, p. 64 ; II, pp. 306, 307.

coloured, but Flandin, in regard to the wall-reliefs at Khorsabad, informs us that he could trace a tint of yellow ochre on all parts not otherwise coloured, while the upper parts of the walls upon which the sculptor had lavished none of his art, were often decorated with frescoes.

But walls plastered with stucco also commanded the attention of the painter as well as those lined with stone bas-reliefs, and Layard discovered the remains of paintings on stucco at Nimrûd, specifically in the upper chambers on the west side of the mound, the rooms of which were constructed of crude bricks coated with plaster and elaborately painted.[1] Most of these paintings do not aspire to anything more than designs, simple or complex as the case may be. In one fresco two bulls are portrayed facing each other ; their bodies are white, the ground from which the bulls are carefully delineated by a pronounced black outline, being yellow, while dark blue plays a leading part in the purely decorative accessories at the top of the fresco. Other evidence of the extensive use of paint for the ornamentation of interior walls, was forthcoming in the discovery on the floor of a chamber in the north-west palace of Nimrûd, of "considerable remains of painted plaster still adhering to the sun-dried bricks, which had fallen in masses from the upper part of the wall. The colours, particularly the blues and reds, were as brilliant and vivid when the earth was removed from them, as they could have been when first used. On exposure to the air they faded rapidly. The designs were elegant and elaborate. It was found almost impossible to preserve any portion of these ornaments, the earth crumbling to pieces when any attempt was made to raise it."[2]

The exteriors of buildings were also sometimes decorated with colour, a notable example being the ziggurat at Khorsabad of which three complete stages together with a part of the fourth were found still

[1] Layard, *Nineveh*, II, p 15.   [2] *Ibid.*, I, p. 130.

remaining. The lowest stage was painted white, the second black, the third red, and the fourth white ; doubtless the remaining stages were also painted, the colours being emblematic of the seven planets, as in the case of the traditional temple of Belus at Babylon.

The best example of the Babylonian painter's art is afforded by the city of Babylon itself. As early as the sixties, the French excavators, Fresnel and Oppert, had collected a large number of single-coloured and multi-coloured fragments of relief bricks. The coating of colour, which was always applied to the narrow sides of the bricks, was sometimes from one to two millimetres thick. Unfortunately this valuable collection was lost, but the statements of the explorers are corroborated by the description of a Babylonian palace wall, contained in the works of Diodorus the historian (*circ.* 44 B.C.) where he refers to " all manner of shapes of animals on rough bricks with colouring very like that of nature " ; and he goes on to say that on the towers and walls were " representations of all kinds of animals, and as far as colouring and shape went, well done. The whole represented a hunt, where everything was full of animals of all kinds, and in size more than four yards. In this was also represented Semiramis, on horseback, in the act of throwing the spear after a panther, and a short distance off her husband, Ninus, stabbing a lion with a lance."[1] Nebuchadnezzar himself further alludes to the pictures of wild oxen and colossal serpents, which he caused to be portrayed on blue enamelled bricks as decorations for the gates. Most of the glazed and coloured tiles found at Babylon resemble coloured bas-reliefs, the figures of the animals standing out in relief on a blue background generally, though sometimes the ground is green. The brick-enameller's art reaches its climax in the Lion-frieze which adorned the Procession Street of Marduk, at Babylon. One of these clay bas-relief lions is seen in

[1] Cf. Delitzsch, *Mitteilungen*, No. 6, pp. 13–17 ; and Diodorus II, 8.

T

Fig. 46.[1] The ground is dark blue, the monotony of which is varied by the introduction of yellow stripes and the white rosettes already so familiar from the enamelled

FIG. 46.—Enamelled brick relief from Babylon. (After Andrae.)

bricks of Khorsabad. The lion itself, the proportions of which are excellent, stands out in white alabaster clay, and the whole work is more perfect in technique than

[1] Cf. Koldewey, *Mitteilungen*, No. 3, pp. 5, 10, 11.

the Persian lion frieze at the Louvre, which it in some
ways resembles.   What detracts from the artistic merit

A

B   FIG. 47.—A (after Andrae); B (after Layard).

of the latter is the disproportion which the body bears
to the forepart and head, both of them being too small,

but the Babylonian lion is almost entirely free from this defect. The discovery of the Ishtar Gate at Babylon added another bounteous supply of material for the study of Babylonian painting : here too the coloured representations on the enamelled bricks were in relief. The walls of the gate were found preserved to a height of thirty-nine feet, the whole of the wall being covered with animals, principally bulls and dragons, of which there were at least eleven rows.

In Fig. 47, A, we have a black and white reproduction of one of the clay relief bulls which adorned the gate of Ishtar at Babylon. The bull is in the act of walking, and exhibits both grace and dignity in his movements, the slightness of his frame only serving to intensify the agility with which he seems to advance. The proportions are excellent and contrast very favourably with the Assyrian bull from Nimrûd (cf. Fig. 47, B). The latter is hard and conventional, while the posture—in itself a sufficiently natural one—is here rendered in a most wooden and inanimate fashion. The body of the animal is white, but the painter has attempted to make his subject stand out upon its pale yellow background, by edging it with an artificial outline of black. When the bull was coloured blue and thrown on to a white background this device was of course unnecessary (cf. Layard. Ser. I, Pl. 87.) The blue bull here alluded to belongs to the same species as the white one reproduced in Fig. 47, B, and is in the same kneeling position, but he is furnished with the wings of an eagle. It will be observed that in the Babylonian bull, as also in both the Assyrian bulls, the artist has evaded the difficulty of drawing the two horns in perspective by portraying only one, the other being theoretically concealed from view by the horn near the spectator.

But the palace of Nebuchadnezzar itself contained a large number of these coloured reliefs, many pieces of the glazed tiles of which they were composed having been found by Koldewey. The fragments recovered, number literally thousands, and Koldewey says that apparently when the bricks were stolen by later builders, the glazed portions were knocked off in order to make them more useful for the common purposes for which they were destined, and we to-day are the beneficiaries of that lack of appreciation. Amongst the animals portrayed on the palace and temple walls may be mentioned the bull, a mythical monster compounded of " parts of a bird of prey," scorpions, serpents, panthers and steers, as well as the ubiquitous lion, while some of the fragments recovered show parts of the human body, and birds are also sometimes encountered. The lions form the most interesting study : there are two main types, (1) lions walking to the left, with white skins and yellow manes; and (2) lions walking to the right (a) with white skins and yellow manes, and (b) yellow skins and green manes ; while there is a third type characterized by lions running to right or left. Sometimes the tail is portrayed standing out straight behind, sometimes it assumes a curved and less rigid form. Great difficulty has been experienced in fitting the various fragments together, but the assiduous efforts of the Germans have not been without success.

The process by which these coloured clay reliefs are supposed to have been made is as follows : a layer or slab of plastic clay of a fair size was taken, and on this surface the complete picture was modelled in relief, the process thus far being the same as that employed in the ordinary stone bas-reliefs, except that a chisel was in requisition there while here the hands would suffice, though it seems probable that moulds were at all events made for some of the lions, many of which are apparently entirely uniform. However that may be, the slab of clay now bearing in relief the figure determined, is supposed to have been cut up into rectangular blocks of the same size as the ordinary bricks, each rectangle being marked, with a view to simplifying the task of fitting each into its right place in the picture ; after this, each piece was painted with a coat of coloured varnish, and then thoroughly baked in the oven—the thoroughness of the baking is attested by the hardness of the enamel—after which the various parts were fitted together. In the same way at Nimrûd, Layard found a large number of enamelled bricks, bearing the figures of animals and flowers as well as cuneiform characters, lying promiscuously upon the floor of the entrance passages to the palace, upon the unpainted backs of which rude designs, chiefly consisting of men and animals, were drawn in black ink or paint, " and marks having the appearance of numbers." The marks alluded to must have presumably served the purpose of guiding the builder in his attempt to reconstruct the picture on the wall.

Coloured clay reliefs were not however the only species of pictorial representation adopted in the embellishment of the city of Babylon, or the palace of Babylon's most illustrious king. On the southern side of the Ḳasr, a large number of beautifully glazed tiles stamped with Nebuchadnezzar's inscription and adorned with flowers, twigs, and in one case part of a human figure —some fourteen inches high—were discovered, together with many sculptured stones bearing similar designs, the workmanship of which however was more perfect than that of the tiles. The latter have a flat surface, but they resemble the relief tiles in general technique. Many other glazed bricks were found on the eastern side of the Ḳasr, painted with various designs and displaying great delicacy—on one of them a human figure is portrayed, clad in a rich garment and holding what appears to be a spear in his left hand—these however Koldewey assigns to the Persian period.

But colour was further employed, as the handmaid of humbler forms of architectural decoration in Babylonia

PLATE XXX

DECORATED ARCH AT KHORSABAD
(cf. Place, " Ninive," Plates, 14, 15)

as well as in the northern country. Thus at Nippur, the walls of many of the rooms were stuccoed with a plaster consisting of mud and straw, and were coloured, the colours used being apparently always solid. The ruins of Nin-makh's temple at Babylon, excavated by the Deutsche Orient-Gesellschaft, similarly showed the remains of white decorations on its walls ; while colour played no insignificant part in the decoration of the famous cone-wall at the Wuswas mound of Erech, the cones of which were coloured red or black and then arranged in a variety of geometrical patterns upon a wall consisting of mud and straw.

As we have already seen, enamelled bricks were used for the purposes of architectural decoration in Assyria as well as in Babylonia, though the enamel used is generally inferior in quality, and is more thinly applied, in consequence of which it does not adhere so well to the clay, and it fades sooner. To Place and Botta we are indebted for the finest and largest specimens of the Assyrian enameller's art as yet discovered. The principal gateways of Dûr-Sharrukîn (Khorsabad) (the town built by Sargon, 722–705 B.C.), which are formed of arches resting on the backs of projecting winged bulls, seem to have been the object of the painter's peculiar attention. These arches were decorated with a semicircle of enamelled bricks (cf. Pl. XXX), the enamel being laid upon one edge of the bricks, the average length of which is about three and a half inches. The ground is blue and the composite winged figures are yellow, while a line of green edges the lower part of the head-gear. The rosettes which form a supplemental decoration are white. These figures which extend over the entire round of the arch are all uniform : they are engaged in some act of worship, or in the performance of some religious ceremony, and at once recall the scenes depicted on the palace wall reliefs, with which they are practically identical. In contradistinction to the method usually employed in Baby-

Ionia, these coloured representations are not in relief, the colour being applied to the flat surface of the bricks, the only exception being the central bosses of the rosettes which are slightly raised. Another good example of coloured tile-work was found on a plinth in the doorway of what Place regarded as the harem in Sargon's palace. The plinth in question is twenty-three feet long and over three feet high. The figures portrayed are the king, standing on one side of the plinth with bare head, while on the other side he wears the usual head-gear, a lion, a bull, an eagle, a tree and a plough, all done in yellow on a blue background, the borders of the whole plinth being decorated with the inevitable rosettes. The leaves of the tree are green, a colour apparently somewhat seldom used by the enamellers of Mesopotamia. Another painted fragment from Khorsabad, interesting for the extreme brilliancy of its colouring (cf. Place, *Nineve*, Pl. 32), is reproduced in Pl. XXXI. The faces of the two human beings are white, the background being green ; the frieze at the top is yellow, the circular decorations consisting of an inner circle of green or yellow, while the outer circle is composed of trapezoidal figures of red and white in the case of those with a green inner circle, and red and green in those with yellow centres, arranged in either case alternately.

Layard also succeeded in recovering many glazed and coloured bricks from Nimrûd (Calah) of even greater interest as regards the composition of the scenes depicted than as regards the colours used, which in their present state in no way compare with those from Khorsabad in brilliancy. The most interesting of these (cf. Pl. XXXI) is one in which the king, followed by the chief eunuch, is seen receiving his chief officer,[1] a scene so often portrayed on the Assyrian bas-reliefs. Above his head there is a " kind of fringed pavilion " and the sole

---

[1] Layard, *Monuments*, Series II, Pl. 55, 6 ; and Layard, *Discoveries*, p. 167.

remaining sign of a cuneiform inscription, while beneath
him is a spiral design seen more frequently on the so-
called Hittite works of art, though it is also found as a
decorative accessory on some of the earliest sculptures in
Babylonia (cf. Fig. 27). The predominating colours are
black and yellow : the hair and beard of the king and his
followers, their sandals, as well as the circular balls found
within each link of the spiral chain are black, the background is light yellow, the dress of the various figures
being of a deeper shade of yellow, and the royal head-
dress white. As Layard says : "This is an unique specimen of an entire Assyrian painting."

Of the remainder, the most interesting are briefly
described by Layard in *Discoveries*, pp. 166 and 167,
and illustrated in colours in his *Monuments*, Series II,
Pls. 53–55. One of these (Pl. 54, 7) contains a picture
of four hairless and clean-shaven captives, whose four
necks are bound together by means of a rope, the end
of which is held by the prisoner in front. Two of the
prisoners wear white loin-cloths, while the other two are
clad in long white shirts opening in front. As regards
the colours, the ground is a pale blue, and the figures
are yellow. Another fragment of great interest is that
reproduced in *Monuments*, Pl. 54, 12, on which are portrayed two horses, an Assyrian warrior, and a man holding a dagger. The latter, who is naked with the exception
of a blue loin-cloth, has apparently been wounded or
killed in battle. The background here is olive-green,
while the horses are blue. On another glazed tile (Pl.
54, 13), we see a picture of Assyrian cavalry, again
on a ground of olive-green, but in this case the horses
are yellow, while the trappings are blue. One of these
painted bricks (Pl. 53, 1) presents us with a picture of
a blue fish on a yellow background ; the scales of the
fish however are coloured white, while on the same tile
there is a man transfixed by two arrows and girded with
a white loin-cloth. On another fragment (Pl. 53, 3), a

chariot to which horses are yoked is being dragged over a naked figure, whose neck has been pierced by an arrow. A fillet to which is attached a feather, encircles the man's head. The horses are blue, their trappings being white, and the wheels of the chariot are yellow. Below are seen the heads together with a portion of the shields of two Assyrian soldiers. The helmets are yellow, but the faces are " merely outlined in white on the olive-green ground," while the shields are blue, but are edged with alternate squares of yellow and blue. All these belong to the same period, but another fragment was found by Layard (Pl. 53, 6) which appears to be of earlier date : the background is yellow, but the outline is black instead of white, while the figures, the heads of which have been destroyed, are dressed in the same way as the tribute-bearers bringing a monkey and other offerings to Ashur-naṣir-pal, as portrayed on bas-reliefs which were taken from the same building. The outer mantle is blue, the inner being yellow, and the fringes white.

But pottery was also sometimes decorated with colours ; thus Captain Cros, De Sarzec's successor at Tellô, discovered black pottery with incised lines filled in with white paste on this site, a style of pottery well known in Egypt and elsewhere, but not hitherto found in Babylonia. At Nippur on the other hand pottery painted with green and yellow stripes was found, while other vases decorated with black and white discs were also brought to light.

Painted pottery has been similarly found in Assyria : at Nimrûd Sir Henry Layard's men discovered various fragments of pottery which apparently belonged to the covers of jars; they were decorated with the spiral design, also honeysuckles, cones and tulips, in black on a pale yellow ground. Prehistoric pottery has moreover been found in the course of the recent excavations at Ashur, the clay vessels in question being decorated with red and black geometrical designs. Clay slipper-shaped

PLATE XXXI

Photo. Mansell. *British Museum*

GLAZED BRICK, WITH FIGURE OF AN ASSYRIAN
KING POURING OUT A LIBATION ON HIS RETURN
FROM A HUNT

GLAZED BRICK
(*cf.* Place, "*Ninive,*" *Pl. 32*)

coffins were also sometimes coloured; many of the sarcophagi discovered at Nippur were covered with a blue glaze, but they belonged apparently to the Parthian period. Glazed sarcophagi were likewise found at Warka (i.e. the ancient Erech) as well as at the city of Babylon, though they also were the products of a late period. Various other terra-cotta objects were not infrequently coated with a vitreous glaze, the colour of the enamel being usually blue or green. Colour was not only used in Babylonia however for decorating buildings, pots and figures, but also apparently for the adornment of the human body, for the German excavations at Fâra revealed the presence of alabaster colour-dishes in the graves, traces of the colour in some cases still remaining. The colours are black, yellow, light green and light red. According to the analysis of the colours of the Babylonian bricks conducted by Sir Henry De la Becke and Dr. Percy, quoted by Layard,[1] " the yellow is an antimoniate of lead, from which tin has also been extracted, called Naples yellow, supposed to be comparatively a modern discovery, though also used by the Egyptians. The white is an enamel or glaze of oxide of tin, an invention attributed to the Arabs of Northern Africa in the eighth or ninth century. The blue glaze is a copper, contains no cobalt, but some lead; a curious fact, as this mineral was not added as a colouring material, but to facilitate the fusion of the glaze, to which use, it was believed, lead had only been turned in comparatively modern times. The red is a sub-oxide of copper."

[1] *Discoveries*, p. 166.

CHAPTER IX—CYLINDER-SEALS [1]

O F the smaller relics of Babylonian and Assyrian antiquity there are none so numerous or so pregnant with interest as the engraved seals which kings and commoners of all periods alike possessed. The universality of their usage in later times is attested by Herodotus (I, 195), who tells us that in his day everyone in Babylonia carried a seal as well as a walking-stick, while abundant evidence of their general use in early times is afforded by the vast quantity of seals discovered in the course of the excavations.

The seal, important as it is in our own day, was an even more indispensable convenience of civilized society in primitive times, and was probably one of the first inventions that owed their origins directly to the mutual recognition of private rights of ownership. The purpose which it first of all served was of course the same as that which it serves with us to-day, though the sealing of the mud plaster covering of a jar of wine, of the string of a registered parcel, or the flap of a paper envelope, in no way prevents the thief from robbing the contents in any of these cases, yet it renders it impossible for such a theft to be perpetrated without detection, detection not indeed necessarily of the thief, but of the deed itself, and that after all is the essential preliminary to the successful establishment of any suit at law. Its use in primitive times was, however, far more extensive, for, as Newberry well puts it,[2] "what locks and keys are to us, seals were to

---

[1] A considerable number of the seal-impressions here reproduced are taken from Dr. W. Hayes Ward's monumental work on cylinder-seals in Western Asia, by the author's generous permission.

[2] *Scarabs*, p. 5.

the people of the Old World." If a man left his house
for the day, and no occupant remained to keep watch,
he probably secured himself and his goods so far as possible by sticking plasters of mud on the door and impressing his seal upon them in such a manner as to make
it impossible to enter the house without breaking the

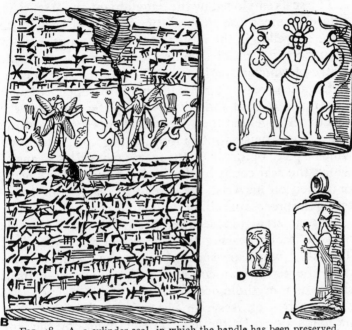

FIG. 48.—A, a cylinder-seal, in which the handle has been preserved.
B, a clay tablet bearing a seal impression.
C, D, illustrate the variation in size exhibited by cylinder-seals.

seal ; at all events Dr. Ward informs us [1] that he saw
in a Khan at Hillah, near Babylon, a door of a room
containing goods belonging to a merchant who was away
from home, carefully sealed up with pats of clay on which
the impress of the merchant's seal had been duly fixed,
thereby rendering access to the house dependent on the
bursting of the seals, and in the conservative East the
customs of to-day are not merely those of yesterday, but

[1] Ward, *The Seal-Cylinders of Western Asia*, p. 1.

generally represent the traditional usage of hundreds, sometimes thousands of years. A few such sealed pats of clay, some of which formed stoppers of jars, have been found, but the principal object for which the cylinder-seal was used, was the authentication of deeds, documents and letters.

The seals employed by the Babylonians and Assyrians differed from those generally employed elsewhere, in shape as well as in the motifs of the engravings. They assumed the form of cylinders or rollers, through the centre of which a single or double piece of wire was inserted, the wire being generally made of copper, though sometimes of gold and silver, while later on, iron also occurs. At one end the wire was clamped, while at the other it was twisted into a loop (cf. Fig. 48, A) through which a piece of thread or twine was passed by means of which the seal could be slung round the owner's neck, or carried on his wrist, the wire at the same time facilitating the process of rolling the cylinder on the moist clay.

The tablet (K. 382) seen in Fig. 48, B, is a good example of a clay tablet bearing the impress of a cylinder-seal. The tablet, which measures $4\frac{1}{8}$ inches by $2\frac{5}{8}$ inches, contains the terms of a contract. The impression itself shows us a mythological four-winged being, such as is seen so often on Assyrian bas-reliefs. In either hand he holds a bird by the leg. The cylinders by the side of the tablet are reproduced to actual size; A, C, and D (Brit. Mus. Nos 89319, 89538, 101974) illustrate the divergence of size which the Babylonian cylinder-seals exhibit, (C) being an unusually large specimen, and (D) an exceptionally small example, the vast majority of seals occupying an intermediate position between these two extremes; in (A) we have a cylinder in which the metal handle is still preserved.

The existence of the same kind of seal in Egypt as early as the time of the first dynasty has been used as an argument in support of the theory that the primitive civilizations of Egypt and Babylonia were to some extent interdependent. It is true that cylinder-seals could only be of use where clay was employed as a writing-material, but there is no direct evidence that the practice of using clay for either writing or building purposes was borrowed from Babylonia, while the similarity in shape of early Babylonian and Egyptian mace-heads is an even more uncertain argument whereon to base an otherwise unsupported theory.

The materials used in the manufacture of cylinder-seals were many and various. The earliest known material is shell, but the most frequently occurring is hæmatite. Among other materials used may be mentioned serpentine, marble, quartz crystal, chalcedony, carnelian, agate, jasper, syenite, jade, obsidian, onyx, limestone, schist, mother of emerald, and amethyst. A few flint cylinders have been recovered, but this material was evidently but seldom employed, while glass is of even rarer occurrence, and metal is unknown. The process by which the required device was engraved upon the cylinder depended upon the material of which the latter was made. The softer materials employed in earlier times, such as shell, marble or serpentine, were possibly engraved with tools made of flint, but the harder stones would require an implement made of some more stubborn material. Ward is of opinion that either emery or a certain stone called corundum was used for the purpose. The latter was employed at a very early period in Egypt and in later times in Greece. The earliest seals appear to have been entirely made by hand, the practice of drilling by means of a bowstring not being introduced till a later period. Within the confines of a single chapter it will of course be quite impossible to review all the innumerable types of cylinder-seals used by the Babylonians and Assyrians of different ages, and we can therefore only single out one or two examples of some of the more interesting classes as being fairly representative of the periods to which they belong.

The most ancient seals are generally made of white

marble, or shell, and sometimes also of lapis lazuli and serpentine. It is impossible to assign a definite or even an approximate date to the vast majority of cylinder-seals recovered from the ruined mounds of Mesopotamia, as most of them belonged to individuals otherwise unknown, but fortunately a number of seals have been brought to light which belong either to kings or officials whose date can be independently computed, and which therefore give us an illustration of the proficiency to which the art of engraving had been brought at the particular period in which the owners of the seals lived, and a comparison of the style of art exhibited on the otherwise undateable seals with those whose age has thus been fixed, makes it possible for us to assign them with some degree of certainty to the period to which they belong in the history of the art of seal-engraving.

The interest of these small relics of the past is of course centred in the scenes depicted, which are very various, and which throw a flood of light upon the mythology, and elucidate many legendary uncertainties in the theological and religious conceptions of the Babylonians and Assyrians. Where a comparison with royal or official cylinder-seals of certain date is not feasible, the similarity between the style of art exhibited on the particular seal in question and that to which some sculptures of ancient patesis or kings conform afford us the necessary clue, while lastly, when both of these tests fail, if the seal bears an inscription, the character of the writing often enables us to place it in its right class.

One of the earliest Babylonian rulers whose seals have been recovered is Lugal-anda, patesi or priest-king of Lagash, and the immediate predecessor of Urukagina, the last king of the first dynasty of Lagash. An impression of one of the seals of Lugal-anda is reproduced in Fig. 49. Part of the seal is divided into two registers, in the uppermost of which we see the eagle with outspread wings

clutching two lions, which together formed the heraldic
arms of the city of Lagash. It is noticeable that the lions
are treated with the same freedom as on the little block
of Dudu (cf. Fig. 27) the contemporary of Entemena,
one of Lugal-anda's predecessors. Here as in the little
block referred to, the lions are treated in a very spirited
manner, and in contrast to earlier representations of the
device, the lions are gnawing at the wings of their cap-
tivator. On the right of the city-arms there is an inscription written in very archaic characters. In the lower
register we have two human-headed bulls, a stag, a
bearded hero resembling Izdubar, or Gilgamesh as por-

FIG. 49.

trayed on other early cylinder-seals, and another figure
who is passing his left arm round the stag's neck and
holding one of the fore-paws of the stag in his right
hand. Unlike the bearded hero, who is similarly engaged in grasping the fore-paw of one of the human-
headed bulls, he is clean-shaven, while his hair is represented by four tongue-shaped projections. On the left
of the two registers there is the body and the lower part
of the face of a large human-headed bull, while on the
right are two lions, one of whom is seen burying his teeth
into the neck of a composite creature, half man and half
beast. It will be at once obvious that this cylinder-seal
of the early Sumerian period, presupposes an indefinite
period of artistic development in the practice of engraving.

U

In the very early seals the scene is of course far less composite and the workmanship infinitely more crude ; we frequently find the same eagle-motif, but the animals which he claws are usually goats, bulls, or ibexes, as seen in Fig. 50, the lions only being introduced at a later date. Here we have a very primitive seal in which we see the eagle grasping two ibexes by the horns, while a hero is grasping the same two animals by the leg. Hero, eagle and ibexes are represented in a highly archaic and crude fashion, though in the symmetrically outspread wings of the eagle we seem to have a foreshadowing of the conventionalism of later days. The ibexes have their hind quarters raised in the air, while the eagle grasps them by the horns, the seat of their strength actually as well as symbolically. The seal itself is both thicker and shorter than usual, and has only one register.

But the simplicity which usually characterizes the cylinder-seals of the earliest period sometimes gives place to an altogether overwhelming complexity, as in the seal represented in Fig. 51. The two registers into which the field of the cylinder is divided encroach on each other in so inordinate a manner that it requires a careful inspection to see that there are two registers. The eagle is the central figure in the upper register, his claws reaching out on the one hand towards a lion attacked by a vulture, on the other towards a lion who appears to be attacking a reversed ibex. Below, a huntsman occupies the commanding position ; he is clad in the short Sumerian skirt, the fringe of which is archaically represented by a series of tags, which recall the fragmentary sculptures of the prehistoric period of Lagash (cf. Fig. 25, C), and he is surrounded by a crowd of lions and antelopes. This seal is clearly the offspring of a more developed art than that reproduced in Fig. 50, but this notwithstanding, it is essentially archaic in character, and belongs to the early Sumerian period.

One of the most popular designs for cylinder seals in early Sumerian times is that of one or two seated deities, sometimes accompanied by the eagle. A very archaic example of this class is reproduced in Fig. 52. The two seated beings are certainly gods, in spite of their being clean shaven and having the same faintly suggested features as the figure in the middle. It will be observed that the fringe of the short Sumerian skirt of one of the deities and also of the worshipper is represented by a series of pointed tags as in Fig. 51.

FIG. 50.   FIG. 51.

FIG. 52.   FIG. 53.

In Fig. 53 we again have two seated gods, but this time they have a large bowl between them, from which they seem to be drinking by means of tubes. They are apparently seated on camp-stools, while before one of them is a sacred tree. Their dress consists in a long robe, which covers one arm while leaving the other exposed and free, and reaches down to the ankle, the bottom of it being decorated with a fringe, and the body of it by a branch-shaped design.

Sometimes, again, we have a representation of a god seated in a boat as seen in Fig. 54. It is impossible to say who the god is, though his divine character is clearly demonstrated by the horned cap. From the emergence of branches, or what may be flames of fire and streams of water from his shoulders, it seems a fair assumption on the part of Dr. Ward that the god is none other than Shamash, the sun-god. The boat is being propelled through the river or canal by two oarsmen, who, together with the god, are standing in the boat. The two men have different head-gears, but all three are clad solely in the old Sumerian skirt. Reeds to the height of the occupants of the boat are growing in the water, and a very primitively executed wild-boar is haunting this quaintly depicted marsh. Both bow and stern of the boat are similarly shaped, and are curved upwards to a great height. If the god be Shamash, it seems probable that here, as elsewhere, he is represented as traversing the heavens in his bark.

Another series of archaic cylinder-seals is concerned with the heroic feats of Gilgamesh and Ea-bani, two mythological beings whose conquests over bulls and lions won for them a reputation and a fame which lasted right down to the latter days of Assyrian history. We have an impression of one of the most primitive of the Gilgamesh seals in Fig. 55. The hero stands between two bisons, one of which is being attacked by a lion and the other by a leopard, while the inhuman and semi-bestial Ea-bani is attacking the lion from behind. The occurrence of the spotted leopard is specially noteworthy, as it hardly ever occurs on later cylinders, while the presence of bisons which only haunt the highlands is an additional archaic touch, and is a further indication of the antiquity of this seal, which must have been engraved at a time when the recollection of his mountain origin was still fresh in the Sumerian's mind, for in the later period of Babylonian art, the bison gives place to the swamp-loving buffalo. All the details of the seal betray the same primitive characteristics, and, as usual, there is no inscription.

We have already seen one royal seal-impression, and

we have in Fig. 56 the seal of a later but far more famous
Babylonian king, Shar-Gâni-sharri, king of Agade. In
the reign of Shar-Gâni-sharri and his son Narâm-Sin,
Babylonian art reached her climax,—the crudeness of
the earlier work had passed away, while there is as yet
no trace of the conventionalism of later days, and freedom is the keynote of her success. The scene is an oft-
recurring one: a hero who to all appearance is Gilgamesh
is kneeling on one knee, and holds in his hands a vase,
from the overflowing streams of which the buffalo seeks

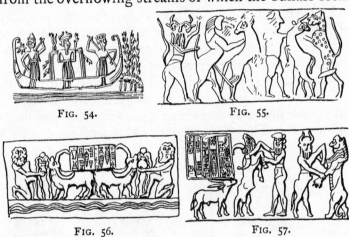

FIG. 54.   FIG. 55.

FIG. 56.   FIG. 57.

to quench his thirst. The seal is engraved with vigour
and precision, the boldness of which is only exceeded by
the natural effect produced. Both hero and animal are
treated with a freedom and fidelity seldom if ever surpassed in Oriental art, while the strength of the picture
lies in the artist's genius, and is in no way dependent
on the subject, which does not lend itself to anything
particularly striking or effective.

In Fig. 57 we have the impression of another seal in
which Gilgamesh and Ea-bani are the prominent actors.
Ea-bani is engaged with a lion, but his comrade is fighting with a massive horned-buffalo. This seal belongs
to the time of Shar-Gâni-sharri and Narâm-Sin, kings of

Agade, its date being fixed alike by the style of art and the purport of the brief inscription, which contains the name of the owner, Bingani-Sharali, king of Agade and the son of Narâm-Sin. This seal, now in the British Museum, was discovered at Cyprus.[1] The movements of Gilgamesh and Ea-bani are portrayed in a life-like manner, though the action of Ea-bani's left arm is somewhat awkward and ungraceful. The same may be said of the overpowered and ill-designed buffalo, and also of the antelope beneath the inscription, but the lion is decidedly conventional, a fact possibly due to the ubiquity of his presence on the cylinder-seals and monuments of the earliest Sumerian times, from which one may perhaps infer that the perpetual reproduction of the same animal, has in time worn off the freshness with which the artist at first approached his subject. But the Gilgamesh seals probably reach their climax in that reproduced in Fig. 58. The hero is engaged in mortal combat with a lion, whom he is endeavouring to throw. Gilgamesh

FIG. 58.

is represented full-face and with the various peculiarities which appear to have been proper to his unique person —the long, curly beard, the equally long hair parted in the centre with the three characteristic ringlets on either side, and the body entirely naked but for a narrow girdle. The action is concentrated and focussed into a point—

[1] Cf. Ward, *Seal-Cylinders*, p. 69.

there are no conflicting persons, animals, or even objects
in the scene to draw away or divide the attention of the
spectator, and the animation with which the subject is
treated is ample justification for the isolated and exclusive position that it here holds.

Another group of Babylonian seals belonging to different periods show the dramatic conquest of the deity over

FIG. 59.

the winged dragon. One of the earliest, best preserved,
and most instructive examples of these, is a shell cylinder
preserved in the Metropolitan Museum, New York, also
published by Ward[1] (cf. Fig. 59). The dragon has the
wings and hind part of an eagle, while his fore-legs and
head are those of a lion ; between the wings upon his
back stands a nude goddess brandishing lightning in
either hand. The dragon is harnessed to a four-wheeled
chariot, the front part of which is higher than the back,
while a god of disproportionate size is driving the chariot
and flourishing a whip in his left hand. The lion-
headed dragon is apparently vomiting, and his action recalls that of one of the expiring lions on the bas-reliefs
of Ashur-bani-pal. It may, however, be meant to represent the ejection of venom, though if this is the case it
has not been very happily rendered. Before this group
of supernaturals, stands the worshipper who is in the
act of presenting an offering of uncertain character upon
an altar.

[1] Cf. *Seal-Cylinders*, p. 48, Fig. 127.

But sometimes gods and heroes are found side by side on the same seal, as is the case on the seal reproduced in Fig. 60. The horn-capped and seated deity is Shamash, the Sun-god, from whose shoulders rays of light proceed, while from his lap issue streams of living water.

The god is clad in a long mantle hung from the right shoulder, while the left arm and shoulder are left bare, and he is seated on a three or four-legged stool. Before him is a crescent, and behind him is a star mounted on a

FIG. 60.

kind of stand, while in his presence a typical scene is being enacted ; two heroes are laying low a lion—one of them has his left foot on the lion's head and is grasping the tail of the upturned beast with his left hand, while he is about to drive a knife into its rear quarters with his right. The other hero is holding himself in readiness with a little hatchet; his head-gear differs from that of his comrade in being spiked, but in all other respects the two are alike. This seal is made of pink marble, and is now preserved in the Metropolitan Museum, New York. One class of deities was intimately associated with the serpent, and a god's body is sometimes represented as being formed of a serpent coil, as is the case in the cylinder-seal reproduced in Fig. 61. The god in this case is sitting opposite to a goddess who is likewise seated, and holds a shallow

FIG. 61.

cup in her hand ; above her arm is the crescent, and behind her is the mounted star as in Fig. 60. The star as here represented is identical with the early Sumerian ideogram and determinative for god, and, doubtless has that signification here. The goddess has a long robe reaching down to the ankles, but her left arm and shoulder are free, as in the case of the god in Fig. 60. Her seat consists in a kind of camp-stool, a form of support which the genius of the Babylonian seems to have invented at a very early date. The serpent-bodied and human-bearded god holds a branch in his hand, the precise significance of which is not very clear, but the prominent place occupied by the sacred tree in Babylonian and Assyrian mythology justifies the assumption that here as elsewhere it has some symbolical meaning. Behind the god is a five-barred gate, which must be intended to suggest the difficulty of access to the divine presence, or else the necessity of an introduction thereto. Unless the gate were opened either by the god himself, or by some intermediary being of divine or quasi-divine character, the worshipper was presumably unable to gain admittance.

As we have already seen, the cylinder-seals frequently present us with the pictorial aspect of a legend already known from the literature. One of the most famous legends of the Babylonians was that which told of Etana's courageous but bootless attempt to ascend to heaven on the wings of an eagle. Higher and higher soared the eagle, till at last heaven's portals were in sight, but the goal, for some reason not indicated, was never reached, and both Etana and his living aeroplane were dashed to the ground. We have an illustration of this bold flight on some of the seal-cylinders in the British Museum, an impression of one of which is given in Fig. 62. Etana is seated on the eagle, who is bearing his burden aloft in the sight of an admiring and upward-gazing dog. On the right a shepherd clad in a long garment —his right shoulder being exposed as usual—is driving a horned sheep and two goats towards a primitive looking fence : both Etana and the shepherd wear beards and long hair, while the latter carries a staff in his left hand. In the background is a naked but likewise bearded

individual, who is seated beside a large amphora with
the contents of which he appears to be entirely preoccupied ; he is presumably performing culinary operations of some kind.

The scene on other Babylonian seals is that of a god
attacking a humanly conceived enemy ; this class comprises cylinder-seals belonging to the archaic period as

well as those of later date. The
impression of one such archaic
seal is reproduced in Fig. 63.
In the centre we have the god,
mounted on a bull, his left hand
raised, his right hand grasping a

FIG. 62.

weapon or a whip ; he is trampling on a prostrate and
suppliant foe, whose figure is sketched in the roughest
and crudest conceivable manner. As Ward says, this
seal must date from the time when the horse was unknown, or at all events not used in battle. On the right
side of the impression, the god is engaged on foot with
an enemy who appears to be armed with a weapon
shaped like a boomerang, such as that with which the
god Nin-girsu is armed
on the Vulture Stele.
The god holds in his
right hand a weapon of
uncertain character,
while between the two
and facing the god is a
diminutive worshipper

FIG. 63.

whose hand is raised—doubtless in token of submission
—towards his divine lord. On the left the god is stabbing
a human-headed bull with a dagger, while from the
god's back, rays, or what appear to be rays, are emitted.

By the time of Gudea, patesi of Lagash, and Ur-Engur
and Dungi, kings of Ur, we find a marked change in
the artistic merits of the seal-engraver's products. Speaking generally, they are executed with far greater care,

and with a wealth of precision entirely absent in most of the earlier intaglios, but what they gain in care and detailed attention, they lose in the conventionalism to which that care and attention have given birth. We have here no rough sketch of a born artist, but the elaborated painting of a copyist. In Fig. 64 we have an impression of one of Gudea's cylinder-seals. The god, who is probably Nin-girsu or Ea,[1] is seated on a box-like throne : he holds a vase in either hand, from each of which issue two streams which pour their contents into three vases resting on the ground, these in turn becoming themselves the generators of living springs of water.

Facing the god is an intermediary deity who is supporting one of the vases with his left hand, and leading the worshipper, probably Gudea himself, with his right. From the shoulders of the in-

Fig. 64.

termediary emanate two serpents, the head of the near one exactly resembling the strange reptiles on the vase of the same patesi (cf. Fig. 90). The identification of the intermediary deity with Ningish-zida is rendered highly probable by Gudea's allusion to this god in one of his inscriptions, where in his description of the manner in which he was introduced to his supreme god, Nin-girsu, he expressly states that " Ningishzida, his god, held him by the hand."

In Fig. 65 we have a seal-impression of Ur-Engur, king of Ur about 2400 B.C. The scene depicted is a familiar one : an intermediary god is in the act of introducing a suppliant worshipper to a superior deity seated on a throne. The enthroned god has a lengthy beard

[1] Cf. Ward, p. 128.

and wears a round hat somewhat resembling the turban worn by Gudea (cf. Pl. 23). He is resting one arm on the back of his throne, while his right hand is extended in apparent invitation to the slowly approaching worshipper. The throne itself, unlike the box-like

FIG. 65.

seats of earlier days, is provided with a back, and the back legs are fashioned after the legs of an ox. The intermediate deities wear the horned cap with which the gods in Gudea's time were usually covered, while horns appear to rise also from out of their heads, the horns oddly enough being identical in shape with those on the terra-cotta head discovered during the recent excavations in Babylonia.[1] The seated deity is clad in a long simple garment reaching down to the feet, his dress being simpler than that of the attendant deities, or even that of the worshipper himself. The latter wears a long tunic, and a fringed mantle over his left shoulder. Both of the intermediaries are likewise apparelled in lengthy garments, which differ, however, from each other and also from that of the worshipper in being more elaborately worked, the divine introducer wearing the richer

[1] Cf. *Mitteilung.*, No. 9, p. 6.

robe of the two. The inscription refers to Ur-Engur, king of Ur, who may conceivably be the figure seated on the throne ; in support of this theory, it is worth noting that the kings of this dynasty were often deified while yet on earth. Ur-Engur was succeeded by Dungi, the impression of one of whose cylinder-seals is given in Fig. 66. Both of these seals are preserved in the British Museum. A bearded and horn-capped god is standing before an altar shaped like a high standing vase, from which arises a feathered branch which may be intended to represent the ascending flame, while two long bare stalks with tufted heads hang over the altar on either side. The god holds in his left hand a weapon, the upper end of which is provided with a lateral semi-circular handle, similar to that found at Tellô by De Sarzec, and also to that represented on the stone vase of Gudea (cf. Fig. 90). In his extended right hand he holds a three-stalked flower, which is an exact replica of that found in the hands of mythical beings on later Assyrian bas-reliefs. On the other side of the altar is the suppliant, clad in the same fringed garment seen

FIG. 66.

in Fig. 65, while his right hand is raised in adoration. Behind him is another worshipper whose dress resembles that of the god, and who is similarly crowned with a horned cap, but in spite of this divine distinction he has both hands raised in worship. Dungi was succeeded by Bur-Sin, one of whose cylinder-seals is seen in Fig. 67. The scene varies little from that found on the seals of his predecessors. A seated god, a worshipper, and another adoring figure wearing a divine head-gear behind. The god wears a turban as in the seal of Ur-Engur (cf. Fig. 65) ; he reposes on a very thickly upholstered seat, while both his own feet and those of his throne rest on a small low platform. The worshipper here has his hands clasped in front in much the same way as Gudea's hands are, in the statues from Tellô, but the third figure, whom Ward somewhat humorously describes as a " flounced goddess," has both hands raised. An impression of a cylinder-seal of Gimil-Sin, the successor of Bur-Sin on the throne of Ur, is reproduced in Fig. 68. The turbaned and long-bearded god is again seated on a richly upholstered divan, and is elevated on a little platform. He holds in his right hand a double-handled vase, while his left hand is concealed in the folds of his flounced robe. The garment of the intermediary is exactly the same as that of the seated god, but a horned cap takes the place of the turban. The worshipper behind has one hand raised like his usher, while the fringed garment hanging from his shoulder is arranged so as to allow his left leg to be seen. A seal of Ibi-Sin, the last of the dynasty (cf. Fig. 69) presents the same subject, while the treatment practically shows no variation. It will have been noticed that the star and crescent find a place on some of these cylinders, while from others they are absent,—from which it may reasonably be inferred that they were mere symbolic accessories, and as such of no vital importance.

All these seals bear inscriptions in contradistinction to those belonging to the earlier period, and a considerable part of the field of the cylinder is occupied with writing instead of scenery. But as time went on this tendency became more pronounced, and during the Kassite period, sometimes nearly the whole of the seal is occupied with an inscription, usually of a religious character. Thus on a cylinder inscribed with the name of Kurigalzu, the Kassite king of Babylonia (*circ.* 1400 B.C.) (cf. Fig. 70) the pictorial element is reduced to one single figure, that of the worshipper.

An extremely interesting seal-impression of the Kassite period is published by Clay in *The Museum Journal*, University of Pennsylvania (I, 1910, pp. 4–6). It is dated in the fourth year of Nazi-Maruttash, king of

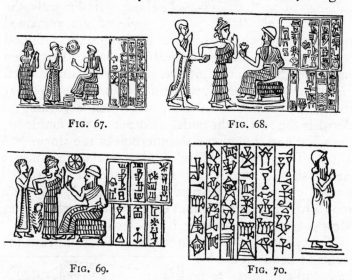

FIG. 67.   FIG. 68.

FIG. 69.   FIG. 70.

Babylon (*circ.* 1330 B.C.) (cf. Fig. 71). Three bearded men are engaged in ploughing; one is urging on the two humped oxen who are yoked to the ploughshare, the second holds the handles, while the third appears to be pouring grain into a drill attached to the plough.

It has been said that this seal-impression gives us the earliest representation of the Babylonian plough, but that statement must be considerably modified in the light of the early seal-impressions given by Ward (p. 132, Figs. 369, 371, 372). The plough is portrayed on all these three cylinders, and they all antedate the cylinder-seal of Nazi-Maruttash (cf. also the votive-tablet from Nippur, Fig. 25, E).

The Neo-Babylonian Empire (625–538 B.C.) inherited the stereotyped traditions of the long period of Kassite

supremacy, and though there was a certain reaction in favour of the pictorial as against the literary element in the later cylinder-seals, the style of art remained

FIG. 71.

more or less unchanged, if not unchangeable. A good example of a Neo-Babylonian seal-impression is that found on a tablet dated in the 26th year of Nebuchadnezzar (cf. Fig. 72).[1] The worshipper stands before a rectangular box which looks like an altar, but which, according to Ward, is the seat of the gods. It supports two emblems, one a dog and the other a thunderbolt of the storm-god Adad. The posture, attitude and general appearance of the worshipper exactly correspond to those found on the Kassite cylinders of Kurigalzu (cf. Fig. 70), and are a good illustration of the conventionalism to which later Mesopotamian art became so hopelessly enslaved.

The cylinder-seal was employed in Assyria from the earliest periods of her history, and continued to be used right down to the time of the Persians, who in turn adopted the same kind of seal. A cylinder-seal belonging to the early

FIG. 72.

Assyrian period, i.e. about 2000 B.C., is shown in Fig. 73. The workmanship is crude, but in the scene itself we see in embryo the military exploits of the late Assyrian bas-reliefs. A warrior, mounted in his two-wheeled war-chariot, is in the act of dispatching an arrow from his

[1] Cf. Menant, *Pierres Gravées*, II, p. 132 ; Ward, p. 193.

drawn bow; his rival, on foot, is doing exactly the same, and it appears to be a question as to which of the two combatants will get his arrow in first. The chariot is drawn by a bull, an indication that the horse was not as yet used for war purposes, while the four-spoked wheels are a further archaic touch—the chariot-wheels of the later Assyrians having eight, twelve, or sometimes sixteen spokes. The bull, in his mad career, is trampling over a prostrate foe, a scene which is frequently represented

FIG. 73.

on the bas-reliefs; it is however interesting to see the symbolical star and crescent of the old Babylonians reproduced on this early Assyrian seal.

We have already seen the winged-dragon on an archaic Babylonian seal (cf. Fig. 59), but it was apparently not till the Assyrian era that the conflict between "Bel and the dragon" was represented in Mesopotamian art.[1]

FIG. 74.

On an early Assyrian cylinder-seal, now preserved in the Metropolitan Museum, New York (cf. Fig. 74), we have a primitive picture of the conquest of Bel-Merodach as the representative and very incarnation of order, system and method, over the dragon— the personification of disorder and tumultuous chaos. The god is drawing his bow — not apparently at a venture, but with the deadly certainty with which the gods can presumably aim. This notwithstanding, the god has taken the precaution of carrying a quiver-full of arrows on his back, while he is further armed with an axe. The winged-dragon of composite character is reared upon his hind legs, his face turned towards his omnipotent adversary, as on the

[1] Cf. Ward, p. 197.

x

famous Marduk and Tiâmat bas-relief. The god is accompanied by another beast with wings, who is doubtless ready to come to the assistance of his divine lord when called upon. Behind the god we see the winged disc, and what appear to be two eyes, while the

crescent of Sin, the moon-god, and the star of Ishtar are engraved in front. Behind the dragon is a sacred tree, resembling a palm-tree. The sacred tree played a very important part in Assyrian art, and is one of the most fre-quently recurring objects on

FIG. 75.

the palace-wall reliefs. It is likewise often to be found on Assyrian seals, a good example of which is afforded by a cylinder-seal in the British Museum reproduced in Fig. 75. The sacred tree in its most conventionalized form occupies the central part of the picture; on either side stands the king with hand raised in adoration; his dress—for an Assyrian king —is comparatively simple, but his headgear is a re-plica of the pointed hat so frequently seen upon the heads of Assyrian kings on the palace wall-reliefs. Above the sacred tree is the god Ashur with his winged disc, from which two cords descend which seem to form the outward con-necting link between the god and his worshipper, and recall the rays which emanate from the disc

FIG. 76.

of Aten, and terminate in hands bearing the Egyptian symbol of life, on the famous stele of Khuenaten, the so-called " heretic king " of the eighteenth dynasty of Egypt. Behind the king is the winged eagle-headed genius so constantly represented on the bas-reliefs This strange mythical creature has one hand raised while in the other he carries a basket of the ordinary Assyrian type.

In a number of seals, one of which is reproduced here (cf. Fig. 76), a man-fish, or a fish-god, resembling the figure found by Layard in sculptured relief at Nimrûd (cf. Pl. IV) occupies the most prominent position. Ashur in his winged disc is again casting the shadow of his divine protection over the sacred tree; on either side stands the Dagan-like worshipper with one hand raised and holding a basket in the other. He is followed by an attendant worshipper, while behind, is a warlike-looking personage—possibly the god Marduk—who is about to execute vengeance on an ostrich; with his left hand he firmly grasps the ostrich's long neck, and in his right he holds a scimitar with which he apparently intends to remove the bird's head.

FIG. 77.

The seated deity found on Babylonian seals of all periods is also found on the cylinder-seals of the Assyrians. We have a good specimen of an Assyrian seal of the kind referred to in Fig. 77. A bearded god is seated on a chair with a high back such as is never found on Babylonian cylinders: the legs of the chair are strengthened to support the weighty person of the divine occupant by means of cross-bars, while the back is somewhat grotesquely decorated with balls. In front of the god is a table or stand with double folding legs and covered with a cloth upon which a shallow bowl and two flat cakes of bread are set; above the table is a fish—its head turned towards the god. Behind the enthroned god stands a goddess, from whose body proceed four ray-like projections which terminate in stars, the general ap-

pearance of the projections being not unlike that of four
starry rockets. Before the loaded table stands the worshipper with one hand raised, while in the field of the
cylinder there is an ibex, an eye-shaped design, seven
balls and a crescent.

CHAPTER X—SHELL-ENGRAVING AND IVORY-WORK

(A) SHELL-ENGRAVING

THE art of engraving on shell in Mesopotamia dates back to the earliest days of Sumerian civilization. The most ancient of these engravings are executed on shells with rough surfaces, of which those of the oyster seem to have been the most popular.

Some of the fragments recovered are clearly shaped and fashioned for inlaying purposes, while others, of curved shape, can be fitted together and once formed part of an engraved and delicately moulded vase or cup. Some time later mother-of-pearl became the popular material among engravers, who used it to great advantage. Mother-of-pearl is undoubtedly more effective and striking than ordinary shell, but it has its disadvantages and drawbacks, for it is both brittle and scaly, and in consequence of this the engraver seems to have been compelled from the necessity of the case to confine himself to the use of flat blades or flakes when employing this material.

One of the most ancient specimens of the shell-engraver's art as yet discovered is that reproduced in Fig. 78. This fragment is convex in form and a truncated triangle as regards its shape. A lion is seen in the act of strangling a bull ; with one of his fore-legs he is grasping his victim round the neck, and the other is thrown around and over the bull's back, while he is burying his teeth in the bull's neck. The general style to which this engraving conforms, the full-face view of the lion, the act in which he is engaged, and the combined vigour and crudeness which characterize this production, vividly recall the mace-head of Mesi-lim, king of Kish (cf. Fig. 26). The comparison between the two is so striking that we can hardly be wrong in assigning this engraved shell to approximately the same period, i.e. to the time before Ur-Ninâ, the founder of the first dynasty of Lagash. It was discovered at Tellô in the neighbourhood of Eannatum's well and is just under three inches in height. In Fig. 79[1] we have another fragment of a very archaic shell-engraving; a human-headed and streaky-bearded bull is

FIG. 78.—(Louvre) Cat., p. 389.   FIG. 79.—*Déc. en Chald.*, Pl. 46, 4.

being attacked by a lion-headed eagle; the shell itself is extremely thin, and the engraving very delicate, but the design itself as well as the mode of its execution both testify to its great age. The shell work of the time of Ur-Ninâ and his successors is well illustrated in Fig. 80. We have here a sketch of a man bearing a net; the man is clean-shaven and bald, and his face is of precisely the same type as that so frequently represented on the sculptures of Ur-Ninâ's time. His only clothing is a short "kaunakes" skirt, the fringe of which is portrayed in the fashion characteristic of the earliest Sumerian works of art. In his right hand he carries a

[1] Cf. Heuzey, *Cat.*, pp. 387 ff.

battle-axe, while with his left he holds the ends of two sticks from which is slung the net or basket already referred to. This small relic was found in the same neighbourhood as the preceding, and is just under two inches high. Another interesting specimen of Sumerian shell-engraving is published by Mr. L. W. King in the *Proceedings of the Society of Biblical Archæology*, 1910, pp. 243–5. It represents a bearded hero embracing an ibex. It is worthy of note that the hero's dress does not consist in the Sumerian skirt, but in a loin-cloth. Probably the finest example of early Babylonian shell-

FIG. 80. FIG. 81. FIG. 82.
(Musée du Louvre) Cat., pp. 393, 401.

work is that reproduced in Fig. 81 ; the leaping kid is wonderfully realistic both in form and attitude and has clearly been studied from nature. Of the mother-of-pearl work of a somewhat later date we have a good example in Fig. 82. Here Gilgamesh is depicted in standing posture holding in either hand one of the long " staves " seen elsewhere, and specifically on the famous green steatite vase of Gudea (cf. Fig. 90). Gilgamesh is portrayed full-face and has the long vertically streaked beard so frequently seen on the cylinder-seals. This fragment is just under two and a half inches in height, and emanated from the same place. The engraved oblong mother-of-pearl plaques would appear to have been used for the decoration of the handles of knives or daggers.

In Fig. 83 we have one of the best preserved and most interesting specimens of later shell-work in Mesopotamia. This fragment was discovered at Warka (Erech), but is clearly Assyrian in style: the elaborately caparisoned horses remind us strikingly of the horses sculptured in relief on the palace walls of Ashur-naṣir-pal at Nimrûd (Calah), while the floral decoration betrays Egyptian influence and recalls the carved ivories which were found amid the débris of that king's palace. The ruined mounds of Assyria herself have yielded but few specimens of the shell-engraver's art, and those that have been recovered are for the most part Phœnician in workmanship and Egyptian in conception, sphinxes and lotus - plants assuming the most prominent part in the decoration. The discovery of engraved shells of apparently a yet later date was among the many interesting results attending the German excavations at Babylon; a number of these shells were found on the floor of a building of Nebuchadnezzar, some of which showed Egyptian influence and were decorated with lotus ornaments. Shell was thus used for various decorative purposes, but in early times it sometimes served as a material for the fashioning of even so utilitarian an object as a seal, as we have already had occasion to remark.

FIG. 83. (After Layard.)

(B) IVORY-WORK

Unlike shell, which could be readily picked up on the shores of the Persian Gulf by the inhabitants of the earliest centres of civilization in Lower Mesopotamia, many of which were doubtless seaports in those days, ivory was only procurable elsewhere, and it was not till the dwellers in the valley extended their power outside that they were able to command a supply of this more precious substance, ivory forming one of the principal materials exacted by the later Assyrian kings from their various vassal princes. A large collection of carved ivories discovered in Ashur-nasir-pal's palace at Nimrûd (Calah) affords us the desired opportunity for studying the ivory work of the period, and for ascertaining the proficiency to which that art was brought by the artists of that day. What strikes one instantly, and with overwhelming force, about the little group of carved ivories in Pl. XXXII is their pronounced Egyptian appearance, a sure and certain indication of the intimate relation which must have subsisted between Egypt and Assyria at this period. In the top right-hand corner we have the head of a woman, represented full-face and with an Egyptian head-gear : the head is set within the frame of a narrow window, from which it looks out over a balcony supported by pillars. In the centre we have the fragment of a similar head, below which there is a bull's head. In the top left-hand corner we have an ivory plaque upon which is figured an Egyptian king in standing posture, grasping a lotus plant about his own height with his left hand. The plant rests upon a stand, the top of which is shaped volute-wise and resembles the capitals of the columns on the bas-relief from Sippar (cf. Pl. XIV). Below on the left is a carved ivory sphinx, which in style and character is clearly neither Assyrian nor Babylonian. But the most interesting specimen in this group is the carved ivory panel in which two women are seated opposite each other on either side of a cartouche surmounted by a disc and feathers. The cartouche contains Egyptian hieroglyphs which may be read " Uben Shu," the meaning of which would be " The Sun god riseth," or the " Rising Sun " : the inside of this cartouche is gilded, and the characters within are inlaid. The feathers, which are likewise inlaid, are the emblem of Maat, the god of truth, and the disc is of course emblematic of the sun. The two women are obviously Egyptian, their head-dresses, the folds in their garments and their general attitude all alike testifying to their Egyptian origin, while beneath their seats, which consist of low-backed chairs, there is the "ankh" sign, the meaning of which is "life." This sign, misnamed " crux ansata," or " cross with a handle," has needless to say nothing whatsoever to do with the Christian symbol; it probably represented a girdle, that which used to be regarded as a handle being that part of the girdle which encircled the waist, the long stem being the loose ends, and a girdle as encircling the vital parts would not unnaturally symbolize life, and in picture-language come to signify it. The two seated figures have one hand raised in token of adoration before the sacred emblems in the middle, while in their other hands they firmly grasp a sceptre. Below we have seven more fragmentary specimens of ivory-work, all of which were discovered amid the ruins of the same palace and betray a strong foreign influence. The deductions which these little ivory carvings justify our making in regard to the foreign affairs of Assyria at this period, are rendered certainties by the evidence afforded by the bronze bowls dealt with in the chapter on Metallurgy.

Fig. 84.

PLATE XXXII

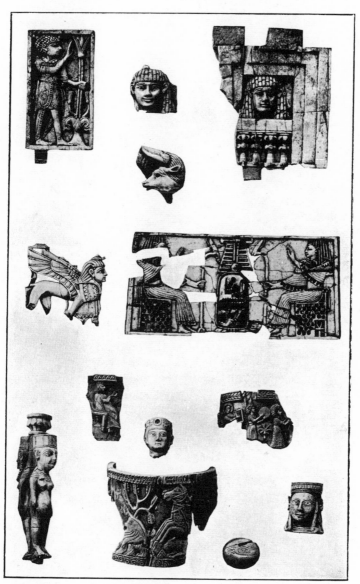

Photo, Mansell

CARVED IVORY PANELS, FROM NIMRÛD

It must not however be supposed that all the ivories discovered in Assyria are the work of Egyptian or Phœnician artists. Some, of which a good specimen is seen in Fig. 84, are as Assyrian in style and conception as any palace bas-relief. The ivory panel here reproduced is just five inches high. The subject is a familiar one—a four-winged mythological being crowned with a horned cap, with the right hand extended in the performance of some religious ceremony, and carrying a basket in the left hand. Not only is the motif entirely Assyrian in character, but the workmanship and manner of execution bears the unmistakable hall-mark of Assyria. The aggressive masculinity of the arms and legs, the folds, arrangement and style of the garments as well as the hair and strongly depicted beard, are all exactly paralleled in the figures so often seen on the stone sculptures of the period. On either side of the panel in which this mythological creature is enshrined there is a scroll-work device which was employed in Babylonia as early at all events as the time of Entemena of Lagash, while his feet stand upon a line of the rosettes which appear so frequently as a decorative accessory in Assyrian works of art. The lower part of this panel is filled in with circular and volute-shaped devices, and at the bottom of all we have another line of rosettes. Among the various subjects carved on the other ivory panels emanating from the ruins of the same palace the following may be mentioned as of especial interest : a hero slaying a lion, some Assyrians gathering fruit, and Ashur-nasir-pal accompanied by deities and attendants.

These ivory panels from Nimrûd were as we have seen, in many cases inlaid[1] with lapis lazuli and gilded, and they were probably used to decorate and embellish thrones, or other stately articles of furniture, and in

[1] For the early history of inlaid jewellery cf. Dalton, *Archæologia*, LVIII, pp. 237-74.

this connection we not unnaturally think of the great throne which Solomon built for himself, which is said to have been made of ivory and overlaid with the best gold (cf. 1 Kings x. 18) as also of the ivory palace erected by Ahab.

CHAPTER XI—TERRA-COTTA FIGURES AND RELIEFS

I T were indeed paradoxical if the Babylonian artists had not invoked the aid of the clay, which they employed so readily and extensively not only in their building operations but also for all ordinary writing purposes, in their attempts to represent human and animal life. Undoubtedly this material was not employed for these purposes so frequently as might have been expected, but this is probably due to the comparative fragility of this substance and its consequent inability to withstand the disintegrating effects of time and climate ; as most of the objects fashioned by Babylonian artists would appear to be of a votive character, it is obvious that durability was one of the most important considerations in their production. Notwithstanding this fact however, a sufficiently large number of terra-cotta figures, some of which belong to the earliest periods of Sumerian civilization, have fortunately been preserved. The most ancient of these terra-cotta models are extremely small in size and crude in workmanship. We have a very archaic example in Fig. 85, A. The eyes of this small figure are the most noticeable features ; they consist of flattened balls ; the bodies of these primitive little models are as unfinished as they can be, sometimes being fashioned merely triangular-wise. In Fig. 85, B, we have another example of the same type and belonging to the same period, though it shows a slight advancement on the preceding figure. A thick head-gear or wig, crowns the head, and in its hands it holds an object of uncertain character, either a child or an instrument of music according to M. Heuzey. The clay, though moulded in the hand, is incised with a number of delicate lines, which are probably due to the application of a sharp and finely pointed tool. These curious figures are about one and a half or two inches high.

The next illustration (Fig. 85, C.) transfers us from the early Sumerian period to that of Gudea. The comparative proficiency attained through long cultivation of the art is sufficiently obvious. The figure is that of a god, his head-gear being characteristically furnished with four pairs of horns, and unlike the copper votive

Fig. 85.—A, B (cf. *Déc. en Chald.*, Pl. 39; 1, 2). C (cf. Cat., Fig. 183). D (cf. Cat., Fig. 193; *Déc. en Chald.*, p. 252). (All Musée du Louvre.)

statuettes of Gudea the god here has bull's ears. The upper part of the body is left bare, but the lower part, which unfortunately is not preserved, was evidently covered by a garment fastened round the waist by a girdle. The god's left hand has hold of a stick or weapon inserted in the girdle, the upper portion of which is seen in the illustration. As usual, the god wears a heavy beard represented by a series of vertical streaks, but the arrangement of his hair in two long tails hanging down over his chest and curled at the ends, is somewhat peculiar. This little plaque is between two and a half and three inches in height.

The Sumerians of early times did not however confine themselves to a portrayal of single figures in their clay reliefs, but sometimes aspired to complete scenes ;

thus in the fragment reproduced in Fig. 85, D, we see a standing woman ; her hands are raised in a devotional manner, and doubtless were the remainder of this clay relief preserved we should see her accompanied by her husband, as so frequently on the cylinder-seals. Her thick, wavy hair hangs plait-wise down her back, and a raised fillet surrounds her head. The relief in which the woman's figure is raised is high, and the workmanship, though crude is not without life. This little fragment is about five inches high and is made of grey-coloured clay. Occasionally these terra-cotta figures were painted, as was the case with the little male statuettes discovered at Babylon in 1910.[1]

Ever faithful in the art of imitation, the Assyrians also turned their attention to the artistic possibilities inherent in the clay which they used alike for the construction of their houses and for writing purposes. Some of the clay figures, or little clay reliefs discovered in Assyria belong without doubt to Assyrian times, but by far the larger half of the terra-cotta figures, lamps and other objects discovered are as certainly post-Assyrian.

Some very interesting terra-cotta figures representing the Fish-god, Dagan, are preserved in the British Museum (cf. Fig. 86, A, B). These small images are only a few inches high, but the humanly conceived face of the god is treated with less conventionalism than is the case with the sculptured portraits of human beings during the Assyrian period, a fact which of course may possibly be due to the plasticity of clay as compared with stone. These little figures are probably Assyrian and not Babylonian in workmanship ; at all events, a fish-god sculptured in relief was discovered at the entrance to a small Assyrian temple at Nimrûd, which, apart from other evidence,[1] is a clear indication that the fish-god was venerated in Assyria as well as in Babylonia. It would

---

[1] Cf. *Mitteilungen*, No. 44, p. 24.
[2] Cf. also the Assyrian seal reproduced in Fig. 76.

seem reasonable to suppose that the Dagan-cult would
naturally find its origin in the alluvial centres of Sumerian civilization in the extreme south of Babylonia,

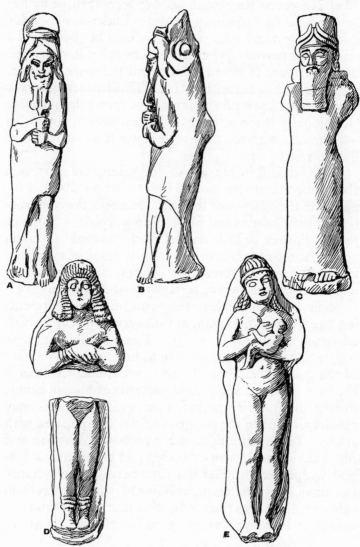

Fig. 86.—A, B (Brit. Mus., No. 91837).   C, E (Musée du Louvre).
D (Cf. *Mitteilung.*, No. 5, Abb. 1).

where the water was an all-important factor for good or ill, but according to Jastrow[1] it was imported from the north to the south, though the name of a king of Isin, Ishme-Dagan, who reigned about 2200 B.C., shows that the god was known and revered in Babylonia at least as early as his time. On the other hand it is equally noteworthy that one of the earliest known Assyrian kings, whose reign must probably be assigned to the nineteenth century B.C., also bore that name. These clay images of the gods were usually buried as amulets in the foundations of buildings. Another terra-cotta image of a god belonging to the Assyrian period, and the work of an Assyrian artist, is seen in Fig. 86, C.[2] This little image was found, together with two other terra-cotta figures, beneath the floor of the court of Sargon's palace at Khorsabad. Each had been enclosed in a brick capsule as a foundation-amulet, where they remained undisturbed until the spade of Botta brought them once more to light. The figure here reproduced is that of an Assyrian god, while one of the other two was a mythical creature, and the third was a demon, but all three must have been buried for much the same purpose, the god to take care of the positive welfare of the inmates of the palace, the demon to act negatively in warding off evil influences, while they all have their stone counterparts in the bas-reliefs recovered from the ruins of Assyrian palaces. This little image is eight inches high and is made of a greyish clay. The god is clothed in a long robe reaching down to his feet ; his head is crowned with a cap encircled by two pairs of horns, and his beard conforms to the usual Assyrian type.[3]

Various terra-cotta figures of nude women or goddesses have been recovered from different Babylonian

---

[1] Jastrow, *Religion of Babylonia and Assyria*, p. 208.

[2] Cf. Heuzey, *Catalogue des Figurines de terre cuite du Musée du Louvre*, Pl. I, Fig. 2.

[3] For the other two, cf. *Ibidem*, Pl. I, Figs. 1 and 3.

Y

and Assyrian sites, but they are for the most part not earlier than the Parthian period, and their consideration does not therefore fall within the scope of the present volume. There are however exceptions to this generalization, one of the most remarkable being that of a terra-cotta figure also preserved in the Louvre and reproduced in Fig. 86, E.[1] This little model is reported to have been found at Hillah, near Babylon ; the place of its discovery was a Greek grave, but it was found in the company of seals and amulets belonging to a much earlier period. The woman, in a standing position, is seen suckling her infant at her breast. The bodies of the mother and her child both exhibit the characteristic fullness of Eastern art, but in spite of this fact, there is a delicacy and refinement, as well as an insight into the charms of human nature such as is seldom seen in the statues and figures of Oriental antiquity. Various terra-cotta figures of nude women were also discovered at Nippur in the strata of Shar-Gâni-sharri and Ur-Engur, while another interesting example of a nude woman or goddess is seen in Fig. 86, D.[2] This little clay figure was discovered during the course of the German excavations at Babylon, a site which has yielded numerous terra-cotta figures of nude women with and without a child ; the lower part of the body does not apparently belong to the upper part represented here, but is the broken half of another clay figure ; it enables us however to form a better idea of the general appearance of these terra-cottas when complete. Both fragments were recovered in the ruins of the temple of the goddess Nin-Makh, and doubtless formed part of clay miniatures of a stone statue of the goddess, which unfortunately has not yet been brought to light. The figure exhibits a certain heaviness, which the thick tresses of hair only tend to accentuate. The hair itself appears to be carefully waved

[1] Cf. Heuzey, *Les Figurines Antiques de terre cuite*, Pl. II, Fig. 3.
[2] Cf. Koldewey, *Mitteilungen*, No. 5, pp. 19, 20.

and curled; the woman's hands are clasped below her breasts, while she wears bracelets on her wrists and anklets on her legs.

During the same excavations an interesting figure of a bearded man, made of unbaked clay and measuring about six inches high, was found in the temple of Adar; his left arm is hanging down, and his right arm is extended and holds what appears to be a staff, while on his head he wears a Phrygian cap or something akin. A similar clay figure was found in the Anu-Adad temple, but it differed from the former in being provided with a golden staff. The figure was enclosed in what is known as a brick capsule; these capsules were sometimes only a few inches high, but at other times reached ed as much

FIG. 87. (Brit. Mus.)   FIG. 88. (Brit. Mus.)

as twenty inches. These capsuled statuettes were generally located before the entrances to rooms. Sometimes figures of animals as well as of human beings were similarly enshrined in brick capsules; thus a model of a clay dove enclosed in this manner was discovered by the German excavators at Babylon.

Among the most interesting of the Assyrian terra-cotta models must be mentioned those of the favourite hunting-dogs of Ashur-bani-pal (cf. Fig. 87) found in his palace at Nineveh; these same dogs can however be so much more readily studied from the stone bas-reliefs of this same king, that it will be best to forgo any detailed consideration of them here. Unfortunately it is impossible to speak with any confidence as regards the date of the vast majority of clay figures yielded by the excavations in Babylonia and Assyria ; they comprise figures of gods and goddesses, as well as of dogs, lions and other animals. Some of these are fashioned in the round, others are portrayed in relief upon small plaques. One of the best preserved of these plaques is reproduced in Fig. 88. This little clay relief was discovered by Sir Henry Rawlinson at Birs-Nimrûd. A clean-shaven and semi-nude attendant is in charge of a large hound which he is leading by means of a strap. The attendant, who is armed with a stick, is more life-like than the attendants on the bas-reliefs of Ashur-bani-pal, but the dog, though spirited, cannot compare with those sculptured in hard stone on the palace walls of that same king. The innumerable terra-cotta lamps which have been excavated from time to time for the most part belong to a late period, it is however interesting to note that clay lamps were apparently in use at a very early period, even as early as the time of Bur-Sin, king of Ur (*circ.* 2350 B.C.), one of whose clay lamps was discovered at Nippur. We have already remarked that clay was probably used extensively for making moulds for casting metal objects, and it is certain that it was sometimes used by the sculptor as a material for rough sketches (cf. p. 118). The clay figures or statuettes of the earlier period were either fashioned by hand, or else stamped in a mould, but in either case they were solid, in contradistinction to the Babylonian terra-cottas of the later Greek and Roman times which were generally hollow in the interior, their outside being coated with a kind of paste by means of which the artist endeavoured to work out the details of hair, clothing, and other externalities, while they were not infrequently covered with a vitreous glaze, the colours used being blue and green. But a consideration of this later work lies beyond the scope of our volume, which is confined to a consideration of the Babylonian and Assyrian period.

CHAPTER XII—STONEWARE AND POTTERY

STONE and clay were the two materials from which the Babylonians and Assyrians as a rule manufactured their vases, pots and bowls, though, as we have seen (cf. Fig. 45), metal was occasionally used for the purpose. Unfortunately the study of Babylonian and Assyrian pottery has never received the attention which it deserves, while in the earlier excavations carried on in Mesopotamia the importance of these uninscribed relics of the past was not realized, and the omission to observe the particular strata of the mounds in which they were respectively discovered, as well as in some cases the failure to note even the sites where they were unearthed, has made anything like a systematic study of Babylonian and Assyrian pottery a virtual impossibility.

Various kinds of stone were used as materials for making bowls and vases from the earliest periods of Mesopotamian civilization. Thus at Nippur the American excavators unearthed a vase made of sandstone, bearing an inscription of Utug, patesi or priest-king of Kish, the writing of which was even more archaic than that on the mace-head of Mesilim, king of Kish (cf. p. 185, Fig. 26) and, therefore, presumably of an earlier date ; it seems to have been dedicated to En-lil as a thank-offering, an incidental testimony to the important place which the god of Nippur must have occupied even at this extremely remote period. So, too, a vase of white calcite stalagmite, bearing an inscription of Urzage, a king of Kish belonging to about the same period, was dedicated to En-lil and his spouse Nin-lil.

Stone vases have similarly been found at Tellô, while the fragments of a number of stone vases made of white calcite stalagmite and bearing an inscription of Lugal-zaggisi, the king of Umma who sacked Lagash in the reign of Urukagina the last king of the first dynasty, were found on the same site, and we learn from the inscriptions on these vase-fragments that they were dedicated by Lugal-zaggisi to En-lil at E-kur. A fragment of an alabaster vase bearing the name of Urukagina is now preserved in the British Museum, and an onyx vase, dedicated to the goddess Bau, was discovered in the neighbourhood of Ur-Ninâ's building, while a large basalt bowl of Eannatum was found on the same site, and the fragments of a limestone vase, bearing an inscription of Entemena, a later king of Lagash, were discovered beneath the temple of En-lil at Nippur. So also at Jôkha, the site of the ancient city of Umma, fragments of vases and objects made of stone were brought to light, while at Fâra, the ruined mounds of which represent one of the earliest sites of Sumerian civilization in the Babylonian plain, vases and cups made of various stones including marble were recovered. These were generally of a simple character, though sometimes they were decorated. But Bismâya, thanks to the scientific excavations carried on by Harper and Banks for the University of Chicago, has probably yielded a richer and more varied harvest of stone pots than any other site in Babylonia. They comprise bowls, phials, dishes, cups, mugs, and vessels of every conceivable shape, the tallest measuring about twelve inches in height, and the largest about twelve inches in diameter, while the thickness of the walls varies from an eighth of an inch to just under an inch and a quarter.[1] The stones from which they are made vary almost as much as their dimensions, and include white marble, yellow marble, alabaster, yellow limestone, pinkish onyx, porphyry, green porphyry, blue

[1] Cf. Banks, *American Journal of Semitic Languages*, Vol. 22, p. 35 ff.

freestone, soft limestone, and grey sandstone. Hardly any of these manifold vessels were found complete, but Banks was able to reconstruct a large number from the fragments that remained. They were all polished; some were engraved with a comparatively simple design, while others were elaborately decorated with the figures of men and animals, and some were inlaid with ivory and precious stones. The inscriptions were few and fragmentary, the name of the king or the temple mentioned being otherwise unknown, while the writing is extremely archaic. That part of the mound in which these stone vase fragments were discovered contains only the plano-convex bricks characteristic of the old Sumerian period, which further indicates the extreme antiquity of this large collection of stone-ware, and indeed stone-ware seems to have been to a great extent supplanted by the more economical and more easily wrought clay pottery, at a comparatively early date, as was the case in ancient Egypt. Most of the vases from Bismâya are circular in shape, though examples of oval, oblong, square, and shell-shaped vases were also found. The stone most commonly used was marble, due no doubt to its comparative softness and adaptability to the chisel. The curvature and general symmetry of these vases is so perfect that, according to Banks, a lathe or something answering the same purpose as a lathe, must have been used. The softer stones at this period were doubtless worked with flint instruments, as in the case of the earliest cylinder-seals. The purposes which these vases served must have been as diversified as the vases themselves. Some appear to have been lamps, others drinking-cups; some were probably used as water, wine, or oil jars, while others may have been used as wash-basins; some were used for articles of toilet, and in one vessel traces of *henna*[1] were still visible in one compartment and traces of *kohl* in the other.

Of the stone-ware of the early period of Semitic

[1] Cf. Banks, *American Journal of Semitic Languages*, Vol. 22, p. 37.

supremacy in the Euphrates valley, a gracefully curved vase of white marble belonging to Urumush[1] king of Kish, which was discovered at Nippur during the course of the excavations carried on by the University of Pennsylvania, and is now preserved in the Pennsylvania Museum, affords us a good example; while of the stoneware of the somewhat later period of Shar-Gâni-sharri and Narâm-Sin, the Semitic kings of Agade, a white alabaster "phial" (cf. Fig. 89) discovered at Tellô and bearing the name of Narâm-Sin is an excellent specimen.

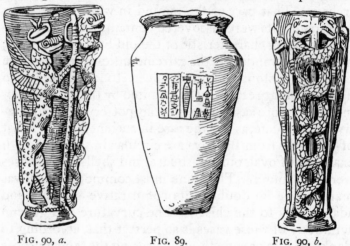

FIG. 90, a.   FIG. 89.   FIG. 90, b.

It consists in a well-rounded flask or phial seven and a half inches high, and is inscribed with the words "Narâm-Sin, King of the four regions." Another small stone vase of this king made of marble was acquired by Oppert during the ill-fated expedition of 1855, the inscription upon which gave the additional information that the stone from which the vase was made came from Magan, but this valuable relic shared the fate of the other monuments and tablets recovered by Fresnel and Oppert, and went down in the Tigris on May 23rd, 1855.[2]

[1] Cf. Hilprecht, *Babylonian Expedition*, Vol. I, part ii, Pl. XX.
[2] Cf. *Découvertes*, *Description*, p. 118; Hilprecht, *Explorations*, p. 170.

Many stone vases of the late period of Sumerian supremacy have been brought to light, but none so interesting or so illuminating as that of Gudea, patesi of Lagash (cf. Figs. 90 *a*, *b*). This unique vase of dark green steatite is between eight and nine inches high, and rests upon a narrow circular base. It is furnished with a very small spout which could only allow but a small quantity of liquid to pass at a time. The decoration is of the most elaborate order : two entwined serpents occupy the central part of the design, their sinuous coils encircled round a long staff traversing the whole height of the vase, while their tongues are seen touching the edge of the vase near the embryonic spout. The serpents are flanked by two strangely composite and highly mythical creatures which face each other; in the grasp of each is a long spear provided with a semicircular lateral handle, an exact replica of the copper weapon discovered by De Sarzec at Tellô,[1] the site where this vase was also found. These winged monsters have the body and head of a serpent, and are provided with claws and talons, while their tails find their fitting termination in the sting of a scorpion; their necks are encircled with twisted tails, and their headgears consist in a kind of horned cap, an indication of the supernatural powers of these extraordinary monstrosities. But in spite of the highly mythical character of these creatures, the artist has not lost sight of the general appearance of the serpent that has, as it were, supplied the material and natural foundation for the unnatural additions which his imaginative mind has superimposed, the scaly skin of the snake being portrayed by means of inlaid fragments of marble. The inscription informs us that this vase was dedicated to the god Nin-gish-zi-da by Gudea for the prolongation of his life.

Another stone vessel of a somewhat unique character

---

[1] Cf. p. 243.

is the dark alabaster bowl in the Nimrûd Central Saloon of the British Museum ; it is sculptured in relief with a scene of Gilgamesh and Ea-bani wrestling with lions, but unfortunately it is in a very poor state of preservation.

But the practice of making vases of stone did not cease with the decline of Babylonian supremacy ; the Assyrians imitated their cultural progenitors in this as in all other matters. The most interesting stone vase belonging to the Assyrian era is that bearing an inscription of Sennacherib (cf. Fig. 91, A). It is a kind of am-

FIG. 91.—A, B, C (British Museum, Nos. 93088, 91596, 90952). D (after Clay).

phora though the two handles are nearly worn away. The shape and proportions of this vase are very artistic, and the curves well rounded off. In general contour it somewhat resembles the little glass vase of Sargon, a yet more remarkable relic of antiquity (cf. Fig. 91, C). Another interesting example of Assyrian stone-ware is seen in Fig. 91, B; the vase, which is decorated round the neck, bears the traces of a well-nigh effaced inscription, and like the small glass vase of this same king is engraved with a small lion. It is shaped differently from most of the stone vases of the period, and has a charm and beauty all its own. Various glass vessels and tubes were recovered from the ruins of Babil, Kouyunjik and elsewhere, but their date is in nearly all cases an uncertain quantity. Assyrian and Babylonian glass would appear to have been made in the ordinary way, i.e. by a mixture of silex or sand with alkalis, while it was fashioned into the required shape by means of a blow-pipe, and finished off with a turning machine, of which the marks are sometimes still visible. This is the case with the little vase of Sargon illustrated above.[1]

Stone-ware of the late Babylonian period is well illustrated by the jar-fragment of Nebuchadnezzar (604–561 B.C.) published by W. L. Nash in the *Proceedings of the Society of Biblical Archæology* (1910, p. 180). The inscription is very brief and apart from the king's name only has the numeral "one," which was probably followed by a measure, but the name of the latter is broken away. This stone jar like the Assyrian jars differs from most of the inscribed vessels of earlier times, which usually bear a dedicatory inscription, while in shape it is not unlike the Assyrian jars seen in Fig. 91.

Allusion has elsewhere been made (cf. p. 86) to the marble vase bearing the name of Xerxes in cuneiform and Egyptian hieroglyphics, but a number of similar vases and fragments bearing an inscription of this same king have also been brought to light. One such vase was found by Newton at Halicarnassus in Asia Minor, the fragments of another being found by Loftus at Susa, while a third (cf. Fig. 91, D) recently acquired by the Babylonian Museum of the University of Pennsylvania, is published by Clay in the *Museum Journal* (1910, 1, p. 6). It bears the royal inscription of Xerxes the Great written in four different languages, Persian, Elamite, Babylonian and Egyptian, the last-named being written in the old hieroglyphics, and the other three in cuneiform. The vase measures nine and seven-eighths inches in height, and eight and fifteen-sixteenths inches in diameter.

[1] Cf. Layard, *Discoveries*, p. 197.

Although stone-ware appears to have been used more frequently in the earlier periods of Mesopotamian civilization, it must be not supposed that terra-cotta pottery was not also used by the ancient Sumerians and early Semites. A vast quantity of pottery comprising bowls, phials, flat vases, chalice goblets, oval pots and vessels of every description, size, shape and form has been r e covered from Tellô, Nippur, Fâra and other recently excavated sites in Babylonia, and indeed so numerous and so manifold are the vessels in question that only a

FIG. 92.—"Pre-Sargonic cup."   FIG. 93.—"Earliest vase from Nippur."
(Hilprecht, *Explorations*, p. 407.)

long and systematic study of the mass of material now available, as thorough and exhaustive as that made by Professor Flinders Petrie of Egyptian pottery, would justify any attempt to classify and date the different specimens. The earlier excavations in Mesopotamia similarly yielded a large number of terra-cotta pots and jars, but unfortunately there is so much uncertainty as to the locality from which many of them came, and even where that is known, there is generally no means of ascertaining in what strata they were found—(as is unhappily also the case with a good deal of the pottery discovered in recent years)—and as they further bear no inscriptions, any attempted systematization in our present state of knowledge is inevitably based largely on unproved and unprovable hypotheses. Two good examples of early pre-Sargonic pottery are seen in Figs. 92, 93. Both the cup (Fig. 92) and the vase (Fig. 93) were discovered in the pre-Sargonic strata at Nippur.[1] Many other interesting specimens of early pottery were discovered on the same site, some being apparently black in colour, others being red. In a room beneath the pavement of Narâm-Sin two vases were brought to light which illustrate the remarkable differences in size and shape exhibited by early Babylonian pottery, one of these vases being bell-shaped and having a flat bottom twice as large in diameter as its mouth, while the other, a little over two feet high and one foot nine inches across the top, was decorated with a rope pattern.[2]

Among the minor results attending the excavations at Bismâya was the recovery of a vast number of terracotta vases, some entire, others only fragmentary.[3] They were found in graves, wells, and drains as well as in the various platforms contained in the mound, and in the plain itself. Between twenty-five and twenty-six feet below the surface two large burial urns were discovered, while at a depth of some thirty-four feet a smaller urn was brought to light. The earliest examples of pottery were found more than forty-four feet below the surface. In the larger vases and urns the clay appears to have been mixed with chopped straw,[4] the clay itself being as a rule of a yellowish brown colour, but according to Banks, the clay was burnt to a deep brown or black colour in the earliest times. The wheel seems to have been used at all periods, though not to the

---

[1] Cf. Hilprecht, *Explorations*, p. 407.

[2] Hilprecht, *The Babylonian Expedition of the University of Pennsylvania*, Series A, Vol. I, part ii, Pl. 27.

[3] Cf. E. J. Banks, *American Journal of Semitic Languages*, Vol. 22, p. 139. [4] *Ibidem*, p. 140.

exclusion of hand-made pottery. One of the pre-Sargonic vases from this site was apparently formed by placing the clay on a flat surface, which the potter revolved with one hand while fashioning the clay into the required shape with the other hand; as Banks suggests, this may have been the origin of the potter's wheel. The vessels from Bismâya vary in height from a little over an inch to just under thirty inches, and they exhibit every conceivable kind of shape. The surfaces of most of them are plain, but some are decorated with dots, squares, concentric circles and grooves. Two large vases are painted with the marks of their makers or owners in black, but these are regarded by Banks as post-Babylonian. Some of the vases are provided with covers, the cover of one of the funeral urns consisting in a kind of dish ; sometimes, in the case of vases which were buried, a woven cloth was fastened over the mouth and sealed with clay. These cloths have of course long since perished, but the marks of the threads on the clay are still visible.[1] One vase is shaped like a boat, while another interesting terra-cotta object discovered on this site is a lamp terminating in the head of an ox.

Some very unique specimens of Babylonian black pottery with incised lines filled with white paste were discovered by Capt. Cros at Tellô. These vases were not only decorated with geometrical designs, but also with fish, boats, water-fowl and other river scenes.[2] This type of pottery is of frequent occurrence in the ancient world. It has been found in Susa on the east, while in the west it penetrated as far as Spain. Of Babylonian pottery belonging to the Kassite period, mention should especially be made of three vases discovered by Peters and Haynes at Nippur. These pots are decorated with

---

[1] Cf. E. J. Banks, *American Journal of Semitic Languages*, Vol. 22, p. 140.

[2] Cf. *Comptes Rendus, Académie des Inscriptions et des Belles Lettres* 1904, p. 115.

PLATE XXXIII

POTTERY, FROM NIMRÛD

Photos. Mansell   *British Museum*

POTTERY, FROM NINEVEH

green and yellow stripes, and were enclosed in an urn together with three small boxes, the largest of which was ornamented with knobs. Along with these articles more than a hundred discs and crescents pierced for the purposes of suspension, and mostly coloured black or white, were also found. One of the best examples of late pottery is the delicately-shaped and well-preserved amphora discovered by Koldewey at Babylon,[1] but it must probably be assigned to the Roman period.

With regard to Assyrian pottery we are in a still greater state of ignorance, in spite of the wealth of material at hand. Large quantities of pottery were brought to light by Botta, Layard and other early excavators, but unfortunately their archæological importance seemed as nothing compared with colossal bulls, sculptured bas-reliefs, or even prosaic clay tablets, and the result of this fortunately bygone apathy is that the site from which they came is sometimes not ascertainable, while on hardly any occasion is it possible to discover the building or immediate locality where they were found.

But the scientific excavations carried on by Koldewey and Andrae at Ashur are calculated to yield more satisfactory results in this connection. These excavations have already thrown light on the early pottery of Assyria, in the discovery of clay vessels decorated with black and red geometrical designs and assigned to the prehistoric period.

Another interesting specimen of Assyrian pottery found on the same site consists in a large round vase decorated about the top and having two handles.[2]

In Pl. XXXIII we have a miscellaneous group of pottery from the ruined mounds of Nineveh, and a similar group from Nimrûd. The pots here displayed show much variation both in size and form, but little more can be said about them. Apart, how-

[1] Cf. *Mitteilungen*, No. 40, p. 8. [2] Cf. *Ibid.*, No. 26, p. 19.

ever, from the complete vessels in clay, a number of fragments of bowls have been recovered bearing inscriptions of kings of Assyria who reigned between 1140–681 B.C. These inscriptions are principally concerned with the various building-operations undertaken during the reign of the king in question. Were these bowls complete they would be of immense importance in arriving at some definite idea as to the shapes and sizes of vases in vogue at the different periods to which they belong. But as fortune or misfortune has it, hardly any of the well-preserved cups and bowls as yet recovered bear any inscription or design at all, and this is one of the great difficulties with which the student of Babylonian and Assyrian pottery has to contend. Sometimes a coloured glaze was applied to the surface of terra-cotta vessels, but to what extent this practice prevailed in early times it is hard to say.

Probably the two most striking pots yielded by the excavations are those numbered 91941 and 91950 in the British Museum collections. The former is a large jar nineteen inches high and eighteen and three-quarter inches in diameter, upon which is portrayed the figure of a man with the tail of a goat and the claws of an eagle, while the broken remains of one handle are still preserved. The latter is a six-handled vase two feet six inches high, on the body of which rude figures and dragon-like animals are depicted, but both of these vases probably belong to post-Assyrian times.

CHAPTER XIII—DRESS, MILITARY ACCOUTREMENTS, ETC.

THE full dress of the earliest Sumerians comprised nothing more elaborate than a skirt fastened round the waist and probably made of wool. But the taste for decoration shown by all primitive peoples is evinced by the Sumerians at a very early date, and they seek to relieve the dead monotony of the skirt by edging the bottom with a fringe (cf. Figs. 25, 52), the fringe on the earliest monuments being formed by a series of pointed tags. In the time of Ur-Ninâ, the archaically fringed skirt has given place to an elaborately flounced and pleated skirt—at least in the case of kings and magnates (cf. Figs. 26, 27), but the upper part of the body was left entirely bare ; people of particularly high rank are however sometimes seen wearing a skirt with an upper part attached, which covered the left shoulder as is the case with the leader of the procession on Ur-Ninâ's tablet (cf. Fig. 26), though it is noticeable that Ur-Ninâ himself here has no clothing on the upper part of his body. Later on the king of Lagash still wears the flounced skirt, but has another garment over it : this upper garment was also apparently made of wool, and passed over the left shoulder and under the right arm (cf. Pl. XII) ; as this is, however, a battle scene, the upper garment may be part of the king's military insignia. This custom of leaving the right arm and shoulder free obtained right down to the time of Gudea (cf. Pl. XXIII) and Khammurabi (cf. Pl. XIV).

The heads of the majority of the figures on the early sculptures are hairless and beardless, though as we have seen (cf. p. 183) long hair and a pronounced beard were not infrequently worn, the hair on the head—possibly a wig—sometimes being allowed to hang down the neck (cf. Fig. 25, B, C), sometimes being gathered up behind and secured by a fillet (cf. Pl. XII). This seems to have been done by the king when on active service, doubtless with a view to making his helmet more comfortable and secure. As nearly all these early figures are without hats or head-gear of any kind, we are almost entirely in ignorance as to the nature of their head-coverings—if, indeed, they had any. Sometimes feathers were worn (cf. Fig. 25, A), while a figure resembling Gilgamesh on one of the most ancient Sumerian bas-reliefs (cf. *Découvertes*, Pl. I, 1) in existence, has a flat head-gear of indeterminate character, the deity on the same archaic sculpture wearing what appears to be an early form of the horned head-dress of the gods in later times.

The dress of early Sumerian women is somewhat uncertain ; if we might assume the form of dress shown on the little stone statuette discovered by De Sarzec at Tellô (cf. Fig. 33, p. 224) to be typical, the feminine dress of the period would appear to have consisted in a flounced woollen skirt hung from the left shoulder, the right arm and shoulder being exposed. The length of the fillet-bound hair in the statuette referred to removes all doubt as to the sex, and it is noteworthy that the dress of this Sumerian woman is exactly the same as that of the individual on Ur-Ninâ's stele referred to above, and of course the personage there may conceivably be a woman also (cf. further p. 186). But the little copper statuettes of women belonging to the same period always show a nude bust, it is therefore probable that the women of the time generally wore an ordinary skirt like the men, the shoulder-suspended garments being reserved for the élite.

The dress of royalties and grandees differed however

from that of the commonalty in quality rather than in character : thus the skirts of all Ur-Ninâ's courtiers— the distinguished leader of the procession alone being excepted—are much the same as that of their royal master ; but the quality is very different, the one being entirely plain, the other extremely elaborate.

In later times what had been the exception seemingly becomes the rule, and in Gudea's period the left shoulder was always covered by the folds of the mantle-like garment then in vogue ; while the Semite Narâm-Sin, of yet earlier date than Gudea, wears a plaid passing over his left shoulder and wrapped around his body, leaving the right arm similarly free. The pleated plaid worn by Narâm-Sin finds a striking parallel in the garments worn by Nin-gish-zi-da and the accompanying deity on a Gudea stele in the Berlin Museum (cf. *Sum. and Sem.*, Taf. VII). The royal head-gear of Gudea differs from that of later times, and probably from that worn by the earlier rulers of Lagash : it consists in an embroidered turban, differing entirely from the conical-shaped cap worn by Narâm-Sin on the Pir-Hussein stele, and the similar shaped crowns of the later Assyrian kings, but bearing some resemblance to that worn by Khammurabi on his famous code-stele (cf. Plates, XXIII, XIV ; Fig. 31).

But while the Semite Narâm-Sin wears a long beard, the Sumerian Gudea is still beardless. So too the Semite Khammurabi wears a long beard, but the mantle slung from his left shoulder is not unlike that of Gudea, while the vesture of the god Shamash on the same stele is pleated like that of Narâm-Sin, though the material would appear to be different. In a later relief of the time of Nabû-aplu-iddina, king of Babylon about 870 B.C., the god Shamash wears a striped robe with sleeves, and the practice of leaving the right arm and shoulder exposed seems to have by this time fallen into desuetude (cf. Pl. XIV).

Of the dress of the women in the days of Gudea we have a good illustration in Pl. XXIII. She wears a gracefully fringed mantle, which was apparently[1] first pressed over the breasts and carried under the arms, after which it was crossed at the back, the two ends being brought over the shoulders and made to hang symmetrically in front.

The grave-deposits have afforded abundant evidence of the extensive use of jewellery even in the earliest Sumerian times, thus at Fâra necklaces of amethyst, coral, lapis lazuli, mother of pearl and agate were found, while other early sites yield similar testimony.

For information regarding the military accoutrements of the early Sumerians we are mainly dependent on the bas-reliefs of the period, of which the Vulture Stele is the most important. The long lance or spear, which was apparently grasped by both hands (cf. Pl. XII), was clearly the principal weapon of offence, while the axe, the dart, a club or mace, a curved weapon—generally hitherto regarded as a throwing-stick or boomerang—and a lance were also in use. Very few Sumerian weapons have been brought to light, but in addition to those enumerated in the chapter on Metals, mention may be made of an archaic axe-head made of agate, now in the American Museum of Natural History;[2] the characters with which it is inscribed are somewhat more wedge-shaped than those found on the monuments of Gudea, and it may accordingly be assigned to a rather later date. Another axe-head, also made of agate, and inscribed with early line characters, is in the Metropolitan Museum, New York,[3] while a number of baked clay balls and some small stone eggs, as well as copper arrows, spears, axes and stone clubs were discovered in the pre-Sargonic strata at Nippur. The

---

[1] Cf. Heuzey, *Catalogue des Antiquités Chaldéennes*, p. 249.
[2] Prince, *Journal of the American Oriental Society*, XXVI, p. 93.
[3] Cf. *American Journal of Semitic Languages*, April, 1905, p. 173.

discovery of arrows belonging to such an early date is of considerable interest, as it has been contended that the bow and arrow were introduced by the Semites chiefly owing to the fact that it has been thought that these weapons were not represented in early Sumerian art. But a very early example of the bow in Babylonian art is afforded by an archaic shell cylinder-seal published by Ward.[1] The human beings and gods on this seal are clad in the Sumerian short skirt and not in the Semitic plaid, while the occurrence of a bison on the top of a mountain, an animal which is only represented on very early seals, further argues the antiquity of the cylinder-seal in question, and therefore of the use of the bow and arrow depicted upon it. The discovery of clay balls and stone missiles similarly appear to afford evidence of the use of the sling at a very much earlier period than was hitherto supposed.

It is interesting to trace the history of the boomerang-shaped weapon shouldered by one of the figures on the archaic fragment of the circular bas-relief reproduced in Fig. 25, B. The curved weapon[2] may have originally been a throwing-stick or boomerang, though its shape is the only argument in support of this theory. But whatever its original use may have been, there is evidence that a weapon of this shape was wielded as a club or primitive sword at a very early period. In a sculpture belonging to a slightly later period than the above-mentioned bas-relief, the weapon in question has lost its simplicity and is no longer made in one piece but is composed of three narrow pieces held together by a number of rings. Were this curiously shaped implement only found in the hands of rulers or dignitaries, the rings might merely be decorative accessories, but its occurrence in the hand of a huntsman attacking a lion, (cf. Fig. 78) makes it incumbent that we should seek

[1] Cf. Ward, *Cylinder-Seals*, Fig. 139 *c*.
[2] Cf. Heuzey, *Comptes Rendus*, 1908, pp. 415–22.

for some more adequate and practical reason for the
existence of these rings. Doubtless this later form was
adopted with a view to increasing the efficiency of the
weapon. The weapon is here used at close quarters, and
was clearly not used as a throwing-stick at this period,
but rather as a kind of sabre. At an early date the
Sumerian must have sought for some means of rendering his weapon more serviceable, and have conceived

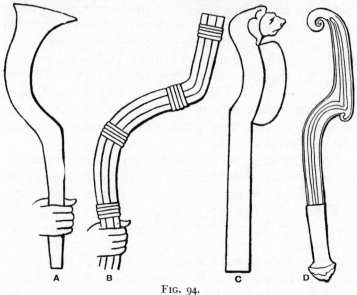

Fig. 94.

the idea of substituting a blade of flint or obsidian, and
in point of fact numerous edged pieces of flint and obsidian as well as primitive saw-blades with teeth have
actually been found in early Babylonian ruins. The
problem of affixing this blade to the handle or shaft,
would find its natural solution in fashioning the latter,
of two or more pieces between which the obsidian or
flint blade might be inserted, both wood and blade being
kept in place by rings ; of its early use as a club or sabre
we have evidence on the archaic shell reproduced in
Fig. 78, where the huntsman is seen holding a curved

implement which is composed of three pieces of wood bound together by rings, as on the Vulture Stele, it is obviously not employed here as a throwing-stick but as a weapon for use at close quarters (cf. also Fig. 94, A. B).

In the later period of Gudea we find the same style of weapon in use. Upon a bas-relief recovered by Commandant Cros from Tellô, and belonging to Gudea, we see a curved weapon (cf. Fig. 94, C)[1] terminating in a lion's head and having a blade which was apparently inserted in a longitudinal slit made in the wood. Sometimes these curved weapons were made of one piece of metal, as was the case with the two examples discovered by Commandant Cros in an early Babylonian grave, one of which is reproduced in Fig. 94, D. Both of these weapons are made of copper and were found in a coffin consisting of two bell-shaped pots cemented together by bitumen. The one in the figure is the more elaborate of the two, and unlike its companion, has the handle still preserved while its total length is about sixteen inches. The edge of the blade was of course on the outside of the curve, the instrument thus resembling a scimitar or short curved sword. It is thus possible that the scimitar, or at least the archetype of the scimitar owes its origin to the Sumerians.[2] The other weapon is of a more primitive character and recalls the earlier examples afforded by the bas-reliefs more vividly, while its blade is double edged. In Assyrian times the curved end becomes quasi-circular in form and the outer edge is furnished with teeth, as is the case with the sceptre which Ashur-naṣir-pal holds in his hand (Pl. XXIV). The arms borne by Eannatum himself as represented on the Vulture Stele are the curved weapon already alluded to, a number of darts some of which are double pointed, and a long lance. Eannatum is in the act of piercing the head of a vanquished foe with his lance, which he holds horizon-

---

[1] Cf. *Comptes Rendus*, p. 418, Fig. C.
[2] Cf. Sayce, *Archæology of Cuneiform Inscriptions*, pp. 65, 66.

tally over his head at the extreme end. According to
Commandant Cros, the lance is used in exactly the same
way by the Arabs of Irak to-day. It is first held loosely
in the middle, while the action consists in throwing it
forcibly through the hand till the lower end of it is
reached, but it is not allowed to escape from the hand
altogether ; the weapon is therefore used in part as a
spear, and in part as a javelin.

For information regarding the military accoutrements
in use at the time of Shar-Gâni-sharri and Narâm-Sin
we are mainly dependent on the stele of the last-named
monarch (cf. Pl. XIII), and the bas-relief fragments reproduced in Fig. 28,B,C. The bow and arrow would appear to be the principal weapons used by the Semites,
though the spear and the axe also occur on early Semitic
monuments. One noticeable feature in these two sculptures is the absence of any kind of shield.

The cylinder-seals contribute little towards the solution of the manifold problems incidental to a study of
early military affairs, as those seals which are engraved
with battle-scenes are for the most part Persian in
origin.

To attempt to describe the complete wardrobe of the
Assyrians would be almost as difficult as to give a full
and comprehensive account of English dress to-day. The
costumes are so various, and often so finely-wrought,
that even a brief review of the different " modes " would
far exceed the bounds of a single chapter. The king's
robes are, of course, the most magnificent and most
elaborate both in arrangement and decoration. In Pl.
XV we see Ashur-nasir-pal, king of Assyria (885-860
B.C.) arrayed in his ceremonial robes. In comparison
with the festive garments of his successors, they are
simple and inornate, and are merely a replica of those
worn by the mythical being behind, the only difference being that those of the king are arranged so as
to conceal both his legs, the exposure of the royal leg

being apparently out of accord with kingly dignity. The under-garment seems to be a fringed robe or chasuble, over which a long, deeply-fringed mantle is arranged ; both the king and his divine attendant wear a broad waist-band into which two daggers are thrust ; but the mantle itself was apparently fastened by means of cords ending in tassels. The king's head-dress, however, is entirely different from that of his follower ; it is shaped somewhat like a mitre, two tails being similarly attached to the back. The royal tiara worn by the later kings of Assyria conforms to the same type, only it is more richly decorated and exhibits some variation in regard to its shape. It would appear to have been coloured, if we may trust the evidence afforded by the enamelled bricks from Khorsabad,[1] the colours being red, white and yellow, the latter perhaps being intended to represent gold braid. Judging from its general appearance, the head-dress itself must have been made of cloth.

Both figures here (Pl. XV) wear a bracelet on either wrist and two armlets on their sinewy arms, while a necklace encircles their bull-like necks. Ashur-naṣir-pal, like all Assyrian kings, has a thick crop of hair and a very strong beard. Shalmaneser II, his son and successor, wears much the same dress as his father and the same conical head-gear (cf. Fig. 44), but Sennacherib one hundred and twenty years later is no longer content with the simple yet dignified dress of Ashur-naṣir-pal and Shalmaneser, but assumes a far richer and costlier set of robes (cf. Fig. 31). The royal mantle is not merely decorated with a fringe but is most elaborately embroidered throughout, while his crown is also far more ornate than those worn by his Nimrûd predecessors, but his attitude is precisely the same as that of Ashur-naṣir-pal in Pl. XV. Both kings are holding a bow in their left hand and two arrows in their right. The regal and ceremonial costume of Ashur-bani-pal con-

[1] Cf. Botta, II, Pl. 155.

trasts similarly with that of Ashur-naṣir-pal and his immediate successors—his dress resembling that of Sennacherib in its general ornateness (cf. Pl. XX) while even the costume which he wears while reclining at meat in his garden is far more elaborate than that worn by Ashur-naṣir-pal on the highest ceremonial occasions (cf. Pl. XXI).

Some uncertainty exists regarding the dress-materials used by the Assyrians. Many garments were doubtless made of wool or woollen stuffs as in the other period, but a kind of cotton was also used, for Sennacherib states that he imported trees that bore wool or hair, from the south, and that the wool or hair was subsequently clipped and utilized for the manufacture of garments.

There is the same uncertainty as to the materials used in embroidery, but there is no doubt about the skill of the embroiderer, who must have been a veritable artist, if we may judge from the bas-relief representations of his work, a good example of which is reproduced in Layard, Pl. 9. He clearly did not confine himself to designs but aspired to artistic representations and scenic effects. Conventional palm-trees, and four-winged monsters are the most conspicuous features. One of these monsters is grasping one of the back legs of a lion in either hand, while the lions are making ruthless attacks on passively resisting bulls.

Women are seldom portrayed on the Assyrian bas-reliefs, but we at all events know that the lady who had the honour of being Ashur-bani-pal's queen was quite as richly clad as her royal master (cf. Pl. XXI), while both wear ornamental fillets round their heads. Jewellery seems to have been prized and loved by the Assyrian king and his courtiers almost as much as by the women of to-day, and the demand for " novelties " must have taxed the jeweller's inventive faculties to the utmost. Not only were armlets and bracelets in requisition, but also necklaces, ear-rings, and trinkets. The latter generally took the form of divine or astrological symbols, one of the most interesting ornaments worn by the king being exactly like a Maltese cross, and closely resembles the cross found on Kassite seals (cf. Fig. 71). The trinkets were suspended on a cord which encircled the royal neck, above which the real necklace is seen. Both bracelets and ear-rings show great variety in design and no little skill in workmanship. Unfortunately but few articles of jewellery (apart from a number of bead-necklaces[1]) have been recovered, and of the majority of these it is impossible to tell the date, but thanks to the bas-reliefs we can gain a very fair idea of the proficiency to which the jeweller's art had been brought at this period, though we cannot be sure of the metals used in each particular case. In Fig. 95 we have a group of bracelets of manifold shapes and designs, the rosette as usual playing the leading part in most of the decorative devices. In A we have an example of a royal necklace ; it is simple and neat in design and presents a striking contrast to that worn by one of the winged figures from Nimrûd (cf. B) which is decorated at the opening with heads of animals. The ear-rings worn by kings, warriors, priests and mythical beings vary quite as much as the bracelets, though there is a certain similarity between most of them (cf. Fig. 95). The drops are in nearly all cases long, and they frequently have a cross piece which gives them the general appearance of a " crux ansata."

The toilet requisites of the Babylonians and Assyrians were doubtless much the same as those in use to-day, though but few articles from the dressing-table have been recovered, the most notable of which are the combs now preserved in the Louvre (cf. Figs. 96, 97). They

---

[1] An interesting bead of black marble, measuring $1\frac{1}{2} \times \frac{5}{8}$ inches was discovered at Ashur ; it bears an inscription of Shalmaneser, the purport of which is that that king brought the bead from a temple in Syria.

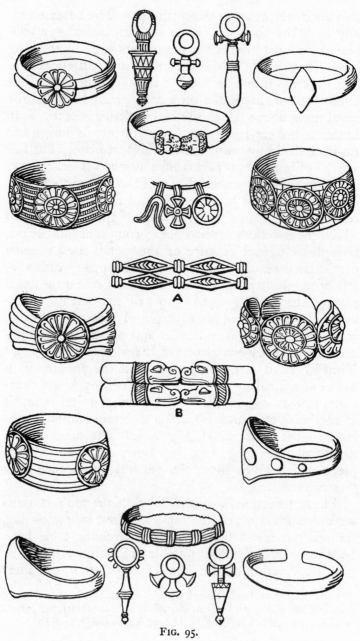

FIG. 95.

are made of ebony and measure about three and a half inches across, while they are elaborately decorated in the centre with the figures of sphinxes or lions, sometimes realized in open-work, sometimes in relief. The teeth on one side are large and few, those on the other being slender and numerous. A similar comb was discovered by Koldewey at Babylon, the centre of which is decorated with the figure of a winged bull.[1]

Sandals formed the principal footwear of civilians— royalties or commoners as the case may be—though the feet were often left bare. The ordinary sandal had a thin

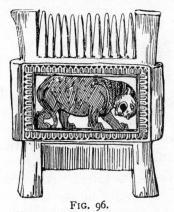

FIG. 96.

FIG. 97.

sole and a small cap for the heel, apparently made of strips of leather which were sometimes coloured red and blue alternately, though more frequently the entire sandal was of a reddish hue, while it was held in position by a loop round the great toe, and by a string which was laced across the instep and tied in a bow. This was the type of sandal worn by Sargon. There was, however, an entirely different sandal in vogue at the time of Ashur-bani-pal; the sole of this later sandal was of consider-able thickness, especially at the heel, while the upper leather did not merely form a protecting cap to the heel but covered the whole side of the foot. But shoes

[1] Cf. *Mitteilungen*, No. 7, p. 18.

were used as well as sandals as early as the time of
Sennacherib; those represented on the bas-reliefs are of
a clumsy make, though finely decorated with crescents
and rosettes, and they were seemingly laced in front.

But the military uniforms of the Assyrians show far
greater variation than the apparel of kings, eunuchs
and attendants. In the early Assyrian period the foot-
soldiers wore a short tunic and a fringed girdle, their
heads being protected by a pointed helmet; the arms,
legs, neck and feet were generally bare, though the latter
were occasionally shod with plain sandals. The infantry
included archers,
spearmen and
swordsmen, while
the archers were of-
ten further armed
with swords and
sometimes with
maces, and appear
to have formed the
pick of the foot-
soldiers. All three
divisions were pro-

FIG. 98.
Foot-spearman (1st
period, Nimrûd).

FIG. 99.
Foot-archer (1st period,
Nimrûd).

tected by small hand-shields, the bowmen often being attended by another warrior armed with a spear, who acted
as shield-bearer. In the reign of Shalmaneser II we frequently see the bowmen clad in a long coat of mail reaching from the neck to the ankles (cf. Fig. 44), but in the
Sargon period the difference in the equipment of the foot-
soldiers becomes more pronounced. There are at least
three different kinds of archer. First of all there was
the light-armed bowman, who was practically naked but
for a loin-cloth, which supported a quiver, and a head
fillet(cf.Fig. 100). Next came the more simply equipped
of the heavy-armed (cf. Fig. 101), who was clad in a coat
of mail reaching from the neck to the waist, beneath
which was a fringed tunic extending to the knees, while

their feet were generally protected by sandals, and the head covered by a pointed helmet. The principal feature which differentiated the appearance of the most heavily armed archers from that of the foregoing was the long deeply fringed tunic (cf. Fig. 102), over which a coat of mail was worn similar to that worn by the archers of the second class.

The spearmen of the period are clad in much the same way as the medium-armed archers, the most noticeable point about them being their helmets, which are surmounted by a crest of one kind or another (cf. Fig. 29), while another frequent peculiarity in their equipment is

FIG. 100.   FIG. 101.   FIG. 102.

the arrangement of their belts which cross each other on the chest and back. Their feet are generally bare, though sometimes they are shod in sandals, and occasionally in a low boot.[1]

Sargon's son, Sennacherib, appears to have largely re-organized the infantry and instituted fresh corps. The slingers seemingly make their first appearance in this king's reign, though the sling was known in Babylonia even before the time of Shar-Gâni-sharri (cf. above, p. 341). On the bas-reliefs of Sennacherib we see him fully armed with helmet, coat of mail, tunic reaching to the knees, close-fitting hose and a short boot, none of which can have added to the efficiency of his services. There

1 Cf. Botta, *Monument*, II, Pls. 90, 93.

were four types of archer, two heavy-armed and two light-armed. The most heavily armed (cf. Fig. 103) wore a tunic, a coat of mail reaching to the waist, hose, short boots, and a conical helmet, and are protected by long shields carried by a shield-bearer. The next class have no shield protection, and their legs and feet are entirely bare (cf. Fig. 104). The better equipped of the light-armed are clad in a short tunic, wear a peculiar kind of fillet round their heads, and sandals on their feet, while they carry short swords at their sides and quivers on their backs. Last come the lightest equipped archers of

FIG. 103.   FIG. 104.   FIG. 105.

all, who wear a striped tunic[1] reaching down to the knees and somewhat longer behind than in front (cf. Fig. 105). Their feet, arms and legs are bare, and fillets form their sole head-gear, while they are seldom armed with short swords like the preceding.

There were apparently two classes of spearmen in Sennacherib's army ; the better equipped wear a coat of mail over their tunics, a conical helmet, hose on their legs, and boots on their feet, while they are generally armed with a comparatively short spear, a rather large convex shield, and the usual short sword. The second division are equipped in much the same way as the light-armed spearmen of Sargon, and wear plain tunics, cross belts, and crested helmets, but unlike the spearmen of

[1] Cf. Rawlinson, *Five Monarchies*, II, p. 49.

Sargon they usually have sleeves to their tunics, wear hose on their legs, boots on their feet, and sometimes carry a long convex shield arched at the top instead of a round one. Yet another class of foot-soldiers deserve a mention; these are armed with double-headed axes which they use to cut down trees and clear the road for the passage of troops. Their equipment closely resembles that of the better-armed spearmen. The army in Ashur-bani-pal's time is much the same as it was in the time of Sennacherib; it comprised bowmen, spearmen, mace-bearers, warriors armed with battle-axes and slingers. In regard to the latter it is interesting to note that the heavy armour of the slingers has been exchanged for a lighter and more serviceable garb.[1]

The principal weapon of the cavalry in the early period was the bow, though sword and shield both occur, but were apparently not much used. It was customary for the mounted archers to be accompanied by another mounted soldier whose office it was to hold the bridle of the archer's horse while the archer was aiming his arrow at the enemy. The attendant wears a plain tunic and an ordinary cap, while the archer has a pointed helmet, an embroidered tunic and a sword belt. Their legs and feet are bare to enable them to sit their horses firmly—the latter being without saddles. In the time of Sargon the cavalry consisted partly of spearmen, partly of archers. Saddles or saddle-cloths somewhat resembling those worn by European cavalry horses to-day were in regular use, while the unarmed attendants were no longer required, both archers and spearmen being able to manage their own steeds. The uniforms worn by the cavalry were similarly much more elaborate than those worn by the mounted archers of the earlier period. Their tunics are close-fitting, but expand below the waist into a kind of fringed kilt, they wear hose on their legs and long boots on their feet,

[1] Cf. Rawlinson, *Five Monarchies*, II, p. 43.

2 A

which sometimes reached nearly up to the knee; the principal weapons borne by the horsemen are bows and spears, but they are frequently armed with a short sword as well, while the spearmen occasionally carry a bow and quiver as well as a spear and a sword (cf. Fig. 106).

In Sennacherib's time, the ordinary cavalry are equipped in much the same way ; some of the regiments however are heavily armed with a coat of mail extending to the bottom of the back (cf. Fig. 107). In the

FIG. 106.

sculptures of Ashur-bani-pal, the horses of the cavalry are sometimes covered with a large cloth similar to that carried by the chariot steeds (cf. Fig. 108), over which the saddle-piece is placed, but the equipment of the cavalry themselves shows little or no variation from that of former times.

The charioteers form the last division of the Assyrian army to be briefly considered. The chariot contained at least two persons—the driver and a warrior ; but when the king took the field in person he was attended by a shield bearer, or sometimes two

shield bearers, as well as by a charioteer. The normal
weapon used by the chariot soldier is the bow, which
he generally has full drawn, the arrow on the string ;
he is however not infrequently girded with a sword,
while a spear is often lying at his side within easy reach.
He is sometimes merely clad in a tunic, sometimes in
a long coat of mail reaching down at least as far as the
knees, but having short sleeves, doubtless with a view
to facilitating the manipulation of the bow. He either
discharges his shafts from the chariot itself, or else dis-
mounts in order to take a more certain aim ; in the latter
case the attendant protects the bowmen by means of a

FIG. 107.

shield which he holds in his left hand, while in his right
hand he holds a spear or sword wherewith to repel any
close attack. The warrior generally wears a helmet which
is occasionally furnished with side and front pieces made
of metal scales, calculated to protect the shoulders, the
nape of the neck, and sometimes even the chin, but the
attendant as a rule has no covering for his head.

The chariots were drawn by either two or three
horses, but there was apparently never more than one
pole ; accordingly when a third horse was harnessed to
the chariot, he must have been attached by a rope or
thong, and was probably taken as a relief-animal to fill
the place of one of the others in the event of either of
them being shot through. The trappings of the horses

were often very elaborate, as may be seen in Figs. 83, while the chariots were also sometimes very ornate. There are two main types of war-chariot represented on the Assyrian bas-reliefs, one being characteristic of the earlier period, when Calah (Nimrûd) was the capital of the empire, the other of the later epoch when the seat of the government was established at Nineveh. The chariots of the early period are low and short, the wheels being comparatively small, and as a rule only having six spokes, while the chariots portrayed on the later reliefs are generally more capacious and also loftier, while the wheels, which would appear to be about five feet in dia-

FIG. 108.

meter, are normally eight-spoked (cf. Fig. 108). A position in one of these later chariots consequently gave the warrior a good vantage ground for aiming at the enemy and also for viewing the situation. The poles of the chariots of both periods frequently terminate in the head of an animal, an ox or a horse as the case may be. Sometimes a cross-bar was fixed to the end of the pole, which also occasionally terminated in the heads of animals, the cross-bar being at times straight, at others curved.

From this brief description of the military equipment of the Assyrians, it will be at once manifest how elaborate must have been the organization of the army. Reference has frequently been made to the conical-shaped helmets of the soldiers, and the similarly shaped tiaras of the kings, but it must not be supposed that all Assyrian head-gears were conical. Some idea of the diversity of head-coverings used in Assyria may be gained from the selection reproduced in Fig. 109. The most noteworthy of these is the horned crown in the centre

(A), which was worn by the colossal winged-bulls. The horns which are the symbol of divinity, occupy a prominent position on the head-coverings of nearly all Baby-

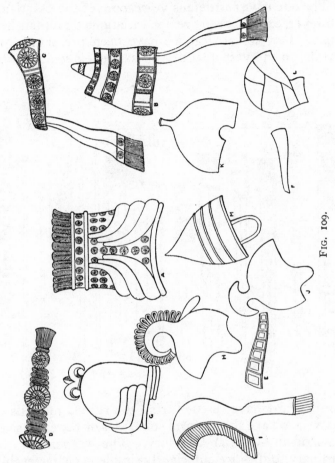

FIG. 109.

lonian and Assyrian gods, and their presence on the head-gear of a human-headed bull is indicative of the divine character with which they endowed these colossi. The top of this massive crown or hat is decorated with a row of feathers, while its face is adorned with the familiar rosettes. In (B) we have a royal tiara, and (C),

(D), (E) and (F) illustrate the different kinds of fillets worn round the head, while (G) to (M) exhibit the various types of helmets used in the Assyrian army.

The offensive and defensive weapons of the Assyrians, however, exhibit even greater variations than their helmets. Few actual weapons have been preserved, but thanks to the vast quantity of bas-reliefs which Botta

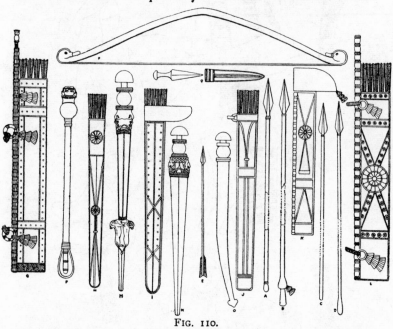

FIG. 110.

and Layard have rescued from the ruined mounds of Assyria, we are able to form some idea of the extensiveness of an Assyrian armoury. The weapons of the ordinary soldier are sufficiently simple in character, but those which kings, demigods, or viziers wear are often most ornate. In Fig. 110 we have a selection of the more striking weapons represented on the bas-reliefs. (A), (B), (C) and (D) show us four different kinds of pike wielded by the warriors of Ashur ; they vary in length and their handles differ, but they all have a more or less diamond-shaped blade, while the arrow-heads (E) are shaped in the same manner. The two extremities of the bow from which the king despatches his unerring shafts into the heart of the enemy, the lion, or the wild bull, and for which he also finds use in the performance of religious ceremonies, often find their termination in the head of a bird (F). But though the arrows themselves are severely practical in their appearance, the quivers in which they reposed when " off duty " are more elaborate (cf. (G)–(L)). The largest of these quivers could accommodate as many as five arrows (cf. (L)), but the normal number seems to have been four. The quiver was slung over the back by means of cords (cf. (G), (J) and (L)). The swords would appear to have been generally straight ((M) (N)), though sometimes curved (O). The sword-hilt was frequently adorned with several lions' heads, while the scabbard itself was often decorated with lions, the result of which is highly ornamental and effective. The sceptre was a ceremonial weapon—inoffensive without doubt, but eloquently symbolic of royalty (cf. (P)), while the dirk (Q) on the other hand is brandished in a most alarming manner by the composite monstrosities portrayed on the palace walls of Ashur-naṣir-pal.

But by far the most formidable military invention of the warlike Assyrians was the battering-ram ; the ram was brought to bear upon the wall of the besieged city by a movable tower, in the shelter of which the ram could be effectively and safely worked, the tower and the battering-ram thus forming together a most potent factor in both offensive and defensive operations. These movable towers were by no means uniform, but varied both in size and height, sometimes they were surmounted by towers (cf. Fig. 111 (A)) from which the attacking forces could shower their arrows upon the beleaguered army with impunity, at other times they were quite low and shaped liked a torpedo, the larger ones resting on

six wheels (cf. Fig. 44), and the smaller on four (Q).
The ram itself also varied—sometimes it was set at an
angle slanting upwards (A), its projecting extremity being

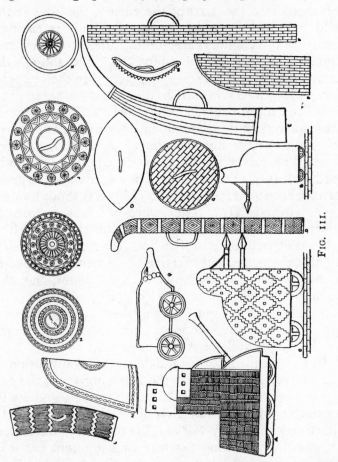

FIG. III.

at the same time heavier and thicker than the shaft, but
more usually the ram was fixed horizontally and pointed
like a spear (B), the tower sometimes being armed with
two of these rams (C). The most noticeable of the
shields here represented are the large shields, from behind the shelter of which the bowman could aim and

shoot at his ease, the shield of course being held in position by a shield-bearer (cf. (D), (E), (F)). These large shields were generally upright (F), but were often curved at the top to protect the head of the archer from the missiles of the enemy (D), while sometimes the whole shield was curved (E). But the lancers required no such protection, a small hand-shield which they could carry themselves being the only type of defence which would not completely nullify their usefulness in the field. These shields varied in shape and size ; they were generally round (cf. (G)–(K)), but sometimes curved and oblong (L), while at other times they were concave in the body, oval at the top, straight at the bottom, and decorated with a boss in the centre and an engraved design round the edge (cf. (N)). Another type of shield was shaped somewhat like a lozenge (O), but they all alike have their handles in the centre. They were often most elaborately engraved, the designs being formed by an arrangement of straight lines ((G) and (P)), geometrical figures ((H) and (L)), or circles of rosettes ((I) and (J)). One of the shields illustrated here differs from the rest in having its outer face notched like the edge of a saw, and must have served offensive as well as defensive purposes (cf. (M)).

But the Assyrians waged war " terra marique,"—on the sea as well as on dry land, and in Fig. 112 (A) we have an example of one of the war-galleys used by Sennacherib in his pursuit of the Babylonian rebels across the mouth of the Persian Gulf. It is a bireme, i.e. a boat with two banks of oars ; below are the oarsmen, while the warriors are stationed on an upper deck. The boat is shaped rather like a cutter in front, but the stern ends off in a sweeping upward curve, and there is a mast and cross-beam secured by yards in the fore-part of the galley. The course of the boat is steered by means of two oars worked from behind, which differ in shape from those used to propel the boat. In (B) we have another variety of this type of craft : here both ends of the boat are curved, the extremities being squared off instead of pointed as in (A), and there is moreover no mast, but in (C) we have a

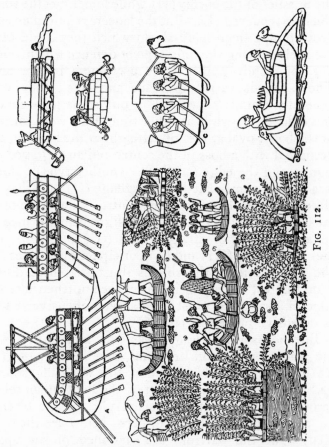

FIG. 112.

different kind of boat altogether ; it is an open boat with only one bank of oars and there are no warriors aboard. There are only four rowers and their oars are totally different from those used in the war-galleys, the oars of the galleys resembling long shafted spades, while those here are not unlike hockey sticks. Both prow and stern are curved, the latter terminating in a horse's head, and in the centre of the boat there is a mast. The custom of decorating the ends of a boat with an animal's head, no doubt originated among the Phœnicians, who were the maritime people of the Oriental world. In one of the scenes on the bronze gates from Balâwât we see Shalmaneser II receiving the tribute of the ships of Tyre and Sidon (D) ; these ships, or rather boats, are curved at either end, while both prow and stern are figured with the heads of camels. Only two men are required to manipulate the heavily laden craft, one of whom is apparently steering, while the other is pulling the boat along with the aid of a very heavy and clumsy-looking oar. But war-galleys were not the only boats in use in the time of Sennacherib ; a lighter and far smaller boat was employed for the transport of goods (E). The cargo occupies the centre of this odd little vessel, on either side of which two oarsmen are busily plying their oars. Strange to say, they appear to be pulling in opposite directions, but we must possibly attribute this anomaly to the sculptor's ignorance of nautical affairs ; the oars are quite different from those employed in the battleships, but they are exactly the same as those used on the cargo raft above (F) ; the raft seems to be loaded with large blocks of stone ; the wooden raft by itself is clearly incapable of sustaining so heavy a weight, and the requisite buoyancy is attained by fastening inflated skins to the nether part of the raft. A kind of reed raft seems to have been used for traversing the marshy districts of Lower Mesopotamia (H), the reeds being tied together by means of osiers, and the water excluded by a covering of leather or a thick coating of bitumen. These reed crafts sometimes assume the form of flat rafts, while at other times they resemble canoes.

CHAPTER XIV—LIFE, MANNERS, CUSTOMS, LAW, RELIGION

(A) THE EARLY SUMERIAN PERIOD

1. *LAWS, MANNERS AND CUSTOMS*

THANKS to the indefatigable labours of Père Scheil and M. Thureau-Dangin, and to the admirable work of M. Genouillac on *Sumerian Society*, in which that scholar publishes, translates and comments on many of the early tablets from Tellô, we are able to obtain a very fair idea of the manners and customs of the Sumerians at the time of the first dynasty of Lagash.

An investigation of the conditions of any society naturally commences with a brief consideration of the laws, which regulated the process of propagation upon which the continuance and prosperity of the community ultimately depends. It would appear that from the earliest Sumerian times marriage was regarded in the light of a legal contract, and divorce could similarly only be effected by legal procedure. But the Sumerian marriage laws of the time of Lugal-anda and Urukagina differed from the European laws of to-day in at least one important point, the contract being made by the man with his father-in-law rather than with his prospective wife, and consequently in the case of divorce it was the father-in-law and not the divorced wife who was entitled to satisfaction.

Polyandry was evidently not unknown, for Urukagina had occasion to apply the utmost rigour of the law to its repression, although it had hitherto been by no means condoned, but was on the contrary already regarded as a criminal offence, and not only was this the case, but even polygamy seems to have been discountenanced, for such expressions as " the wife of the priest of Nin-girsu," or " the wife of the patesi " implicitly suggests that there was only one lady in it, and that there was no liability to confusion in the matter. It is however quite conceivable that the patesi had an official wife, just like the priests of Amen, or the kings of Egypt, the other ladies of the harem not ranking with the royal spouse or enjoying the same distinguishing appellative, but this is of course a matter of conjecture. However that may be, there is abundant evidence to show that the Sumerians compare very favourably with other primitive peoples in their regard for and treatment of women. They could act as free agents in the matter of property, and could be legal witnesses to contracts, while widows were especially safeguarded against the extortion of those in power, and the very poor were legally protected against the rapacity of the priest, who exacted a kind of tithe from the members of the community. Two other social reforms carried out during this reign are noteworthy in this connection, one being the abolition of the tax hitherto laid upon the parties to a divorce, and the other, the reduction of the priests' burial fees. But in spite of the checks that it was thus found necessary to place upon the extortionate priesthood, the service of the gods was deserving of special recompense, and thus it was that in accordance with this principle an orphan, the son of a priestess of the goddess Bau, received a larger pension than other orphans.

But apart from what may be termed domestic and family duties, women were expected to perform other functions even as early as the time of Urukagina. Some women devoted themselves to the more menial services of the gods and attended to the offerings of the sanctuary; others again were employed as weavers, while another class of women attached to the court were occupied with the care of sheep, goats and other small domestic animals. Some again were gate-keepers, and a certain number pursued the art of hair-dressing.

As might be expected, the trades pursued by men were more numerous and various. The boat-building trade engaged a considerable number of the men of Lagash, while carpenters and furniture-makers also appear to have had plenty to do. The currier's trade similarly flourished, and among the more æsthetic trades which were practised, perfumery and jewellery may be specifically mentioned, while of the proficiency to which the art of metal-working and stone-carving had been brought, we have abundant evidence in the numerous bas-reliefs, figures and statuettes that have come down to us. A large part of the working population were gardeners or tillers of the soil, for the Babylonians had long since emerged from the bedouin stage of primitive civilization, and had settled upon the land, which they cultivated apparently with great success. Among the domesticated animals of which they made use, the cow, the sheep, the ass and the goat may be specifically singled out. The ass was used both for riding and also for draft purposes. The ox was the principal beast of labour, his services being required both in the work of irrigation and in the transport of building materials, though the ass was also sometimes employed for these and similar purposes. The ox was further used for food, while cows were seemingly reserved for breeding and for supplying milk, from which they made butter, and possibly also cheese. The sheep was reared for the double purpose of providing wool as a material for clothing, and meat for consumption, some breeds being held in particularly high value for their wool, while others were specially prized for their tastiness as an article of diet, though some were utilized for both of these purposes. It appears to have been the custom to offer the flesh of the sheep in whole or in part to the gods before mortal man ventured to partake thereof, the shorn wool being given over to the female weaver of the harem. The sheep enjoying the especial royal patronage was white in colour, and was therefore presumably the most uncommon and the most highly valued, while the commonest breed was brown. The male sheep or lamb was usually selected for sacrifice to the gods in preference to the female. The kid seems to have been regarded as a medium of exchange, at all events rent was paid by means of kids, or sometimes sheep, while the goat often served as a sacrificial victim as we have seen elsewhere.[1] The kids belonging to the goddess Bau were tended by the women of the harem, though also sometimes by herdsmen. Goats as well as sheep were held in high value for their wool, two species being particularly singled out, one being known as the white-fleeced goat and the other as the black-fleeced. Other animals of a nondescript character also played an important part in the life of the people as well as in the service of the gods. Birds too formed part of the offerings due to the powers above, the principal of which were apparently the goose, the duck, the chicken and the turtle dove.

The fertility of the soil naturally encouraged its cultivation even in the earliest times. Part of the land in the time of Urukagina belonged to the royal domains, the remainder being occupied by private individuals. Cereals, such as corn and barley, were cultivated with success, as in the days of Herodotus,[2] while some of the land was reserved for fruit trees and vegetable products.

But the land was not entirely divided up into crown-lands and landed estates, " small ownership " accounted for a certain amount of the available ground, and it would appear that even poor women sometimes had their little plots ; the small owners were often however the victims of the extortionate capitalist, and their wrongs from time

---

[1] Cf. p. 17.   [2] Cf. p. 10.

to time called for redress. On such occasions the official entrusted with the task of readjusting matters took great care to distinguish between arable-land and land which did not admit of being cultivated. The supervision of the royal estates involved, as might be expected, the employment of a whole army of agricultural officials with different degrees of responsibility and varying duties to perform. Agriculture in the time of Urukagina even as to-day entailed a regular series of operations: the land had to be ploughed, the seed sown, and the harvest reaped, and last, but perhaps the most important and the most laborious of all, there was the work of irrigation, which in a land subject to floods in winter and a rainless semi-tropical heat in summer required constant attention and an infinite amount of hard work. The cutting of canals, even in our own day, with all the appliances at the disposal of modern hydraulic science, is by no means an easy or quickly accomplished task, and we can readily understand that the labour was no less, and the process no simpler some four or five thousand years ago. The work of irrigation, so essential and so arduous, was not left to individual enterprise, but was undertaken by the state and formed one of the principal departments of public works, and the early rulers of Lagash seem to have been as proud of their irrigation-engineering performances as they were of their triumphs on the battle-field. The persons employed were either regular engineers, or else navvies turned on to the work for the time being. But the work of irrigation was not finished with the cutting of the canals ; some means had to be devised for conveying the water from the canals to the soil. No doubt in earlier times this was done by means of a hand machine, perhaps consisting in a bucket attached to a pole, to the other end of which a counterpoising weight was suspended. In Assyrian times,[1] these machines were set by the side of

[1] Cf. Johns, *An Assyrian Doomsday Book*, p. 19.

a "pit" or cistern, which was often a depression in the bed of the stream, into which the buckets were lowered and from which they were raised when full, or else a pit dug actually on the field into which the water of the canal flowed by means of a runnel. The machine itself in its simplest form resembles the modern "shadûf," such as was used in ancient Egypt[1] and is in common use among the fellahin of Upper Egypt to-day. But on big estates some more efficient apparatus would be obviously required, and was undoubtedly used, at all events by the Assyrians. What the larger machines were, we do not know, but as Johns suggests, they may have very possibly consisted in a set of buckets fastened to a wheel, which was revolved by oxen, the buckets taking up the water as the wheel brought them to the bottom, and emptying their contents on their way round: but whatever the machine was it must have been fairly elaborate, for it sometimes required as many as eight oxen to work it.

The important part which agriculture played in the life of the community is shown by the name of one of the months which was called "the month during which the oxen labour." The rainy season of November and December over, the labourers proceeded to sow the seed, the harvest of which was to be reaped in the summer during the "month of harvesting." The corn was cut with a kind of sickle, after which the grain was beaten or else trodden by oxen on the field itself. Next it was passed through a sieve, and was then ready to be distributed or stored in the granaries.

As we have already seen, much the same animals were reared for the maintenance and comfort of man some five thousand years ago as to-day. Human nature and human requirements vary but little compared with the marked differences which separate one civilization from another, and one stage of culture from one more primi-

---

[1] Cf. Erman, *Life in Ancient Egypt*, p. 426; and Wilkinson, I, p. 281.

tive or more advanced, though these differences are indeed superficial rather than fundamental, but the elementary laws upon which human life depends essentially belong to those things which are fundamental, and in that sense they are eternal. Thus it was that the members of Urukagina's community partook of beef, mutton or lamb according to the season, as we do to-day ; his bill of fare however not only comprised joints but also poultry and birds—chicken, duck, goose, or turtle as the case might be. Fish of all kinds, including both fresh-water and salt-water fish, were prepared in various ways for food, while milk, butter and cheese all appear to have been in regular use. Wheat and barley, as we have several times had occasion to note, were grown on a large scale, and without doubt formed the staple food of the people, providing them with an ample supply of material for cakes and different kinds of bread, including milk loaves and black bread. The principal fruits which were cultivated at this period, were dates, figs, pomegranates and grapes : they were eaten cooked and uncooked, sometimes forming part of a fruit salad, at other times being made into fruit cakes.

The date-palm flourished everywhere and was a principal means of support to the poor, while the dates themselves seem to have been used as a medium of exchange. The apple appears to have been cultivated and to have furnished certain drink,[1] while the tamarisk provided a kind of sweet gum. As regards vegetables, onions, radishes, cucumbers and beans appear to have been the most favoured, though various other vegetable products, which have not as yet been identified, are mentioned in the texts. At this early period the art of fermenting cereals was already known, and beer, date-wine, and other alcoholic drinks were to be found in the Sumerian cellars.

[1] Cf. Genouillac, p. xlix.

With their arts and crafts we have dealt elsewhere, as also with their architectural remains, which however afford us little or no information regarding the structure of private dwelling-places, but from the literature we learn that wood as well as brick was used more extensively in their building operations than we should suppose. Wool formed the principal material for making clothes, though linen was also possibly manufactured,[1] while fur was sometimes worn, presumably in the cold weather.

Business transactions were made by contracts, the transactions in question usually having reference to the sale of slaves, animals or other property. The validity of the contracts apparently depended upon their being duly attested, as in later times, the witnesses receiving gifts for their services. In regard to the purchase of slaves, and the price which they fetched in the market, it is a significant fact that according to the stele of Manishtusu, an ass and a slave were worth exactly the same, which betrays a lack of appreciation of the superiority of the working capacity of a human being over that of a brute beast.

But the crown and the church took good care not to allow the laity the full possession of their own property, and managed to make a very comfortable livelihood for themselves by means of various impositions and taxes. Farm produce, garden fruits, fish, cattle, wool and perfumes were all levied as royal or ecclesiastical dues, while the temple sacrifices were of course for the most part mere perquisites of the priests, though the latter had to hand a goodly proportion over to their royal patron.

A civilization such as this, with its commercial enterprises and its legal transactions, of course presupposes the invention of systems for ascertaining the weights and measures of the various objects and different forms

1 Cf. p. 346.

of property with which those transactions were immediately concerned. There was a square or area measure, a sine quâ non in property-conveyancing ; there was a long measure, equally necessary for the sale and purchase of wood or stuffen goods, the smallest unit of which appears to have been the thumb. Then again the daily requirements of man made the invention of a measure of capacity an absolute necessity. Other modes of reckoning besides the regular metrical systems were however sometimes adopted, thus fishermen appear to have sold their fish either by number or by the basket, while liquids were measured by means of different sized vessels. Lastly there was a weight measure, which was the same in Urukagina's time as in that of the later dynasty of Ur.

2. *RELIGION*

The religion of the Babylonians and Assyrians was polytheistic throughout the whole course of their history. It is true that in later times a certain tendency towards monotheism was exhibited, but it never became forcible enough to create such a revolution in the religious ideas of the people as the change from polytheism to monotheism necessarily implies. The gods worshipped in the later period of Gudea were, with the exception of Nin-gish-zi-da the personal god of Gudea, known and venerated in the time of Urukagina.[1] It is further an interesting and noteworthy fact that the name Gishgibilgemesh (Gilgamesh) is sometimes accompanied by the determinative for " god " in the literature of the time, a clear indication that even at this date the hero of Babylonian folk-lore was accredited with divine or quasi-divine attributes. The local god of Lagash was Nin-girsu ; to him the land belonged, and it was he who entrusted the government of it to the king ; the people of Lagash are indeed identified with their divine lord, their triumphs are his, and their wrongs are crimes

[1] Cf. Genouillac, p. lii.

against his godhead. The priest of Nin-girsu ranked immediately after the patesi himself, and his temples are entirely national in character. The very palace of the patesi was in reality the house of Nin-girsu, while that of his queen was the dwelling-place of Nin-girsu's divine spouse, the goddess Bau. Another goddess who was deeply revered and worshipped even as early as Ur-Ninâ's day was the Lady Ninâ, from whom the founder of the dynasty derived his royal name, while the goddess Gatumdug, in whose honour Ur-Ninâ built a temple, was regarded as the "Mother of Lagash." En-lil, the ever famous lord of Nippur, also occupied a prominent place in the assemblage of gods at this time; he is mentioned first in the royal protocols of Eanna-tum and Entemena, and is also first in the divine invocations on the Vulture Stele of the former ruler.

But the influence of the powers unseen upon the minds and lives of the people is reflected in the authority of the priests. The priest, minister or servant is not in truth "greater than his lord," but his authority and his power are entirely proportional to those enjoyed by his heaven-born master. The temptation on the part of earthly emissaries to abuse the power which their position gives them is generally found to be irresistible, and the priests of Lagash were, as we have seen, no exceptions to the all but universal rule. The power enjoyed by the high priest of Nin-girsu may be judged from the fact that both Enlitarzi and Enetarzi occupied this position before they ascended the throne.

Sacrifice formed the principal part of early Sumerian worship; animals, birds, fruit, vegetables, bread and cakes all contributing to the heavily-laden altars of the gods, and incidentally to the rapacious appetites and pockets of the priests; offerings were also made to the statues of the living and the dead, the offerings being placed on an altar close to the statue; thus a certain Shagshag seems to have derived satisfaction by placing offerings before her own effigy, while the statue of the deceased Ur-Ninâ was similarly honoured. Another interesting practice in vogue at this period was that of burning oil-lamps before the statues. The latter were apparently votive in character, and they seem to have performed the religious obligations required of the people whom they represented, to have actually offered the prayers inscribed on their lifeless bodies, and, in short, to have played the noble part of a vicarious worshipper. Without doubt this is the real explanation of the devotional attitude displayed by Gudea in his statues. Magic and divination, the ever-ready handmaids of all primitive religions, were cultivated and fervently believed in at this period as in later times, prophets, seers, and dream-interpreters being almost as much in demand as they are to-day.

A special order of priests was appointed to take funerals and perform the necessary rites and ceremonies, and they received fees or honoraria for their services. The dead required sustenance in the grave, and it was customary to place seven jars of liquor and four hundred and twenty loaves of bread beside the corpse; this custom had become virtually binding and obligatory upon the unfortunate relations of the deceased, and one of Urukagina's reforms was the reduction of these dues.

The temples themselves, which sometimes stood in their own grounds and were surrounded by a sacred wood, were enriched with statues, vases, inscribed slabs, treasures of silver and precious stones, and luxuries of all kinds.

The actual and inward piety of the people of Lagash, as of the Babylonians and Assyrians of a later period is evinced in the divinely-compounded names which they bore, names which were clearly intended to secure the assistance and favour of the god whose earthly namesakes they were, and in whose honour these names were compounded. Thus the designation of one individual is "En-lil is my defence," of another, "Bau is my mother," and of a third "Enki is my companion," names which vividly recall some of the proper names in the Old Testament. Another striking testimony to the reality of what may be termed the individual religion of those days, is the prevailing belief in the beneficence of one particular god towards oneself ; it is clear that the personal element in the religious feelings and aspirations of the times was not satisfied by the oblations and ceremonies of the official cults, but sought and presumably found satisfaction in the comforting belief that some one god really understood the peculiar circumstances, difficulties and perplexities of the aspirant, and, understanding, might be counted upon to render help in time of need.

(B) THE KHAMMURABI PERIOD

1. LAWS, MANNERS AND CUSTOMS

The reign of Khammurabi is in some respects the half-way house in the history of Mesopotamian civilization. The king was of course the supreme head of the state, and indeed he was not only "the first gentleman" in Babylonia, but also enjoyed the unique privilege and blessing of being a demigod. The deification of kings was a practice in vogue centuries before the time of Khammurabi, and it was doubtless a practice assiduously cultivated by the kings themselves. Some of the early Semite kings of Kish were deified after death, while the name of Shar-Gâni-sharri of Agade is often written with the divine determinative, and the name of his son Narâm-Sin is hardly ever written without it. But during the later dynasty of Ur the practice grew up of deifying the king while still alive, instead of waiting for him to take his seat on the bench of gods after death. Of Khammurabi's divine nature we have evidence in the use of such names as " Kammurabi-ilu " (=Khammurabi is god), as well as in the frequent coupling of his name with those of the gods in oaths.

After the king, but a long way after, come the nobility and gentry, a class which not only comprehended the men of high birth but also those who, though artisans, had the distinction of belonging to old trade guilds, among which may be mentioned carpenters, tailors, builders, or potters. Next came what may be termed the lower middle classes, while at the bottom rung of the ladder—if indeed he can correctly be said to have been on the ladder at all—was the slave, who was nothing more than a piece of goods or a chattel.

The full extent of Khammurabi's empire is not known, but his claim to immortality rests not on the ever-shifting sands of territorial aggrandizement, but on the solid rock of moral progress. To form an accurate estimate of the influence which Khammurabi's code of laws has had on the Mosaic code and indirectly on the European codes of to-day is beyond our power, but one fact is indisputable, and that is that the legal code of Khammurabi some four thousand years ago enshrines many of those principles of justice and mercy which we are apt to regard as the peculiar offspring of our own enlightened age.

Many however of the laws embraced in this world-famed code show little or no variation from those in force if not actually systematized in the time of Urukagina. The laws relating to marriage are almost a replica of those which obtained among the early Sumerians, the contract being still made between the suitor and the father of the prospective bride, to whom he normally paid a price for his daughter's hand, the price of course varying according to the station in life of the parties concerned. The sum given to the father was often handed over by him to his daughter, but if no children were born of the marriage the man was entitled to receive back the price he had paid for his wife on her death, if it had not been returned to him previously.

The father in his turn usually gave his daughter a dowry or marriage-portion, which on her death reverted to the family in the event of her having no children. The dowries often comprised various kinds of property including gold and silver, slaves, furniture and apparel, and generally appear to have exceeded in value the marriage-price paid by the husband. If children born of the marriage survived the wife, her dowry was divided amongst them. Even if the woman was divorced she retained her marriage-portion, though it was forfeited in the event of gross moral misconduct on her part. In the eyes of the law a married man and woman were one, each being held accountable for the other's debts, not excepting even prenuptial liabilities. But though the Babylonian of Khammurabi's day, as in the time of Urukagina, was apparently a monogamist, he was permitted to have a concubine in the event of his wife not providing him with an heir, the children of the concubine being regarded as legitimate, and the concubine being entitled to all the respect and consideration due to a wife. There are various clauses in the code dealing with special cases, such as the marriage of a free woman with a slave, or the marriage of votaries, but for a detailed account of these, reference must be made to the standard works on the Khammurabi Code, among which may be specially mentioned Harper's *Code of Hammurabi*[1] and John's translation of the code in his *Babylonian and Assyrian Laws, Contracts and Letters*.

As in the earlier period, the Babylonians of Khammurabi's day were essentially an agricultural people, but since the time of Urukagina, agriculture had developed enormously, and the relationship of landlord to tenant, and of employer to labourer, was regulated and fixed by a number of legal enactments embodied in the code.

[1] This work comprises an autographed text, transliteration, translation, glossary, index of subjects, list of proper names, signs and numerals, together with a map, frontispiece, and photograph of text.

Ordinary arable land was let at a fixed rental, the rent being paid in corn, but the owner was entitled to a deposit, and non-payment of the rent was a legal debt. The code contains two special provisions, the effect of which must have been to make the tenant postpone the payment of his rent as long as possible. The one enacted that if the rent had not been paid, or if the land had been lent on the share-profit principle and the crops were destroyed by a storm, the damage done was shared either equally or proportionally by landlord and tenant. If on the other hand the rent had been already paid, the tenant could claim no compensation. The share-profit system was very common, and in such cases the landlord generally received a half or two-thirds of the crop. But the inequalities calculated to arise from such a system were obvious, for though it safeguarded the tenant to some extent, it left the landlord without remedy in the event of his tenant being an idler, and to provide for such a case a clause was inserted to the effect that the negligent small owner should pay an average rent " like his neighbours." Often the landlord further secured himself by stipulating in the contract for the erection of a cottage on the land, or insisted on the tenant renting a cottage already built there, the cottage to be vacated on the termination of the lease.

The tenant was empowered to sub-let his ground, the principal landlord's consent apparently not being necessary. The landlord was of course legally entitled to the rent agreed upon in the contract with his immediate tenant, but provided that was forthcoming, and the ground properly cultivated, he could raise no objection. Sometimes the landlord found the seed, the necessary tools, and also the oxen, and in addition paid a wage to the farmer; in this case the status of the tenant somewhat resembled that of a gardener in his cottage on an estate to-day. The seed, the oxen, and everything belonged to his master, and the penalty for

any embezzlement of the same on the part of the tenant
was the amputation of the latter's hands.   Again, if a
tenant of this kind were a rogue, he might hire out the
oxen, purloin the provender he had received from his
master for the said oxen, and at the same time produce
no crop : in this case he was liable to a heavy fine, and
if he were insolvent, he was torn to pieces by the oxen
on the field which he had neglected to cultivate.

The laws and regulations which applied to agricultural land-tenure, applied for the most part to the leas-
ing of plantations and gardens as well.   Thanks to the
extraordinary fertility of Babylonian soil the owners of
land became very wealthy ; this notwithstanding, the
money-lender was not without clients.   Unforeseen dis-
asters occurred, which crippled the landowner, and but
for the money-lender he would not be able to tide over
the trouble.   As security for the loan he frequently mortgaged his land, but the code enacted that he should at all
times reap the crop himself, and pay off the debt and the
money-lender's expenses from the produce.   Moreover
the money-lender was legally bound to accept such produce or corn in settlement of the debt, and could not in-
sist on being paid in money, unless, as was frequently the
case, he had stipulated in the contract that the loan was
to be repaid in the same form as that in which it had
been received.   As a further safeguard for the unfortunate money-borrower it was made illegal to exercise distraint for rent or anything else upon a working ox.   This
was a humane law, for the watering of the ground, as
well as the ploughing of the soil and the threshing of the
wheat, was largely done by oxen.

The laws regulating the irrigation of the land were
stringent owing to the disastrous consequences resulting from negligence on the part of any concerned.
Once the canals had been made, it was the bounden duty
of each landowner, whether small or great, to keep that
part of the canal which passed by or through his land

in good repair. If that part of the bank of the canal for which he was responsible gave way, and the water thereby flooded his neighbour's land, he had to pay damages in full, and if he were insolvent he could be sold up. He was entitled to open a runnel to water his field, but if the water swamped the adjoining fields through some inadvertence or negligence on his part, he had to give full compensation.

The wages, presumably the minimum wage of the labourer, was fixed by law, as also was the hire-price of oxen and wagons. The hirer of animals was under a legal obligation to take proper care of them, and omission to do so involved a penalty. But if an accident occurred which the hirer could not be expected to foresee or prevent—such as an attack by a lion—the owner had to bear the loss. This was also the case if the person in charge of the animal was a shepherd or herdsman in the owner's employ, the principle being the same in both cases. Wilful negligence was not to be condoned, but on the other hand, the consequence of unforeseen and unavoidable accidents was not to be visited upon either hirer or employee.

The larger half of the working population in Khammurabi's time were probably engaged in agricultural pursuits while the remainder were occupied in trade or commerce. Now the expansion of trade depends upon the existence of an adequate means of transport, whereby exports can go out and imports come in. Before the invention and introduction of locomotives, water was the unrivalled medium for conveying large quantities of goods from one place to another, and even to-day with our interlacing networks of railways we still find use for the canals of primitive days. It was undoubtedly the two rivers, the Tigris and the Euphrates, that were accountable for the development of the trading faculty of the Babylonians, a faculty which ultimately made them the great commercial people of the Oriental world. We are accordingly not surprised to find that already, even in the time of Khammurabi, shipping was an important trade. A sure and certain indication of this fact is to be found in the number of laws directly concerning ship-builders and boatmen in the Code. The ship-builder, or rather the boat-builder,—for ships properly so-called were a very much later invention,—was absolutely responsible for his workmanship, and was required to give a year's guarantee to the purchaser ; if it proved faulty during that time he had to provide another. As in the case of the agricultural labourer, the hired boatman was responsible for the boat and cargo in his charge, and any negligence on his part was penal. If a ship collided with another ship riding at anchor, the colliding ship was liable for all damages.

Business was carried on largely by means of agents as it is with us to-day. The agent gave a receipt for the goods or money he received from his chief, and then went off to trade with them. The agent generally appears to have received an ordinary commission, which on his return he was expected to repay with a reasonable profit, the profit sometimes being a definitely fixed sum, at others, a prearranged share of the actual proceeds. As in our own day, some merchants were speculators, and all the uncertainty incidental to any kind of speculation seems to have surrounded the prospects of the agent, who doubtless at times scored well, while on other occasions he lost heavily. But any loss resulting from an untoward event which the agent could neither foresee nor prevent, had to be borne by the merchant. Thus if an agent were robbed in the course of his travels, he could clear himself from all liability in the matter by taking an oath to that effect. But this law might clearly lead to sharp practice on the part of a dishonest agent ; and accordingly any false claims on his part had to be repaid threefold, but a false claim by a chief in regard to the goods entrusted to his agent had to be repaid six-fold. All business transactions had to be drawn up in writing to make them legal.

The obvious advantages of partnership were soon recognized by the commercially sagacious Babylonians, and business-partnerships were well known in the time of Khammurabi. In arriving at the dividends, the usual arrangement was for the partners to withdraw their capital and interest, and then receive equal shares of the superfluous profits. The dividends were made yearly and the withdrawal by each partner of his capital virtually dissolved the partnership, which could of course be renewed from time to time if desired.

As in all commercial enterprises, capital was the one essential, and the need of immediate cash was supplied by the money-lender. The rate of interest charged in Khammurabi's time is not known, but the rate charged on loans of corn was often as much as forty per cent. Such loans were however generally in demand at seed-time, and if repaid at harvest, no interest seems to have been charged. A debtor could repay his loan either in the form of corn or sesame, and the value of each was fixed by law. If a debtor was insolvent, he could hand over a servant to his creditor to work off the debt which was due. The ownership of such a servant was, however, still vested in the debtor, and the servant was protected by law against maltreatment at the hand of the creditor. If he were a free man, the creditor had to restore him to his original master at the termination of three years, and the same rule applied if a wife or child of the debtor were the pledge or surety.

Distraint was not unknown, but it was the last expedient which the creditor was entitled to adopt after all other means had failed. Distraint on corn without the previous consent of the debtor was illegal, and illegal distraint *ipso facto* forfeited the right of any further claim on the part of the creditor, while the execution of a distraint where no claim had been substantiated was penal, and the theoretical creditor had to pay a fine. As before-mentioned no distraint could be levied on a working-ox, and indeed distraint of any kind could apparently only be issued subsequently to the consent of the debtor. In short, the interests of the humbler and poorer members of the community were safeguarded in every way possible. Not only were the small farmers protected, but even the working-classes received the attention of the legislators of Khammurabi's time. Thus at harvest-time there was evidently a tendency to put up the price of beer, and accordingly a clause in the code enacts that drink was to be sold at a cheap rate in spite of the increased demand.

Again, everyone in the community is practically at the mercy of the housebuilder, and accordingly any damage caused by the use of faulty materials or bad workmanship, had to be made good by the builder. If the house collapsed and the owner was killed, the builder was put to death, while if the owner's son or servant was killed, the son or servant of the builder was similarly put to death, in accordance with the primitive law of retaliation. House-tenure in the time of Khammurabi was generally on the repairing-lease system, the tenant being required to leave the house in the same condition in which he found it, while it was customary to pay rent half-yearly instead of quarterly, the rent being paid in advance.

The ultimate sanction and enforcement of these various laws concerning the relationship subsisting between capitalist and workman, owner and hirer, and landlord and tenant, was to be found in the courts. Strange to say, the chief scene of jurisdiction was the temple, the god himself adjudicating through the mediumship of his earthly plenipotentiaries. The precise form of legal procedure in the time of Khammurabi is not known, but certain facts in regard to the institution and conduct of suits have been elucidated.

One great difference between law-suits in the time of Khammurabi and those of our own day was that the cases were not apparently conducted by counsel, but by the parties themselves, an arrangement which must have considerably accrued to the advantage of the abler of the two suitors. The more important cases were heard by a bench of judges somewhat resembling our Court of Appeal, while the minor suits were heard by a single judge, as in our High Courts and County Courts. The plea had to be set down in writing in the form of an " affidavit " ; whether the defendant was able to file a counter-affidavit does not seem quite clear. At the trial itself the plaintiff and defendant both summoned their witnesses, and the judgment was signed by both parties. Appeal to a higher court was the only remedy for the loser of the suit, the judge in the lower court not being allowed to hear the same case a second time under pain of being struck off the list, and at the same time mulcted for twelve times the amount of the fine he had previously ordered, or the damages he had assessed.

The date of the trial was fixed by the judge, but it had to be within six months of the filing of the affidavit. This time was allowed in order to enable the plaintiff to procure his witnesses in the event of their being absent from home. The appointment of the judges, or at least of some of them, was vested in the crown ; whether they were paid or not is a matter of doubt. Sometimes judgeships were hereditary. But whether judges received fees or not they appear to have been regarded as professional men and retained their title even after they had ceased to exercise their judicial functions. The supreme judge was the king himself, to whom cases of primary importance were occasionally referred, while the principal officers of state often acted as judges.

The following crimes were capital offences, though the precise form in which the death sentence was to be carried out is not always quite clear :—a false accusation of witchcraft ; perjury on the part of a witness in a capital case ; burglary of a temple, palace, or private house ; kidnapping a free-born child ; highway robbery ; theft of the goods of a man whose house is on fire ; adultery ; various forms of incest ; rape of a betrothed maiden ; persuading a slave to flee from his master, or being an accessory after the fact by harbouring him ; various forms of theft and fraud ; and building a house so badly that it collapsed and thereby killed the owner. The penalty of death appears to have been inflicted either by burning, impalement, dismemberment, or drowning.

Criminal offences of a less serious character were treated differently. Among the penalties enumerated in the code, mutilation, branding and scourging are the most barbarous. Mutilation was a punishment based logically on the " eye for an eye," and " tooth for a tooth " principle, its application being primarily to those who had mutilated their neighbour. But its application was extended to cover other forms of crime or offences adjudged in those days as crimes, thus insolence on the part of an adopted child to his foster-parents was effectually stopped by the removal of the child's tongue ; while an adopted son who is unduly inquisitive into the origin of his birth has his eye plucked out ; lastly—and what perhaps to us seems the most amazing of all—if a surgeon performed an operation and the patient died through any carelessness or lack of skill on his part, the surgeon's hands were amputated—a law which must have considerably cooled the ardour of any of the surgeons of those days particularly addicted to the use of the knife. Branding was the outward and visible sign (usually imprinted on the arm) of degradation to slavery,—the punishment for slandering a votary or a married woman. Scourging was the penalty for striking a superior ; the scourging was to be performed in

2 C

public, the strokes numbering sixty, and the implement used a cow-hide whip ; while banishment from the city was the very fitting and meet punishment for incest.

2. RELIGION

The one outstanding feature of the Babylonian religion of Khammurabi's time was the unique position assigned to Marduk in the Babylonian pantheon. Marduk owed his exaltation to what we may without undue levity call local interest. The dynasty of which Khammurabi was so illustrious a monarch was the first dynasty of the city of Babylon itself; and Marduk the local god of Babylon naturally shared in the good fortune and prosperity of the people over whose welfare he presided. To Marduk belonged the real credit, honour and glory of his people's success, what wonder then that he should be accorded the post of honour in the hierarchy of heaven ! Other gods indeed existed, and received such attention as befitted their inferior position, but their light was as that of a planet compared with the dazzling radiance of the midday sun, while a monotheistic tendency sprang up, fostered by a desire to attribute to Marduk such marvellous performances as the creation of the world, performances which had hitherto been ascribed to the older gods of Southern Mesopotamia.

But reverence and respect for the traditions of a heroic past precluded the possibility of dishonouring the gods who had made that past so glorious, and the only way to satisfy the religious aspirations of Marduk's devotees on the one hand, and maintain the loyalty due to the time-honoured gods of Babylonian infancy on the other, was to identify the latter with Marduk ; had this process of identification been carried to its logical conclusion it would have resulted in the evolution of a monotheism as exclusive and as simple as the most dogmatic Unitarianism of to-day.

Fortunately or unfortunately such was not the case ; the practical sequence of the tendency was realized in the identification of Marduk with the ancient god of Nippur, but apart from that, the tendency remained a tendency and nothing more. Notwithstanding this fact however, Marduk's supremacy was so firmly established, and his position so impregnably secured, that the passing changes and chances of some two thousand years were unable to oust him from his high estate, and it is to Marduk that Cyrus, the vanquisher of Babylon's last native king, and the fated heir to her evanescent empire, ascribes the triumphant victory which attended his arms. He recorded the acknowledgment of his obligations to the lord of E-sagil on a clay cylinder now preserved in the British Museum.

The inscription is written in cuneiform characters, and states that Marduk " sought out a righteous prince, a man after his own heart whom he might take by the hand, and he called his name Cyrus. And Marduk the great lord, the protector of his people, beheld his good deeds and his righteous heart with joy." Thus 1500 years after the time of Khammurabi, the cult of Marduk was still intimately bound up with the prosperity of his people, and it was owing to the neglect of his worship and to the mal-preservation of his fanes that Nabonidus the last king of the Neo-Babylonian dynasty was unable to withstand the onslaughts of a foreign conqueror.

Although Marduk was thus the supreme god of Babylon, to whose shrine all true patriots were wont to resort, other gods were still the subjects of veneration, and it was still thought prudent to seek their favour and assistance. The sun continued to pursue the even tenor of his way, and after all, the sun is an important factor in the manifold operations of agriculture, it therefore behoves man to pay his respects to a god whose mere momentary absence behind a cloud of displeasure may bring about such momentous consequences. Among other deities worshipped at this time, mention should be made of Ishtar, the mother of the gods, and the goddess of love and war, Anu the lord of heaven, and Ea the god of the deep, of Sin the moon-god and the specific patron of the people of Ur, of Ninib the god of war, and Adad the weather deity.[1]

The great religious movement which characterized the establishment of the first dynasty of Babylon, naturally brought in its train all the paraphernalia required by and incidental to a highly-organized state religion. The priesthood became a power, and the temples commercial centres as well as seats of learning. The revenue of the temple was very large ; its principal source seems to have been the endowments and royal bounties of the kings. As in earlier times, it owned a large number of cattle and sheep, and the administration of its property seems to have caused Khammurabi a considerable amount of anxiety. A great many priests and laymen were attached to the service of the temple, and the spiritual labourer of those days seems to have deserved an altogether exorbitant hire. It was clearly a most profitable concern, and the privilege of serving in the temple was a positive asset which could be bought, sold, or mortgaged. This valuable privilege which brought such pecuniary advantages with it, was, needless to say, very jealously guarded by the elect, who firmly adhered to the hereditary principle—then in full swing. These privileges were in fact inalienable and were transmitted from father to son.

The financial prosperity of the temple and its attachés is shown by their opening their doors for financial business pure and simple, money-lending in time becoming quite an important branch of the temple work. The loans however seem to have generally been free loans, no interest being exacted.

---

[1] Cf. Jastrow, *Religion*, pp. 116 ff.

But the temple had its obligations to perform as well as its privileges to enjoy, one of the duties incumbent upon the temple authorities being the ransoming of a fellow townsman who had been taken prisoner by the enemy.

(C) THE ASSYRIAN ERA
1. *STATE OF SOCIETY*

In Assyrian times the same explicit or implicit regulations in regard to the family seem to have been in force, or tacitly agreed to, as those which obtained in the older Babylonian period. Apparently a man was only expected in the normal way to marry one woman, though it seems probable that in the event of the first wife proving childless it was regarded as quite justifiable and legitimate for a man to take to himself another woman, in view of the desirability of his having an heir.[1] Accordingly monogamy seems to have been the general rule, though polygamy was by no means unknown. When a man married, he left his father and mother and was expected to " cleave " unto his wife, and they became " one flesh " and inhabited " one house " ; in short, the Assyrian " home " was normally the same as the English " home " of to-day. As in the time of Khammurabi, women could be legal owners of property, and often owned farms and occupied vineyards.

The general pursuits of the people were much the same as those followed by the earlier inhabitants of Mesopotamia. The population was, as then, largely agricultural ; the land required the same careful and elaborate irrigation while the ground had to be ploughed, the seed sown, and the harvest reaped as heretofore. A corn-land holding[2] usually had a house attached to it, and also a court where the corn was stored, which thus served the purpose, if not resembling the appearance, of a barn. A large number of people were evidently employed in

[1] Cf. Johns, *Doomsday Book*, p. 26.   [2] *Ibid.*, p. 20.

the vineyards, which must sometimes have been very extensive, for the number of plants in a single vineyard in one case was as many as 49,300, and it is a significant fact that the most celebrated wines in Babylonia came from the north, while it is also worth noting the frequency with which the vine occurs on Assyrian bas-reliefs. Orchards and gardens also abounded, though what grew in them is to some extent a matter of conjecture; if however we may assume that the list of plants mentioned in the Babylonian *Garden Tablet* published by Meissner, holds good also for the Assyrian garden, leek, onion, garlic, lettuce, coriander, hyssop, turnip, cabbage, and radish must have been familiar garden products.

Cattle and sheep were reared as in the old days, the latter both for their wool and also for food, while goats provided milk, as well as meat and hair, goat's hair being used even to-day in the East for the coverings of tents. Oxen were used largely for working the irrigation machines, while asses also served as beasts of labour. The camel was not unknown, and is often named in connection with the sales of estates. The horse at this period was in common use, but was seemingly reserved for riding and driving.

The legal paraphernalia of Assyrian times was the natural development of the Babylonian law code of which it was the off-shoot. In the ownership of land the hereditary principle seems to have been the dominating factor, and probably farms and vineyards passed automatically from father to son in the same way as crown lands and larger estates. The peasant was still a serf, bought or sold with the land to which fate had attached him ; he was not permitted to migrate elsewhere, but on the other hand he was under the protection of the state ; he could not be ousted by invaders, and his living was a first charge on the estate. It is certain that estate-slaves were sometimes requisitioned for military or other state purposes, the owner being of course compelled to meet the demand, while the produce of his land was also subject to taxation. Some estates were however exempt from dues of this kind, the exemption doubtless being granted by the royal favour and confirmed by royal charter.

Among the smaller land-owners we find a number of farmers or vine-owners who have forsaken business or industrial pursuits, and have left the bakery and the scribe's office to return to the soil.

The landlord frequently did not reside on his land, but let it out to tenants, whom he expected to pay rent in due season. The original ownership of land was no doubt largely if not entirely the gift of the king, while conquests would continually place fresh tracts of land in his hands. Probably some of the newly acquired property went to swell the extent of the crown lands, while the rest or part of the rest was distributed among the king's ministers, generals and other court favourites.

2. RELIGION

The Assyrian religion was Babylonian both in origin and character. Anu, Bel, and Ea, Marduk, Nergal, Adad, Shamash and Sin, Nanâ and Ishtar were all held in esteem, and temples were erected in their honour. The supremacy of Assyria and the corresponding decline in Babylonian power scarcely affected the authority and influence of the time-honoured gods of the Babylonian pantheon. But the new political situation required some recognition in the religious life of the nation, and the exigencies of the present demanded some consideration, as well as the hallowed traditions of the past. These two conflicting interests had to be reconciled, and the reconciliation was effected and a way of escape devised similar to that adopted by the earlier Babylonians when confronted with a like dilemma. The local god of Ashur was exalted to the first place in the pantheon, and became as it were the Marduk of Assyria, though his position was even more unassailable than was that of Marduk in Babylon, for the latter[1] was bound to acknowledge Ea as his father, whereas Ashur is above all ties of this kind ; the Babylonian-Assyrian pantheon is recognized by him, but it in no way touches his lofty estate.

The cult of the god of Ashur goes back to the earliest known period of Assyrian civilization, while he gave his name to the first known capital of the country, and ultimately to the country itself. Ashur is the divine impersonation of Assyria, as Marduk was of Babylonia, only the identification was more pronounced, for the decline of Assyrian power and the death of her empire meant virtually the death of Ashur, whereas Marduk maintained his influence during the time of Babylon's adversity as well as during that of her prosperity ; foreign conquerors sought to do him honour, Cyrus the Persian ascribes his conquest of Babylon to the lord of E-sagil, and even Antiochus Soter (280-260 B.C.) restores his renowned temple. But another difference between the Ashur-cult of the north and the Marduk-cult of the south must also be noted. Ashur was worshipped in temples erected all over the Assyrian empire, whereas Babylon was the place " where men ought to worship " Marduk, just as in later times Jerusalem was the only authorized centre for the worship of Jehovah. But in spite of the universality of his presence, Ashur had a principal seat of worship, the locality of which was the same as that of the then centre and capital of the empire, Ashur, Calah, Nineveh or Khorsabad as the case might be.

The adaptability displayed by Ashur in regard to his earthly home may, as Jastrow suggests, be partly due to the fact that a statue was not the only, or even the principal symbol of his divine presence, as was the case with

[1] Cf. Jastrow, pp. 191 ff.

Marduk and the other great gods. His usual emblem was a standard consisting of a pole surrounded by a winged disc to which is attached an archer with drawn bow. It is impossible to say the exact time when a military standard came to be regarded as the natural and fitting symbol of the patron god of the country, but the nature of the symbol itself makes it quite clear that Ashur was regarded as a god of war. Indeed the patron deity of a people as warlike as the Assyrians, could not but reflect the military spirit of his people. The Assyrian warriors were the " troops of Ashur," their enemies being his enemies and their friends his friends. Ashur's spouse was Bēlit (=" the Lady "), but the same goddess sometimes appears as the consort of Bel[1] and sometimes also as the wife of Ea, in the Assyrian inscriptions, while at other times again Bēlit is merely a designation of Ishtar. The last-named goddess occupies a very prominent place in the Assyrian pantheon, only coming second to Ashur himself. There were indeed no less than three Ishtars in Assyria—Ishtar of Nineveh, Ishtar of Arbela, and Ishtar of Kidmuru, but the Assyrians do not appear to have preserved any definite distinction between them, so that for all practical purposes we only have one goddess to consider in this connection.

It is hardly to be wondered at that Ishtar, the goddess of war as well as of love, should have been held in high reverence by the Assyrians, who not unnaturally accentuated her warlike attributes. But the Assyrians were not responsible for the origin of Ishtar's warlike character ; she had been regarded in this light at least as early as the time of Khammurabi,[2] while her fighting spirit is strongly painted in the early Gilgamesh epic, but it remained for the Assyrians to develop this aspect of her character to the virtual exclusion of all other aspects. As the Assyrians extended their sway on every side, the power of Ishtar the *Bēlit*, or " lady " of battles,

[1] Jastrow, *Religion*, p. 226.   [2] *Ibid.*, p. 83.

advanced also ; she is the goddess of kings and people alike ; in times of danger she vouchsafes her counsel and her timely words of encouragement to the king through the medium of dreams. She is "perfect in courage" and incomparable in splendour ; her appearance is like unto flames of fire, and she rains streams of fire upon the enemies of Ashur-bani-pal. Unlike other goddesses she reigns in her own right, and not in virtue of her position as the spouse, counterpart, or reflection of any of the important gods. She is their equal in rank, power and dignity, while her very name becomes almost a synonym for "goddess," and in later times all goddesses, whether native or foreign, came to be regarded as so many forms or manifestations of Ishtar.

But apart from the advancement to honour of the warlike deities of Babylonia, and the further development of the military character which they already bore, the Assyrian religion varies but little from that of the mothercountry. The civilization and culture of the Assyrians was imported *en bloc* from Babylonia, and this wholesale appropriation of the manners and customs of the people of the south displays itself in Assyrian art, religion, law and architecture. Their temples and palaces were more or less faithful copies of those erected in Babylonia; their beliefs, rites and ceremonies were derived from the same source, while their literature shows hardly any originality at all. When Ashur-bani-pal resolved to collect a library in his royal palace at Nineveh he was obliged to dispatch his scribes to the south to make search in the archives of the ancient temples which contained the prayers and hymns addressed to the gods, the legends and epics of the remote past, the astronomical reports and medical formulæ of the immediate present. A large part of Ashur-bani-pal's library consisted in practically verbatim copies of these original texts, but the debt which we owe to Ashur-bani-pal's bibliographical propensities must not be measured by the originality of the volumes of his library, but by the large contribution which they make to the Babylonian and Assyrian litera-aature now at our disposal.   In a great many cases the Babylonian originals have not been recovered, and we are entirely dependent on the copies of Ashur-bani-pal's scribes, and but for this great king's assiduity in this direction we should be in entire ignorance regarding the contents of a large part of the Babylono-Assyrian literature.

(D) BABYLONIAN AND ASSYRIAN SYMBOLISM

In all religions, whether ancient or modern, material representation forms the connecting link between the natural and the supernatural, the physical and the spirit-ual.   The medium sometimes assumes the shape of an image of a naturally or unnaturally conceived deity, at other times it takes the form of an emblem, astronomical or otherwise, with which the god is associated.   We have had abundant evidence of the prominent part played by images in the worship of the Babylonians and Assyrians, and it will perhaps not be unfitting to devote two or three pages to a brief consideration of some of the em-blems of the deities to whom reference has been made.

The chief sources for the study of Assyrian and Baby-lonian symbolism are the cylinder-seals, the Babylonian Boundary-Stones, and the monoliths of Assyrian kings. In a brief review of Mesopotamian cylinder-seals we have had occasion to observe the frequent occurrence of emblems, many of which are also found on the mono-liths of Assyrian kings, e.g. Sargon, Sennacherib and Esarhaddon.   Among those of which the signification is certain we may mention the crescent, obviously em-blematic of the Moon-god Sin, and the star of Ishtar, while the deity armed with thunderbolts is certainly Adad.   The winged disc which occurs on a stele of Esarhaddon, as well as on other Assyrian monuments, is clearly symbolic of Ashur, though in earlier times it apparently emblematized Shamash, the Sun-god,[1] and if this be the case we have a useful piece of evidence in support of the theory of a solar origin for Ashur.

But the Babylonian *kudurrus* or boundary-stones provide far more material for the study of Babylonian symbolism than do the Assyrian royal sculptures, for the emblems of the gods, as well as the gods themselves, were for the most part borrowed from Babylonia and adopted with variations by the people of the north. We have the emblems which are scattered about sporadically on the Babylonian cylinder-seals collected together in more or less large groups on the boundary stones. On one of

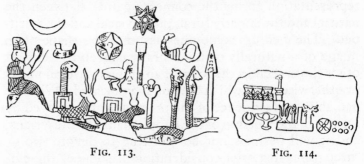

FIG. 113.   FIG. 114.

these boundary stones (cf. Fig. 113) the name of the god with whom the emblem is associated is inscribed by the side, thus giving us definite data instead of hypothetical conjecture upon which to base our investigation. Unfortunately all the names inscribed on this kudurru are not legible, but among those which are certain, the following should be noted : Shamash the Sun-god who is represented by a circle within which are four rays of light alternating with four streams of water. Ishtar is represented by a star, and Sin the Moon-god by a crescent as usual. Ea is symbolized by a ram's head on a column, the column being set on a rectangular throne beneath which lies the fish-tailed capricorn. Marduk is represented likewise by a column, the top of which how-

[1] Cf. Ward, *Cylinder-Seals*, pp. 391, 392.

ever is shaped like a lance. Nergal, the god of the dead, is symbolized by a lion-headed column, while the seated goddess is Gula, who has been identified with Bau.

Another important monument in this connection is the rock-relief of Sennacherib near Bavian (cf. Fig. 114). The inscription mentions twelve gods, and the same number of emblems, presumably corresponding to the twelve gods, are sculptured on the rock. But the important point is that not only does the number of emblems portrayed tally with the number of gods mentioned, but there are definite indications that the order of sequence is the same in both cases.[1] Thus the crescent which obviously symbolizes the moon-god occurs fifth, the same place occupied by Sin in the list of names. Again, the star, the undoubted emblem of Ishtar, similarly comes eleventh, the name of the goddess also being eleventh in the list. Lastly, the thunderbolt, which is the certain symbol of Adad, occupies the seventh place and corresponds with that occupied by the god in the inscription. These three coincidences can hardly be regarded as accidental, and it is reasonable to assign the remaining symbols to the corresponding gods in the list. Following out this method we can provisionally assign the emblems as follows : Ashur, Anu and Bel are represented by horned hats ; Ea by a column with a ram's head ; Sin by a crescent; Shamash by a winged disc ; Adad by a thunderbolt ; Marduk by a column with a pine-apple termination ; Nabû by a simple column ; Ninib (?) by a column surmounted by two lions' (or two bulls') heads ; Ishtar by a star ; and Igigi by seven dots.

Probably the finest specimen of a Babylonian stele of this character is that of Nebuchadnezzar I (circ. 1120 b.c.) (cf. Fig. 115). In the upper register we have the crescent, disc and star of Sin, Shamash and Ishtar respectively, the second register being occupied with a row of three emblems each consisting in a divine seat

[1] Cf. Ward, Cylinder-Seals, pp. 391 ff.

surmounted by a horned turban. The last-named seemingly represent Anu, Bel and either Ashur or Ea.[1] Next in succession we appear to have the emblems of Marduk and Nebo, while in the fourth register we have the double-headed column of Ninib, a horse's head resting on a seat and surmounted by a vaulted arch, (this is

of particular interest, as according to Ward, it is probably the earliest representation of the horse in Babylonian art); an eagle on the top of a column, and another column surmounted by a hawk's head and representing Zamama. In the fifth register is the goddess Gula seated on a throne and accompanied by a dog; a scorpion-man or Sagittarius; while last of all we have the thunderbolt of Adad over a calf, a tortoise which is possibly an alternative emblem for Ea,[2] a scorpion, and the lamp of Nusku, the god of fire. Finally the whole of one side of this remarkable stele is traversed by a gigantic serpent. Other monu-

FIG. 115.

ments exhibit different varieties of the same emblems, while among those not included here, are the club, the arrow, the sparrow and plough, the sheaf, the vase, the bull, the goose, the man-fish, the dove, the rod and ring (cf. Pl. XIV), and the coiffure and knife of the goddess Ninkharshag, for a full and exhaustive study of which the reader should refer to Ward, *Cylinder-Seals*, pp. 389 ff. Of the burial customs of the Babylonians and Assyrians, so far as they are known, we have treated elsewhere (cf. pp. 62, 69, etc.), but it will perhaps not be superfluous for us to briefly consider their eschatology.

[1] Cf. Ward, *Cylinder-Seals*, p. 398.
[2] *Ibid.*, p. 407.

(E) BABYLONIAN ESCHATOLOGY

Man's ideas and thoughts are very largely determined by his environment, so too his beliefs regarding the next world have as their material basis and setting the world in which he now lives ; the unknown but vaguely guessed at, can only be defined, or rather depicted in terms of the known, the unseen in terms of the seen, heaven in the terms of earth, God in the terms of Man — in short, the doctrine of the Incarnation underlies all religion and all religious systems.   As we have already seen, the early Babylonians in all probability came from the mountainous country of Elam, for they used the same picture-sign or ideogram for both "mountain" and " country " ; the earth was therefore conceived by them under the form of a mountain, and if this world be shaped like a mountain, the world beyond must also doubtless bear a similar shape, hence one of their names for the other world was E-KUR, which signifies "mountain-house," the same name being also applied to the present world.   In the early days of Babylonian mythology, the gods themselves were believed to inhabit E-KUR, the mountain-house of the world, and it is perhaps not unnatural to find the gods so intimately associated with mother-earth, when one recalls that the Babylonians believed the gods themselves to have been evolved from the same watery chaos from which the earth as it were emerged—the gods and the earth were children of the same parent, and were brought into being in the same way.

But this mountain-theory with regard to the other world in no way excluded or apparently even collided with other views of quite a different character ; indeed the most popular conception of the next world, as the realm of the dead, was that of a hollow, or cave situated underneath the earth, which was believed to be shaped somewhat after the fashion of an in-

verted saucer : this cave was called " Aralu," and was
poetically described as " irṣitum la tarat "—" the land
without return "—a description which is strangely negative, and which illustrates how little the Babylonian
concerned himself with the life after death compared
with the Egyptian, who may with some truth be said
to have devoted his attention more to the life beyond
than to the life which now is.   The locality of Aralu
under the earth may also be inferred from the story of
Ishtar's descent into Hades ; this practically universal
conception is so natural a one that it hardly calls for an
explanation.   The association of the realm of the dead
with the grave beneath the earth where the remains of
the dead were deposited—is almost inevitable, and the
corresponding association of the abode of the gods, or
heaven with the regions of light and brightness above
this earth—the ever-visible sun and moon being gods
themselves—is equally natural, but in passing, it must
be remarked that in the system—for lack of a better
word—which set the abode of the gods in the regions
of the sky, the heaven which they inhabited was not
accessible to mortal man, be he ever so good or vir-
tuous ; it was apparently only in earlier times when the
home of the gods was located in or on the earth that
the souls of the departed are regarded as dwelling with
or near them.

This is further corroborated by the application of the
term E-kur—" mountain-house "—to the earth itself as well as to the abode of the gods and the realm
of the dead, while at the same time it was used to designate the earthly abodes or temples of the gods ; the
theory which located the home of the gods upon the E-
kur is probably the earlier, and it was only in later
times, when Babylon had made herself more or less
supreme in the Euphrates valley, and had thereby gained
for her god Marduk a similar supremacy, that the circumstances seemed to demand, as it were, a more uni-

versal and less local home for the god whose sway thus
extended all over the country; if Marduk confines himself to his temple-home in Babylon, how can he watch
over the fortunes and receive the homage of his devotees
all over the empire ?

Moreover, as has been already stated, on grounds
independent of this the temptation to assign a heavenly
or sky-home to the gods has been yielded to almost
universally ; this view of course did not exclude the
possibility of the god's presence in the temples erected
to his honour, it only excluded the idea of his exclusive
presence in the temple.

But there were yet other names besides Aralu and
E-KUR, used to designate the abode of the dead, one of
which was " Shualu " ; this term signifies " enquiry "
and comes from the same root as that from which the
proper name " Saul " (" asked for ") is derived, itself
being the equivalent of the Hebrew " Sheol " which the
Greeks rendered " Hades," and English translators unfortunately rendered " hell " ; the world of the dead is
accordingly regarded as a place of enquiry, the enquiry
being presumably of the nature of an oracle. The dead
are thus supposed to be endowed with the power of
answering questions addressed to them by people on
earth ; and in this capacity they resemble the gods, the
only difference being that the gods grant oracles through
the hands of their priests, while the dead use necro-
mancers as their mediums, as was the case when Samuel
manifested himself to Saul through the agency of the
necromancing witch of Endor. Thus in connection with
the E-KUR home of the gods and of the dead, it will be
observed that the dead are not only regarded as with, or
near the gods, but, like the gods they are also empowered
to assist earthly mortals with their oracular utterances;
this pre-supposes that the dead are endowed with a
greater knowledge than the living, and accordingly however gloomy Aralu, Shualu or E-KUR (as the home of the

dead) may be, the dead are at all events drawn nearer to the gods in this respect, and partake more freely of the Tree of Knowledge than the living.

Having arrived thus far, the deification of the dead is but a short step, which the Babylonian found no great difficulty in taking; as however the deification of the departed was the exception rather than the rule, the exceptional cases of such deification must have had a special raison d'être of their own, and that raison d'être was probably the power of granting oracles which the Babylonian attributed to those highly-favoured individuals, whose heroic achievements on earth had won for them the greatest honour accorded to mankind in antiquity. The kings indeed were often deified after death and even during their lifetime, but that was the natural corollary of the belief that the next world is similar in order and in its mode of government to this world, albeit it was much more gloomy and also of a comparatively negative character.

But though the dead are thus regarded as more akin to the gods than the living, and more the objects of their special care, yet their very affinity to the gods seems to place them more beyond the power and control of the latter, and the priests whose delegated divine authority is paramount over the living, have no right of influence whatever over the dead.

Another name for the under-world was " Ki-gallu " which signifies " great land," " Ki " being the regular ideogram for " earth " generally, or " land " specifically, the two being to the early oriental mind practically synonymous; this term, like E-KUR, thus associates the abode of the dead with the abode of the living, the abode of the living being on the earth, and the abode of the dead being under or within the earth. Other epithets applied to the under-world were—" the dark dwelling," " the house of death," " the grave," " the great city," " the deep land," and the above-mentioned " irṣitum la tarat," "the land whence there is no return," the latter occurring in the well-known story of Ishtar's descent into Hades, where the nether-world is further described as a house of darkness in which the dead, clothed in feathers like birds, depend upon dust and clay for their nourishment. This account of the world beyond the grave tallies well with the account given by Ea-bani, when called up from the realms of the dead to speak to his friend Gilgamesh ; Ea-bani shrinks from paining his friend by describing the horrors of the underworld, but is at last prevailed upon to do so, and his description of Hades is that of "a place where the worm devours and all is cloked in dust"—"Dust thou art, and unto dust shalt thou return." The idea of the dead being clothed with feathers like birds recalls the characteristically Mesopotamian monsters of composite form, half-bird and half-man, themselves apparently connected directly or indirectly with the nether-world.

It was believed however that the pitiable lot of the dead could be to some extent mitigated by acts of devotion and charity practised by those that remain ; thus it was of primary importance to the deceased that he should receive a respectable and decent burial, and furthermore his needs did not stop there, for in E-kur—whether the term be applied to the earth as the home of mortals, or to the land of the dead, man requires both food and drink for his sustenance. The condition of the hapless man who receives no burial and is provided with none of the necessaries of life in the next world is described at the close of the Gilgamesh Epic, where we are informed that such an one is consumed by gnawing hunger and has perforce to satisfy his appetite with the offal on the streets ; but not only was the unburied shade a curse to himself so to speak, he also became a curse to the living by assuming the form of an "ekimmu" or demon, possessed with malignant intentions towards mankind, and furthermore endowed with the regrettable power of carrying those intentions into good effect ; it therefore behoved the living to attend to the requirements of the dead from the point of view of self-defence quite apart from any considerations of pious charity.

There was no distinction made between the faithful and unfaithful departed in the halls of Aralu, the only difference there was, lay between the lot of those who received the rites of burial and the means of sustenance at the hands of their surviving friends and relatives, and the lot of those to whom were denied the last rites and offices ; it should however be observed that the future life of those who perished on the battlefield was believed to be fraught with greater happiness, or at least less un-happiness than that of the generality of mankind.

Thus to the Babylonian the sting of death was very far from being removed, and their funeral dirges consisted chiefly in lamentations on account of the pitiful plight of the departed one rather than for their own personal loss ; for them there was no swallow-ing up of Death in Victory, the only possibility of future bliss lying in immunity from death, an immunity which had only been offered to one or two mortals, and of which only one had apparently succeeded in avail-ing himself, that single exception being Ṣit-napishtim whose exaltation to the godhead apparently exonerated him from the necessity of dying. The prevailing note was thus one of pessimism, a pessimism from which "the dwel-lers in Mesopotamia " have never succeeded in entirely emancipating themselves, a pessimism which is more-over discernible in the sacred writings of the Hebrews long after their emigration from Babylonia to the land of Canaan. To Job the lot of a tree is preferable to that of humanity, for " it hath hope, if it be cut down, it will sprout again ; but man lieth down and riseth not ; till the heavens be no more, they shall not awake nor be raised out of their sleep " ; so too the Psalmist begs that he may be allowed to recover his strength—"before I go hence and be no more," the general inference being that to the Hebrew mind the life beyond the grave resembled bare existence rather than a life with positive activities and positive functions to perform.

The tendency to regard the unknown with suspicion and doubt is incidental to the laws of our nature, and history demonstrates that only a courageous buoyancy won through the ceaseless efforts of mankind to combat the Mother who bore them, can overcome this as all other tendencies inherent in human nature. To the peoples of antiquity the world beyond was unknown and dark, for primitive man perforce regards as dark a state of existence concerning which he is in the dark, just as he has invariably attributed the causes of physical phenomena outside his ken to the powers of darkness, but the very darkness of the other world so far from diminishing the reality of its existence in his primitive mind, seems to have contrariwise, intensified it; he regarded the unseen through the medium of a mental telescope—to him it loomed dark but big; seeing was by no means the necessary condition of his believing, he believed where he did not see, and his imagination proved quite adequate to the occasion. In the twentieth century on the other hand there is an inclination to regard the unknown as *ipso facto* non-existent, but it must be confessed that the tendency exhibited by early man to accredit the unknown with an even greater reality than the known, accords more closely with the archetypal idealism of Plato and others whose mental development is at least of no mean order, and whose theories have not as yet stood convicted at the bar of Logic.

A SHORT BIBLIOGRAPHY

THOSE readers who may desire to enlarge their information on any particular subject referred to in this volume cannot do better than consult the following works. For a history of the excavations, Hilprecht's *Explorations in Bible Lands* (T. & T. Clark, Edinburgh), is a most useful book. For further details regarding the excavations at Nippur Peters' *Nippur, or Explorations and Adventures on the Euphrates* (Putman) should be consulted, and also Fisher's *Excavations at Nippur* (Philadelphia). For a study of cuneiform writing and the inscriptions, Sayce's *Archæology of the Cuneiform Inscriptions* (S.P.C.K.) should be read. It is the most recent work on the subject, is full of interest and original ideas. For the literature of the Babylonians and Assyrians, see Harper's *Literature of the Assyrians and Babylonians*, (Aldine Library), which contains the translation of a thoroughly representative selection of the literary products of both countries.

An account of the excavations carried on during the last decade by the Deutsche Orient-Gesellschaft at Babylon and Ashur will be found in the official reports of Koldewey and Andrae in the Mitteilungen of the Society (published by J. Hinrichs' sche, Buchhandlung Leipzig), while for a detailed account of the Anu-Adad temple at Ashur Andrae's *Der Anu-Adad Tempel* (also published by Hinrichs) should be consulted. The works of De Sarzec and Heuzey (published by E. Leroux, Paris) should be studied by those who wish to gain a full and comprehensive account of the excavations at Tellô ; of these the *Découvertes en Chaldée* is the most important. This magnificently illustrated work, which contains a complete statement of the early discoveries made on this site, and also a critical and well-balanced judgment of the deductions which we may make from those discoveries, is unquestionably one of the most important contributions to the study of Sumerian art. Of M. Heuzey's smaller works, *Une Villa Royale Chaldéenne* (Leroux, Paris) is calculated to be of special interest to the student of Babylonian architecture, while his numerous articles in the

Revue d'Assyriologie (Leroux, Paris) and papers in the *Comptes Rendus de l'Académie des Inscriptions et Belles Lettres* solve many of the problems which beset the study of oriental art. In regard to Cylinder-seals, the monumental work which has recently been published by W. Hayes Ward, *The Cylinder-Seals of Western Asia* (Carnegie Institute) is by far the most comprehensive on the subject, and is the culmination of a great many years' research in the public and private collections of Europe and America.

For the study of Law, the reader should consult C. J. Johns' *Babylonian and Assyrian Laws, Contracts and Letters* (Edinburgh), *Assyrian Deeds and Documents* (Cambridge), and *An Assyrian Doomsday Book* (Delitzsch and Haupt, *Assyriologische Bibliothek*, Band XVII, Leipzig), while the student of Babylonian and Assyrian Religion should refer to Morris Jastrow's *Religion of Babylonia and Assyria* (Boston, U.S.A), which is the only exhaustive work on the subject. For a detailed and comprehensive treatment of the arts and crafts of the Babylonians and Assyrians in the light of the material available when the book was published, Perrot and Chipiez, *History of Art in Chaldaea and Assyria* (Chapman & Hall, London; A. C. Armstrong & Son, New York) should be read.

In regard to manners, customs and general mode of life, reference should be made to the standard works of Maspero—*The Dawn of Civilization, The Struggle of the Nations*, and *The Passing of the Empires* (S.P.C.K., London), to the same writer's (Maspero) *Life in Ancient Egypt and Assyria* (Chapman & Hall) to Sayce's *Assyrians and Babylonians* (J. C. Nimmo, London); and to Delitzsch's *Handel und Wandel in Altbabylonien* (Deutsche Verlags-Anstalt, Stuttgart), while for military matters, the reader should consult J. Hunger's *Heerwesen und Kriegführung der Assyrer* in *Der Alte Orient* 1911.

This volume does not deal with the history of the Babylonians and Assyrians, but those interested in that branch should read Rogers' *History of Babylonia and Assyria* (Eaton & Mains, New York; Jennings & Pye, Cincinnati), Goodspeed's *A History of the Babylonians and Assyrians* (Smith, Elder & Co., London); and the standard-works of Maspero—*The Dawn of Civilization, The Struggle of the Nations* and *The Passing of the Empires* (S.P.C.K., London) for a general history, while for the early period King's *Sumer and Akkad* (Chatto & Windus) and Radau's *Early Babylonian History* (Oxford University Press) should be studied,

LIST OF THE MORE IMPORTANT
KINGS AND RULERS
AND A BRIEF CHRONOLOGICAL SUMMARY

Approximate
dates
B.C.

Mesilim, king of Kish, suzerain of Southern Babylonia   3000

FIRST DYNASTY OF LAGASH.

Ur-Ninâ, the founder of dynasty   3000
Akurgal
Eannatum
Enannatum I
Entemena
Enannatum II
Enetarzi
Enlitarzi
Lugal-anda
Urukagina, defeated by Lugal-zaggisi, king of Erech   2800
    and Sumer

DYNASTY OF KISH.

Sharru-Gi   2750
Manishtusu
Urumush

DYNASTY OF AGADE.

Shar-Gâni-sharri, established empire embracing Assyria,   2650
    Syria and Palestine
Narâm-Sin

SECOND DYNASTY OF LAGASH.

Ur-Bau   2500
Gudea   2450

408

DYNASTY OF UR.

Approximate
dates
B.C.

Ur-Engur   2400

Dungi, sacks Babylon, exercises suzerainty over Babylonia, extends his sway to Elam

Bur-Sin I

Gamil-Sin

Ibi-Sin

DYNASTY OF ISIN.   2300–2100

FIRST DYNASTY OF CITY OF BABYLON.

Khammurabi, king of Babylon, establishes a powerful   1900 kingdom in Babylonia, expels the Elamites who had effected a settlement in Ur and Larsa, restores Shar-Gâni-Sharri's empire in Palestine and embraces Assyria within the sphere of his influence

This dynasty is brought to an end by an invasion of the Hittites, who captured Babylon

The Kassites from the mountainous district, east of the Tigris, invade Babylonia and establish themselves as kings of Babylon. About a century after the Kassite invasion Assyria asserts her independence and becomes a separate kingdom

(?) Ushpia,[1] the probable founder of the temple of   2100 Ashur

(?) Ki-Ki-a, the first builder of the Dûru at Ashur,   2000 restorer of the temple of Ashur, and builder of the Adad-temple

Shalmaneser I   1300

Tukulti-Ninib I, king of Assyria, conquers Babylonia   1275

Ashur-rêsh-ishi   1140

Tiglath-Pileser I   1100

Ashur-naṣir-pal extends the limits of the empire   885–860

Shalmaneser II becomes master of the whole of   860–825 Western Asia. The Israelites under Jehu acknowledge his suzerainty

Tiglath-Pileser III recovers the ground lost by his   745–727 immediate predecessors, carries the tribes of Reuben, Gad, and the half-tribe of Manasseh into captivity

Shalmaneser IV besieges Samaria   727–722

---

[1] Cf. *Mitteilungen*, No. 21, p. 49.

Approximate
dates
B.C.

Sargon, the usurper, takes Samaria and transports 722–705
most of population ; defeats Egyptians and
Philistines at Raphia ; reduces Babylonia,
carries on war in Elam ; builds great palace at
Khorsabad

Sennacherib reduces rebellious Babylonia ; defeats 705–681
Egyptians at Altaku in Dan ; carries on war
in Palestine ; Hezekiah of Judah acknowledges
his suzerainty ; destroys Babylon (689)

Esarhaddon conquers Lower Egypt (672) 681–668

Ashur-bani-pal invades Egypt, the latter having 668–626
thrown off the Assyrian yoke ; sacks Thebes,
the Egyptian capital (666) ; entirely subjugates
Elam ; defeats and puts to death Shamash-
shum-uk'in, Viceroy of Babylonia

Egypt and Lydia assert their independence

The Medes made raid on the eastern borders
of the empire (*circ.* 634)

Ashur-bani-pal dies 626

Shortly after his death the Median king
Cyaxares defeats Assyrians and besieges
Nineveh. Invasion of Scythian hordes momentarily checks Cyaxares, but soon after
Cyaxares and possibly Nabopolassar, an Assyrian general in Babylon, besiege and ultimately capture and destroy Nineveh (*circ.*
607)

Assyria goes to the Medes, Babylonia to
Nabopolassar, who founds the Neo-Babylonian
Dynasty

NEO-BABYLONIAN DYNASTY.

Nabopolassar 625–604

Nebuchadnezzar II defeated Necho, king of Egypt, 604–561
before his accession ; captures Jerusalem and
takes Judah into captivity

Nabonidus, entrusts Babylon to his son Belshazzar. 555–538
Cyrus, the Persian, invades Babylonia, captures
Babylon and destroys the Neo-Babylonian
Empire

INDEX

Abêshu', k. of Babylon, 33
Abû Adham, 163
Abû Habba, 3, 60, 68 ; cf. also
  Sippar
Abû Hatab, 77
Abû Shahrein, 121, 134, 156,
  157, 163, 242, 263
Acacia, 12
Accounts, lists of, 109
Achæmenian inscriptions, 86
Adab. Cf. Bismâya
Adad, 263, 388, 391, 397
Adad-nirari I, 78, 81, 254
Adad-nirari II, 81
Adad-nirari III, 43, 81, 233,
  268
Adar, 232, 323
Agade, 7, 29
Agate, 76, 287, 340
Agents, 381
Agglutinative languages, 105
Agriculture, 13, 14, 367, 368,
  377, 389
Ahab, 36, 316
Ahaz, k. of Judah, 36, 111
Akkad. Cf. Agade
Alabaster, 14, 75, 76, 83, 146,
  225, 226, 326
Alashiya, 109
Alcohol, 370
Alexander the Great, 3, 39
Altaku, battle of, 37
Altars, 135, 141, 184, 206, 301
Amen, 365
Amenhetep III, 21, 108
Amenhetep IV, 108 ; cf. Khue-
  naten

Amethyst, 287, 340
Amphora, 298
Amran, 71, 72
Amulets, 116, 321
Amurru, land of, 130
Andrae, excavations and discover-
  ies by, 69, 77, 140, 142, 149–
  51, 176, 254, 335 *et passim*
Animals, 14–24, 244, 270, 271
"Ankh" sign, 314
Antelope, 16, 19, 184, 291
Antiochus Soter, 59
Anu, the god, 102, 388, 391 ;
  Temple of, 397
Anu-Adad Temple, 141–4, 323
Apil-Sin, 110
Appeal, Court of, 384
Arabia, 114
Arad-Sin, 32
Arakhtu canal, 74
Aralu, 400
Aramaic brick-inscriptions, 70
Archers, 195, 261, 350–6
Arches and arched structures,
  156, 168–80, 210
Architecture, 119–80
Armenia, 10
Arrow, copper heads, 242 ; em-
  blem, 398
Artaxerxes I, 66
Ashdod, 53, 112, 113
Ashur, 141–4, 178, 180, 200,
  229, 232, 254, 261, 263, 335
Ashur, the god, 25, 79, 146, 306,
  307, 391, 392, 397
Ashur-bani-pal, 2, 38, 39, 56, 64,
  71, 73, 114, 150, 218–22, 268

Ashur-bêl-kala, 35, 48, 229
Ashur-etil-ilâni, 43
Ashur-naṣir-pal, 20, 24, 35, 48, 78, 80, 81, 140, 141, 145, 199, 201, 202, 205, 230, 239, 240
Ashur-rêsh-ishi, 81, 142
Askelon, 37
Ass, 14, 18, 220, 366
Assyrian army, 350; buildings, 140–48, 151–58; civilization of, 3, 34; cylinder-seals, 304; laws, customs, etc., 344, 389–95; sculpture, 200, 229
Astrolabæ, 116
Astrology, 104, 109
Aten, disc of, 306
Axe, 254, 340

Babil, 59
Babylon, 29, 59, 69, 114, 116, 241, 268 et passim; cf. also Kasr
Babylonia, 3, 4, 10, 156, 181, 222, 375, 386
Balâwât, 15, 55, 258
Bandlets, 216
Bank, artificial, 208
Banks, E. J., excavations and discoveries by, 6, 82, 172, 223, 326, 333, 334
Barbaro, Josafat, 85
Barbel, 27
Barley, 11
Barton, G. A., 96, 98
Basalt, 14, 81, 167, 198, 232, 240, 326
Baskets, 190
Basket-carriers, 247
Bas-reliefs, 181–200, 201–22, 271, 272, 273, 274
Battering-rams, 203, 208, 261, 359 f.
Battle-axes, 188, 193
Bau, the goddess, 326, 365, 367, 373, 397

Baumgarten, 74
Bavian relief of Sennacherib, 81, 397
Bazu, land of, 23
Beans, 370
Bearded and beardless Assyrians, 239
Beef, 366
Beer, 383
Behistun inscription, 90
Bêl, 17, 71, 391, 397
Bêlit, 71, 393
Bells, bronze, 255
Bel-Merodach, 305
Belshazzar, 39, 51
Belus, temple of, 138
Berosus, 150
Bey, Bedri, excavations by, 68
Bilingual tablets, 104
Bingani-shar-ali, 294
Bint-el-Amir, 64
Birch, 261
Birds, in Mesopotamian art, etc., 24, 115, 184, 367
Birs-Nimrûd, 18, 29, 51; cf. also Borsippa
Bismâya, 6, 82, 83, 121, 123, 159, 223, 251, 326, 327, 333
Bisons, 2, 3, 23, 292
Bitumen, 124 f., 226, 243, etc.
Black Obelisk, 15, 267; 93
Blow-pipe, 331
Boars, 19, 24
Boats, 14, 259, 334, 361 f.
Bone, implements of, 74, 178
Boomerang, weapons shaped like, 183, 188, 298, 340, 341 ff.
Booth, A. J., 94
Borsippa, 29, 59; cf. Birs-Nimrûd
Boscawen, 254
Botta, discoveries and excavations by, 41, 279, 321, 335, 345 etc.
Boundary-stones, 16, 101, 111, 395
Bows and arrows, 193, 203, 204, 205, 208, 216, 219, 341

Bracelets, 202, 212, 230, 233, 261, 268, 347, 348
Branding, 385
Bread, 11, 370
Breccia, 70, 71
Bricks, 120–3
Bridge of boats, 259
Bronze, 13, 54, 55, 103, 150, 242, 251, 252, 253, 254, 255, 256, 261, 262, 267
Budge, E. A. Wallis, excavations by, 68
Buffalo, 2, 3, 23, 45, 293
Bull, 15, 17, 24, 213, 214, 236, 237–9, 257, 272, 275, 276, 280, 289, 298, 305, 310, 398
Burials, 62, 69, 74, 75, 77, 80, 176–8, 190, 365
Burnouf, Emile, 90
Bur-Sin, 77, 104, 253, 301, 324
Business-contracts, 371
Bustard, 26

Cabbage, 390
Calah, 35 ; cf. also Nimrûd
Calf, 192, 398
Camels, 15, 390
Camp-stools, 291, 297
Capital offences, 384
Capsules, 158, 323
Carchemish, 39
Carnelian, 287
Carpenters, 227, 366
Carts, 214
Case-tablets, 106
Cavalry, Assyrian, 281, 353 f.
Caylus, Count, 86
Cedar-wood, 2, 73, 130, 131, 150, 161, 258
Chalcedony, cylinder-seals of, 287
Champollion, 89
Chardin, 85
Chariots, 15, 188, 203, 204, 219, 220, 259, 281, 295, 304, 354 f.
Chickens, as offerings, 367

Chinese art and language, 10
Chosroes, 41
Cilicia, 38
Clark, C. H., 63
Clay, 75, 77, 95, 103–18, 252, 273, 274 ff., 324
Clay, A. T., discoveries by, 65, 303, 331
Clay, E. W., 63
Cloth, coverings of clay urns, 334
Club, emblem, 398
Cock, 26
Coffins, 49
Colour boxes, 77
Colours, 270, 283
Columns, 160–8, 396, 397
Combs, 349
Commagene, 34
Commercial tablets, 110
Cones, 111, 112, 123, 148, 202, 249
Copper, 75, 77, 180, 242–7, 249, 252, 286
Coral, 340
Coriander, 390
Corundum, 287
Cosmologies, Babylonian, Egyptian, Hebrew, 4
Cotton, 347
Couch, royal, 221
"Country of the Sea," 33, 34
Cow, 366
Crane, 26
Creation legends, 53
Cremation, 62
Crenelated walls, 152, 203, 211, 227, 261
Crescent, 296, 302, 305, 306, 308, 395
Crews for transport-barges, 107
Cros, Gaston, excavations and discoveries by, 84, 235, 334, 344
Crown-lands, 391
"Crux ansata," 314
Crystal, 287
Ctesias, 141

Cucumbers, 370
Cuneiform inscriptions and literature, 85–116, 203
Cups, 184, 205, 221, 326, 327
Cutha, 29
Cyaxares, 39
Cylinder-seals, 284–308
Cypress, 2, 73
Cyprus, 294
Cyrus, 39, 74

Dabigu, 260
Daggers, 202, 219, 281, 298, 311
Dagon, 307, 319, 320
Damascus, 114
Darius II, 66
Date, 12, 13, 370
Dating, Babylonian method of, 110
Dead, future state and offerings for, 374, 399 f.
De Bruin, 85
Deer, 3, 24, 220, 265
Deification of kings, 375
Deities on seals, 291 f.
Deity seated, 198; cf. also Gods
De la Becke, Sir H., 283
Delitzsch, Friedrich, 61, 71, 74, 261, 264, 273
Deluge story, 53
Demons, 140, 262, 321
De Morgan, J., 226
Dêr, 68
De Sacy, 86
De Sarzec, excavations and discoveries by, 13, 56–8, 161, 171, 187, 195, 227, 234, 243, 244, 248, 253, 329
De Saulcy, 93
Diarbekr, 195, 200
Diodorus, 59, 90, 127, 273
Diorite, 14, 81, 146, 227, 228, 229
Disc, of sun, 206
Disc, winged, 395

Distraint, 382
Divorce, 365
Dogs, 14, 18, 19, 220, 235, 297, 398
Dolerite, 14, 57, 69, 91, 241
Domes, 155
Dove, 26, 323, 398
Dowries, 376
Dragons, 275, 295, 305, 336
Drains, 158–60
Dress, 181, 198, 216, 221, 223, 226, 230, 232, 233, 281, 337–56
Ducks, 367
Duck weights, 26
Dudu, 192, 266, 289
Dungi, 6, 32, 50, 82, 101, 110, 247, 298, 301
Dûr Sharrukîn, 41, 279; cf. also Khorsabad
"Dûru," the, 81

Ea, the god, 27, 73, 299, 388, 391, 392, 396, 397
Eabani, 2, 292, 293, 330, 403
Eagle, 24, 25, 280, 291, 306, 310, 398
Eagle, Etana and, 297
Eannatum, 27, 57, 187, 188, 326
Earrings, 252, 264, 347, 348
East India House Inscription, 140, 150
Ebony, 349
Eggs, stone, 340
Egypt, 3, 4, 38, 256, 258, 268, 269, 286, 312, 313
Egyptian hieroglyphics, 5, 331
"Ekimmu," 403
Ekron, 37
Ekua, 73
E-kur, 399
Elamites, 2, 31, 32, 37, 38, 114, 199, 247
El-Hibba, 61, 148
Enlil, the god, 17, 62, 133–6, 325, 326, 373

Enlitarzi, 373
Entemena, 12, 30, 137, 191, 265, 326
Enubi-Marduk, 108
Envelopes, 105, 106
E-pa, 133, 136
Eponyms, 114
Erech, 9, 29, 30; cf. also Warka
Eridu, 27, 29; cf. also Abû Shahrein
Erman, 369
E-sagila, temple of Marduk, 71-3, 115, 199
Esar, k. of Adab, 223
Esarhaddon, 13, 23, 38, 43, 73, 78, 114
Eschatology, 399-405
Esneh, 4
Etana, 297
E-temen-an-ki, 73, 138
Eulmash-shakin-shûm, 205
Euphrates, 10, 11
Euting, Prof., 122
Exchange, mediums of, 367
Eyes, 181, 191, 202, 308
E-zida, 51, 59, 115

Face-masks, 264
Fâra, 74, 121, 157, 172, 242, 250
Feathers, 181, 403
Feudalism, 390, 391
Field, Mr., 63
Figs, 13, 217, 370
Fish, 26, 27, 115, 281, 334, 370
Fisher, C. S., 10, 63, 136
Fish-god, 307, 319; cf. also Dagon
Fishing-hooks, 76
Flandin, 272
Flint, 75, 242, 287
Flowers, 13, 277, 278, 301
Fly-flaps, 205, 216, 221
Foot-wear, 202, 271, 280, 349
Fortress, assault of, 210

Foundation-cylinders, 50, 51
Fox, 20
Frazier, W. W., 63
Freestone, blue, 326
Fresnel, expedition of, 47, 273, 328
Frog, 20
Fruits, 370
Funerals, 374
Furniture-makers, 366
"Future Life," 76, 399 f.

Gardeners, 366
Garlic, 390
Garnet, 267
Gates, double-leaved, 210
Gates, on seals, 297; cf. also Balâwât
Gate-sockets, 57, 65, 83, 102, 259, 267
Gatumdug, the goddess, 228, 235, 373
Gaza, 37
Gazelle, 16, 19, 184, 256, 257
Geere, H. V., 63
Genouillac, 364, 370
Gezer, 254
Gilgamesh, 3, 53, 191, 289, 292, 293, 311, 330, 338, 372, 393, 403
Gimil-Sin, 302
Gishgibilgemesh, 372
Glass, 42, 76, 180, 286, 331
Goats, 14, 17, 18, 184, 250, 265, 290, 297, 366
Goddess, nude, 295, 321 f.
Gods, 102, 104, 111, 197, 318, 321, 324, 372-5, 386-9, 391-5
Gold, 6, 72, 73, 74, 79, 83, 139, 150, 263, 264, 286, 323
Goose, 867, 398
Grammatical tablets, 104
Granite, 59, 83
Griffins, 256, 257
Grotefend, G. Friedrich, 87

Gudea, 6, 13, 22, 31, 57, 61, 62, 84, 133, 136, 149, 227, 228, 235, 243, 298, 299, 318, 329
Guilds, trade, 376
Gula, the goddess, 397, 398
Gum, 370
Gungunu, 32

Hadadnadinakhe, 149
Hades, 400
Hair, arrangement of, 183, 188, 190, 216, 224, 225, 226, 230, 233, 244, 338
Halévy, Joseph, 105
Halicarnassus, 331
Handles, lateral, 243
Hanging gardens, 127
Hannon, 37
Hare, 20
Harper, R. F., excavations and discoveries by, 63, 82, 94, 97, 123, 131, 142, 264, 267, 377
Harrison, Provost, 63
Hatchets, 75, 76, 242, 296
Hawaiians, war-gods of, 263
Haynes, excavations and discoveries by, 125, 133, 135, 157, 171, 334
Head-dresses, 198, 202, 203, 206, 216, 228, 233, 249, 271, 321, 338, 339, 345, 356, 396
Hebrews, 404 f.
Heifers, 266
Helmets, 187, 188, 193, 195, 212, 281, 350 f.
Henna, 327
Hereditary principle, 390
Herodotus, 10, 13, 127, 131, 138, 157, 284
Heroes, 289, 290
Heuzey, Léon, discoveries, etc., by, 25, 169, 184, 186, 187, 191, 192, 251, 246, 310, 321
Hezekiah, k. of Judah, 37, 38, 208
Hillah, 285, 322

Hilprecht, H. V., excavations and discoveries by, 16, 57, 59, 60, 63, 66, 117, 136, 148, 169, 184, 252, 328, etc.
Hincks, 91, 92
Hindiyah Canal, 11, 12

Historical documents, 104, 110, 111
Hit, 124
Hittites, 33, 35, 69
Holtzman, 91
Hommel, F., 98, 139
Honey, 11
Honeysuckle, paintings of, 282
Horns, symbolic (?), 211
Horse, 14, 15, 16, 28, 281, 397
Hoshea, k. of Israel, 36
House-building, 383
Houses, 156-8
Hunting-scenes, 204-5, 218-21
Huts, 169
Hyenas, 24
Hyksos kings, 16
Hymns, 104
Hyssop, 390

Ibex, 3, 19, 257, 290, 308
Ibi-Sin, 302
Igigi, 397
Ili-Ippalzam, 108
Ilu-Ittia, 114
Iluma-ilu, 33
Imgur-Bêl, 139
Imgur-Marduk, 67
Impalement, 208
Implements, 252
Inlay work, 236, 249, 250, 251, 254
Inundation, 4
Irak, 344
Irishum, 3, 79
Iron, 255, 268, 269, 286
Irrigation, 368, 390
Ishme-Dagan, 143
Ishme-Dagan, k. of Isin, 321

Ishtar, the goddess, 70, 306, 388,
391, 393, 395, 396, 397
Ishtar's Gate, 271, 274, 275
Isin, dynasty of, 32
Israel, 36
Ivory, 13, 83, 223, 254, 312
Ivy, 14

Jackals, 24
Jackson, Sir John (Ltd.), 11
Jade, 287
Jasper, 287
Jastrow, Morris, 65, 321, 388,
392, 393
Jehoiakim, 39
Jehu, 15
Jerusalem, 37, 39
Jewellery, 76, 252, 261, 267, 323,
340, 346, 348
Job, 404
Johns, C., 369, 377, 389
Jonah, 14
Josephus, 151
Judah, 36, 38, 39, 112

Kalat Sherkat, 48, 59, 69, 77,
78, 94, 158, etc.; cf. Ashur
Kallima-Sin, 16
Kampfer, 85
"Kanephores," 246
"Karduniash," 34
Karûn, river, 22
Kasr, 149–51; cf. Babylon
Kassites, 33, 303, 335
"Kaunakes" garments, 310
Khabour, 129
Khammurabi, 32, 50, 107, 108,
110, 141, 198, 376
Khipa, 116
Khorsabad, 41, 131, 160, 174,
239, 272
Khuenaten, 306
Khukhnuri, land of, 110
"Ki-gallu," 402
King, L. W., excavations and dis-
coveries by, 84, 252, 311, 408

Kinneir, 90
Kish, 5, 29, 30, 310
Knife, 75, 242, 311, 398
Kohl, 327
Koldewey, R., excavations and
discoveries by, 61, 68 f., 125,
127, 130, 144, 146, 149–51,
164, 276, 322, 335, 349
Kouyunjik collection, 104
Kudur-Mabuk, 32, 112, 247,
248
"Kudurrus," 396; cf. Boundary-
stones
Kurdistan, 16
Kurigalzu, 303

Labour, 377
Lachish, 38, 215–17
Lacouperie, 10
Lagash, 6, 9, 29, 191, 192, 265,
289, 290; cf. also Tellô
Lamassi, 238
Lamps, 177, 334, 398
Lance, 243
Landlord and tenant, 108, 377 f.
Lapis lazuli, 76, 102, 225, 250,
288, 315, 340
Larsa, 17, 29, 30; temples, 139
Lassen, 90
Layard, Sir Henry, excavations
and discoveries by, 18, 22, 23,
42–7, 54, 129, 140, 166,
167, 175, 253, 255, 262, 271,
280, 335
Laws, 198, 384, 398
Lead, 253, 255, 267, 268
Leases, 398
Lebanon, 130
Leek, 390
Legal contracts, 105, 106 ff.
Leopard, 24, 257, 292
Letters, 107, 108
Lettuce, 390
Lever, 214
Lexicography, 104
Libations, 205

Libyan languages, 5
Limestone, 14, 70, 145, 153, 182, 183, 224, 230, 287, 326, 327
Linen, 346
Lions, 20, 21, 22, 24, 185, 218, 219, 234–43, 251, 255, 257, 265, 270, 275–6, 280–9, 290 –1, 293, 309, 324, 330
Liver, omens derived from, 116
Locusts, 26
Loftus, W. K., excavations and discoveries by, 49, 51, 123, 156, 158, 163, 331
Longperier, 94
Lotus-plants, 13, 312
Löwenstern, 94
Lu-enna, 267
Lugal-anda, 288
Lugal-banda, 111
Lugal-Kigub-nidudu, 30, 102
Lugal-Kisali, 30
Lugal-shar-engur, 29
Lugal-Tarsi, 102
Lugal-zaggisi, 30, 326
Lydia, 39
Lynxes, 24

Maat, 314
Macalister, 254
Maces, 191, 200, 230, 287
Magan, 328, 335
Magic, 104, 109, 374
Mail, coats of, 350 f.
Manasseh, 38
Man-fish, 398
Manishtusu, 31, 226, 371
Marble, 42, 55, 83, 223, 287, 326, 328, 347
Marduk, 33, 48, 71, 73, 199, 273, 306, 386, 391, 392, 397
Marriage, 364, 376, 389
Maspero, 269, 408
Mathematics, 104
Measures, 372
Mechanics, 214, 215

Medes, 39
Medicine, 104, 109
Meissner, 69, 390
Memphis, 38
Mesilim, k. of Kish, 29, 30, 185, 310
Mesniu, the, 4
Messerschmidt, 62
Metals, Babylonian work, 242– 53; Assyrian work, 253–69; cf. also pp. 83, 103, 131, 132
Meyer, M. L., excavations by, 61, 69
Military arrangements, 188, 195
Milk, 366, 370, 390
Millet, 11, 13
Mitani, 109
Mohammerah, 3, 22
Mohl, 41
Money-lenders, 379, 388
Monkey, 20, 282
Monotheism, 372, 386
Moritz, B., 61
Mortar, 124–6
Mortgage, 108
Moschians, 34
Mother of emerald, 287
Mother-of-pearl, 83, 249, 250, 309, 311, 340
Moulds, 252
Mounds, 6
Mountain-sheep, 20
Mukeyyer, 50, 120, 156, 159, 242
Mule, 17
Münter, 86, 87
Murashû Tablets, 66
"Mushlala," 78
Musical instruments, 197, 204, 205, 221, 222
Mutilation, 385
Mutton, 366
Mythology, 104

Nabonassar, 110
Nabonidus, 5, 6, 50, 60

Nabopolassar, 34, 39, 73, 112, 150, 207
Nabû. Cf. Nebo
Nabû-aplu-iddina, 118, 205, 207
Nails, 243-4, 245, 253, 258
Nairi, 35
Names, divinely-compounded, 374
Nanâ, 391
Napir-asu, 262
Narâm-Sin, 5, 7, 8,30, 31, 57, 64, 67, 83, 84, 117, 135, 193-4-5, 293, 328
Nash, W. L., 331
Nebi Yûnus, 14, 56
Nebo, 48, 51, 77, 78, 84, 139, 232
Nebuchadnezzar I, 16, 397
Nebuchadnezzar II, 39, 50, 51, 73, 115, 138, 140, 149, 150, 243, 331
Necho, 39
Necklaces, 197, 264
Neo-Babylonian Empire, 304
Nergal, 73, 391
Neriglissar, 74
Nets, 310
Newberry, 284
Newton, 331
Niebuhr, Carsten, 86
Nile, 4
Nîmit-Marduk, 67
Nimitti-Bêl, 139
Nimrûd, 13, 42, 55, 56, 140, 175, 232, 235, 239, 268, 280, 281, 307, 312, 313, 319
Ninâ, 13
Nineveh, 14, 34, 84, 239, 335
Ningal, 197
Ningirsu, 29, 133, 183, 186, 191, 266, 299, 372
Ningishzida, 22, 299, 329, 372
Ninkharsag, 227, 398
Ninib (Adar), 42, 388, 397
Nin-lil, 325
Nin-makh, 71, 136, 137, 278, 322

Ninsun, 111
Ninus, 273
Nippur, 6, 29, 99, 30, 62-8, 116, 121, 132-6, 161-3, 184, 304, 322, 333
Norris, Edwin, 91
Nusku, 398

Oaks, 13
Oannes, 27 ; cf. Ea.
Oars, 363
Obsidian, 75, 287
Olive, 11, 13
Oliver, 90
Omens, 104 ; Cf. Pigs, Dogs, etc.
Onions, 370, 390
Onyx, 83, 287, 326
Opis, 29
Oppert, 47, 94, 273, 328
Oryx, 3, 20
Ostrich, 25, 307
Ovid, 141
Oxen, 14, 16, 253, 273, 366
Ox-hoof, 115, 254
Oyster shells, 309

Padî, k. of Ekron, 113
Painting, 270-83
Palaces, Assyrian, 151-6 ; Babylonian, 148-51
Palm-trees, 129, 158, 221
Panther, 273
Partnerships, 382
Pehlevi, language and inscriptions, 16, 86, 87
Pepper, Wm., 63
Percy, Dr., 283
Perfumery, 366
Perrot and Chipiez, 140, 238, 271, 408, etc.
Persepolis, 86, 87, ff.
Persian cuneiform, 86, 87, ff.
Persians, 39
Peters, J. P., excavations and discoveries by, 63, 161, 162, 334, etc.

Petrie, W. Flinders, 269, 332
Phœnician characters, 21, 255, 312
Picture-writing, 96–100
Pigs, 14, 20
Pinches, T., 139, 140, 261
Pir-Hussein, 339
Place, Victor, excavations and discoveries by, 41, 42, 153, 160, 173, 279
Planetary colours, 138
"Plano-convex" bricks, 120
Plans, 116
Plants, 115
Pliny, 59
Plough, 16, 184, 280, 303, 304
Polyandry, 364
Polygamy, 364, 365
Polytheism, 372
Pomegranates, 12, 370
Poplar, 12, 129
Porcupines, 20, 24
Pork, 19
Porphyry, 326
Porter, 90
Potter's wheel, 334
Pottery, 84, 282, 333–6
Prayers, 104
Prestwich, 10
Priests, 373, 388
Prisms, 112, 113
Pul. Cf. Tiglath-Pileser III
Pyramids, 141

Quartz, 287
Quivers, 188, 195, 358

Rabbit, 20
Radau, 187, 408
Radishes, 370, 390
Rafts, 363
Ram, 178, 396, 397
Raphia, battle of, 37
Rassam, H. H., excavations and discoveries by, 46–9, 54–6, 59, 61, 258

Raven, 26
Rawlinson, G., 200, 222, 352, 353
Rawlinson, Sir H., discoveries by, 18, 51, 90 f., 324
Reeds, 13, 14
Religion (early), 372–5; (Khammurabi period), 386–9; (Assyrian), 391–5
Rent, 378
Repoussé-work, 258, 259 ff.
Rezin, k. of Damascus, 36
Rich, C. J., discoveries by, 40, 59
Rîm-Sin, 32, 101, 247, 248
Ring and staff, 103, 198, 206
Riparian obligations, 379
Rivets, 252
Rogers, R. W., 94, 408
Roofs, Assyrian, 153, 154
Ropes, 206, 214, 281
Rosettes, 14, 78, 202, 233, 260, 274, 279, 315, 357

Sacrifices, 244, 373
Saddles, 353
Sagittarius, 398
Sammuramat, 233
Samsu-iluna, 50, 68, 108, 110
Sandals. Cf. Foot-wear
Sandstone, 69, 70, 163, 325, 327
Sanskrit, 90
Sarcophagi, 74, 75, 180
Sargon, 37, 53, 79, 112, 144, 151–4, 209, 212, 330
Saws, 75, 242
Sayce, A. H., 89, 94, 407, 408 et passim
Sceptre, 197, 230
Scheil, Père, 68, 364
Scimitar, 254
Schist, 287
Schrader, 61
Scorpion, 26
Scorpion-man, 398
Scourging, 385

Scroll-design, 192, 315
Sculpture, bas-reliefs (Assyrian), 201–22 (Babylonian), 181–200
Sculpture, in the round, 222–41
Seals, 285, 286, 324
Semiramis, 233, 273
Semites, 5, 30
Senkereh, 49; cf. also Larsa
Sennacherib, 37, 38, 46, 47, 56, 78, 113, 213–17, 330, 397
Serpents, 22, 23, 273, 296, 299, 329, 398
Sesame, 11
"Shadûf," 369
Shagshag, 373
Shalmaneser I, 35, 78
Shalmaneser II, 15, 36, 55, 81, 143, 207, 232, 259, 268
Shalmaneser IV, 36, 37
Shamash, 1, 60, 139, 205, 296, 396–7
Shamash-Killâni, 116
Shamash-shum-ukîn, 38, 73, 110
Shamshi-Adad, 79, 143, 167
Share-profit system, 378
Shar-Gâni-Sharri, 5, 7, 8, 23, 67, 102, 117, 293
Sharru-Gi, 30, 31
Shatt el-Hai Canal, 224
Shatt en-Nîl Canal, 133
Sheaf, 398
Shêdi, 238
Sheep, 14, 17, 18, 115, 297, 366
Shell, 72, 75, 76, 236, 250, 287, 341
Sheol, 401
Shields, 208, 211, 281, 360
Shipping, 381
Shualu, 401 f.
Shutruk-Nakhunte, 194
Sidon, 114
Silver, 72, 73, 76, 150, 251, 264, 265, 267, 286
Simmash-shipak, 205
Simon, L., 61

Sin, the Moon-god, 50, 306, 388, 391, 395, 396, 397
Sin-eribam, 106
Sin-Gamil, 101
Sin-gashid, k. of Erech, 111
Sin-idinnam, k. of Larsa, 107, 111
Sin-ikisham, 106
Sin-muballit, 110
Sin-shar-ishkun, 81, 144, 145 ff.
Sippar, 3, 29, 139; cf. also Abû Habba
Sit-napishtim, 26, 404
Skins, 203, 211, 363
Slaves, 376
Slings, 341
Smith, George, excavations and discoveries by, 52–4, 128, 138
Solomon, 316
South-west wind, 262
Spain, 334
Sparrow and plough, 398
Spasinus Chorax, 3
Spearmen, Assyrian, 350–6
Spears, 76, 193, 211, 219, 242
Sphinxes, 312
Squeezes, 90, 117
Stag, 20
Stage-tower. Cf. Ziggurat
Stalagmite, 325, 326
Standards, 193, 204, 244
Star, 296, 302, 305, 395
Statues, offerings to, 373
Steatite, 197, 235, 252, 329
Stone, uses of, 74, 75, 100, 101, 115, 126–9, 224, 245, 246, 325–31
Stork, 26
Storm-god, the. Cf. Adad
Strabo, 127, 157, 158, 168
Stucco, 278
Stylus, 227
Sumerians, 1, 2, 10, 29, 290, 291, 364, 372
Sumu-abu, 32, 110
Sumu-ilu, k. of Ur, 235

Sumu-la-ilu, k. of Babylon, 110
Sun-god, 111 ; cf. also Shamash
" Sun-Tablet," 164, 205
Surgeons, 385
Surghul, 61, 157
Susa, 1, 2, 32, 38, 193, 199, 226, 262, 331, 334
Swallow, 26
Swan, 26
Swimming, 203
Swords, 212, 254, 350 f.
Syenite, 287
Syllabaries, 109
Symbolism, 395
" Synchronous History," 111
Syria (northern), 35, 36

Table, 307
Tablets, 103, 105, 286
Talbot, 94
Tamarisk, 130, 370
Tarsus, 38
Taylor, J. E., excavations and discoveries by, 50, 51, 120, 123, 124, 133, 134, 156, 159, 163, 176, 200, 242, 263
Tell el-Amarna letters, 108
Tell el-Hesy. Cf. Lachish
Tellô (Lagash), 13, 56–8, 61, 84, 161, 187, 195, 224, 234, 248, 301, 310
Tell Sifr, 50
Temples, Assyrian, 140–8 ; Babylonian, 132–40
Temple-towers, 1 ; cf. also Ziggurats
Terebinth, 13
Terra-cotta, 321, 322, 324
Te-Umman, k. of Elam, 114, 222
Thebes, 38, 114
Thistle, 14
Thompson, R. C., excavations by, 84
Thrones, 197, 216, 217, 235, 264

Thunderbolt, 79, 395
Thureau-Dangin, 364
Tiâmat, 306
Tibet, 18
Tiglath-Pileser I, 34, 35, 112, 142, 200, 267, 268
Tiglath-Pileser II, 79
Tiglath-Pileser III, 36, 43, 81, 111, 208, 268
Tigris, 10
Til-Garimum, 113
Tin, 253, 255
Tirhakah, k. of Egypt, 38, 114
Toilet, 327, 347
Tortoise, 20
Trades, 366, 380
Trees, 12, 280, 291, 306
Trilingual inscriptions, 86
Tubal, 113
Tukulti-Ninib I, 21, 34, 72, 78, 79, 81, 179
Tukulti-Ninib II, 35
Tulips, 282
Turbans, 228, 300, 302
Turks, 12, 68
Turnips, 390
Turtle-doves, 367
Tychsen, 86
Tyre and Sidon, 363

Umbrellas, 205
Umma, 29, 30
Ungnad, 19
Untash-gal, k. of Elam, 262
Ur, 6, 29, 30, 31, 133 ; cf. also Mukeyyer
Ur-Bau, 149, 227, 249
Ur-Engur, 6, 31, 32, 50, 64, 67, 82, 133 f., 299
Ur-Ninâ, 9, 30, 120, 130, 149, 186, 235, 244, 310
Urukagina, 13, 27, 30, 326, 374
Urumush, 30, 31, 328
Urzage, 325
Ushpia, 78
Utug,

Valle, Pietro della, 85
Vases, 226, 229, 302, 398
Vegetables, 373
Vestments, 206
Vetches, 14
Vines, 13, 112, 217, 218, 221
Votive figures, 244
Vultures, 24, 25, 57, 187, 188 ff., 204, 290

Wages, 380
Ward, W. Hayes, 2, 15, 16, 63, 284, 285, 287, 292, 295, 298, 304, 305, 341, 396–8
Warka, excavations and discoveries at, 9, 49, 156, 163, 312
Water-fowl, 334
Weapons, 188, 202, 221, 252, 259, 340–4, 350–9
Weavers, 365
Westergaard, 91
Wheat, 11
Wilkinson, 369
Windows, 160, 211
"Window Inscription," 85
Wine. Cf. also Alcohol, 11

Winged Being, 202, 286
Winged Disc, 306
Winged monsters, excavation and transport of, 43–5
Witnesses, 384
Wolves, 24
Woman, 224, 225, 226, 229, 244, 245, 338, 340, 365, 366, 389
Wood, 129–31
Wood-carving, 236
Wool, 337, 366 f., 390
World, map of, Babylonian conception of, 116
Wuswas façade, 157

Xerxes, 86, 331

Yôkha, 121

Zabum, 72, 110
Zamama, 398
Zaquriu, 268
Zarpanit, 73
Zedekiah, 39
Zend-Avesta, 86
Ziggurats, 42, 142, 143, 148
Zoroastrian faith, 86